FARCE AND FANTASY

FARCE AND FANTASY

*Popular Entertainment in
Eighteenth-Century Paris*

Robert M. Isherwood

New York   Oxford
OXFORD UNIVERSITY PRESS
1986

Oxford University Press

Oxford   New York   Toronto
Delhi   Bombay   Calcutta   Madras   Karachi
Petaling Jaya   Singapore   Hong Kong   Tokyo
Nairobi   Dar es Salaam   Cape Town
Melbourne   Auckland

and associated companies in
Beirut   Berlin   Ibadan   Nicosia

Library of Congress Cataloging in Publication Data
Isherwood, Robert M., 1935–
Farce and fantasy.
Bibliography: p.
Includes index.
1. Paris (France)—Social life and customs—18th century.
2. Performing arts—France—Paris—History—18th century.
3. Music-halls (Variety-theaters, cabarets, etc.)—France—Paris—History—18th century.
I. Title.
DC729.I84   1986   790'.0944'36   85-3072
ISBN 0-19-503648-4

The following journals have kindly granted permission to include in this book articles that were first published
in their pages in somewhat different form:
Proceedings of the Western Society for French History, "Entertainment in the Parisian Boulevards in the
Eighteenth Century" (1984, XI): 142–52.
Journal of Modern History, "Entertainment in the Parisian Fairs in the Eighteenth Century" (March 1981):
24–28.
International Review of the Aesthetics and Sociology of Music, "Popular Entertainment in Eighteenth-Century
Paris" (December 1978, IX): 295–310.

Printing (last digit): 9 8 7 6 5 4 3 2 1

Printed in the United States of America
on acid free paper

TO
Nicholas
and
Aaron

Preface

This book deals with entertainment as an important dimension of French culture. It explores aspects of the entertainment world of the Parisian marketplace, though certain subjects such as government-sponsored festivals, provincial entertainment, religious fêtes, and ballooning have been omitted because they require full-scale, independent studies. My book, except to a limited extent, does not investigate the careers of commercial entrepreneurs or of their performers. Since the archival and other sources do not lend themselves for the most part to statistical analysis, this is not a computerized study.

Unlike most histories, this one does not examine eighteenth-century France from the standpoint of the philosophes or of the Revolution. The philosophes, with the exception of Frédéric-Melchior Grimm, had very little interest in popular entertainment. As for the Revolution, I have deliberately tried to forget that it occurred and have chosen the late 1780s as an arbitrary point of termination out of the conviction that too many scholars have looked at the eighteenth century with the hindsight that the Revolution was coming. Attitudes, ideas, commitments, and tastes that developed during the Revolution are too often projected into the pre-Revolutionary mentality. It seems more appropriate to attempt to view the cultural world of pre-1789 as its people did.

Moreover, although I have tried to be as exact and concrete as possible, I have avoided the *histoire événementielle* of politics and economics. I am persuaded that daily or yearly events had less bearing on popular entertainment than the weight of its tradition. People had known farce and fantasy before 1700 in the fairs of the Middle Ages and Renaissance and in carnival, charivari, and the Feast of Fools. They would know it in later years, as they still do today, in circuses, wax museums, fire-eaters, football halftime shows, the entertainment myriad that surrounds Beaubourg, flying saucers, and, of course, television. Not long ago, Professor David Pinkney sent me an advertisement that Professor Bertier de Sauvigny found in his mailbox. It described the wonderful powers of M. Nebaly Sylla, "Grand Marabout de la Casamance Pacao Darsaime." Sylla, a resident of the rue de la Glacière, promises in this advertisement to "cure every physical and moral complex." He "strengthens, induces, attracts the sentiments of affection, sympathy, consideration." He guarantees results in bringing his patients to good health, sincere love, and social success and in expelling "ill-omened and evil influences." In Milan, Italy, in May 1982, my son, Nicholas, and I picked up from the sidewalk a leaflet advertising the services of a medium, Mister Giglio, with the announcement that "occult forces exist since the earth was born; it has always been this way; whoever knows them can use them." Anyone with doubts is advised to consult Mister Giglio, who promises to use his powers in parapsychology, astrology, and spiritualism along with his magnetic fluid to resolve problems caused by occult influences. Giglio's residence is given as 40 Via Plinio in Milan.

The key questions this book seeks to answer are, What sort of popular entertainments were available to Parisians, what was their social setting, who enjoyed them, and why? In the realm of popular entertainment, is the now fashionable distinction between elite and popular culture valid, and, if so, what was popular entertainment? Was the distinction sociological? That is, if a distinction existed, was it based, as most scholars have held, on a division of taste and interest between the wealthy, educated highborn and the poor, unsophisticated lowborn? Determining the social composition of audiences and crowds at the centers of popular entertainment is crucial to the commonly accepted sociological separation of cultural worlds. I will also look into what role, if any, politics played in shaping a distinction between cultures and taste publics. Since a case has been made by Peter Burke and others that the end of the century saw a growing separation of popular and elite culture, that issue must also be addressed. Its more difficult corollary is whether entertainment helped to widen the social and cultural stratification structure or, on the other hand, helped to break down that stratification and bring people together.

Finally, the most interesting aspect of popular entertainment, then and now, is the one least frequently asked by scholars: What made it enjoyable to so many people? What kind of satisfaction did spectators derive from the farces of the fairs and boulevards; the equilibrists and funambulists; the conjurers and charlatans; the dabblers in magic, optical illusion, mechanics, and phantasmagoria? Not only must the Parisian *spectacles* be examined carefully to discover if they had common elements that made them appealing, but the total atmosphere of the popular marketplace must be evoked and analyzed in order to find out what made it tick and what made it enticing.

This book challenges the findings of many scholars and reaches different conclusions on many points of fact and interpretation. Readers are advised to remember that its focus is entertainment, not culture as a whole. It is to be hoped that some will be induced to conduct their own investigations into this very rich subject.

Numerous individuals and organizations have contributed enormously to my work on this book. The latter include the Vanderbilt University Research Council, the Camargo Foundation, the American Council of Learned Societies, and the National Endowment for the Humanities. I am also grateful to Madame Simone Brunau and the Cité Internationale des Arts for providing inexpensive apartments in Paris. I want to thank Orest Ranum for giving me the idea for this book. He and Robert Darnton have suggested bibliography and approaches from time to time that have been quite valuable. As the research progressed, several individuals have steered me to sources and literature. This study would have been much less rewarding without their generous assistance. They include Jack Censer, William Weber, James Hunn, Peter Ascoli, Emmet Kennedy, James Patty, James Leith, David DiPietro, Stephen Rombouts, Susanna Barrows, and Edward Gargan. I am indebted to my former wife, Nita, for locating the engravings for this book in virtually every repository in Paris. Thanks are inadequate for expressing my sincere appreciation to the Bibliothèque Nationale and to the Bibliothèque Historique de la Ville de Paris, the Bibliothèque de l'Arsenal, and the Archives Nationales. None of these bears any responsibility for whatever errors there are in this book.

Finally, for their patient labors in the editing and typing of my manuscript, I am grateful to Elizabeth Litzinger, Mary F. Moore, Cheri Radford, Sally Miller, Frances Potts Hale, and Patricia Gayden.

Nashville, Tennessee   R. M. I.
March 1985

Contents

I

THE BRIDGE,
THE FAIRS,
AND LYRIC COMEDY

1

The Singing Culture of the Pont-Neuf

FOR OVER A CENTURY after its construction in the reign of Henri IV, the Pont-Neuf was the center of popular life in Paris. It benefited from its location in the heart of the city, but even more from its identification with a king who had become a folk hero. Henri was a symbol of benevolence and well-being, and the equestrian statue on the bridge was a popular shrine. The carnival atmosphere of the Pont-Neuf embodied many of the defining characteristics of marketplace culture: the street peddlers shouting their characteristic chants; the parade of strollers and carriages across the bridge; the crowds clustered around charlatans, grimacers, and tumblers; and musicians providing a show in which everyone participated. There was little differentiation between the actual life of the passing crowd and the representation of life offered by the public entertainers on the bridge. Sharing a common language, uttering the well-known cries of the streets, responding to common symbols, the people on the bridge, like those of the fairs and boulevards, participated in their own culture, one that enabled them to escape temporarily the restraints, rituals, and regimentation of official life.

Indeed, it was a culture unified by derisive laughter at the world outside. The festive scene along the bridge and in the fairs mocked organized civil society through the coarse language and gestures of the people, in the maliciously derisive songs of the ambulant musicians, through the burlesque satire of the farceurs and marionettists, and, above all, in the social familiarity encouraged by an open, public place. Contact in the street among people normally separated by social rank, occupation, wealth, age, and sex was free and familiar. If derisive laughter was the common trait of street culture, integration was its social norm. "All the classes rubbed elbows,

3

bumping into each other, exchanging greetings and punches, gibes and bows".[1] Amid the clatter of wooden shoes and carriage wheels on the pavement, young girls and abbés, attorneys and nuns mingled with beggars, colporteurs, and dandies who carried parasols sold at each end of the bridge to protect their pale complexions from the sun. Hundreds of young lovers expressed their affection openly, rubbing shoulders with ostentatious bourgeois and prostitutes from the Butte de Saint-Roch who browsed along the boutiques, stopping perhaps to drink eau-de-vie from the jug of a porter shouting

> *Vi, vi, vi, vi, à boire, à boire,*
> *Excellent petit cabaret,*
> *Rempli de blanc et de clairet,*
> *De Rossolis, de Malvoisie,*
> *Pour qui n'aime point l'eau-de-vie.*[2]

The cries of the vendors were the most characteristic sound on the bridge and along the streets of Paris. Carrying their wares on their backs, the merchants beckoned customers with a crescendo of sounds. Louis-Sébastien Mercier wrote of them:

> The little people are naturally excessively noisy; they shout with a gross discordance. From every direction one hears raucous, shrill, deafening cries. *Voilà le maquereau qui n'est pas mort; il arrive, il arrive! Des harengs qui glacent, des harengs nouveaux! Pommes cuites au four! Il brûle, il brûle, il brûle!* These are cold cakes. *Voilà le plaisir des dames, voilà le plaisir!* This is a biscuit. *A la barque, à la barque, à l'écailler!* These are oysters. *Portugal, Portugal!* These are oranges.
> Join to these shouts the confusing clamor of the strolling old-clothes peddlers, the parasol vendors, the merchants of old scrap-iron, the water porters. The men have women's cries, and the women the cries of men. It is a perpetual yapping, and one would not know how to characterize the tone and accent of this wretched shouting when all these jumbled voices cross in an intersection.
> The chimney-sweeper and the whiting merchant still sing these discordant cries in their dreams when they sleep. . . .[3]

The cries expressed the festive culture of the people. They formed what Jean-Georges Kastner called "a *social music*, a *popular music* in a much broader sense than is generally given to this word. It is the ensemble of cries at once collective and individual which are like the voice of the people and which in certain civilizations become symbols, traditional phrases assumed by certain groups, certain distinct professions."[4] There were special verses, intonations, and chanting tunes for every item of food, wine, and merchandise. Many of the cries dated to the thirteenth century and contained images of food, excrement, and sex. Often abusive and profane, they were intended to provoke joy and laughter. Since they expressed the collective life of the people and were full of broad humor and double entendres, they were useful to opéra-comique writers such as Charles Favart and Charles-François Panard, who turned them into vaudevilles.

Bouquinistes were once a common sight on the bridge and, as they are today, along the neighboring quais.[5] In the early seventeenth century their stalls stretched along two broad parapets although in later years the regular booksellers of the city obtained a royal edict that drove them from the bridge and curtailed greatly the sale of old, cheaply priced books. Realizing that the book peddlers of the bridge were dispensing subversive *mazarinades,* Cardinal Mazarin enforced a ban on them. During the early decades of the eighteenth century, the bouquinistes returned to the bridge, but in 1742 Louis XV issued an edict charging that literature opposing the political and religious order was entering France illegally from foreign countries and was being circulated in cafés, in private homes, in the streets, and on the bridges. The books were said to be peddled by children and servants. Alleging that these acts violated the regulations pertaining to booksellers and printing, the edict prohibited portable boutiques on the bridges, parapets, quais, and other public thoroughfares. The departure of the bookdealers contributed to the decline of the bridge in the later decades of the century.

Still there was much to see and buy on the bridge and its environs. There were cafés at both ends of the bridge where strollers could watch the crowd, play dominoes, and listen to recitations of epigrams and poems. Boutiques on the nearby streets and on the quai des Orfèvres sold trinkets, fabrics from the Indies, toys, hardware, engravings, jewelry, English pistols, cutlery, and canes. On the bridge itself one could purchase dogs, face powder, wooden legs, glass eyes, false teeth, violets, tulips, roses, and fruits of all sort. The oranges of the Pont-Neuf were celebrated. Mercier wrote: "The beautiful yellow fruit is on its amphitheater in the middle of the Pont-Neuf! The passersby stop complacently in front of its numerous pyramids; its delightful smell puts a sensual smile on every lip."[6]

The bridge was a choice spot for beggars. Usually huddled near the equestrian statue of the king, they eked out a livelihood by entreating alms from the strollers or by selling verses to the singers and information to the pamphleteers. Describing a trip to Paris in 1788, an anonymous author reported a beggar appealing to him for "charity, please, for the love of the good Lord!" Getting no response, he tried invoking the name of Jesus Christ, then the Virgin Mary, also without effect. Only when he uttered the magic name of Henri IV did his appeal prove irresistible and elicit from the visitor a generous offering.[7]

Less harmless were the thieves, murderers, and gangsters who also populated the bridge. Despite the fact that Louis XIV made sure that a squad of *guet* (constables of the watch) were on duty at all times on the Pont-Neuf and that sentinels were stationed on the quais, the bridge was the scene of many crimes. The low elevation of the parapets enabled assassins to commit murder and escape easily, and thieves found the bridge an easier place to work than others because it had no houses, unlike other bridges in Paris. The band of Louis Dominique Cartouche perpetrated nightly robberies around 1720.[8] Moreover, the bridge was the favorite hunting ground of recruiting sergeants, whose headquarters were nearby on the quai de la Ferraille, where the bird market was located. Luring their victims by jingling sacks of *écus*, these flesh peddlers pressed drunks and ne'er-do-wells on the bridge into the royal military service, often applying force if the poor fellows later had a change of heart.

Despite its seamy side, the passing parade of Pont-Neuf strollers, merchants, and beggars was a bustling outdoor show in which everyone played a role. It rang with the laughter, shouts, and familiarity of the marketplace culture that had for years pervaded the fairs and eventually spread throughout the city. Paul Scarron perhaps caught the mood best, identifying the principal entertainers who made life hum on the bridge—the singers and the charlatans:

> *Vous, rendez-vous des charlatans,*
> *Des filoux, des passes-volants,*
> *Pont Neuf, ordinaire théâtre,*
> *De vendeurs d'onguents et d'emplâtre:*
> *Séjour des arracheurs de dents,*
> *Des fripiers, libraires, pédants,*
> *Des chanteurs de chansons nouvelles,*
> *D'entremetteurs de damoiselles,*
> *De coupe-bourse d'argotiers,*
> *De maîtres de sales métiers,*
> *D'opérateurs et de chimiques,*
> *Et de médecins spagiriques,*
> *De fins joüeurs de gobelets,*
> *De ceux qui rendent des poulets.*[9]

Song peddlers usually congregated at the edge of the bridge near the Samaritaine, the hydraulic machine that pumped water to that quarter of the city. With its bronze-colored religious statuary that gleamed in the sun, its galleries, clock tower, and carillon, the Samaritaine was perceived as a monument of the people. Louis XIV had the structure rebuilt late in his reign, and it was repaired in 1776 before being destroyed in 1813. For the song peddlers and their clients, it was a symbol, like the equestrian statue, of good King Henri. Perched on stools or shaded by umbrellas, the singers told coarse jokes and regaled the crowd with salty songs about the latest scandals of the court and city. Some sang hymns, and others offered ribald couplets.

As Mercier said, one provides a scapular to drive away the Devil while the other joyfully hails his victory. The latter attracted much larger crowds. "The singer of the outcasts hails wine, good living, and love, and celebrates the attractiveness of Margot."[10]

The best-known singers of Louis XIV's time were a blind man named Philippot, called Le Savoyard, a collection of whose songs was published in 1665, and Monsieur Etienne, coachman of a magistrate named Verthamont, who appeared daily near the Samaritaine wearing his livery long after he had quit his former occupation. The Savoyard was nearly always surrounded by a crowd that included cooks, lackeys, clerks, bourgeois, soldiers, and pickpockets. Memories of the coachman were still vivid when Alain-René Lesage composed a prologue about him called *L'Ombre du cocher poète,* which was performed at the Saint-Germain fair in 1722.[11] Arriving on the Pont-Neuf, Polichinelle tells a cobbler he is going to organize a show to replace the Opéra-Comique of the fair. When Polichinelle proves incapable of singing, however, the enchanter, Gribouri, summons the ghost of the coachman, the master of "itinerant opera." To the cracking sound of a coachman's whip, the "Apollo of the Samaritaine" emerges from hell in a spout of flames wearing his green livery costume and singing, "Flon, flon, la rira dondaine," the "march of the Pont-Neuf." He snaps his whip and Polichinelle and his players are miraculously transformed into singers. Unlike the Savoyard, who usually sang licentious or patriotic couplets on vaudeville airs, the coachman specialized in satires and in a macabre sort of song: laments about current criminal assaults and murders.

Many of the singers had an infirmity like the Savoyard, and all wore unusual clothing. The most popular singers in the early eighteenth century were Michel Le Clerc and Charles Minart.[12] Le Clerc wore a hood, cape, and large boots. The verses of many of his songs told of the agony of criminals who had recently been hanged, prompting Mercier to observe that "in Paris everything is material for a song; and whosoever, marshal of France or hanged person, has not been sung about . . . will remain unknown to the people. I maintain that the rakes in the street of the capital are more illustrious than Voltaire."[13] Minart, violin in hand, was dressed in tattered, patched clothing and wore a tricornered hat. A basket strapped to his back contained his songs and books of the Bibliothèque Bleue. He bawled his ribald songs lustily at the crowd, who could buy them for two liards each or three for a sou.

Most of the verses were scathing commentaries about the scandalous activities of prominent people or about current events. Some dealing with the king, his mistresses, and high-ranking churchmen and ministers could not be sung openly on the bridge, but the singers concealed them under their coats and sold them to the bemused throngs of people. Writers found appropriate

1. Charles Minart. Courtesy of the Bibliothèque Nationale Cabinet des Estampes (hereafter BN CE). (Oa 135c, TI, or photograph 76C75121.)

material in themes such as religious quarrels, the failures of royal politics, the immorality of polite society and of the notorious *filles d'opéra,* economic crises such as the Mississippi Bubble, the vanity of intellectuals, the pretensions of courtesans, the Comédie-Française's jealousy of the Opéra-Comique, and the dismissal of ministers.

Songs of derisive laughter and mockery of a social order that lay outside the marketplace culture of the people were an expression of popular liberation from that order. "Brushed aside from affairs by shyness, the people were compensated for their strained inactivity by some fleeting sparks where spirit and mischievousness often played a greater role than reason. They jeered in verse at despotism or the incompetence of their rulers, and they consoled themselves from any abuse by an epigram, from an insult through a song; that was the usual way of flouting bad luck."[14] The writers and hucksters of songs were less restrained and inhibited than other groups in the marketplace. The highest-placed persons of French society felt their invective the most, and the rimers had no compunctions about lying and defaming. Their excess is understandable when it is realized that songs were almost their only form of protest, their only way of expressing their contempt for the high orders and their irritation at having to submit to a political order not run in their interests. Their verses must have stung, because the ancien régime depended greatly on public respect and the songwriters resorted to every form of caustic derision to subvert that respect.

Since the songs were salacious and scandalous, not many writers identified themselves, and few verses were published, though they were copied over and over in manuscript. Songwriters known to the authorities often were arrested. Cardinal Fleury threatened songwriters with the galleys and had many incarcerated for their libels and antireligious verses. Louis XV ordered the lieutenant general of police to arrest songwriters when they maligned Madame de Pompadour. Attempts to suppress the malicious songs served only to increase the demand for them. And by Pompadour's time, being sent to the Bastille was practically a guarantee of fame. One writer who slandered Chancellor Maupeou fled to England to avoid arrest. He later wrote Maupeou that the attempted arrest was worth 30,000 livres to him in sales of his song. Anything forbidden was eagerly sought after, especially by a public whose principal source of scandalous news was songs.

The tunes themselves were often of popular origin; and the verses, as their crudeness of style suggests, were in many instances probably written by the singers, peddlers, and lackeys of the bridge. Certainly, they were aimed at the crowd on the bridge and expressed its derision of polite society. But ordinary people could not have written many of the "Pont-Neufs" because the verses contained information about the lives of high-placed individuals to which the lower ranks would not have been privy.[15] Indeed, it is a fact that many of the

2. Song merchant. Engraving by Jacques Juillet about 1768. Verse:

Que je suis malheureux
Qu'el indigne metier
D'être le ventre creux
Obligé de chanter.

(BN CE, Oa 135 c, T1. See also MC. Moeurs, P.C. 62 bis.)

verses were composed by people of rank. They included the D'Argensons, the princesse de Conti (daughter of Louis XIV and Mme La Vallière), the duchesse de Bourbon, the comte de Maurepas who was secrétaire d'Etat for most of his life, and Louis XVI's brother, the comte d'Artois. Courtiers themselves, thus supplied the crowd with the malicious news that formed one of the cornerstones of marketplace culture.

Not only were popular songs written by nobles, but they also enjoyed a great vogue among the high ranks of society, especially in the second half of the eighteenth century. Reviewing a collection of songs by Antoine-Pierre-Auguste de Piis with verses by several authors, which Piis presented to the king's sister, the *Journal de Paris* commented: "From the first to the last orders of society, everyone sings or likes to hear singing; and in order to please most of these amateurs, it is not always necessary for the words to be delicate: some puns, some equivocations are sufficient to fulfill the purpose."[16]

Charles Collé became the favorite songwriter of *le monde*, for whose private theaters he also composed licentious *parades* fashioned on those of the streets. Collé brought the Pont-Neufs into the salons. The couplets he wrote were nearly always bawdy, erotic, and derisive, as these two verses indicate:

> *L'Eventail à la main,*
> *J'entre dans un jardin;*
> *Ma juppe flotte en l'air et s'élève avec grâce.*
> *Je crois que c'est un vent badin*
> *Qui vient, qui folâtre et qui passe:*
> *C'était, ma chère, au lieu du vent,*
> *Un Cordelier du grand couvent.*[17]

> *Au Dieu d'Amour, une Pucelle*
> *Offroit un jour une chandelle,*
> *Pour en obtenir un amant.*
> *Le Dieu sourit à sa demande,*
> *Et lui dit: Belle, en attendant,*
> *Servez-vous toujours de l'offrande.*[18]

In 1783, Mercier complained that from the time that the court began to sing popular songs, they had become too coarse, spiteful, and acrid.[19]

An inspection of the surviving song collections of the seventeenth and eighteenth centuries readily shows who the public's favorite villains were. One of the best collections provides no fewer than 22 songs about the maréchal de Villeroy, many of which dealt jeeringly with his defeat in Italy at the hands of Prince Eugen.[20] Prominent figures such as Bishop Jacques-Bénigne Bossuet and Madame de Maintenon were treated even more extensively, and most of the songs written in the years 1709–1715 commented on

France's military and diplomatic defeats. The atmosphere of the court in 1709 was evoked in these stanzas to the very popular air "Reveillez-vous, belle endormie":

Louis toujours de gloire avide
mais de périssant à veue d'oeil
Par l'ambition qui le guide
Se fait escorter au cercueil.

Sa sempite cruelle maîtresse
Plus souveraine que jamais
Malgré le mal qui nous oppresse
Ne veut point qu'on fasse la paix.

Le Dauphin bourgeois de Versailles
Chasse, mange, et se divertit
La Chouine cette vieille médaille
Seul l'occupe et le ravit

Bourgogne dévot et stupide
Passe ses jours en oraison
Plus rassoté d'Adelaide
Qu'un aveugle de son baton.

Pour lui dissimulant sa haine
Elle contraint tous ses désirs
Et déjà voudroit entre Reyne
Pour goûter de libres plaisirs. . . .

Monsieur ayant la foiblesse
De proscrire la Dargenton
Qui voudroit être sa maîtresse
Qu'une élève de la fillon.

Il fait succéder à la gloire
La musique et la volupté
On le nommera dans l'histoire
Héro de sensualité. . . .

A la foire à la Comédie
Conti tous les jours est fiché
Le goût du théâtre étudie
Pour se voir à Sceaux recherché.[21]

Spared throughout most of his reign, Louis XIV speedily became a victim of acerbic attack on his death in 1715. A verse from "Louis XIV aux enfers" shows the typical tone of these pieces:

Sur les bords de l'Achéron,
L'invincible monarque
Criait fièrement à Caron
Hé! qu'on prépare la barque

> *Ne parlez pas si haut, Bourbon,*
> *La faridondaine, la faridondon,*
> *Ici vous serez obéi, biribi,*
> *A la façon de Barbari, mon ami.*[22]

And another, on the air "Des pendules":

> *Les uns le nomment Louis le Grand*
> *Et d'autres Louis le tyran*
> *Louis banqueroutier Louis l'auguste*
> *Et c'est raisonner assez juste*
> *Car n'eut d'autres raisons jamais*
> *Qu'il faut, nous voulons et vous plaît. . . .*
>
> *Son confesseur qui le savoit*
> *Pour pénitence lui donnoit*
> *D'exterminer les Jansenistes*
> *Dont empêché il avoit la liste*
> *Et chaque pêché pardonnoit*
> *Pour une lettre de cachet.*[23]

The regent, his successor, fared no better, being subjected to scornful epitaphs and funeral orations on his death. His personal iniquities occupied the songwriters more than his politics, especially the incestuous relationship the duc de Saint-Simon reported between the regent and his daughter, the duchesse de Berry:

> *Que notre Régent et sa fille*
> *Commettent mainte peccadille,*
> *C'est un fait qui semble constant,*
> *Mais que par lui elle soit mère,*
> *Se peut-il que d'un même enfant*
> *Il soit le grand-père et le père.*[24]

Saint-Simon was upbraided in return, however:

> *Régent, que veux-tu peine*
> *De ce petit Simon, boudrillon?*
> *Vil insecte de terre,*
> *Vrai gibier de lardon boudrillon*
> *Petit boudrillon, boudrillon don don*
> *Petit boudrillon, boudrillon don don.*
> *Tout le monde s'étonne*
> *Que tu souffres Simon*
> *Qui chez toi se cramponne*
> *Comme un petit morphion.*

The songwriters found ample grist for their mill in the scandals of the Mississippi Bubble, the Parlement of Paris, the Jansenists, and the convulsionaries of Saint-Médard. The latter were treated to this verse:

> *Chaque malade en silence,*
> *Cachant sa convalescence,*
> *Sur son tombeau s'ecriera:*
> *Miracle-ci*
> *Miracle-là*
> *Là, là, là, là.*[25]

The favorite whipping boy of this period was Cardinal Fleury. Fleury was ridiculed for his attempt to enforce the papel bull Unigenitus, for the decline of French trade and a weak foreign policy, for appointing poor officials, and for his own avarice. He retaliated by urging Maurepas, who wrote songs for the court, to flood the streets with verses attacking his enemies.[26]

The reign of Louis XV was the apogee of the era of derisive laughter through song. More songs appeared during his reign than in any previous one. The crowd's favorite victim was the king's mistress, Pompadour. For 15 years the songwriters reviled her unmercifully, mainly for her intrusion in politics. She was blamed for the Seven Years' War, and all of her favorites —Soubise, Richelieu, Clermont, for example—were criticized. Not even Madame du Barry, whom Parisians despised and for whom a familiar old tune "La Boulonnaise" was renamed "La Bourbonnaise," was raked so mercilessly as Pompadour. Reporting the public's anger at Pompadour in 1749, D'Argenson noted that people at Versailles complained to Berryer, the lieutenant general of police, about the flood of "horrible songs" dealing with her and the king.[27] D'Argenson quoted the verses of one song on the air of "Les Trembleurs":

> *Les grands seigneurs s'avilissent,*
> *Les financiers s'enrichissent,*
> *Tous les poissons s'agrandissent:*
> *C'est le règne des vauriens.*
> *On épuise la finance*
> *En bâtiments, en dépenses;*
> *L'Etat tombe en décadence,*
> *Le roi ne met ordre à rien, rien, rien.*
>
> *Une petite bourgeoise*
> *Elevée à la grivoise,*
> *Mesurant tout à toise,*
> *Fait de la cour un taudis*
> *Le Roi, malgré son scrupule,*
> *Pour elle follement brûle;*
> *Cette flamme ridicule*
> *Excite dans tout Paris, ris, ris, ris. . . .*

> *Si dans les beautés choisies,*
> *Elle étoit des plus jolies,*
> *On pardonne les folies,*
> *Quand l'objet est un bijou;*
> *Mais pour si mince figure,*
> *Et si sotte créature,*
> *S'attirer tant de murmures,*
> *Chacun pense le roi fou, fou, fou.*

The vogue for these songs has become such "a great rage," D'Argenson insisted, that they will soon be as abundant as the *mazarinades* once were.

As for Louis XV, his death was treated as a welcome release from oppression. A song of 1774 had this harsh judgement:

> *Etais-tu bon? c'est un problème*
> *Qu'on peut résoudre à peu de frais;*
> *Un bon prince ne fit jamais*
> *Le malheur d'un peuple qui l'aime;*
> *Car on ne peut appeler bon*
> *Un roi sans frein et sans raison*
> *Qui ne vécut que pour lui-même.*[29]

In the last decades of the ancien régime, the songwriters dealt with the American war, the dismissal of Necker, the Estates General, the early balloon flights, the duc de Chartres' alterations of the Palais-Royal, Gluck and Piccini, womens' hairstyles, and Beaumarchais' *Le Mariage de Figaro,* among other topics. The Pont-Neuf was still the home of songwriters although their vogue had passed.

In their heyday the singers were rivaled on the bridge by charlatans. Indeed, in this age of skepticism and scientific progress, Parisians found no type of entertainer more fascinating than a charlatan. Perhaps the charlatans spoke to and for the people more realistically than did the vaunted philosophes. The charlatan in the comédie-parade *Le Charlatan ou le docteur Sacroton* (1780) asks: "Who is it that speaks to the public today? No one, my friend, no one but us."[29] The name probably derives from *scarlatano* because a well-known charlatan of the early seventeenth century, Desiderio-Descombes, who sold antidotes for snake bites, wore scarlet clothing.[30] Charlatans sold ointments, lotions, herbs, elixirs, and tonics guaranteed to cure everything from baldness to warts. They had opiates and plasters for stomach ailments; electuaries and roots for toothaches; oils for deafness; pomades for sore feet; potions and balms for itching and bad temper; grease for burns; unguents made from butter, oil, wax, herbs, and the fat from phoenixes, they claimed. Some charlatans hawked earth alleged to be from Bethlehem, which they said helped to give milk to wet nurses. They bandaged wounds, set broken bones, and sold crystal eyes and wooden legs. They had soaps and powders to whiten teeth, pastes for corns, and slings for cramps. Popular belief in the healing and regenerative powers of their drugs was widespread. They catered to the same taste for the marvelous and the magical that the public displayed throughout the century in its fascination with such phenomena as mesmerism, necromancy, phantasmagoria, and other forms of white and black magic. Their remedies were mysterious and seemed miraculous. The Pont-Neuf charlatans waxed eloquently on the curative qualities of their medications, usually insisting they came from the Orient. Their harangues were peppered with Italian, Spanish, and Latin phrases. Nearly all had someone in their entourage dressed like a Moroccan to enhance the exoticism. Many asserted that they had *lettres patentes* from foreign rulers confirming the efficacy of their medications or that they had learned their formulas from the Prince of Transylvania or the ruler of some other remote country.

Though charmed by their elixirs, the public clustered around the charlatans because they provided a free show as part of the sales pitch. They employed monkeys, musicians, acrobats, and grimacers to entertain the people and arouse interest in their wares. They attracted the crowd with guitars or violin music. Wearing bizarre, multicolored costumes, they often performed little farces and concerts with songs and dances. The shows of the charlatans were, of course, free and were not very different from those of the fair actors performing on their *tréteaux*. Indeed, they borrowed material from each other and sometimes moved from one occupation to the other. In the 1720s an actor named Toscano of the Comédie-Italienne quit the theater and got rich as a medicine man.

Many of the seventeenth-century charlatans were Italian. The best-known was Hieronimo de Ferranti from Orvieto. A group of veiled girls harangued the crowd about the therapeutic value of his oils and salves. All were made with a drug that became known as *orviétan*, after his birthplace, whose formula was supplied to Ferranti by an apothecary of the rue Dauphine. The *orviétan* became the standard designation for various medications of later charlatans such as Christophe Contiegi and Monsieur Barry, who set up his act on the quai near the rue Guénégaud. Contiegi with his performers and the crowd were engraved in 1649.[31] This verse appeared on the engraving:

> *L'Orviétan est bon*
> *Contre toute sorte de vermin.*
> *Contre beste vénimeuse, et chiens enragés*
> *Contre la peste. Contre les vers qui nous mange*
> *Contre la petite verole et autre. . . .*

French charlatans, most of whom came from Normandy and Picardy, often passed themselves off as Italians or were attended by servants whom they referred to as Italians. Like Moors, Italians were considered exotic. Barry, about whom Dancourt wrote a comedy (*L'Opérateur Barry*) in 1702, was the successor of the first important French charlatan of the ancien régime, Tabarin. Appearing around 1620, Tabarin set up his stage on the Place Dauphine. He sold pomades and an opium electuary, and he amused the crowd with coarse burlesque routines.

In the early years of the eighteenth century the principal charlatan of the bridge was Cavanel, who sold a balm much in demand called Simone, also the name of his little, long-tailed monkey who did an assortment of tricks. His contemporary, Turpin, hawked his drugs while his associates, dressed as Pierrot and Scaramouche, performed *parades*. They were accused of being pickpockets as well, and their elixirs contained poisons that sometimes caused illness, even death. Periodically, ordinances were issued against charlatans, but they were never enforced for very long until the end of the eighteenth century.[32] Many charlatans became very wealthy, notably Monsieur Willars, who sold bottled water from the Seine that he promised would prolong life to the age of 150. A member of the French Guards named Printemps got rich before the Faculty of Medicine stopped him from selling a decoction of hay.

Not infrequently charlatans gained the attention of the royal court. In December 1739 the *Gazette à la main* announced the arrival in Paris of a Saxon charlatan from England who enjoyed the protection of the duc d'Orléans.[33] Specializing in cataract operations, he allegedly cured people of blindness. He treated the blind father of a young man attached to the duc's train until the blind man's wife complained that her husband's incapacity was worth 600 livres a year to them and that he would lose this trade if he recovered his sight.

By the late eighteenth century, charlatanism became more closely identified in the popular mentality with various forms of magic, and the Pont-Neuf charlatans combined the sale of elixirs with other, nonmedicinal preparations and magic tricks. In 1776 a Venetian named Rupano had powders to clean teeth, stain removers, and wax to heal corns.[34] Signora Francisca hawked her grease pomades to prevent falling hair and graying with a show of six Asian snakes walking the tightrope and wrapping themselves around her neck and body. Sieur Martini told fortunes by cards and palmistry; and Sieur Jouanaux analyzed dreams, explained the means of becoming invisible, and promised to prolong life for over 5,000 years. Specializing in dog and cat ailments, Monsieur Mochine and his two female assistants, Demoncy and Varechon, hawked cures for inflammations, gall, nasal congestion, cancer, ulcers, and gangrene. They set the broken bones of dogs and cats; clipped and bled them for one livre, four sous; and also sold them.

By the 1780s the king's doctor had managed to drive from the bridge most of the *orviétan* sellers and those who dealt in elixirs and powders with an opiate base. A decree by the Parlement of Paris in May 1781 banned the sale of new remedies.[35] Charlatans, therefore, turned more and more to magic.[36] One had a theory of the cause of attraction and planetary motion; another claimed discovery of a universal agent capable of modifying any sort of matter; still another explained the secrets of generation and the mechanism of nature. The popular mind was captivated by "science," especially physics, mechanics, and botany, and by its close relative, magic.

Public tooth pulling had long been one of the favorite exhibitions of the Pont-Neuf charlatans. In the seventeenth century Monsieur Cormier accompanied his operations with conjuring tricks, grimaces, and hooting. Seigneur Rondin sold unguents and replaced the teeth he yanked with false ones. By far the most celebrated and revered tooth-pulling charlatan of the eighteenth century was a fellow known as "le grand Thomas," who from 1711 until about 1733, performed with a monkey on an iron cart on a platform near the bronze horse bearing the people's king. A man of large girth, Thomas always wore a tricornered hat with a great plume, a Basque jerkin, a long vest with buttons, a white tie, and a large plaque like a badge on his chest. His bellowing harangues poured from an earnest and cheerful face. Thomas told horoscopes; sold a medicine for five sous to cure liver and kidney ailments, gout, and fever; and yanked the public's teeth with tremendous force, gusto and ceremony, often lifting his patients several feet off the ground. Jean-Baptiste Gouriet wrote of him: "Big Thomas operated effortlessly whenever the tooth held on a little; but when it proved unyielding, it is said that he made his man fall to his knees and lifted him from the ground up to three times with the force of a bull. That is for the lower jaw. It is not known how he attacked the upper jaw; perhaps he used a winch."[37]

The people who frequented the Pont-Neuf adored Thomas not only because he provided a valuable service and put on a fine show, but also because he was an amiable fellow and a generous one. On occasion he extracted teeth for nothing, and he gave large banquets on the bridge for the poor. In 1728, ostensibly in order to express his happiness about the king's recovery from an illness, Thomas pulled teeth at no charge for three days on the Pont-Neuf and in the prisons and hospitals, where he had once been a surgeon's assistant. In 1729, in celebration of the birth of the dauphin, Thomas dispensed his medicines and his dental services freely for fifteen days. He also planned a gigantic banquet around the statue of Henri IV. He bought beef, lamb, and goose for the occasion. Although he had police permission to hold the affair, on September 19 at the last minute they stopped it, seized the food, and ordered Thomas not to show up. Several days earlier Thomas had posted signs announcing the gala repast. Unaware of the cancellation, thousands of people flocked to the bridge, the quais, and the

3. Grand Thomas, Courtesy of the Musée du Carnavalet (hereafter MC).
(Moeurs, p.c. 11.)

Place Dauphine. The joyful fête turned into an angry demonstration against this popular hero. The poet Alexis Piron, who frequented the Pont-Neuf and the Place Maubert in order to pick up the marketplace language and to gather subject matter for his opéras-comiques, has left an eyewitness account of the event:

> Meanwhile, the guests arrived, having for a bridal gown only their dirty shirt, some muddy caps, leather aprons, and wooden shoes. These gentlemen, having found on the Pont-Neuf neither soup pots nor clean bowls, fell back to the quai Conti, where the host lived. They banged insolently and said that the public was sacred and that it would not be mocked in such a way by him. The great Thomas, appearing at a window as if he were at a tribune, believed he could calm these famished people by the sight of his august face and the public eloquence that he has put to good use for so long. An empty belly has no ears. The guests rebelled to such an extent that the great Thomas was pushed to this extreme of dragging outside the only plate that the inspector of police had left him.[38]

Refusing to be appeased, the crowd smashed Thomas' windows. The guard finally intervened to stop the demonstration. Two days later a song, "Sur le repas du grand Thomas," was sold on the bridge.

> *De toute part*
> *Tout le peuple accouroit en foule,*
> *De toute part,*
> *De Paris et de Vaugirard,*
> *De Ménilmontant et du Roule*
> *Croyant que le bon vin y coule,*
> *De toute part.*
>
> *Y pensois-tu?*
> *Thomas faisant cette dépense,*
> *Y pensois-tu?*
> *Ah! voilà les gourmands à cul:*
> *Point de repas, point de bombance,*
> *L'on en rit par toute la France;*
> *Y pensois-tu?*

Doubtless the most festive occasion in Thomas's career was his procession to Versailles for an audience with the king and queen. He made quite a show of it to the delight of the bridge people. Thomas appeared with his entourage on the bridge wearing an enormous silver hat with a globe and a singing *coq* on top. A lappet at the base of this headgear displayed the arms of France and Navarre along with an emblem of the sun with the words "Nec pluribus impar." His scarlet costume cut in Turkish style was ornamented with designs of gems, jaws, and teeth. Teeth also adorned the drapery of his horse. A sword six feet long was clasped to Thomas's waist. The crowd acclaimed him as he rode off with an entourage including a trumpeter, a drummer, a flag-bearer, a tisane merchant, and a pastrycook.

Thomas was a folk hero, a symbol of the marketplace culture of Henri's bridge. Numerous engravings and songs commemorating his feats testified to his enormous popularity. When he died, an "Apothéose du docteur gros Thomas" was sung on the air "Un jour, le malheureux Lysandre":

> *Sur un char ceint de garde-fous,*
> *Construit d'une forme nouvelle,*
> *Et y débutoit pour cinq sous*
> *La médecine universelle;*
> *Le foie et les reins entrepris*
> *Par son remède étoient guéris,*
> *Et, par une secrète cause*
> *Qu'il connoissoit, dans tous les maux*
> *Il ordonnoit la même dose*
> *Pour les hommes et les chevaux.*[39]

2

Raillery in the Fairs

LONG BEFORE Thomas tickled the crowd with his buoyant good humor, long before Henri IV's bridge was built, the Parisian fairs rang with the carnival aura of popular life. But only during the first several decades of the eighteenth century did they become the heartland of popular entertainment. There were many fairs in or near Paris. The fair of Saint Clair was held in late July and August for the benefit of the merchants on the rue Saint-Victor. In the more rustic setting of the park of Saint-Cloud on the Seine to the west of Paris, boutiques and taverns were set up in the vicinity of the grand cascade designed by Antoine Lepautre in the seventeenth century. Lasting only eight days, this fair offered such recreations as balls, fireworks, marionettes, and plays performed by provincial actors.[1] Tickets to these shows, which were often drawn from the repertoire of the Parisian theaters, cost as little as 12 or 2 sous. The eighteenth-century version of the modern *fête des loges* held at Saint-Germain-en-Laye was the *foire de Bezons*, a small wine-growing village west of the city.[2] Parisians flocked there every year on the first Sunday in September, and it was customary to gather at the Etoile of the Champs-Elysées for a festive, processional return to the city. The throng of people from all orders of society amused themselves among the tents and carts strung out on the prairie of Bezons. Fairs were also held in most Parisian parishes on patron saints' days. Religious images and books were sold along with spiced breads and wafers.

All these fairs, which were of short duration and offered minimal paid entertainments, paled, however, alongside the two great ones of the age—the fairs of Saint-Germain and Saint-Laurent. Both were begun by monks in the Middle Ages to accommodate pilgrims who congregated in churches on certain specified days to honor relics.[3] The monks rented stalls to merchants to sell food and wares and eventually permitted entertainers to perform. Part of their profits were given to the crown in return for its guarantee of the privilege of the fair. The Saint-Laurent fair was situated after 1662 on five acres of land above the church of Saint-Laurent between the faubourgs of Saint-Denis and Saint-Martin, where the Gare de l'Est is today. In 1663 the priests of the mission of Saint-Lazare, whose proprietary rights over the fair had been upheld several times since the fourteenth century, built eight tent-covered markets for the merchants. Over a hundred boutiques, renting for two sous a *toise* (6½ feet), were set up along the intersecting alleys. The merchants sold pots of rich soil and sandstone, crockery, crystal, and toys. At the eastern edge of the fair, cabarets, restaurants, and *spectacles* were installed in a spacious yard (the *préau*) surrounded by gardens. Six passages were cut through the walls surrounding the fair. The grounds were lined with acacia trees, and after 1706 chestnut trees from India were planted. The fair opened in late July and closed on the feast day of Saint Michel in September though it was often prolonged.[4]

The more fashionable fair of Saint-Germain,[5] which ran from February 3 until Palm Sunday, extended over an area of crisscrossing streets, including the rue du Four, the rue de Buci, and the rue des Quatre-Vents. Two huge markets, 130 steps long and 100 wide, were covered by a magnificent timbered roof built in the sixteenth century at the instigation of the abbé of Saint-Germain, a roof that the composer Charles Favart called "one of the marvels of Paris."[6] The entire terrain was sunken, six to eight feet deeper in some places than the surrounding land, forming what one observer called "a pit or rather a mere hole in the middle of the faubourg. . . ."[7] Visitors complained about the dangerous, narrow passageways that had to be crossed to gain access to the seven doors into the fair. Louis-Sébastien Mercier, who called the door on the side of the rue de Tournon "the most perilous spot in Paris," noted that people were in danger of being hit by carriages as soon as they descended into "this narrow gorge."[8] Still, the pit did not deter thousands from attending the fair every day.

Although the monks had sold the booths of the fair to various entrepreneurs over the years, they still zealously guarded the seigneurial rights they had exercised for centuries. They were entitled to six deniers in taxes, three livres rent per loge, the *lods et ventes*, and a few other charges. Accusing the monks of imposing excessive entrance fees on the merchants, Henri Sauval grumbled that "the abbé who is not satisfied with his rights of entrance comes back to the cost under other pretexts."[9] Usually, the monks had their way. In 1718, for example, they protested to the Conseil d'Etat that entertainers were moving their shows into the streets outside the enclosure of the fair, thus avoiding the abbey's fees.[10] Claiming that the *préau* was less occupied than earlier because of this tactic and that the merchants were suffering, the abbé asked the crown to intervene. The regent complied promptly, ordering the suppression of *spectacles* not occupying a loge inside the fair.

Nowhere in Paris could a more sumptuous array of products be seen than at the Saint-Germain fair. Food items included pastry, spiced breads, jams, waffles, fruit, candy, lemonade, fruit drinks, tisane, beer, and eau-de-vie. Two Armenians, assisted by a garçon named Francesco Procopio di Coltelli, began selling coffee for two and a half sous a cup in the early 1670s. Joachim Nemeitz warned his readers against eating too many glazed chestnuts, pistachios, truffles, jams, and tuna fish. High fever and illness, he suggested, might result from drinking the wines in vogue—Frontignac, Muscat, and Saint-Laurent.[11] The merchants who had stalls in the fair, some from Paris, but many from Amiens, Rheims, Beauvais, and other communities, included wigmakers, bakers, linen sellers, cask makers, coopers, druggists, cabinet-makers, carpenters, and locksmiths. The most expensive items were mirrors, perfume, gloves, porcelain, jewelry, Moroccan leather, lace, paintings, sculpture, and engravings. Charles Sorel declared that the fair "was a place of joy and even debauchery where one must certainly sell merchandise which would serve intemperance and vanity."[12] Although books were no longer sold at the fair in the eighteenth century, Sorel claimed they were purchased in his time as status symbols. People who could scarcely read their native language bought books in Greek and Latin. They also bought works of art. Sorel added that "peasants and other people of low stock take as much pleasure in the grotesque paintings made to distemper as people of taste get in seeing the most beautiful tableaux."[13]

The fair merchants also relied on gambling as a source of revenue. Some at Saint-Germain earned several hundred livres a day from operating dice and card games in their boutiques.[14] It was a blow, therefore, when the police tried to stop these games by ordinance in 1708, 1716, 1722, and 1741. The latter imposed a fine of 500 livres on violators. Gambling, whether in the form of dice, spinning wheels, lotteries, cards, or skittles, was so widespread in eighteenth-century Paris among all social levels, however, that the fair merchants were soon back in business, along with others who made a full-time occupation out of gambling. Germain Brice noted that at Saint-Germain "professional gamblers never fail to go there in order to deal deadly blows to the purses of suckers."[15] Since these gambling boutiques were usually packed with people, they were favorite haunts of thieves who stole "everything that was in the pockets of those near them. They cut the back of women's dresses and the coats of men who were extremely surprised to see themselves in this apparel."[16] In 1778 the secrétaire d'Etat for Paris cracked down hard on games of chance in an effort to put teeth into the many *arrêts* of the Parlement of Paris and the ordinances of the police against them.[17] It may have had some effect because the fairs declined in the last decade before the Revolution.

The prohibitions against gambling constituted only a small knot in the tangle of edicts issued over the years governing the Parisian fairs. There were laws prohibiting fair operations on Sundays and fêtes, yet there were often entertainments on those days despite an ordinance of 30 June 1732 stipulating a fine of 100 livres for violators. There were edicts against drawing swords in the fairs, cursing, prostitution, vagrancy, bearing arms or canes, and causing public disturbances. Persons obstructing the public thoroughfare or attempting to shunt people into loges or *spectacles* were subject to arrest. An edict required boutiques to close at 10 P.M. The job of enforcing this thicket of often conflicting legislation fell principally on the *commissaires* of the Châtelet. They had the awesome responsibility of preserving order in the fairs and of arbitrating disputes among fair people. There were 48 of these officers of the long robe assigned to the various quarters of the city. Functioning somewhat like justices of the peace, the *commissaires* combined police work with the execution of civil and criminal justice. Reporting regularly to the lieutenant general of police, they could settle disputes at their residences and receive written protests from contesting parties. They interrogated persons summoned by writs of subpoena; determined whether police ordinances were being obeyed; certified bankruptcies, deaths, and injunctions; and kept accounts of incorporation and trusteeships. But for those assigned to districts where the fairs were held, the maintenance of order in an atmosphere of café brawls, pickpocket robberies, brouhahas, and scandals in the theaters was the main task of the *commissaire*.[18]

Most violations of law and disruptions of the peace occurred unsurprisingly in and around the cabarets of the fairs. Often adorned with wall hangings, pictures, chandeliers, and mirrors, the cabarets sold eau-de-vie, hard cider, muscat, liqueurs, and hippocras, in addition to wine. "The cafés are magnificent," Liger wrote, "as much through the illuminations that light them as through the neatness of the furniture with which they are decorated."[19] Some of the cabarets became celebrated. In their *opéra-comique Les Désespérés* (1732), Lesage and d'Orneval referred glowingly to Madame Dubois's cabaret, which was renowned for its wines:

> J'ai des vins de chaque canton,
> Du pays Bourguignon;
> J'ai de l'excellent Mâcon,
> Des vins de Grave et d'Oléron;
> J'ai du Champenois,
> De l'Orléanois
> Vins d'Anjou, de Blois,

> *Avec du Nantois;*
> *J'ai du vin d'Auxerre,*
> *De Tonnerre,*
> *Délicat;*
> *De l'incomparable Auvergnat,*
> *Du bon Sancerre*
> *Et bien d'autres vins*
> *Fins*
> *Qui chassent les chagrins.*[20]

But if the cabarets were adored by the crowds and the entertainers, they were a trap for naive provincials and a headache for the police and the *commissaires*. The French Guards were often obliged to remove drunkards forcibly from these places, sometimes several times an evening, and they frequently had to close down cafés.[21] There were occasions when more than 25 people were arrested at one time in a cabaret.[22] After-hours sales of alcohol were apparently a major problem. Ordinances of 21 April and 28 November 1724, 31 May 1726, and 19 May 1731 prohibited tavern keepers and wine merchants from serving after 10:00 P.M. An ordinance of 30 June 1739 referred specifically to illegal sales of liquor in the *préau* of Saint-Laurent.[23]

Prostitution was a natural complement to cabaret life. Wooden partitions in the cabarets separated people engaged in sexual activity. Liger, who referred to the cabarets as Venus's academy, wrote of eavesdropping on a girl at a Saint-Laurent café who "sacrificed to her lover the rights that conjugal fidelity authorizes only for the husband."[24] When not doing business right in the cabaret, the girls adjourned with their clients to rooms supplied by the cabaret proprietor or the owner of one of the houses located in gardens behind the cafés and boutiques.[25] Commissaire Joseph Aubert reported on 14 June 1743 that several proprietors in the area of the Saint-Laurent fair were renting rooms and boutiques "to some men and women of suspect conduct for occupancy during the time of the said fair Saint-Laurent, who, under the pretext of selling beer, coffee, and liqueurs there, provide refuge for thieves, vagabonds, men and women of the evil life and provide this commerce only in order to sanction a public debauchery, as a result of which several disorders occurred."[26] The *commissaire* added that many merchants leased their boutiques in the fair to people who "engage in a scandalous commerce" while appearing to sell drinks. Aubert's report resulted in an ordinance prohibiting leases without the *commissaire's* consent. Yet ordinances referring to scandalous activity later in the century indicate that the police were unable to control prostitution. Des Essarts commented that "there is no capital where this crime is more common, less hidden and even public, than in Paris."[27]

The *commissaires* were kept constantly busy by the freewheeling behavior that prevailed inside the fair *spectacles*. The police regulations governing conduct at the Opéra-Comique provide an idea of the problem. These stipulated that only hairdressers, maids, and people necessary "to their adjustment" could enter the dressing rooms of female performers; that actors and especially actresses and female dancers could appear on stage and in the wings only to perform their roles, after which they must return to their dressing rooms, taking care to behave modestly and not to meander; that performers must be at rehearsals on time or pay a fine of six livres for the first offense and dismissal for the second.[28] The same fine and threat of discharge were specified for drunkenness. The fines were to be collected by a comptroller, who would turn the money over to the most needy supernumeraries of the troupe. Finally, actors were forbidden to take a seat in a box in the hall during performances.

It is rather surprising that serious crime was not more prevalent in the fairs. There were, to be sure, many incidents arising from the raucous atmosphere of this marketplace setting. Nemeitz urged people not to go to the fairs more than twice a week because in the press of the crowd one could easily become involved in dangerous quarrels.[29] Curses, insults, shoving, and obscene gesturing were characteristics of the scene and led to occasional disturbances. In 1721 there was an uproar when several royal pages prevented the pages of foreign ambassadors from entering the theater of the *danseurs de corde* at Saint-Germain. For three days, dozens of people carried canes in the streets.[30] On 31 May 1738, two attractive girls walking with a cavalier in the fair were approached by a duke and his friends. When the duke put his hand on one of the girl's breasts, the cavalier knocked the intruder down, then fled with the girls into a boutique.[31] On 6 March 1764, the French Guard arrested Robert du Vau, custodian for Monsieur le Ma'al d'Isenghyen, for urinating in public in one of the streets of the fair Saint-Germain. The *commissaire* later sent him to jail.[32] These kinds of incidents occurred frequently in the fairs. Pushing and shoving in the *spectacles* was normal behaviour, and spectators had to be constantly alert against pickpockets after money, watches, handkerchiefs, jackets, and hats. François Colletet warned against challenging thieves who were usually prepared to pull a knife or sword. No one has characterized the scene better than he:

> En vérité, nous pouvons dire,
> Que l'on a grand sujet de rire
> De ce que l'on voit tous les jours
> Dans la ville, dans les fauxbourgs:
> Un homme qui n'a rien à faire,
> A qui sa maison peut déplaire,
> Et n'a point matière de rire;
> N'a qu'à faire un tour de Paris,

En moins de quatre promenades,
Il verra faire des gambades
A des foux et des Arlequins
A des ivrognes, des coquins.
Au peuple cet hydre à sept têtes
Qui suscite mille tempêtes,
Met en rumeur tout le quartier,
Et lui seul fait le bruit entier:
Tantôt il verra dans la boue
Un fou qui se roule et joue,
Un voisin qui se battra,
Un autre qui s'injuriera,
Une femme dans son ménage,
Qui cruelle humeur, fera rage,
D'autres (exemple trop honteux),
Qui s'arracheront les cheveux,
Se chanteront dix nulles pouilles,
Se frapperont de leurs quenouilles,
Et se diront leurs vérités,
A toute heure, et de tous côtés,
Je t'en ai, dans une sortie,
Déjà fait voir une partie;
Tu verras l'autre assurément,
Avant qu'il soit nuit seulement;
Je vois déjà dans cette rue
Cent gens qui font le pied de grue.[33]

The job of arbitrating conflicts among fair merchants, entertainers, administrators, and entrepreneurs was just as burdensome for the *commissaires* as keeping order. These disputes were usually between the merchants and groups of syndics who provided the capital for the fairs and managed them. A dispute over the charges the syndics imposed on the merchants at Saint-Laurent in 1778 illustrates the point.[34] The documents showed that, for the rental of nearly 200 loges covering a space of 30,000 square feet at 2 sous 6 liards a foot, the merchants owed the syndics 3,750 livres, but they had actually assessed the merchants much more based on what the merchants regarded as new and exorbitant charges. The merchants complained to Commissaire Mutel and to Le Noir, the lieutenant general of police. They cited such items as flowers for the opening of the fair, lodging for the guard, fees for the syndics, and posters, all of which they regarded as superfluous or as the responsibility of others.

The problem of arbitration was complicated by the fact that one of the merchants had copied the ledger that he found on the syndics' desk. You will note, the merchants declared, that "these gentlemen have too generously disposed of the money of the poor unfortunate merchants. . . ."[35] There followed a long list of specific complaints about the ledger's receipts and expenditures. When Mutel took all these complaints to the syndics, they responded with a terse rebuttal of some of the charges.

On 5 October 1778, Mutel summed up the conflict in a letter to Le Noir. The two main complaints, he said, were that the merchants were not consulted by the syndics and the general costs were too high. Mutel stated that everything pertaining to the management of the fair that had come to his attention indicated the syndics' zealous pursuit of the merchants' interests. He denied that the merchants had any right to negotiate the expenses of the fair with the syndics. Mutel cited the procedures followed by the syndics of the fair Saint-Ovide. Since those procedures had been ratified by the *commissaire* of that quarter and by the lieutenant general as recently as June and July 1771, they were judged correctly by the syndics of Saint-Laurent to be official police policy on the fairs. The syndics had been faithful to that policy. As for the ledger, Mutel called it an estimate that could be modified in the interests of the merchants in the future if receipts went up and costs down. He concluded that the syndics should be upheld against the merchants whose complaints were not well founded and whose motive was the jealousy and animosity of a few. Thus Mutel opted for capitalist-manager over shopkeeper. But if, as everything indicates, the government was anxious to see Saint-Laurent thrive in this period, Mutel did not serve its interests. The year 1778 was the critical stage in Saint-Laurent's history, and the reversals for both merchants and entertainers, who also coughed up 3,759 livres to the syndics, in that year spelled the imminent demise of a fair battling to regain life.

Mutel's reference to the regulations of 1771 is important. It revealed that, in ancien régime law, it was not always clear whether new ordinances reversed, supplemented, or replaced old ones and that a *commissaire* believed his primary duty was law enforcement. Although his responsibility in the fairs was enormous, he was reasonably successful most of the time. There was little he could do, however, to contain or control the raucous crowds milling about in the free, gregarious, unsegregated atmosphere of the marketplace.

Typically, the fairs were clogged with soldiers, beggars, guardsmen, prostitutes, clerks, lackeys, students, shopkeepers, porters, and *petits-maîtres* (fops). Everyone mingled in a jangling din of shouts, insults, and banter amid a cacophony of whistles, tambourines, flutes, and street cries. "It was a continual ebb and flow of people who pushed each other from one side to the other," wrote Charles Sorel.[36] "It seemed that that day had been chosen by all the people of low rank in Paris to come there. . . . One heard those who suffered from the discomfort screaming from every direction, and in vain pregnant women imagined that they would be more spared than others; one could not have lightened their burden if one had wished to." For Joachim Nemeitz, who wrote an instructional guide for visitors to Paris, everyone at

Saint-Germain moved "helter-skelter, masters with valets and lackeys, thieves with honest people. The most refined courtesans, the prettiest girls, the subtlest pickpockets are as if intertwined together. The whole fair teems with people from the beginning to the end."[37]

These crowds generated their own marketplace culture, one of license, as the *Mémoires secrets* dubbed it, built on humorous mockery of the ranks, restraints, and privileges of the official world. In the fairs there was little distinction between spectator and performer, between the actual life of people in the streets and the representation of life and mentality in the *spectacles*. The fair was itself a show in which everyone participated in derisive laughter at the behavior of civil society and in which the entertainments incorporated the songs and cries of the people, their gestures and postures, their language, and their aspirations and fears. Audiences and entertainers profaned and satirized the accepted standards of etiquette and decency, helping to create a familiarity in the fairs among people often separated by occupations, wealth, age, and sex.

Derisive humor was expressed most commonly in erotic posturing and grotesque grimacing, insulting language or song, and bodily imagery associated with eating and defecation. As Mikhail Bakhtin has shown, the body in marketplace culture symbolized the material existence shared by all human beings.[38] Representing fertility, nourishment, and renewal, the body was an image of the collective mass of humanity, a positive symbol of the festivity of the streets. In the fair theaters of the eighteenth century the characters were always defecating and copulating. They were usually hungry or thirsty. Arlequin's plate of chicken became a trademark.

The satirical celebration of material existence and what Bakhtin calls the "grotesque realism" arising from folk humor were evoked most typically in *parades*. *Parades* were coarse, slapstick farces performed by fair mountebanks (*bateleurs*) on balconies over the entrance to their shows. They were presented free of charge and were intended to give the crowd a sample of the major fare and to attract people to the production inside, usually an *opéra-comique*.[39] Wearing masks and gesturing obscenely, the actors portrayed voluptuous women who deceived their husbands, zany pranksters, crotchety old cockolded men, and young girls who invented new ways of making love. Drawn from commedia dell'arte, the main characters included Léandre, the male lover; Isabelle, the amorous coquette on the verge of pregnancy; Cassandre, the father; and his foolish valet, Gilles, whose manner of speech was usually the coarse jargon of the marketplace. Many of his words were preceded by *t*'s and *z*'s. Obscene equivocations were achieved by suspending sentences and by gesticulations usually mimicking bodily functions. The lewd plots revolved around petty crimes, greed, licentious games, trickery, and deceit. The *parade* derived its appeal, according to Thomas-Simon Gueullette,

4. Arlequin. Painted wooden statue. Courtesy of the Bibliothèque de l'Opéra (hereafter BO). The statue is in the museum of the Opéra.

a barrister who wrote many of these pieces, from capturing the manners of
the ill-bred. Although his highborn friends enjoyed these raucous farces as
much as the people, Gueullette left little doubt that they were written to
appeal to the lowest level of taste. In order to succeed, he averred, the *parades*
must be vile and obscene.[40]

Parades lifted the streets to the stage, capturing the derisive laughter and
the material life of the marketplace. In Gueullette's *Le Marchand de merde*,
for example, which was typical of the genre, Léandre entreats Arlequin to
help him solve a problem: A mischievous rascal named Gilles defecates every
morning on Léandre's doorstep. Arlequin's solution is to pose as a merchant
of excrement and to persuade Gilles that he has hit on a lucrative profession
that no one had thought of before. When Arlequin dupes an apothecary into
buying his barrel of excrement for seven écus, Gilles, who is seeking a trade
that will enable him to marry his beloved Catin, is taken in by the ruse and
resolves to be a *marchand de merde*. Offering his excrement for ten écus a
barrel to the apothecary, Gilles cries: "Qui veut de ma merde? Argent de ma
merde; c'est de la fraiche."[41] The apothecary's response, however, is to flail
Gilles with his stick. Bemoaning the misfortunes of honest commerce, Gilles
seeks consolation from Catin, but she rejects him as a hopeless fool. Léandre
warns him to keep his merchandise to himself, while Arlequin will have
nothing to do with a man so inept at business.

The conclusion of *Le Marchand de merde* seems to carry us out of the folk
humor of the marketplace with its suggestions of charivari, where excrement
was an image of renewal and fertility. We enter the world of eighteenth-
century duplicity, commerce, and bourgeois conventions. Yet enough
billingsgate is preserved in the derisive mockery of the excrement dealer and
in the popular cries and gestures of charlatans, porters, tumblers, and
Arlequins to remind us that the eighteenth-century fairs and their entertainers still belong to the familiar, regenerative culture of the streets.

Does the crude humor focusing on bodily necessities and deceit in social
relationships that this *parade* captures so well suggest that the culture of the
fairs was popular in the sense that it was intended solely for the lower ranks
of society? Do the vulgarities and obscenities of fair theater, the jangling
carnival atmosphere punctuated by the raunchy cries of street vendors, and
the low cost of tickets to the fair *spectacles* point to an elite/popular distinction based on levels of taste and sophistication or on social composition,
whether pegged to wealth, profession, or education? One thing seems clear:
Fair entertainments were perceived as being intended for the people. Most of
the sources that deal with fair shows use these kinds of expressions: from
Pierre-Thomas-Nicholas Hurtaut's *Dictionnaire historique de la ville de Paris*
(1779)—"spectacles du peuple"; from Nicolas-Toussaint Le Moyne's *Dictionnaire universel de police* (1786)—"spectacles destiné pour le peuple"; from the

Mémoires of Charles Favart—"spectacles inférieurs"; from Nicholas Rétif de
la Bretonne's *Les Contemporaines* (1785)—"un spectacle propre à une
certaine classe de citoyens"; from *Le Nouveau spectateur* (15 May 1776)—
entertainment for "les gens oisifs"; from Thomas Rousseau's *Lettre sur les
spectacles des boulevards* (1781)—"spectacles pour les Parisiens de rang
inférieur"; from the *Affiches, annonces et avis divers*—"spectacles aux classes
inférieures de la société"; and from the king's Conseil d'Etat simply "spectacles populaires." The fair entertainments were understood by most commentators of the age to be shows aimed at ordinary people, at the lower ranks
of society. This understanding derived from the genre and the fair setting. But
it does not mean that *spectacles* intended to appeal to "le bas peuple" did not
appeal to people of high rank, wealth, learning, and sophistication. It does
not mean that we can blithely separate taste publics and draw distinctions
between elite and popular culture, which in the works of many recent scholars
have become too neat and too sharp.

In his recent study of popular culture, Peter Burke seems to be on the right
track when he takes exception to Robert Redfield's distinction between the
"great tradition" of the social minority possessing access to learning and the
"little tradition" of the uneducated, often illiterate majority, on the grounds
that "it omits upper-class participation in popular culture."[42] But Burke
moves off track in his contention that during the early modern period the elite
minority "gradually withdrew from participation in the little tradition. . . ."
He cites a remark of Louis-Sébastien Mercier, who derides popular entertainment as the taste of pigs; yet it is Mercier who provides us with some of the
amplest evidence that it was also the taste of the Parisian elite, however
greatly he may have deplored that. If Burke is right that the elite shed their
belief in magical healing, prophecy, and witchcraft, he neglects to mention
the popularity of mesmerism among the highborn and their financial support
of a charlatan from Lyons who claimed he could walk on water.[43] In fact, by
the late eighteenth century, if not before, popular entertainment embraced all
segments of society, including the elite, however they are defined. The
evidence for this is substantial.

The sources stress the mixed social composition of fair audiences and
crowds. In his tourist guide *Le Voyageur fidèle* (1716), Louis Liger spoke of
"a great concourse of people from every social rank" at the Saint-Germain
fair, and Germain Brice noted that the fair attracted "people of all kinds."[44]
Later in the century, the *Mémoires secrets* noted that the low cost of tickets
at the popular theaters enabled everyone to go, "so that the duchess and the
savoyard rub shoulders there without distinction."[45] Jean-Baptiste Nougaret
emphasized that the fair attracted artisans as well as the "dregs of the
population,"[46] and Rétif de la Bretonne observed that a crowd watching
a *parade* at the fair included workers, scrubbing women, gauze makers,

seamstresses, pickpockets, and prostitutes, but also uncorrupted apprentices, children of good families, and artisans' daughters.[47] An English visitor to the French capital, Mrs. Anna Cradock, was astonished in 1784 to see "ladies of society" at Saint-Germain, adding that "it appears that this is allowed."[48] Soon however, Mrs. Cradock learned that "it is good form" to stroll in the fairs. She observed that a café at Saint-Laurent where the 30-piece orchestra played "God Save the King" in her honor "filled up with the most varied public from the little bourgeois to the great seigneur."[49] One senses the same social mix in Dancourt's play about the Saint-Germain fair, in which a merchant of chamber robes, a marquise, a provincial noble, a thieving lackey, a procureur, an abbé, a financier, actors, a valet, a singer, and a customs officer are all present.[50]

The fancy clothing that one sees on ladies in the crowd in engravings may have adorned genuine marquises or *filles d'opéra*. It is impossible to tell though written records indicate that both were part of the scene. They stood in the same turd-strewn lanes as poor Savoyard girls in wooden shoes playing their hurdy-gurdies. While Sorel found Saint-Germain to be a jarring marketplace for the dregs of society and Paul Scarron commented on its thieves and prostitutes, the Parfaict brothers called it "an enchanted palace where all the fashionable people are gathered at a rendezvous."[51] The *Gazette à la main* observed in 1739 that "there are a great many people at all the *spectacles* at the fair and especially at the Opéra-Comique, where the house was full and taken up by the highest society of Paris."[52] In 1741 it declared: "The *spectacles* of the fair ended yesterday with a great sparkle; never has such a large and illustrious gathering been seen as at the Opéra-Comique: princes, princesses, dukes, and all the marshals of France."[53] These observations about fair crowds, to which many more could be added, indicate that *le monde* found the fairs as enticing as *le bas peuple*.

Moreover, if the highborn went to fairs to see and participate in the spectacle of the unregimented marketplace, they also began bringing this culture into their homes, a phenomenon that casts considerable doubt on the notion that *le monde*'s increasing infatuation with popular entertainment was a form of slumming. It became fashionable by the middle of the eighteenth century for people of the high ranks to have private theaters in at least one of their residences, where the bawdiest, most obscene farces and *parades* of the streets were performed.[54] There were private theaters at the *hôtels* of Sourdéac, Soyecourt, Clermont, Villeroy, Chaussée-d'Antin, and at the chateaux of Sceaux, Bagatelle, and Chantilly, to name but a few. Quite a circle of *robins* as well as sword aristocrats formed at Auteuil and Choisy-le-Roi around the barrister and royal procurator, Thomas-Simon Gueullette, the same Gueullette who wrote *parades* for the fairs. He made these farces a modish entertainment of *le monde*, attracting, he insisted, "an astonishing crowd of spectators of the first rank,"[55]

In addition to Gueullette, the principal playwrights of the society theaters included Charles Collé, Charles-François Racot de Grandval, and Jean Baptiste Isoard, known as Delisle de Sales. The son of a counselor of the king and a treasurer, Collé worked for a receiver of the *généralité* of Paris and became the director of the duc d'Orléans' *menus plaisirs*. He admired the plays of Charles-François Panard and Prosper Crébillon, whom he met at the Caveau, a singing club, and he wrote his first *parade*, *Cocatrix*, in 1731. Subsequent works, including *Le Galant escrocs* and *La Vérité dans le vin*, established Collé as the darling of society theater.[56] Baron Grimm excused him on the grounds that his licentiousness was spontaneous rather than premeditated or hypocritical.[57]

Rascot de Grandval, the son of a harpsichord player, wrote heavy-handed *parades* for Mademoiselle Dumesnil's theater. His works bear such titles as *L'Eunuch ou la fidèle infidélité* (1750) and *Sirop-au-cul, ou l'heureuse délivrance* (1754), which he labeled a "tragédie héroï-merdifique."[58] Once an Oratorian, Delisle de Sales became a member of the Académie des Inscriptions, and he published essays on tragedy and on the history of humanity as well as a dictionary of hunting and fishing. Delisle was the principal author of erotic plays performed at the hôtel of Charles-Alexandre-Marc-Marcelin, prince d'Hénin, and his mistress, the celebrated soprano Sophie Arnould.[59]

The main patrons of the *théâtre privé* were the duc de Chartres, the prince de Conti, the comte de Clermont, the maréchal de Richelieu, Président Hénault, the duc de Noailles, the marquis de Montalembert, the duc de Grammont, the duc de la Vallière, and the comte and comtesse de Rochefort. Even the comte de Maurepas, a royal minister entrusted with the supervision of the Opéra, presented lewd *parades*, many of which he wrote, at his *hôtel* on the rue de Grenelle, He was a regular spectator at the fairs.

The most vigorous proponent of private theater in the eighteenth century, whose son in future years would be more responsible than anyone else for making marketplace entertainment the taste of *le monde*, was doubtless the duc de Chartres.[60] Before inheriting the Orléans chateau at Bagnolet, the duc de Chartres installed his group of entertainers in a small house on the rue Cadet in the faubourg Montmartre. Prominent nobles and a veritable harem of pretty girls were attracted to his suppers, which were followed by obscene *parades*. After his father's death, the duc outfitted the chateau of Bagnolet with a *salle de spectacle*, hired Collé to direct his entertainments, and bought two houses with theaters, one near the entrance to the fair Saint-Laurent, the other in the faubourg du Roule, where the Parc Monceau is today. There the duc and his friends, including his mistress from the Opéra, sang vaudevilles and cavorted in the *parades*, *divertissements*, and comedies written for them by Collé and Pierre Laujon. After 1763 responding to the more elevated taste of his mistress, later his wife, Madame de Montesson, Chartres abandoned the libertine ways and the obscene theater of his youth. He tried to get Collé to compose moralistic plays for her coterie at Chaussée-d'Antin, but the playwright rejected the offer with the slur that "pedantic decency leaves me cold as an andiron,"[61]

Chartres' theaters were rivaled chiefly by those of the comte de Clermont (the son of Louis III de Bourbon and Mademoiselle de Nantes, the legitimized daughter of Louis XIV and Madame de Montespan) and the prince de Conti, also of the Bourbon family. Clermont, once an abbé commendataire of Saint-Germain-des-Prés, set up a sumptuous theater in the 1740s in his chateau at Berny near Paris, a residence that in the past had belonged to such luminaries as Pomponne de Bellièvre, Huges de Lionne, and Cardinal Fürstenberg. Amateur and professional actors performed *parades*, *opéras-comiques*, *opéras-bouffes*, and plays taken from the repertoires of the grand theaters for the entertainment of Clermont's mistresses, the actress Adrienne Lecouvreur and the dancer Marie-Anne Camargo. Collé and Laujon were hired not only to provide new pieces, but also to season those of other authors that the comte felt were not spicy enough. Laujon flavored Antoine-Alexandre-Henri Poinsinet's *Gilles garçon peintre*, for example, with these lines, which echoed the marketplace:

> Quand z'un galant vient galamment
> Nous dir'queut' chos' de ben charmant
> Et qu'on s'amus' de son queut' chose,
> Y'z'est d'un' fille à sentiment
> D'ben cacher l'plaisir qu'ça lui cause,
>   Plus l'on en sent,
>   Plus l'on en prend,
> Moins faut l'montrer à son amant.[62]

Each of eight hundred snuffboxes and four thousand rings left in the estate of the prince de Conti allegedly commemorated one of the prince's sexual conquests.[63] This notorious libertine of the high peerage inherited the seigneuries of Ile-Adam, once the possession of the Montmorency family. There, in the company of his intimate circle, including the comtesse de Bouffleurs, the prince de Beauveu, the vicomtesse de Cambis, the duc de Lauzun, and Président Hénault, Conti was entertained by the feculent pieces of Nicolas-Médard Audinot, who directed his theater in 1762 and after became the prince of the boulevard theaters.

The works presented on these private stages were not always *parades*, nor were they always lewd, but the *parade* genre seems to have enjoyed the greatest popularity. Its equivocations and eroticisms in many instances went far beyond the boundaries of the fair shows. For example, in *Les Plaisirs de cloître* by M. D. L. C. A. P., Marton, a novice in a convent, is flogged 40 times in the nude for reading an obscene book. She is comforted by Agathe in a display of sapphic love. Her heterosexual desires are quenched in the final act by Clitandre, who has sneaked into the convent with a Jesuit priest. The Jesuit becomes so aroused by watching the intercourse that he sodomizes his companion, Clitandre.[64]

Even *Les Plaisirs du cloître* appears tame, however, when compared to Delisle de Sales' "théâtre d'amour," which, he tells us, were performed at his prince's theater by "the rakes of his little court and ladies of quality worthy of being courtesans. . . ."[65] *Junon et Ganymède* was typical of Delisle's productions, for which he always provided explicit stage directions. On Olympus, Juno awakens from sleep complaining that she is still a virgin and longing for the adolescent charms of Ganymède, who enters. After removing her clothes, he fondles and sucks her breasts, sending her into a state of ecstasy. But despite their passion and an erotic dialogue, her virginity resists his various means of sexual attack. The exhausted Ganymède is finally revived by Juno's flagellations, and he achieves his conquest.

Obviously, nothing like this would have been tolerated in a public theater. In the private theaters *le monde* adapted the comedy of the streets to its own libertine requirements, clearly borrowing its lewd tone and much of its marketplace imagery celebrating material life. This stage, too, reflected the social realities. The highborn husbands of marquises and comtesses favored actresses, dancers, and singers as mistresses in the eighteenth century. It was for the *filles d'Opéra* that they and their companions launched the private theaters.[66] The actresses and dancers of the public theaters, who often chose their careers because it was an easy entrée to the favors of the rich, lived as regally as anyone in the eighteenth century. For their part, the ladies of high birth found it deliciously evil to play the role of slut and actress. They did not have to bear the stigma of prostitution because they could consort with actresses and enjoy sexual freedom under the guise of being patrons of the arts. The theater served as a "link between the gallantry from above and prostitution from below."[67] For the ladies who simply wanted to watch the action while preserving their anonymity, grilled loges were provided in many of the theaters, though the *Mémoires secrets* noted that they were soon "deciphered."[68]

Both society theater and fair theater flourished in the late eighteenth century, evidently at the expense of the grand theaters. The Opéra from which Jean-Baptiste Lully made a fortune in the seventeenth century was 500,000 livres in debt by the middle of the century. The Comédie-Italienne floundered badly until it literally stole the Opéra-Comique in 1762. Both theaters blamed the little *spectacles* for taking their audiences, doubtless with some justification, and the Opéra began exacting large fees from the fair shows as early as the second decade of the century. As the audience at the Comédie-Française steadily declined, the theater waged a relentless campaign lasting from the time of Louis XIV until the Revolution to suppress the fair entertainers (see Chapter 3).[69] Apparently, the classical theaters bored people of title and position while market slang and gutter morality were amusing. Henri Alémras and Paul d'Estrée wrote:

> The lowest water carrier who spoke coursely . . . entertained them infinitely more—on the stage—than Pompée or Cinna. By withdrawing from this pompous literature of Corneille and Racine, they felt the need to adopt low habits of living—literally—with men who from their perspective had the advantage of resembling them through meanness of instinct and yet of being human. Gilles, Arlequin, Cassandre, Isabelle, Janot, Jocrisse, or Manon, this was life and truth under borrowed names, daily life and gay, very picturesque truth.[70]

Thus, crowds embracing all social ranks thronged to fair entertainments aimed at *le bas peuple* while the high ranks brought the vulgar *parade*, the theatrical genre that most faithfully captured the raillery of the fairs, into their homes. If taste, therefore, cannot be tied to social rank, if fair crowds and audiences engaged in a ritual of derisive laughter at the world and an exuberant celebration of material existence came to include just about everyone, what meaning, then, does "popular" entertainment have in the context of eighteenth-century Paris? Certainly, the fashionable popular/elite distinction should be viewed with greater skepticism, if not discarded altogether. The elite did not define a separate culture for themselves; they began to appropriate the one of the marketplace that by the end of the century belonged to everyone. Perhaps different kinds of questions should be asked about marketplace entertainments. What was the nature of their appeal? What sort of gratification were audiences seeking and receiving from them? The fair *spectacles* themselves must provide the answers.

In addition to *opéras-comiques* (see Chapters 3, 4, and 5), there were five main types of fair shows: acrobats, marionettes, exotic animals, freaks and exhibitions of mechanical and optical devices. Acrobats, tumblers, equilibrists, and what were called *danseurs de corde* or funambulists had been the principal showmen of the fairs since at least the sixteenth century although there had been funambulist exhibitions in France as early as the thirteenth century.[71] The *sauteurs*, who were often referred to as *saltimbanques* (showmen) or *bateleurs*,[72] performed mute, depending heavily on postures, grimaces, and gesticulation. They frequently wore masks and were dressed as lions and tigers, thus enhancing both the comic and exotic aspects of their shows.

Although there were many variations, in the standard leap one of the acrobat's legs was bent obliquely on the ground and the trunk of his body was twisted low to the ground. From this position he quickly contracted his muscles and sprang, uncoiling, into the air. A leaper named Grimaldi vaulted to the height of the chandelier at Saint-Germain in 1742. Most of the acrobats did their handsprings, contortions, somersaults and cartwheels on platforms or planks extended across the *tréteaux*, planks mounted on stiltlike supports or trestles.[73] Some performed on ladders or chairs. Most of the leapers had a speciality: Du Broc did reverse somersaults from a springboard, holding a torch in each hand; Crépin, who always appeared as Gilles singing a comic song and feigning fear, specialized in the broomstick vault; Evince was the first *sauteur* to leap over barrels in France. In 1726, Nemeitz reported seeing a two-year-old child whirling rapidly like a rope while swords were pointed at her eyes, throat, and stomach. He expressed shock at these acrobatic shows, assailing "the indecent, lascivious postures of the girls who dance, shocking reason and decency."[74] An acrobat known only as the Turk climbed a rope to the ceiling of the theater, where he perched on a wooden disk attached to a mast. There he executed contortions, spins, and head-stands. In 1754 one of the troupes introduced a novelty—a company of "Femmes-Fortes." These girls walked barefoot on hot iron or smoldering coals, held hot melted lead in their mouths after lining them with oil, and supported an anvil or rocks or several men on their stomachs while stretched out with their heads resting on one chair and their feet on another.[75] The more any stunt seemed physically impossible, daring, and miraculous, the better the crowd liked it. For this reason, funambulism, an awesome physical feat, was especially relished and may have had associations with magic in the crowd's mind. Jean Bodin called tightrope walkers sorcerers in his *Démonologie*, and a century later Claude-François Menestrier, in his study of ballet, remarked that the "ancients gave the name miracle . . . to these rope dancers who dangle in the air and turn over and over holding themselves only by one foot. . . ."[76]

Like the *sauteurs*, the funambulists had their assortment of stunts. In one, the performer flew around the rope holding himself by his hands or feet, while in others he raced back and forth on a horizontal rope or climbed one stretched at an angle.[77] The most spectacular trick was leaping and whirling from the rope. The funambulists also did their acts while playing violins behind their backs or over their heads. The Dutchman did his contortions on the tightrope wearing iron shoes. He also swung from a slack rope to a tight one. Antony de Sceaux was famous for his dance of the drunkard. Laurent walked the rope with chains or baskets fastened to his feet, while Lavigne, costumed as Scaramouche, danced on the rope without using a balancing pole, playing a violin over his head and between his legs. In 1718, Madame Gaultier de Saint-Edme, one of the founders of the Opéra-Comique, whose permission to present lyric comedies had been revoked, introduced the odd novelty of an ass sliding on a rope from one side of the stage to the other.[78] The songwriters had great fun using this episode to ridicule the Comédie-Française and its rivalry with the Opéra-Comique in a song called "L'Ane de la foire":

> *Paris trouve fort à son gré*
> *Le grand voltigeur d'Arcadie:*
> *L'âne de foire est préféré*
> *Aux ânes de la Comédie;*
> *A meilleur titre il le sera*
> *Aux bourriques de l'Opéra.*
>
> *A la foire, Destouches en pleurs,*
> *Se plaint que l'Opéra-Comique,*
> *Malgré les soins du directeur,*
> *Echoue auprès d'une bourrique;*
> *Faut-il qu'un si sot animal*
> *En mette-tant à l'hôpital!*
>
> *A la foire tout Paris va,*
> *Pour voir l'âne de la Saint-Edme;*
> *Pour ceux du Comique Opéra,*
> *On ne s'empresse pas de même.*
> *L'un pourtant n'est qu'un faux baudet,*
> *Les autres le sont en effet. . . .*
>
> *Autrefois Paris admira*
> *Corneille, Racine, Molière;*
> *Lulli, dans son moindre opéra,*
> *Trouvait le grand art de lui plaire.*
> *Ces grands hommes du temps passé*
> *Par un baudet sont remplacés.*[79]

In 1728, Mignard executed feats of strength on the tightrope, and an Italian woman known as Violente danced the "Folies d'Espagne" on a plank stretched across the rope.[80] Because these acts were given in a small wooden theater with sets and painted decorations, the director increased the price of tickets: 3 livres for the first loge, 40 sous for the second, 24 for the third, and 10 sous for the parterre.[81]

Speculating on why the public derived so much pleasure from such performers, Nougaret and Rétif came up with this explanation: "To delight, to renew the people: an object more important than a young person can sense. Entertainments that are suited to them are necessary for the people, material *spectacles* like *danses-de-corde, tours de force. . . .*"[82] The key word here is material. These were entertainments focused almost entirely on the human body, the symbol of material existence, the universal denominator of humanity. It was an afirmative symbol of the strength and renewal of life. The *sauteurs* and funambulists suggested the dexterity and power inherent in the human physical being.

But there is more to it. These exhibitions at times seemed to reach beyond the physically possible. They were daring, occasionally death-defying, suggesting something miraculous. It is not surprising, therefore, to find rope-walking and vaulting combined with other forms of entertainment where the marvelous played a role, enabling spectators to make an imaginative leap from admiration of physical prowess to something fabulous and magical. Thus, plays where the action unfolded by means of magic carpets, talismans, and superhuman victories were easily adapted to the acrobatic shows. Real and fictitious marvels were natural partners.

An excellent, early example of this combination was a piece called *Les Forces de l'amour et de la magie*, performed at the tennis court of the duc d'Orléans not far from the Saint-Germain fair in 1678 by a team of 24 acrobats led by a Dutch *sauteur* named Maurice Vondrebeck (or Von der Beck).[83] Merlin's opening monologue about his tribulations as the valet of the devilish, toadeating magician Zoroastre was preceded by acrobatic stunts performed on pedestals and followed by the menacing contortions and "perilous" leaps of demons who came to fetch the shepherd girl, Grésinde, to a tryst with their evil leader. Arriving at his howff, Grésinde fails to pacify the threatening sorcerer with dances by her shepherd companions, who include Arlequin, played by Charles Alard, one of the great *sauteurs* of this period. Merlin also fails to prevent Zoroastre from terrifying the girl with his black magic: A wave of his wand releases somersaulting monkeys from a goblet and flying serpents from an unctuous pâté. Grésinde realizes that she must submit. But at the last moment, she appeals to the goddess Juno, who substitutes a leaping demon for the girl just as the wicked magician is about to seize her. Zoroastre is compelled to recognize Juno's stronger magic. The play was little more than a vehicle for the acrobatics, but it enhanced the thrilling, suggestively magical aspect of the physical stunts.

The combination of real and fictitious marvels continued to appeal to fair audiences throughout the eighteenth century. When the Comédie-Italienne was expelled from France in 1697, the gymnastic troupes began appropriating the Italian repertoire, which they grafted onto their acrobatic shows, hiring actors and actresses at 20 sous per day to perform the spoken parts. "The public, who missed the Italians, rushed in crowds to see their imitators, and enjoyed themselves there very much."[84] When the Comédie-Française complained angrily that the *forains* were not confining themselves to tumbling and vaulting, in violation of the Comédie's exclusive right to present spoken dramas in the French language, the acrobatic troupes resorted to singing and dancing, leading to the creation of *opéra-comique* (see Chapter 4). Thereafter, whenever the privileged theaters were able to suppress the Opéra-

5. Outside Nicolet's theater at the Saint-Laurent fair, showing a crowd watching a *parade*. Notice soldiers arresting a thief to the right. Watercolor by Tauney, (MC. Topo 149E. See also BN Ca, Va 290, fol. T 7, or photograph 77374462.)

Comique or when this *spectacle* was held exclusively by one troupe, the fair players returned to the mime and acrobatics that had always been their stock-in-trade.

The *sauteurs* enjoyed a great resurgence in the late 1740s, when the Opéra-Comique was suppressed. In 1747 two Turks, Sieur Ally and Mahomet Carhata, were listed on the bill of fare at the Saint-Germain fair.[85] Presented in the theater of the Opéra-Comique, the show included a play in mime with ballets entitled *Le Dieu de silence à la foire*. In 1748, La Grand Troupe Turque performed flying leaps and slackrope gymnastics while La Grande Troupe des Danseurs, Sauteurs, et Voltigeurs de Corde executed new leaps with their star, Mahomet Carhata, as well as the pantomime *Rien n'est difficile en amour*.[86] A company of English and Italian children executed rope drills, leaps, feats of strength, and an English show, *Arlequin amant désespéré*, at Saint-Germain in 1749 while La Grande Troupe Turque at Saint-Laurent offered acrobatics on planks and pyramids of ten men. It was La Grande Troupe Turque that Jean-Baptiste Nicolet took over about a decade later, making it one of the foremost popular theaters on the Parisian boulevards during the second half of the century.

Like the *sauteurs*, marionettists, who for years had entertained fair crowds, found lyric comedy appropriate for their shows. When Dominique de Normandin, a stable master, obtained the right in March 1675 to open a marionette show, the *lettres patentes* stipulated that he could present plays with machines, songs, and dances.[87] Under the name Troupe Royale de Pygmées, this company opened in a *hôtel* in the Marais with a five-act tragicomedy with music called *Les Pygmées*, played with puppets four feet tall. Changing their name briefly in 1677 to Opéra des Bamboches, they moved to the Saint-Laurent fair in 1678. They were too successful, however, and the Opéra was able to suppress the show as a violation of its privilege. A few years later in 1684, the Opéra again invoked its monopoly over music to suppress the musical marionettes of Alexandre and Jean Bertrand. The Opéra was not as unrelenting, however, as the Comédie-Française which fought to prevent Alexandre Bertrand, a master gilder by trade, and later his son-in-law, Nicolas Bienfait, from converting to live actors. In the early decades of the eighteenth century, marionette shows in fact became a form of retreat for the producers of *opéras-comiques* when their pieces with live actors were suppressed by the Comédie-Française. Alain-René Lesage wrote *opéras-comiques* for marionettes at the fairs in 1722 rather than abandon the genre, and Charles Favart's first piece, *Polichinelle, comte de Panofière* (1732), was written for the puppets of Nicolas Bienfait, whose family held forth at the fair for three generations. The Bienfaits were rivaled only by Carlo Perico, the founder of the Jeu des Fantoccini, which performed at Saint-Ovide and on the boulevard in the 1760s and 1770s, and the Nicolet family—Guillaume (b. 1687), a violinist, and his two sons, François-Paul and Jean Baptiste, the founder of Les Grands Danseurs de Corde. The enduring enthusiasm of Parisians for these springy puppets suspended from strings by a *saltimbanque* behind a curtain is indicated by a police report of May 1763 stating that long after the other *spectacles* had closed for the season at Saint-Germain, indeed after the legal closing date, Bienfait's marionettes were still performing.[88] The patrol thought it advisable to let the show continue rather than risk angering the crowd, but Lieutenant General Sartine was advised to punish Bienfait to set an example. The Bienfait success also may have been due to the mechanical and visual effects of the decorative tableaux that they usually presented after the puppet show. In 1748 their poster announced that they would represent the assault and pillage of Berg-op-zoom. Tickets could be purchased for 6 and 12 sous.[89]

But the marionettes might have had their own special appeal, one that was more prevalent in ancien régime Europe than in modern times. Magical power, especially when the wooden model possessed the traits of a real person, may have been attributed to these animated figures.[90] Linked to black magic, specifically to voodoo, they were for a long time denounced by the Church. Persons accused of being witches were often charged with using dolls and puppets to work their maleficent, supernatural evils. Yet the Church did not always discourage credence in wooden statues crying or oozing blood. Even after they began to appear in Parisian salons and in public places, marionettes were still associated in popular belief with prodigies. No doubt most people by the seventeenth century saw them more as vehicles of amusement than as mysterious androids. Paul Scarron in 1643 noted that people believed the puppets of Pierre Datelin were enchanted, and in 1649 Datelin was still denounced as a magician working with devils. Audiences may also have been fascinated by the size of the marionettes. Small figures, especially when they came to life in the make-believe world of the theater, appealed to the imagination. Like dwarfs and figurines, they evoked sympathy because they were fragile. To many, they probably seemed charmed.

Yet for others, it seems likely that the appeal of the marionettes lay in the salty pieces full of double entendres that were often performed at these shows. In his *Dictionnaire universel de police*, Nicholas-Toussaint Le Moyne expressed concern about the impression the puppet shows made on children: "Nearly all the farces that are played by the marionettes," he wrote, "are embroidered with equivocations, jokes, and indecent situations. . . . Children who attend these shows retain all too easily the impressions they received in these dangerous places. Parents are often astonished to find them informed about things they should not know about; they ought to blame the lack of prudence they have shown in permitting their children to be taken to shows that should have been forbidden them."[91] On one occasion, the Parisian guard intervened in the marionette show of Monsieur Ribier at Saint-Laurent to prevent him from showing "a little figure who was indecent, who pissed in front of the spectators and who has all the bodily parts of a man, and very visible."[92]

Throughout the century, fair crowds were attracted to exhibitions of exotic animals. Lions, bears, tigers, and leopards were unfamiliar sights to Parisians, among whom they generated considerable curiosity and excitement. Although elephants had been seen in Europe since the sixteenth century,[93] they were certainly not common. One, eight or nine feet tall with toenails five inches long, was seen at Saint-Germain in 1698.[94] Elephants were still uncommon enough in 1770 that the one on display that year, said incorrectly to be the first seen in Paris in 103 years, was the subject of engravings and verses:

> *Sans peine je quitte l'Asie*
> *Pour vivre à jamais sous les lois*
> *Et sans regret, renonce à ma patrie*
> *De plus puissant, de plus aimé des rois.*[95]

6. Engraving of a rhinoceros at the Saint-Germain fair. The inscription states that the animal was captured in Asia in the Etats de Mogol and that he allowed everyone to pet him like a dog; that a ship brought him from Bengal in 1741 to Amsterdam; that he ate 20 livres of bread and drank 14 buckets of water and 14 of beer per day; that he weighed 5,000 livres. It adds that the rhinoceros fought constantly with an elephant, whom it defeated by getting beneath the elephant's belly. Indians used the claws, tusks, teeth, flesh, and blood of the rhinoceros to combat apoplexy and other maladies. (MC. Topo PC 10 8H.)

Perhaps the greatest sensation of the age was the appearance of a rhinoceros at Saint-Germain in 1749. The animal, which became the subject of engravings and naturalist tracts, was brought from Asia to Holland and then transported by a horse-drawn van to Germany and France.[96] Baron Grimm reported that it weighed 5,000 livres, was 10 feet long, 10 feet in girth, and over 5 feet high. It drank 14 buckets of water a day and ate 60 livres of hay and 20 of bread. Although rhinoceroses had been seen in Lisbon in 1515 and in London in 1684, according to Grimm, this was the first in France.[97] Tickets to view the animal cost 24, 12, and 6 sous. Apparently, the rhinoceros died along with its master when the ship taking them from Rome to Naples sank in November 1749.[98]

Seals were still so rare in France that when one died in June 1779, the cadaver was embalmed and remained on display.[99] A few years later, after a visit to Saint-Laurent, Mrs. Cradock remarked on an unusual animal (a seal) with the head of a leopard that had been caught in the Strait of Magellan.[100] Perhaps the most exotic animal show at Saint-Germain, and certainly one of the most successful, was that of Monsieur Ruggieri, who became a celebrated pyrotechnist. The nature of his exhibition and of fair menageries in general can be grasped by the "Avis du Public" that he sent for advertising purposes to the newspapers and perhaps made into a poster:

Sieur RUGGERY [sic], who last year was at the booth where the chapel of the Fair Saint-Germain-des-Prés was previously located, with the otter or white bear from the icy sea, gives notice to the public and especially to amateurs of natural history that this year the said RUGGERY has a booth at the fair between the two doors on entering by the rue de Tournon. He proposes to show a new menagerie consisting of 10 animals coming from foreign countries among which are two which appeared in the year 1771. The first is L'OUISTITI who is commonly called the ladies' favorite, or the little monkey. The one that the said RUGGERY sold in 1771 for 35 louis weighed 5 ounces: he was admired by the public. The one that he has this year will satisfy the curious even more; he weighs only 3 ounces. The second is the same leopard from the last fair; he is twice as large. He is going to perform some tricks which will surprise spectators. The third is l'ASPATULLE, an animal who lives entirely on fish. The fourth is a monkey called LE CAPUCIN because of his beard. He cracks nuts with a stone with unusual skill. The fifth is a MAKIS; he deserves to be seen; nothing equals his beauty and gentleness. The sixth and seventh are two PIERROTS from China, male and female. The eighth is a very rare species of monkey; his name is not found in dictionaires of natural history. The ninth is a very little flying squirrel; he is not a quarter as large as ordinary ones. His wings are placed just like those of the bat; this animal deserves the attention of connoisseurs. The tenth is a very rare animal whose loss is greatly regretted; he died at Royes coming from Holland. Since this animal had never appeared in Europe dead or living, the said RUGGERY has had him stuffed with the greatest care by sieur Mauvé. Here is the name and the description of this animal according to the *Histoire Naturelle* of Buffon: "The TARIR of l'AUTA from America, the largest amphibious animal which appears in this region, it has a very small tail; strong and uniform fur, brown. It is female, has only two breasts like the mare, and the color and mane of a horse; its head held like a rhinoceros; it has one horn which it uses to eat a little like the elephant. The rest of the body approaches and resembles that of a pig; it has four claws on its front feet and three on its rear; this animal swims better than it runs; its skin is arrow and ball-proof."[101]

The public was frequently lured into the animal exhibitions by posters promising exotic animals that turned out to be common ones or animals so strange as to defy credulity. In 1689 one booth advertised beasts from India bearing unusual names that in reality were a leopard and a raccoon.[102] Two wild animals allegedly from the "mountain of Barbery" were displayed at Saint-Germain in 1748.[103] One was described as having the head of a sheep, the back of a Spanish horse, the face and neck of a deer, the barbels of a goat, the ears and breast of a hind, a coat of fine wool, the croup of a horse, and the tail of a dog and front feet of a calf. It was reportedly 6 feet tall and ran with the speed of a horse.[104] The other animal, just 2 1/2 feet tall, had the appearance of a human being. He did acrobatic stunts and conjuring tricks. The same year the *Affiches* also called attention to an American cow that was 26 years old with 5 legs and 2 heads, one resembling a man's head with white hair and a black beard that had to be shaved every day. It had the legs of a deer and the claws of an eagle.[105] In 1773, *L'Avant-coureur* noted the curiosity aroused by a monkey playing the hurdy-gurdy.[106] People were astonished to see him playing an allemande with great accuracy, but when someone threw him a nut, the monkey jerked his paw from the keys though the music continued. The crowd's credulity was really tested by a menagerie called "Le Pongo-orang-outang, ou l'homme sauvage" where a unicorn, devils from Peru (really monkeys with faces painted red and a false horn), male and female satyrs, a ferocious Brazilian ocelot, and a mongoose from Surinam were on view.

The *Avant-coureur* observed that crowds were often embarrassed by being duped at these shows, but it predicted that the fair public would continue to be fooled by the promise of prodigies. Louis-Sébastien Mercier, who was disdainful of most fair attractions, agreed. He scoffed at such deceptions as a giant wearing platform boots and a sultan's headdress; a shaved, depilated female bear dressed in breeches, shirt, and jacket who was passed off as a "unique animal"; and a large wooden dummy who could speak because a small boy hid in his stomach. Yet Mercier understood why such shows were appealing:

> A revolution lasting several years is necessary in order to draw the eye of the naturalist to something worthy of his attention. Gross charlatanism is on its throne there. The impudent *saltimbanque* has obtained the privilege of duping the public; since he has paid for this privilege, what does it matter then that he gives fools to the Parisian? People are so taken in that they expect in advance that a fake marvel will transport them no less than if it were true.[107]

Savant animals evoked even greater curiosity than bizarre ones. In the seventeenth century, Jacques Bonnet told of seeing rats holding miniature balancing poles like a funambulist dance in cadence on their hind feet. Eight of these rats performed ballet figures to violin accompaniment on a table, and a white rat danced a saraband "with as much accuracy and seriousness as a Spaniard would have demonstrated."[108] The show cost 15 sous. Bonnet also mentions a monkey named Divertissant, dressed as a woman, who danced a minuet with his master and performed a comic routine while riding a dog. Nemeitz was struck by a monkey in a musketeer's costume who executed military drills, danced a minuet, and did tricks on a dog's back.[109] He also described a show in which pigeons turned roasting meat by pulling a chariot attached to a spit.[110] In the decade of the 1770s there were birds who could count and tell time. A Troupe Volatile featured birds doing somersaults, skinning the cat, forming pyramids, and doing military drills.[111] Finally, a "scholarly" deer guessed people's ages, played cards, loaded cannons, and trotted like a Spanish horse; and a Dutch lady played with snakes said to be from Cayenne that wrapped themselves around her, caressed her, and put their heads into her mouth. One was a flying snake with an 18-inch wingspan.

It was but a short step from exotic animals to freaks. The gazettes throughout the century recorded the curiosity such people aroused in fair crowds. A giant said to be 8 feet tall was seen at Saint-Germain in 1731.[112] In 1777 a 28-year-old Westphalian named Roose appeared at the fair.[113] He measured 8 feet 1 inch and was reported to be well proportioned. Earlier "la grande géante Algérienne," 6 feet 8 inches tall, and a dwarf, 2 feet 4 inches, named Moreau, who later joined one of the boulevard theaters as an Arlequin, were displayed at Saint-Germain.[114] Probably the most unusual of these people was the "giant dwarf," whom the *Mémoires secrets* described as "a 4-year-old child who, formed as fortunately as the most vigorous man beyond the finest proportions in the virile organ, has the diverse abilities of it such as erection, ejaculation. . . . It is especially at the approach of a woman that his virility manifests itself. . . ."[115] Although his waist was larger than a 4-year-old's, his age was verified by his birth record, teeth, and lingual ability.

There are no references to bearded ladies, but people deformed from birth were frequently on display. A German without arms and legs appeared at Saint-Germain in 1716. He was able to write, play a drum and make houses out of cards. A certain Paschal Discol, described as a handsome 16-year-old Venetian with hands growing from his shoulders and feet from his haunches, executed bodily gyrations for the crowd at Saint-Laurent in 1752.[116] In 1779 in a booth next to a refreshment bar at Saint-Germain, a Liégeois schoolmaster without arms performed stunts with his feet.[117] He ate, drank, uncorked bottles, smoked, wrote, tied knots, threaded needles, played cards and cup and ball, loaded a pistol, spun wool, hurled a baton 40 feet behind him, carried a chair, and planted a garden.

If they found the physical feats of acrobats to be spectacular and if they enjoyed being fooled by strange animals, eighteenth-century Parisians became even more fascinated by gadgets with moving parts. In the fairs, as in the salons of the aristocracy, there was a rage for *automates*—paintings with moving figures, birds flying out of clocks, little houses whose doors opened, miniature funambulists, mechanical people popping out of the wall to pour a beverage, figures of Turks dispensing pastry and candy, and automated musicans. These gadgets appealed to the sense of wonder aroused by lillipution images, the illusion of live objects and people, and mechanical wizardry.

Automates had existed at the fairs since at least the early eighteenth century.[118] In 1727, Nemeitz described an "Invention Méchanique" that represented the Opéra. The mechanism enabled paper figures of actors to move about on stage, a chariot to descend, and a conductor to beat time.[119] The vogue for *automates* really set in, however, when Vaucanson first displayed his mechanical duck and flute player at the fairs in 1738. His mechanical flutists also gave concerts of bird songs in the Tuileries, where the public was admitted for 24 sous.[120]

Antoine Boudet's *Les Affiches de Paris* indicates the remarkable enthusiasm for machines, often combined with what were called "experiments in physics," in the late 1740s. He reported that the police authorized Le Nouveau Spectacle Pantomime to present a "pièce phisique-méchanique" called *Le Temple de Mémoire* at the Hôtel de Soissons in which a ball appearing to be in motion by its own force moved about a miniature temple.[121] The following year Sieur Pauliny promised "marvelous phenomena of the forces of attraction, repulsion, and suspension" at his show at the Saint-Germain fair.[122] At Saint-Laurent in July a geographical table representing all the kingdoms of the world was on display.[123] This apparatus was equipped with pistons that propelled balls across it and with a motorized drum that mixed and withdrew numbers placed inside it. Bourgeois de Chateaublanc's *automate* show in 1748 at Saint-Germain included a cyclops working at a forge, a Moor hitting a bell with a hammer, and a peasant with a pigeon on his head emitting wine from its beak.[124]

In 1775 the Swiss Droz brothers presented a figure taking dictation with pen and ink, a child painting portraits, and a clavichordist. Their "Automates organisés et harmoniques" were still performing at Saint-Germain at the Café d'Armand in 1783. Admission cost 1 livre, 4 sous.[125] A watchmaker from Brittany brought his "pièce méchanique" to Saint-Germain in 1777. This gadget depicted a stormy sea with moving ships and various sights of maritime life such as sea gulls, fisherman, and windmills. The borders of the machine contained pictures of the phases of the moon and the hours of high tides for several port cities. The *cabinet* of Monsieur Aubin offered the crowd a strange assortment of things, including a simulated rocket firing with multicolored smoke and flames; a warship fully equipped with rigging, masts, ropes, and 64 cannons of different sizes; a Chinese pagoda made of shells with a carillon that played 10 different tunes; and a moving bust of a wicked dervish. Seats for this odd sequence of curiosities sold for either 24 or 12 sous. In the late 1770s Abbé Mical used ventriloquism for his exhibition of talking *automates*. A Hungarian named Anton de Kempelin invented a chess-playing *automate*, which was seen at the fair, and in 1784 an *automate danseur de corde* was featured. Sieur Perrin displayed an *automate* hunter at Saint-Germain in 1785 who shot his arrows into numbers selected by the audience and also a "moulin sympathique," which moved and stopped on command of the crowd. He charged 3 livres, 30 sous, and 1 livre for admission.[126]

Although these *automate* exhibitions remained popular, fair entertainers by the middle of the eighteenth century began combining mechanics with electricity, optics, and prestidigitation. Calling their booths *cabinets de physique*, they discovered that the mechanical wizardry that made lilliputian figures and objects appear to be alive was more effective when joined with catoptrics and electricity. The aim of these sideshows, billed as "experiments in physics," was not really to clarify the laws of physics, but rather to make science mysterious and awesome. They must be put in the context of white magic, the art of producing the illusion of superhuman prodigies by natural means. Spectators probably understood the phenomena they observed in the *cabinets* although there is a human predilection to want to be fooled, and white and black magic were often confused in popular belief. There did not seem to be that much difference between the black arts of necromancy, mesmerism, and divination and such equally mysterious phenomena as gravity, electricity, hypnotism, and ventriloquism. The practitioners of white magic in the fairs took advantage of the mounting curiosity about natural science that developed among all levels of society in the eighteenth century. They took advantage of the lingering belief in sorcery and the occult and of the human delight in being awed and fooled just as those who wrote for the popular theater filled their shows with magic wands and sorcerers. Henri Decremps, whose book *La magie blanche dévoilée, ou explication des tours surprenants* (1784) explained all the optical and mechanical devices used in illusions such as dancing goblets, mind-reading *automates*, moving tables, and disappearing coins, grasped quite well why crowds were attracted to magic.[127] People attribute the striking effects produced by optical and mechanical illusions, he insisted, to imaginary causes that make them marvel.

One of the earliest of these shows was a magic palace said to be inhabited by "invisible spirits" that was on display at Saint-Laurent in 1747.[128] The miniature palace was rigged up with mind-reading *automates* and optical devices designed by Servandoni. Promising spectators that he would produce "terrifying sparks drawn form the surface of the water," the entrepreneur of this show, Blaise Lagrelet, made small figures from elder pith that he placed on metal plates. One was grounded; the other, connected to a machine, enabled him to vault the dolls or jacks from plate to plate. His *spectacle* was rivaled in 1750 by the *cabinet* of Monsieur Rabiqueau, who presented ships sailing in a pool of water in directions commanded by the audience, copper balls propelled into the air where they remained without apparent support; and a "machine de l'année merveilleuse," in which the spectator saw himself disappear in a mirror or change from a man to a woman.[129] In the 1780s a certain Monsieur Pinetti, billed as a physicist from Rome, brought his "bouquet philosophique" to Paris. An orange tree enclosed in a bottle blossomed and bore fruit when sprinkled with Pinetti's special water. His speciality, however, was an act with a pigeon that he dangled alive by the head from a cord. A candle cast the bird's shadow on a piece of cloth. Sticking the shadow of the bird with his dagger caused its blood to drip into a plate, leaving the impression that the bird itself had been stabbed. One could see his performance for only 6 sous.[130]

Shows featuring optical illusions became the most popular of the various types of fair magic. They drew on optical discoveries and technology of the seventeenth century. In his *Muse historique* in 1656, Jean Loret noted that he crossed himself several times while watching "flashes of bodies fleet like ghosts" twisting and dancing noiselessly on a wall.[131] He was describing one of the first exhibitions of a magic lantern invented by the Jesuit scientist Athanasius Kircher—a box containing lenses that projected luminous, seemingly animated tableaux.[132] Perfected in the eighteenth century by Abbé Jean-Antoine Nollet, a physicist who invented an electroscope and improved the Leyden jar, the magic lantern was one of several optical contraptions used in the *cabinets de physique*.[133] Shows featuring optical illusions in fact became the most popular of the various types of fair magic. There were several kinds of lanterns in use by the late eighteenth century. One, usually just called an *optique*, was a box about 4 feet high containing a mirror inclined at a 45-degree plane and a double convex glass. This contraption enabled the entertainer to make objects appear very flat or thin and to invert objects. Yet another version of the optical box, one attributed to Louis Carrogis, known as Carmontel, made use of transparencies. Carmontel produced tableaux depicting landscapes, wild animals, genre scenes, flaming palaces, hurricanes, and caricatures. He unrolled long bands of these transparencies in front of an illuminated pane of glass, so that they appeared to the spectator as an animated drama. By mid-century, the Parisian fairs were full of Savoyards who made a specialty of these forms of optical magic, carrying on their backs their lantern boxes, which they exhibited whenever a small crowd could be lured by the sound of their hurdy-gurdies.

Two versions of optical magic eventually found their way into the theaters of the fairs and boulevards—*ombres chinoises* and phantasmagoria (see Chapters 7 and 8). Frédéric Melchior Grimm has provided a good description of the technique used in *ombres chinoises*.[134] A piece of tautly stretched oilpaper or white linen cloth was used as a curtain. Actors—later on, cutout figures—were placed behind the curtain, and the light from a candle seven or eight feet back projected their images onto the cloth, so the audience saw moving shadows. The *spectacle*, Grimm observed, "lends itself to magic, to the marvelous, and to the most terrible catastrophies. If, for example, you want the devil to carry someone off, the actor who plays the devil has only

7. A magic lantern called "L'Orgue de Barbarie." Sketch by Edme Bouchardon. (MC. Moeurs, p.c. 75.)

8. *Ombres chinoises* showing ambulatory merchants. (MC. Moeurs, p.c. 30.)

to jump with his victim over the candle behind, and on the cloth he will have the appearance of taking off with him through the air."

Ombres were an appropriate vehicle for a drama, as Grimm discovered when he saw a play written for the medium at a private residence in 1767. In the play, *L'Heureuse pêche* by Abbel Tinchet, technique was linked to subject matter as the magic of fairyland genies, ghostlike characters, and mysteriously flying objects dominated the action. The play concerned the magical assistance rendered by a genie to a humble fisherman.[135] Unable to marry Lisbette because he earns only enough to feed himself by fishing day and night, Colin catches a gold vase in the river. The genie Elemaliga emerges in a puff of smoke from the vase, grateful to Colin for releasing him from his imprisonment for having rebelled against Solomon, prince of the genies. Elemaliga's fate was to remain sealed in the vase until the day when the most attractive girl in the universe was born. Colin tells the genie that that particular day is the fifteenth birthday of the seigneur's daughter, who is the prettiest girl, aside from his own Lisbette. In return for this hope of deliverance, the genie gives Colin the valuable vase as a means to get Lisbette's father, Lucas, to approve the marriage of his daughter to the fisherman. The genie also presents Colin with a magic wand giving him the power to fly and to become invisible. This he uses to make love to Lisbette in her bedroom while avoiding Lucas. Colin also uses his power to harass Philippe, Lisbette's wealthy suitor, who has given Lucas a sack of money for his daughter. Colin manages to terrify Philippe with his invisible antics, and it is finally revealed that Philippe has stolen the money and is deeply in debt.

This "comédie à scènes changeantes" was accompanied by vaudevilles and original music composed, according to Tinchet, by "one of the most celebrated musicians."[136] It had all the ingredients necessary to satisfy the taste of illusion and magic inherent in the *ombre* technique and embellished by the subject matter. The work also supplied humor in the physical, burlesque form the public seemed to enjoy the most, and it contained the perennial social theme of the popular theater—the love of two poor, simple villagers overcoming the efforts of a corrupt noble with the aid of a beneficent fairy.

After watching the play, Grimm expressed hope that the *ombres chinoises* would be made available in public theaters. He got his wish. *Ombres* joined other forms of optical magic at the fair Saint-Germain in 1774 and were soon presented in the boulevard theaters. A certain Monsieur Bernard, who charged the public 24 sous for a seat in his cabinet and 2 sous to stand, used lanterns behind a cloth curtain to project images of temples going up in flame. By 1776 the *cabinet optique* had become a standard attraction at the fairs and boulevards.[137] The most successful *ombres chinoises* show was that of Dominique-François Séraphin, a marionettist, who established his *spectacle* in the Palais-Royal in 1784. Like Grimm, Séraphin found the *ombres* useful as a dramatic vehicle and hired several minor playwrights, including Dorvigny, Guillemain, Gabiot de Sallins, and Duplessis to compose pieces for his theater in the Palais-Royal.

Why were the fair entertainments—the *parades*, acrobats, funambulists, marionettes, exotic animals, freaks and magic shows—so popular among the mixed social groups who thronged to Saint-Germain and Saint-Laurent? Did these *spectacles* have something in common that helps to explain their attraction?

All appealed in one way or another to the human fascination with the marvelous, the predilection to be awed by something incredible and fantastic.[138] Playing on the senses and the imagination through what were largely visual media, the marvelous permitted an escape from reality into dreamlike experiences. Perhaps the fair shows enabled people to project into adult experience the fanciful worlds all children create and play in. The wonderful moments of childhood revery in which the laws of nature and the constraints of society can be cast aside were rekindled in the entertainments of the fairs. The *spectacles* enabled people to accept the illusion of the incredible, to dream, and to marvel—if only for fleeting moments. Moving gadgets, electrical charges, and animated, luminous creatures seemed miraculous, arousing astonishment not unlike that evoked by strange beasts from unknown regions of the earth or animals seemingly gifted with human intelligence. The equilibrists, tumblers, and ropewalkers—the Wallendas and Evel Knievals of their day—performed amazing feats that raised the specter of crippling accident or death.[139] It was not such a great leap from peasant lore about werewolves, spells, and goblins to the seductive marvels of fair conjurers, illusionists, freaks and tumblers. The appeal of popular entertainment was that it stirred the lingering childhood need to dream and fed a human desire to marvel.

Yet the social setting of these entertainments in the marketplace and their retention of the real speech, gesture, chant, and derisive humor of marketplace existence made them fun, even credible, as well as wonderful. Everywhere the fracas of the marketplace rang out: Strollers teased monkeys; girls were insulted; café garçons were beaned with metal plates; people cursed, jostled, and shoved amid the piercing cries of the merchants; lackeys were beaten. All this formed part of the show at the fairs. And these expressions of the abusive mockery of the marketplace were hoisted to the *tréteaux*, where they became a mere extension of the general raillery along the streets. The *spectacles* of the fairs were appealing because they combined derisive humor and fairyland enchantment, the material and the magical. They joined the sense of renewal gained by physical imagery and derisive laughter at regimented society with the sense of escape from actual existence into a world of marvels, whether real or factitious.

The fairs of Saint-Laurent and Saint-Germain declined in the later decades of the century. The two principal reasons for this were the development of other places of entertainment and promenade, notably the boulevards (see Chapter 7), and the departure of the Opéra-Comique from the fairs after its merger with the Comédie-Italienne in 1762 (see Chapter 5). Although some observers suggested other reasons for the decline, including the prohibition of dice games in the boutiques, all agreed that the loss of the Opéra-Comique was an irreparable blow. Edmond-Jean-François Barbier said flatly that if the merger were allowed to stand, both fairs would collapse.[140] Indeed, many merchants sustained heavy losses and were obliged to leave the fair in the wake of the demise of the Comique.[141]

Moreover, fire destroyed the Saint-Germain fair on 17 March 1762.[142] Breaking out at 3 A.M. on a cold, windy night in a marionette loge where fireworks had been used, the fire spread rapidly through the fair, consuming the boutiques of the rue de Lingerie and on to those on the rue des Quatre-Vents, scorching the walls of the houses on the rue de Petit-Bourbon behind the fair. When the roof collaped, the explosion sent flames skyward that threatened the vaulting of the chapel of the Virgin at the rear of the church of Saint-Sulpice nearly 200 feet from the ground. Part of the church roof burned. The police marshaled all their forces, including soldiers of the Guard and the Watch. Monks and magistrates of the quarter pitched in. Joined by the first president of the Parlement, the procurator general, the lieutenant general of police, and two *commissaires*, they worked most of the night and the next day trying to stop the blaze. Guardsmen and soldiers were sent to fetch well water and pumps and to warn the clerics of Saint-Sulpice. But the fire could not be contained. All the merchandise and the boutiques were destroyed. What did not burn was stolen although many of the thieves were caught, and some of the goods were recovered. Many of the fair people were given refuge in nearby *hôtels* owned by the wealthy. Damages were estimated at 2,000,000 livres. Charles Favart described the scene as one of "terrible desolation" with people burning, parents frantically trying to rescue their children, lions and tigers roaming freely, and thieves everywhere: "In a word, there remains no vestige of the fair" although the theater abandoned by the Opéra-Comique was ironically saved.

After the fire there was speculation that because of the departure of the Opéra-Comique the fair would not be rebuilt. The king, however, remitted 200,000 livres to indemnify the fair merchants for their losses from a fund given to the crown to construct a new ship for the royal navy by the six merchant corporations of Paris. Within a year, the fair was restored, though on a small scale and without a roof, which made it less appealing for strollers because the fair was held in the nasty-weather months. The glorious era of the fair as the hub of popular entertainment was over.

The decline of Saint-Laurent was more severe than that of Saint-Germain. The *Almanach forain* claimed that it was the liveliest place in Paris before 1762, but after that year it was frequented only by muslin merchants and trinket peddlers and had just a refreshment stand and a billiard hall for entertainment.[143] The *Almanach* blamed the theatrical merger.[144] It ceased reporting on Saint-Laurent with the 1777 volume. Also acknowledging the low attendance at the fair, the *Correspondance secrète* offered as an additional reason the fact that the quarter was too remote from the center of Parisian life.[145]

Efforts were made to revive the fairs, but their success, especially at Saint-Laurent, was short-lived. At Saint-Germain, the Ruggieri brothers, who were celebrated pyrotechnicians, opened what was known as the winter Waux-Hall in 1769, modeled on one established earlier on the Boulevard du Temple;[146] and the dramatist Roger-Timothée-Regnard de Pleinchesne founded an equally elaborate entertainment fairyland at Saint-Laurent in 1781 called La Redoute Chinoise. Described by one observer as a "charming grove in the shape of an oval," the Waux-Hall was a sumptuously appointed dance hall.[147] Built at a cost of over 100,000 livres,[148] the main structure was

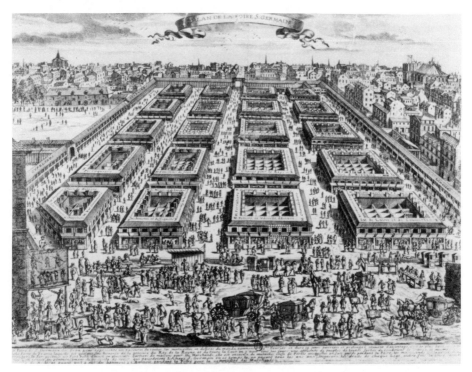

9. The fair of Saint-Germain. The text beneath the engraving calls attention to the marvels of the new fair, which is dubbed "the most beautiful and richest fair of France. . . ." It mentions the attendance of the king, queen, and court and of people from all ranks of society and also the careful supervision of guards at the doors of entry. In the left foreground one can see charlatans and showmen on the *tréteaux*. (BN photograph C59731. See also MC. Topo, p.c. 108H, G., C. The BN côte is Va 122.)

an amphitheater at an incline of seven degrees, with the dance floor at its base. Twenty-four columns in the Doric order linked by latticework and garlands of flowers formed a colonnade above the amphitheater. Marble figures of women bearing cornucopias and mirrors with painted fountains decorated the spaces between the columns. A chandelier was suspended by wreaths of flowers from the arching. Spectators could watch the dancers from the amphitheater or from a second story lined with benches fronting a promenade area. There were also stove-heated salons decorated with pilasters, arcades, fountains, statues, mirrors, girandoles, and chandeliers at both ends of the Waux-Hall, behind one of which was a café ornamented in the Turkish style. Luc-Vincent Thiéry observed that "it would be difficult to imagine anything more elegant and pleasant than this delightful place, which recalls to us and brings together all the charms of fairyland." The *Mémoires*

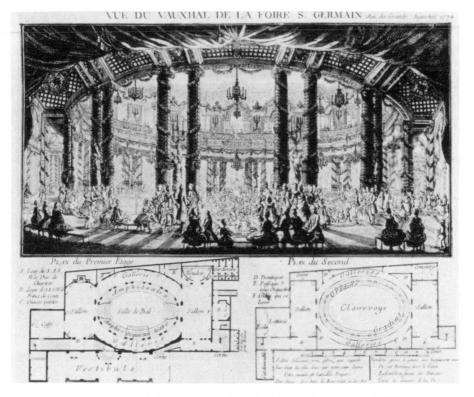

10. The Waux-Hall at Saint-Germain. (BN Va 267d and photograph 77B76603.
See also MC. Topo, p.c. 108H.)

secrets declared that "one believes himself to be in one of these enchanted
chateaux of which the ancient Romans give us such marvelous descriptions."[149]

Masked balls, to which the archbishop of Paris objected because they
continued during Lent,[150] but in vain, were featured at the Waux-Hall, where
the entry fee was 30 sous or 72 livres for a subscription. The large crowds
included courtesans but also "women of quality."[151] An English visitor
complained of the advances made by attractive women. Accusing the French
of lacking modesty and decency in their pleasures, he charged that the
gathering spots of "refined Epicureans" had been turned into "Amsterdam
music-halls."[152] The bishop of Orléans was seen at the Waux-Hall in 1773,
prompting the bishop of Marseilles to charge that other clerics were following his example and to order the clergy of his diocese not to go there.[153]

The Ruggieri often accompanied their balls with displays of fireworks.
Anna Francesca Cradock, an Englishwoman who wrote a lively account of
her visit to France, described such an evening at the Waux-Hall in 1784.[154]

The multicolored lanterns dangling from trees that lighted the dance floor were extinguished at 9:30 for the fireworks, which featured a snake "glittering with 1,000 flames" uncoiling around a fixed star. She estimated the size of the crowd to be 2,000.

In addition to balls, the Waux-Hall featured gladiator bouts, quadrilles, ballet *entrées* danced by children dressed as Provençal sailors, Polish cossacks, sword-fighting tournaments, and colorful *divertissements*.[155] Concerts were also held periodically when the admission fee was raised to 6 livres. A concert held on 3 May 1775, honoring the elector palatine, included a symphony by Gossec, an Italian aria by Méhul, an oboe concerto, and an operatic scene performed by Monsieur Le Gros of the Opéra.

Just as it is easier to conceive of colporteurs, lackeys, and pastrycooks milling about at the freak and animal shows than aristocrats, judges, and tax officials, it is difficult to imagine the former as patrons of the Waux-Hall. One wonders if the fair crowd in general had begun to resemble the clientele of the Waux-Hall and, if so, whether a decline in participation by ordinary people might help to explain the waning of the Saint-Germain fair. In any case, the sources certainly suggest that the Waux-Hall was not for journeymen and clerks. The *Almanach forain* reported that the Waux-Hall attracted an array of distinguished people from the city and the court.[156] Referring to its clientele as "the most brilliant company," "a select society," the *Gazette à la main* noted that "princesses of the blood themselves have not disdained to dance there."[157]

However elite the patrons of the Waux-Hall and the Redoute might have been, they could not prevent the decline of the two venerable fairs. The boulevards captured the crowd, and by the 1780s the Palais-Royal had become the new marketplace of Parisians. In 1787 the *Almanach forain* pronounced the final benediction on Saint-Germain:

> We could not refrain from reflecting sadly on the vicissitudes of this world, when we wandered through the deserted and barely lighted streets of this fair once so celebrated, and on entering we saw in the darkness the ruins of the elegant winter Waux-Hall, which will soon be demolished.[158]

3

The Opéra-Comique

For many decades in the eighteenth century the fairs were the center of Parisian marketplace entertainment. That the merchants fought hard to gain locations near the entertainers is indicative of their importance to the fairs. But at Saint-Germain and Saint-Laurent, neither lace maker nor marionettist, neither *limonadier* nor acrobat would have enjoyed so much prosperity if it had not been for the Opéra-Comique. From its inception in the first decade of the century until its removal from the fairs in 1762, the Comique was the fair public's favorite diversion. It had roots in the obscene farces of the late Middle Ages, the comedies of Molière, and commedia dell'arte, from whose French descendant, the Comédie-Italienne, the fair players took over a ready-made repertoire in 1697.[1] Moreover, the Comique borrowed musical airs, dramatic situations, and the *merveilleux* from its illustrious sister the Opéra, parodying the former and using the latter for humorous mockery of the allegorical theatrical world of elite culture.

In the early decades of its existence, five elements of the *opéra-comique* stand out because they were present in almost every production, usually simultaneously—vaudevilles; physical humor in the form of slapstick, plays on bodily necessities, and sexual innuendo; a regular cast of sympathetic, foolish, and villainous characters; the marvelous; and the omnipresent struggle of the *forains* with the privileged theaters. No doubt these aspects of the *opéras-comiques* account for their appeal and enormous success in the first half of the eighteenth century.

The first of these elements, vaudeville, has been defined as "any song whose melody had long since passed into public domain."[2] Many such songs were probably medieval in origin; others, dating from the sixteenth and seventeenth centuries, were originally associated with historical figures such as Mazarin or historical events such as the wars of religion.[3] New verses were constantly written for these popular airs although they were usually identified by a word or phrase of the original refrain, such as "Lanturulu" or "Biribi," or by an event, for example, "Air de la Fronde." The verses were usually epigrammatic, and the music was spirited and simple. The regular, animated rhythms, usually in 2/3 or 3/4 time, could easily be adapted to new texts and changing note values. Shifting meters and accents in mid-measure did not obscure the basically firm dance rhythms of the vaudevilles. Melodic phrases were often repeated, and the first phrase recurred twice again at the end, making vaudeville tunes easy to remember. Intervals were seldom greater than a third although in the refrains, always the liveliest parts of the music, modulations were freer, intervals were larger, and onomatopoeia—in the form of imitations of drumbeats and trumpet fanfares—was added.

The example provided here, used frequently in *opéras-comiques* in the eighteenth century, shows the vaudeville style. It is the well-known song "Biribi."

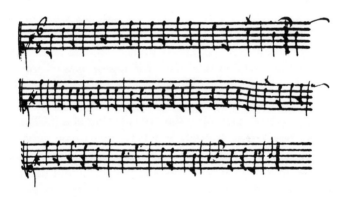

The musical simplicity that made vaudevilles easy for ordinary people to remember and to sing established the popularity of these songs. As early as 1636, Marin Mersenne wrote: "Now this great easiness causes songs to be called vaudevilles because the lesser artisans are able to sing them insofar as the author does not usually follow the curious refinements of figured counterpoint, of fugues and syncopations, and is content to give a rhythm and an air pleasing to the ear, which one designates by the name of *air,* as its principal and almost sole attribute."[5] Most subsequent writers agreed with Mersenne. Claude Brossette, the noted jurist and historian who delivered the first discourse on vaudevilles at the Académie de Lyon in 1725, insisted that the ease of remembering them ensured the endurance of these songs, which sprang from "the mouth of the people."[6] The *Journal des théâtres* noted that the "lower class [*bas peuple*] remembers more easily vaudevilles and romances than the composed song" and that simple tunes help it "to endure patiently the fatigue of work and the heat of the sun."[7] This simplicity made them ideal for the Opéra-Comique, whose actors were not trained musicians and even had to rely occasionally on the audience itself to sing the vaudeville couplets. In the time of Brossette, Lesage, and Favart, it was widely believed by those who wrote for the popular lyric theater that because vaudevilles were recognized quickly and because they conveyed so exactly every sentiment and action, they were superior to original compositions. In their *Dictionnaire des théâtres de Paris,* Claude and François Parfaict expressed the prevailing view: "No matter how agreeable Music composed expressly [for a play] may be, it is not possible that it be considered the equivalent of the Vaudeville, whose words are known by all . . . and which tunes . . . consecrated by usage . . . explain to the Spectators what the actor seeks to communicate by gesture and even his innermost thoughts."[8]

Aside from their musical simplicity, the popularity of vaudevilles can be attributed to their historical association with satire and ridicule. This association was so close that it was virtually unthinkable in the eighteenth century to set a vaudeville air to a text that was not satirical. Contemporary definitions of vaudeville usually referred to its satirical and derisive character. Lesage defined it as "a species of poetry peculiar to the French, esteemed by foreigners, loved by everyone, and the most appropriate to bring flashes of wit, to hold up to ridicule, to correct morals."[9] In his *Dictionnaire de musique,* Jean-Jacques Rousseau stated that "the vaudeville is a kind of song in couplets that turns on playful and satirical subjects. . . . The *vaudeville* belongs exclusively to the French, and they have some very biting and amusing ones."[10] Brossette insisted that vaudevilles were the satirical means by which the people could speak freely and publicly about the faults of the nation. The scandalous news of the court and the city was transmitted in these songs, where it was treated with total irreverence. No event occurred, according to Louis-Sébastien Mercier, that was not recorded in songs. The vaudeville, he noted, "responds through sarcasm to everything useful that is proposed to them" [the people].[11] Mercier believed that vaudevilles provided a better picture of the "true movement of affairs" and the character of a people than narrative histories.

The century's greatest testament to the vaudeville was that of Michel-Jean Sedaine, whose *opéra-comique* texts were written at a time when these popular tunes were no longer used by that theater:

> *Mais des moyens qui dirigent l'affront,*
> *Le Vaudeville est certes le plus prompt.*
> *Humble, rampant, mais guidé par l'injure,*
> *Il parle bas, à l'oreille il murmure;*

Puis tout à coup s'élançant dans les airs,
Ses fiers accens remplissent l'Univers.

Les Souverains, les auteurs et les belles;
Ont ressenti ses atteintes cruelles
Dans tous les temps; et le premier César
Le vit marcher à côté de son char.

L'ambitieux qu'irrite la puissance,
Et l'indigent qui blesse l'opulence,
Et la laideur qu'offusque la beauté,
Versent le fiel par ses mains apprêté.
Le Peuple rit; et cruel sans malice,
Prête à ses sons une bouche complice;
Et peu sensible aux pleurs qu'il fait verser,
Est, s'il les voit, prêt à recommencer.

Ce vil essaim qui dans Paris fourmille,
Qui, tout entier au travail de l'instant,
Va, trotte, vole, agit, boit et babelle,
A vu souvent expire en chantant
Ses grands projets, ses complots, ses allarmes.
Un bon couplet dans un cas important
En ris moqueur a transformé ses larmes,
Donné le change à ce peuple inconstant,
Et fait tomber sa fureur et ses armes.
Le prudent Law, et l'adroit Mazarin
Laissoient chanter, et s'empâtoient du grain
Que repandoient Monsieurs de la musique
Le vaudeville aidoit leur politique.[12]

Sedaine's appreciation of the vaudeville tradition was shared by most eighteenth-century Frenchmen, though it also had its prudish critics, most notably Voltaire. The sage of Ferney declared: "Through what disgraceful custom has it become necessary that this art [music] which is able to lift the spirit to great feelings is used by us only to sing some vaudevilles? It is to be wished that some genius strong enough to cure the nation of these abuses would appear and give to a *spectacle* that has become necessary the dignity and the morals that are lacking in it."[13]

If the vaudeville did not amuse the century's greatest satirist, its derisive character nonetheless endeared it to numerous individuals and groups. The song peddlers of the the Pont-Neuf, of course, wrote couplets to these tunes mocking magistrates, actors, courtiers, and Jansenists and making "the incident of the previous night, . . . a vaudeville the next day."[14] Some individuals, notably Pierre-Philippe-Emmanuel de Coulanges (1631–1716), a close friend and correspondent of Madame de Sévigné, a councillor in the Parlement of Paris, and a songwriter, wrote diaries in vaudevilles recording their adventures. Coulanges scoffed at his dismissal from the office of *maître des requêtes* in a verse written to the popular air "Nous dites, Marie." He recorded the attempts of three men to seduce his wife in another vaudeville. When the pendulum of his clock broke, he composed a parody, "Pendule est morte," on Lully's operatic air "Alceste est morte." And he described his travels throughout France and Italy in vaudevilles.[15] Relating through vaudevilles anecdotes that ridiculed people and obscene descriptions of their private lives became a popular activity during the regency. The surviving manuscript collections of songs testifies to this.[16]

Vaudevilles were also used to express political disgruntlement, social criticism, and just plain foolishness and merrymaking by an unusual group organized in 1702 known as Le Régiment de la Calotte. It was founded by Louis XIV's coat-bearer with the king's secret support and to his great amusement.[17] Made up mainly of persons who had served in the military, the regiment adopted a coat of arms and elaborate paraphernalia to express their irreverent contempt for the world they lived in. Momus, personifying ridicule, was their patron saint; they chose a stick mounted with a grotesque puppet head with a jester's collar as their scepter; their shields bore the image of a *calotte* or cap, one flap turned up to hear the gossip, the other turned down to shut out the world's unpleasantness. A rat, symbolizing whim or folly, perched on top of the cap. The members of the regiment, known as the Calotins, wrote many satirical couplets to the vaudevilles. Circulated around the city, these airs or *calotinades* mocked everyone including the king and the regent who followed him. They were a means of letting off steam. Dorothy S. Packer writes:

> The panorama of French society as it existed in the first forty years of the eighteenth century is unrolled before us with an astonishing freedom of expression in these vaudeville texts. Here is "le genre humain" under a microscope. Insincere lovers, jealous husbands, parasitic courtiers, irreligious abbés, faddists, fops, vain actors, misanthropes, prudes, coquettes, courtesans, lawyers, pedants, censors, nobles,—none are spared. The Regiment of the Calotte and the vaudevillistes exempted no one, from the king himself to the lowest comedian, from the Pope (referred to as "Jupiter Calotin") to the most obscure curé.[18]

Although singing societies such as Le Caveau founded by Alexis Piron, Charles Collé, and Claude-Prosper Jolyot de Crébillon in 1733 perpetuated the vogue in vaudevilles, the real home of popular songs in the eighteenth century and the institution responsible for their enormous popularity was the Opéra-Comique. Sedaine was probably correct in writing that the Comique owed its very life to the vaudeville:

> *Les Triolets, les Rondeaux, les Brunettes,*
> *La Ronde alerte, et les tendres Musettes,*

Les Lanturlu, *les* Lon-la, *les* Fon-flon,
D'autres encor, jusques au Mirliton,
Ont par leur sel et leur tour ironique
Donné naissance à l'Opéra-Comique.[19]

But it is no less certain that the Comique did more to preserve popular culture in song than any other institution or group.

Vaudeville melodies were easily sung by actors with no musical training and were quickly recognized by the audience, but the key to their success in a Comique production lay in selecting just the right ones to suit each episode and character of the piece. This was especially true by the eighteenth century, when there was a vast stock of these tunes (the Lesage collection contained about 1,100), and musicians could incorporate 40 or 50 and even as many as 100 airs in a single piece. Some of the vaudevilles were repeated several times in one production.[20]

In the early decades of the eighteenth century, in addition to composing the musical accompaniments and the ballet *entrées*, Jean-Claude Gillier, a violinist at the Comédie-Française and an *ordinaire* of the music of the royal chapel, selected and arranged most of the vaudeville tunes in close cooperation with Lesage and his colleagues. Both Gillier and Lesage were masters at picking the vaudeville that would best evoke the mood or subject of the text or kindle humorous associations.[21] Quite often a tune was selected on the basis of the original text of the refrain because using the original in conjunction with new verses in new situations enabled authors to evoke satirical references or double entendres in listeners' minds. Many of the tunes were so familiar that, for 165 of the 369 vaudevilles in volume 7 of his collection, Lesage could print a single word or the first line of the original verse or a phrase from the refrain (the *timbre*) rather than the full notation.[22]

In addition to the vaudeville tunes that had accumulated over the years, the creators of *opéra-comique* found operatic airs by Lully and other composers valuable musical resources as well as effective forms of satire. Airs were lifted freely from an opera, then set to new verses quite out of keeping with the originals. Airs that became popular quickly joined the growing vaudeville repertoire.[23] Quite often *opéra-comique* authors parodied dramatic material as well as the music from an opera, enabling them to poke fun at the alleged boredom of opera, paganism, word repetition, the feud over the respective merits of Italian and French music, and the quarrel of the ancients and moderns. The effect of combined parody was often devastating. In the second act of *Arlequin, roi de Serendib* (1713), considered the best of the musical comedies of this period,[24] Lesage burlesqued the contemporary opera *Callirhoé* by André Destouches and Pierre-Charles Roy. Mocking the scene where Callirhoé and Corésus pledge their loyalty, Arlequin, following the melody of Destouches' aria, sings to his slave:

> *Je porterai mon hommage*
> *De la table à vos beaux yeux;*
> *Ne craignez point ce partage:*
> *J'en aimerai trois fois mieux.*[25]

Then together they sing:

> *Sur ces couverts, sur cette nappe blanche,*
> *Sur cet autel redoutable aux poulets,*
> *Par ce couteau, la terreur de l'éclanche*
> *Je fais serment d'être à vous à jamais.*

Like Callirhoé, the harem girl faints, but Arlequin revives her, whistling and tapping his knife on the table as officers rush in bearing meats and sauces.

In addition to vaudevilles and parodies, the Opéra-Comique used instrumental music, performed by an orchestra originally quite small in size but expanded as the authorities would allow and as the productions came to include overtures, interludes, dances, and vaudeville finales.[26] Overtures and pieces accompanying stage action depicted storms, battles, and bucolic settings. Instruments were used to describe natural sounds, such as a flute for the song of a nightingale, or to evoke a mood, as when trumpets and drums heralded a ceremonial entrance. Various types of marches, dance tunes, and instrumental combinations were associated with mythological characters, descents, processions, and pastoral scenes. Although symphonic interludes were rare, fair pieces almost always had one danced *divertissement,* which for years made use of the talents of the *danseurs-de-corde,* accompanied by vocal and instrumental music. Musicians often appeared on stage in these *entrées,* which seldom had much relationship to the main plot. During these little intermissions, the performers played gigues, Allemandes, chaconnes, cotillions, passepieds, and branles, sometimes newly composed, but often borrowed from operas.

Although the dances and instrumental music certainly enhanced the appeal of an *opéra-comique,* it was the vaudeville that lay behind the great success of the fair theaters. These familiar tunes, so easily sung by both performer and crowd, so firmly associated with popular entertainment and its satirical derision, were perfect musical vehicles for the theater of the fairs. Peddled for years along the Pont-Neuf, sung by people in the streets, cafés, and clubs, these airs were in every sense "voices of the city." They linked the rollicking banter of the marketplace to the stage. The vaudeville, Julien Tiersot has written, served "as an act of union, as an active and all-powerful intermediary between the theater and the simple and sometimes rather gauche popular song."[27] The long-established popularity of the vaudevilles virtually guaranteed the success of the Comique.

As a dramatic genre, the *opéra-comique* was an anarchical gallimaufry. Its creators threw the rules and style of classical drama to the winds. Their breathless farces disregarded the classical unities of time and place, declamatory speech and Alexandrian verse, and what Lesage called those "scenes of languishing transition that must always be endured in the best comedies."[28] The early *opéras-comiques* had no consistency or unity of form and structure or even mode of performance, in part from design and in part because of the stratagems the *forains* had to employ to avoid suppression. The pieces were shapeless and episodic, an excuse for the tumblers to perform their stunts and regale the crowd with pratfalls. Their material consisted of snippets of this and that—monologues, fragments lifted from the Comédie-Italienne, vaudeville couplets, jargon, *divertissements* modeled on those at the Opéra, pantomime, grimaces, tumbling, burlesque—all glued together in one-act prologues or *parades,* two-act pieces in which one act served to introduce the characters and the other to present amorphous intrigues, or three-act comedies. Lesage preferred short pieces. Typically, his productions consisted of a prologue announcing the main bill of fair, establishing rapport with the audience, and appealing for the crowd's support against the high-status theaters, followed by two short pieces concluding with a finale of dances, choruses, and a sequence of couplets sung by the principal performers.[29]

In the preface to the printed collection of their works, Lesage and D'Orneval wrote that "the title alone of *Théâtre de la foire* carries an idea of lowness and vulgarity. . . ." Lesage and his colleagues believed that the fair setting and atmosphere required a theatrical genre that reflected the coarse, physical banter and scornful humor of the marketplace. Therefore they put the lyric vulgarity of the streets onto the *tréteaux.* Obscene gesticulation, sexual innuendo, buffoonery, physical assault, and toilet humor were built into every production. Though audiences, like fair crowds generally, were socially mixed, Comique performers played in the marketplace and catered to the taste of *le bas peuple.* Looking back in 1760 to the formative years, Charles Favart, a master of the Comique genre, wrote: "The *opéra-comique* at that time spoke the language of the people, it was the way of the time, and its license should certainly be attributed less to the authors than to the public itself whose depravation it was necessary to stroke in order to win its approval."[30] Favart's condescending attitude suggests by implication that "the people" found their thirst for vulgarity quenched at the Comique rather than at the Opéra and the Comédie-Française, which were morally elevated.[31]

Sexual innuendo combined with slapstick and toilet talk figured in just about every Comique production of the first half of the century. The sex could never be too explicit for fear of censorship. But productions were often built around sexual themes, and, at the very least, double entendre could be employed freely. Equivocal language, according to a contemporary, was a major device to elicit laughter:

> The slip, the surprise, or the free expression of things that ought to be veiled are here the principles of laughter. Ironical remarks, a displaced composure, a gesture or an expression that constrasts with the action, an unexpected recognition . . . , finally anything that arouses spite by ridicule or surprise by some peculiarity becomes a source of comedy.[32]

Pierrot's song at the beginning of *Le Remouleur* (1722) by Lesage is typical of the sexual equivocation used by Comique writers. Cast as a knife grinder on the Parisian streets, Pierrot chortles that even the tough jobs do not worry him:

> *Quand femme gentille*
> *Vient à m'appeler*
> *Vous voyez un drille*
> *Prompt à travailler.*[33]

Similarly, in *Arlequin à la guinguette* (n.d.) a faithful wife, whom a merciful fairy turns into a turtledove, complains of having been forced to feel her husband's chisel.[34] In *Les Festins de Pierre,* Colombine rejects some cheese that Pierrot offers her because it is limp. When Pierrot assures her that he has something else in his pocket she would like, Colombine assures him that she has been pricked too often to die of hunger.[35]

Fair audiences were titillated not only by the Arlequins and Pierrots clutching none too subtly after their teasing coquettes but also by promiscuous girls snaring an innocent male prey. In *Scaramouche dedans* (1711, anonymous though probably by Fuzelier), Isabelle, thinking that young Léandre has never seen a girl, sings this verse:

> *Mon maître a fait un bouquet*
> *Vous allez à voir le fouët,*
> *Venir avec violence*
> *Corrompre mon innocence*
> *Le fouët, le fouët*
> *Vous allez à voir le fouët.*[36]

References are made to Léandre's falling into a gorge from which he cannot get out, and there is a scene in which the old pedant Scaramouche seduces Colombine after trying to instill modesty in her by covering her breasts with his handkerchief. *Scaramouche dedans* had an unusually heavy dose of horseplay in the form of kicking, pushing, and especially *bâton* beating, probably because, since the actors were forbidden to speak, visual comedy and song were doubly important.[37] Octave, Isabelle's wealthy suitor, kicks his valet in the rear end; the doctor empties a chamber pot on Octave; Scaramouche clubs Léandre with his *bâton,* and the lover returns the pounding when he catches the pedant with Colombine. The *bâton* was significant in Comique productions as a physical agent of comedy. Used in every farce of the fairs, it may have had childhood associations with the sticks, balls, pebbles, and pieces of string that for children momentarily become implements of play.[38] Children do not see the *bâton* objectively as a piece of wood or plastic; they see and feel their muscles at work, and their manipulation of it in imaginative play is a subjective affirmation of their being and value. Perhaps the ever-present *bâton* in the Comique was still a mirthful affirmation of the worth of human life, and the sexual equivocations and horseplay less a prurient humor than a celebration of the common life-force of humanity.

By far the most common sexual theme in *opéras-comiques* was the loss of virginity, usually a woman's. One of the first *opéras-comiques* ever produced at the fair, *Le Marchand ridicule* (Saint-Germain, 1708, anonymous), depicts the seductions of a cloth merchant's daughter. The merchant, Janbroche, entrusts his boutique to Pierrot and warns his daughter not to admit anyone lest her reputation and honor be lost.[39] She is to say, "Vraiment nenni" to anyone who approaches her. Unable to get any other response from the girl when he attempts to purchase some cloth, Polichinelle asks her if she is a virgin. She replies as instructed, "Vraiment nenni." The bemused Polichinelle asks: "If a good big boy like me, who isn't crazy for virgins, asked to sleep with you, would you turn him down?" "Vraiment nenni." Polichinelle takes her off to bed and suffers a *bâton* whipping from Janbroche.

Alexis Piron built a career at the Comique using the loss of virginity as his principal theme. His masterpiece was *La Rose, ou les jardins de l'Hymen,* first performed on 5 March 1744. The work was approved by the censor but held up by the lieutenant general of police, causing Piron to protest to the comte de Maurepas, the king's minister for Paris. In his letter to Maurepas, Piron pointed out that his work had not only been passed by the censor, but it had also been read aloud and praised by a private group that included two sexagenarian bishops and several ladies. Admitting that he used some suggestive language, Piron declared: "The words *rose, rosebush, shepherd's crook,* and *garden* have caused some little thing to be thought; but they were all so fitting, as the Examiner has indicated, the veil of allegory was so successfully woven that there was not the smallest hole through which one could see nudity."[40] Piron suggested that the subtlety of his piece would be greater for those seeing it than for readers. The rose tree, he insisted, was an innocent image, and the shepherd's dispute over the girl's bouquet was one of those "commonplaces of pastoral silliness." The author concluded with a reminder that Louis XIV helped Molière when *Tartuffe* was questioned.

The setting of the prologue of *La Rose* is a grove near the temple of Hymen, where Cupid tells Mercury he poaches every day to get even with Hymen, who has shown scorn for his laws. Mercury reminds Cupid that the season of childhood has passed; the shepherd girls must offer Hymen the first flowers and fruits of their gardens. Worried about the young girls' mothers, Mercury is reassured that Cupid's first law is freedom—for husbands, wives, girls, and mothers. The first act opens in a garden enclosed by a grill where two gardeners attend one of the flowers of a rosebush that has begun to bloom. Rosette, a girl of 12, confides to the 20-year-old shepherd girl Sylvie that she feels the first flutterings of love, the first "tourlourirette." Sylvie is dubious about whether Rosette, with her youthful physique, can carry a shepherd's crook; but Rosette, who has been promised the keys to the garden when the first rose blooms, rushes off to ask her mother if she may clip the fresh flower. As the mother hurries away to fetch Hymen before it is too late, Rosette, to the vaudeville "Je ne suis né ni Roi, ni Prince," sings:

> *Fi donc; c'est un monstre farouche;*
> *Prenez bien garde qu'il n'y touche:*
> *Pour l'Hymen laissez la fleurir;*
> *C'est à lui que je la destine:*
> *L'Amour vient-il à la cueillir,*
> *Il ne reste plus que l'épine.*

Colin, a peasant, is left behind to guard the rose that Rosette offers to cut for him, but he refuses, fearing that Hymen will not want it if it is even slightly disturbed despite Rosette's protestations that they could fool Hymen with an artificial rose:

> *Elles n'ont dit qu'en pareil cas*
> *Une fille ne manque pas*
> *De roses artificielles,*
> *Où les plus fins seroient dupés:*
> *Les yeux de l'Hymen, disent-elles,*
> *Tous les jours même y sont trompés.*

Sylvie introduces Rosette to some shepherds, who try to induce her to cut the rose. One offers her "flowers of rhetoric," which will spread her fame from the Seine to the Mississippi. An impotent old man nearly succeeds in getting the rose for a golden apple; his song is a parody of the air "Que devant lui tout s'abaisse et tout tremble" from Lully's *Atys*. Finally, assisted by Cupid, a young rosebush trimmer wins the girl by promising to "ornament" her rose with "my shepherd's crook." She agrees on condition that he renounce his craft and cut only her rose. Cupid, Hymen, and the mother give their blessing to the marriage as the shepherds warn about the passage of youth in the vaudeville finale:

> *Quand l'Hymen cueilloit une rose,*
> *Jadis il s'y piquoit les doigts:*
> *Aujourd'hui c'est toute autre chose,*
> *Il n'est plus d'obstacles à ses droits.*
> *Avec ses flêches badines*
> *L'Amour épluche un rosier:*
> *L'Amour fait si bien son métier,*
> *Qu'Hymen n'y trouve plus d'épines.*

The sexual imagery in *La Rose* was more subtly treated than in most pieces of this period. It was, in fact, rare for a Comique writer to build an entire work around the loss of virginity or to use images such as the rose and the crook rather than the more facile play on words and pat on the rump. *La Rose*, Piron's last work for the Comique and one of the last that theater staged before its demise in 1745, marks a significant advance in Piron's own treatment of sexual themes. The contrast can be seen by looking briefly at *Tirésias* (1722), which did get the *forains* into trouble.

Jupiter is bent on punishing Tirésias (the actor appeared as Arlequin dressed as a *petit-maître*) because he would not turn over his voluptuous mistress, Cariclée, for the god to seduce. Jupiter gains his revenge by turning Tirésias into a girl, but Tirésias discovers that he enjoys the transformation: "I take greater pleasure in my roguishness, in my fickle conduct, my prattle, my coquetry, my obstinacy, and in all the other similar qualities that adorned my last sex. . . . Now that I am utterly capricious, I am, thank God, my own mistress."[41] In an intricate commentary on women, Tirésias tells Jupiter how nice it is to have nothing in his head and to be freely promiscuous. Juno reminds him that, having lost his manhood, he is no longer free to acquire the dignities reserved for males and that his destiny as a woman is to be the plaything of unfaithful lovers or the victim of a churlish husband. Men are like mute puppets before women, Tirésias replies, destined to cut their throats for the sake of honor. Determined to have sexual relations with a man, Tirésias happens upon Cariclée, who has donned male clothing. But Juno's magic spoils his fun by restoring his manhood.

The entire Comique troupe of Francisque Molin, an acrobat for whom Piron wrote *Tirésias* and whose daughter, Mademoiselle Sallé, later starred at the Opéra, was arrested following the first performance. The *commissaire* charged the *forains* with presenting a scandalous *spectacle*. Taking the charge as a personal rebuke, Piron responded with a long, stinging letter to the lieutenant general, admitting that there were a few "traits libres" in *Tirésias* but denying that they were excessive and insisting "the taste of the public demands it of our pieces . . . ."[42] These witticisms, he reasoned, go in one ear and out the other; "they go straight to the imagination in order to entertain it and not to seduce it." No spectator will get the wrong idea if he sees Arlequin for what he is instead of looking for hidden meanings. Much worse goes on at the Comédie-Italienne, Piron insisted: Polyphême jumped on a nymph in a recent piece of "dissolute buffoonery"; the Cyclops rolled around on stage with the same nymph for a quarter of an hour; Arlequin cracked that "la force de l'amour" required three acts, not one; an old man tried to seduce several girls in order to regain his virility; a character called La Foire told the crowd, "I have seen you this morning in my toilet in better dispositions." All this occurred not in an "ambulant theater" but in one that supposedly respected morality, one that enjoyed certain prerogatives that went far beyond the Comique. Why, asked Piron, if the *commissaire* was so concerned about public decency, did he not act against the Italian players? Piron answered his own question:

> But the politics of the latter and their resources well beyond mine have known all too well how to use my prosecutor to their advantage; and nothing is more obvious than his spirit of hatred and partiality. His zeal has injured me, the enjoyment of coming to close the loge with all the glare he could muster, arms in hand, when all that would be reduced to nothing at the sight of the order that he hid maliciously, the violence, finally, that he used on my comrades and on me; all that certainly marks less an amateur officer of the order than a man carried away who uses odiously the sacred arms of justice in order to satisfy a personal dissatisfaction. And I dare not entreat against him this same justice that he abuses!

When D'Argenson sent Piron's letter to the *commissaire,* he demanded retributions in the form of damages, but, instead, the lieutenant general released the *forains,* obliged Francisque to return to marionettes, and took no action against Piron.

The characters in Piron's *opéras-comiques* may have behaved more outrageously than in other productions, but they were well known to fair audiences. Indeed, the characters were as predictable as the sexual allusions and physical banter. To the crowds they doubtless symbolized both the quagmire of life and the charming fantasy of magical escape. Unlike their heroic counterparts singing of battlefield victories at the Opéra, they had to connive to survive, regaling each other with the taunting profanities of the streets. Their social relations were coarse because they lived in a different world from Amadis and Thésée. They brought the bodily functions of eating, defecating, and copulating to the stage where these material needs were juxtaposed with wonders beyond the mundane—a world of enchanted utopias and magical transformations corresponding to childhood dreams and fears.

From the Italians the Comique appropriated Arlequin, Scaramouche, Colombine, the gentle Isabelle, and the handsome Léandre. Arlequin was the great favorite of the crowd. Costumed in his traditional checkered outfit with a *bâton* at his side, he was transformed in the French theater from the foolish, rough valet from Bergamo to a sly, impudent rogue. He was industrious, usually amorous, often cynical, very giddy, and full of pranks.[43] He had a standard collection of gestures (*lazzis*) useful in improvised comedy, and the actors or acrobats who portrayed him had to be good at the pratfalls and agile stunts for which he was known. Always engaged in intrigues, usually cast as a servant though appearing in many disguises, Arlequin was the consummate burlesque character.

Polichinelle, a French character relegated to the marionettes, was also a wonderfully comical figure. He laughed raucously and played tricks on his wife, his neighbors, the local *commissaire,* and the apothecary. He was snub-nosed, wide-eyed, red-faced, with a crooked chin and a big stomach. Polichinelle wore a bright, spangled costume of red and blue with a cape and a three-cornered hat.

No *opéra-comique* was complete without a coquette, and Colombine was the crowd's favorite. Always a maid and the confidante of respectable women, Colombine had as her aim carrying on an affair with an ageing financier for the purpose of ridiculing him. She was a moralizer, giving advice to young girls and helping to reconcile lovers, and she was courted by valets. These and other characters had allegorical associations. Arlequin with his snakelike body, monkey muzzle and black mask, and spangled suit represented spirit, love, and mobility. Colombine represented the pursuit of a dream or ideal. Cassandre, usually an old man, personified the family; and the thin, pale Pierrot symbolized passivity.

These well-known characters of the Italian stage and the French marionettes mingled with conventional characters such as peasants, shepherd lovers, princes, and magicians; but much of the popularity of these shows stemmed from the characters, albeit satirical stereotypes, drawn from everyday life, such as lawyers, doctors, impertinent lackeys, pretentious aristocrats, arrogant *petits-maîtres,* greedy tax officials, and adventurous abbés. Audiences recognized and reacted to such types. They enjoyed seeing rough and rude characters outwit or ridicule persons of title and rank, government officials, and egotistical academicians. Jacques Lacombe was probably wrong in maintaining that audiences did not recognize their own ridiculousness.[44] Fair crowds probably did see their own gross behavior and their own foibles in the antics of Arlequin. Piron insisted that the spectator and the actor "constantly intermingle in the action and suppose that they are objects of the jests of the moment."[45] The crowd delighted in self-ridicule, but they also relished the derisive mockery of social types who existed outside their world or who preyed on it.

Lesage, especially, was a gifted social critic, the real master of marketplace derision. He exposed the profligacy of regency society, the moral corruption of persons of high rank, the fury for speculation in stocks and for gambling in general, the feuds of literary men, the greed and injustice of magistrates and financiers. His aim, however, was not to reform, but to reveal, to unmask, and to amuse. Perceiving that his audience wanted entertainment, not instruction, he gave them comic characters whose morals were disreputable and who were destined for folly. He showed the world as it looked to him with its crooked procurators, ignorant doctors, and vain intellectuals. His point was that we can bear such a society only with derisive laughter and a touch of the absurd.

One of Lesage's favorite targets was the *grande dame.* Extremely self-indulgent, Lesage's dame travels about from theater to ball to château. She loves slumming but insists on the homage due to her by rank. She eschews household responsibilities and fidelity to her husband as demeaning. Lesage showed even less mercy in portraying male nobles, especially *robins.* In *Le Tombeau de Nostradamus,* two young *petits-maîtres* query the prophet on which of them had the oldest noble lineage.[46] Agreeing to reveal the previous three ancestors of each, Nostradamus exposes in succession a country gentleman, a village bailiff, and a miller for the first noble, and a fat rich man, a *petit comis,* and a coachman for the second.

Lesage held up the bourgeoisie, especially lawyers, to even greater ridicule. Surely he must have given the crowd a feeling of revenge for their mistreatment at the hands of dishonest officials. These were treated as cutthroats, cunningly swindling the people, cheating defenseless orphans and widows with no fear of retribution. They dreamed only of becoming ennobled, and this made them conform to established beliefs and customs. Equally bad, the procurator's wife mistreated clerks and ruined her husband through a life of dissipation and extravagant spending. Moreover, Lesage's talkative, obsequious *avocats* were thoroughly disreputable in encouraging people to give false testimony.

But Lesage reserved his sharpest barbs for doctors. The English doctor Gabbanon in *Les Enragés* (1725) cures all the furies of the mind and body.[47] An enraged poet locked in an iron cage because he bites people is cured by suffocation. In *L'Obstacle favorable* (n.d.), Lesage, D'Orneval, and Fuzelier spoofed the contemporary feud between the Faculty of Medicine and the School of Surgery.[48] A Dr. Lavisière, who claimed the power of healing by looking into a patient's eyes, was Lesage's subject in *Les Spectacles malades* (1729), which also satirized the grand theaters.[49] Gazing at the Opéra, which has sought his help, he sees a discordant orchestra and muck in the flute section. When asked what ordinary doctors have prescribed, the Opéra replies:

> *Trois d'entr'eux m'avoient donné*
> *De la racine de* Pyrame.
>   *Ce remède fortuné*
> *Vint m'empêcher de rendre l'âme;*
> *Mais pour mon malheur il leur plut*
> *Dans du sirop de* c, sol, ut,
> *Mettre une drogue que je pris;*
> *C'étoit du chiendent de* Tarsis.
> *J'ai beau reprendre du solide*
> *De la rhubarbe d'*Amadis,
> *Du vrai catholicon d'*Armide,
> *De la confection d'*Atis,
> *De l'elixir de* Proserpine;
> *Ces drogues de vertu divine*
> *Qui m'ont jadis fait tant de bien,*
> *Aujourd'hui ne me font plus rien.*

Telling the Opéra that its malady results from the immunity built up to these medications, Alizon, the doctor's governess and apothecary, prescribes leaves of patience and sugar of hope. The Comédie-Française is diagnosed as being partially paralyzed while the Comédie-Italienne, full of black bile, is told to take her native air. Threatened by a malady that ends in "i, i, i, i, i, i, ie," the Opéra-Comique is cured by an African plant, an emetic called *Corsaire de salé,* the title of a new work by Lesage.

However stereotyped and satirized, Lesage's aristocrats and bourgeois had a ring of truth missing from his portrayal of the lower social ranks. He was least successful in depicting peasants, perhaps because he had little knowledge of peasant life. Most of his peasants were simple bumpkins, either overly crafty or overly naive, sometimes too sensible or too foolish. They seldom emerged as individuals. Using provincial dialect, Alexis Piron was more successful in depicting peasants, with whom he grew up. Piron's social satire in general was sharper, with a harsher critical thrust than Lesage's. He opened *L'Antre de Triumphus* (1722) with a confrontation between Arlequin and two collectors of the *taille.* Arlequin protests that he is not a taxable subject, but replying that they are Arabs who make no distinction between a noble and a *roturier,* they declare: "Inequality would introduce among us only moral corruption."[50] Although Arlequin has no money, they seize everything he is carrying, having learned the practices of the *fermiers généraux.* In the ninth scene of the *opéra-comique,* Piron took on the prestigious gazette of court news, the *Mercure.* Mercury, whom Arlequin dubs the god of thieves, having rid the countryside of brigands (who withdrew to the cities, taking the titles of financiers and merchants), has become a miserable colporteur called Mercure-Galant. Boasting that he hawks obituaries, genealogies, drinking songs, and logographs to the court, Mercury tells Arlequin his *opéras-comiques* do not please everyone because they are too truthful and violate the rules of drama. Calling the marionette show, to which Lesage had repaired in 1722, a "laboratory open to little malicious minds," Mercury informs Arlequin of its popularity with the nobility. The marionettists cry: *"Enter ladies and gentlemen; here is the gathering spot of all the nobility*. And seeing indeed 100 carriages planted at the door of the residence of Seigneur Polichinelle, I went in and I have not seen without surprise that the crier did not exaggerate."

In 1731, Charles-François Panard joined the Opéra-Comique and tried to fashion a lyric comedy with more elevated characters and subjects. His moral allegories and satires were gentle commentaries on the hedonism of the higher orders of society. Sticking to inoffensive, if sometimes banal homilies, Panard avoided farcical intrigues, censorious references to contemporary events, even Italian masks and ambiguous imbroglios. He preferred allegorical characters like Cupidity, Hypocrisy, and Scruple. Dubbed "the fountain of the vaudeville" by Jean-François Marmontel,[51] Panard attempted to free the Opéra-Comique from the stigma of base farce by commenting on the moral condition of humanity in general. But he also knew how to poke fun at his own reforms. In *La Critique* (1742), a lawyer has been sent by his colleagues to rebuke the Comique for satirizing them and depicting them as Arabs and corsairs.[52] Mademoiselle Raimond, an actress, assures him that the Comique will not put him on the stage again because it is tired of him. A Gascon noble complains that the *opéras-comiques* have been "stuffed with Gascons" for 20 years, making a mockery of his sophisticated province. The Gascon is appeased when Raimond assures him that their humor is directed at the old coquettes who make a fool of him, the merchant who flatters him, the imbecile who believes him, and the widow who gives him money. Mademoiselle also dismisses a doctor from the stage after realizing she will live longer without him. Finally, Raimond appeals to Momus and his daughter, a critic, to supply them with new epigrams to enliven their show. They agree, but having blasphemed Apollo, Juno, Minerva, Neptune, Pluto, Mars, Venus, and Bacchus, they are ordered to use words of no more than three syllables.

The characters of the Opéra-Comique played out their absurd intrigues in fanciful worlds filled with the marvels of magic wands, apparitions, metamorphoses, demons, and fairies. Anchored in the lore of peasant societies and nurtured by the human need to return to the fantasies of childhood dreams, the marvelous was the quintessential element of the early *opéra-comique*. The *sauteurs* had earlier discovered the enormous appeal of mixing stage marvels with real ones. The Comique perpetuated that tradition, borrowing heavily from the *féerie,* mythology, allegory, and deus ex machina of the Opéra. The marvels at the Comique, however, were always associated with natural needs and feelings and were usually used for derisive purposes. It was the combination of satirical buffoonery with astonishment and awe that gave the Comique its bounce.

There were several means of arousing curiosity about the strange and miraculous. The simplest was to cast pieces in exotic settings. These were often Oriental. In *Arlequin, roi de Serendib* (1713), Lesage's familiar hero, after being washed up on a strange shore, is robbed by three turbaned thieves who mutter, "Gniff, gniff"; sealed in a barrel; and left in the desert.[53] In a feat combining dexterity and magic, Arlequin escapes from the barrel, only to be captured by the palace guards of the grand vizier, who with the chief of the eunuchs, prepares to sacrifice him to the gods. Lesage introduced his irrepressible toilet comedy, one of the constants in the celebration of physical being in the marketplace, in the sacrificial scene, in which Arlequin interprets the crowd's chant, "Tragizo, trapeza, porphyra, kecaca," to mean that he is to use his turban as a chamber pot as part of the ceremony. Prior to the sacrifice, Arlequin is treated to dancing slave girls and a mountain of food, which he gobbles up quickly, not realizing it is all intended for his consumption. A doctor trying to save Arelquin from gluttony gets a cream pie in the face for his efforts. In the sacrificial scene, a parody of Lully's opera *Iphigénie,* the great priestess glorifies the god Kesaya for preventing virgins from seducing their tutors. The priestess prepares to stab Arlequin, but at the last instant she recognizes him as Arlequin and reveals herself to be his compatriot, Mezzetin. After pillaging the temple, Arlequin and Mezzetin head for Paris in her flying vessel as Kesaya, having left them with a suckling pig, is swallowed up by the earth.

Three years after this production, Lesage and D'Orneval depicted the dilemma of Taber, the Muslim son of Moussafer. Having rejected his wife, Dardané, Taber cannot reclaim her, according to Mohammedan law until she has been scorned by a hulla—a second husband.[54] They employ Arlequin for the job after realizing that he is a "miserable foreigner" because he sings that courtiers are slaves, merchants are wretched, magistrates are restrained, and only beggars enjoy life. Although Arlequin promises Taber to reject Dardané after the wedding, Taber tries to prevent him from seducing her by giving him food (which he eats so rapidly he chokes), getting him drunk, and then having him arrested for violating Muslim law.

The preoccupation of *opéra-comique* writers with the marvelous went much further than Eastern exoticism.[55] Lesage resurrected the sixteenth-century French astrologer Nostradamus in an *opéra-comique* at Saint-

Laurent in 1714.[56] Having stabbed the lover of his wife, Isabelle, Octavio seeks a reversal of his fate at the tomb of Nostradamus. A monster vomiting flame engulfs Octavio as he opens the tomb, but the magician appears in the mausoleum bearing a wand and wearing a white robe covered with talismans and a bonnet with long ears. Nostradamus summons his demons to fetch Isabelle.

The fable of the flood provided Alexis Piron with excellent material for his *opéra-comique Arlequin-Deucalion* in 1722, a tale selected no doubt because the single genuinely spoken part enabled Piron to stay technically within the restriction to monologues placed on the *forains* in 1722.[57] He used the legend to satirize the grand theaters and French society. Three people have survived the flood: Arlequin as Ducalion, the son of Prometheus, who is washed ashore on Parnassus as the lightning and thunder crackle around him; his mute wife, Pyrrha, who in the second act descends from the flies on Pegasus, which has the ears of a donkey and the wings of a turkey, and is tethered with posters of new works given in 1722 at the major theaters; and Polichinelle, a puppet claiming to be Momus, king of the fools, speaking gibberish, whom Arlequin takes from his pocket. The first act focuses on the encounter of Arlequin, leaping about the stage passionately uttering, "Hélas" and "Dieu," and, in Roman dress, Melpomène snaking across the stage with convulsive gestures, with her dagger, the attribute of tragedy, in one hand, and a trumpet, the attribute of epic poetry, in the other. Piron deliberately mixed attributes to satirize the epic tone of Comédie-Française productions in that period. Melpomène disdains Arlequin's proposal of marriage. In the second act, after Apollo has awakened Pyrrha by playing the slumber aria from Lully's opera *Issé,* Arlequin leaps, cavorts with Pegasus, defecates in his hat, hurls two pistols into the sea so that posterity will not have firearms, and learns from Polichinelle how to repopulate the earth: he must throw stones, symbolizing bones, from the earth, the symbol of his grandmother, over his head. Magically, four girls and five men emerge from the ground—a *laboureur,* an artisan, a sword noble, a *robin,* and an oddly dressed person who was not paired with one of the girls. To each Arlequin gives advice and offers predictions: the *laboureur,* who is scorned by the others but necessary for their existence, should live in peace and innocence and learn to mock the others; the artisan should follow the *laboureur,* avoid towns, and do useful work; knocking the sword noble's plumed hat off, Arlequin reminds him that he is not better than his father and that he should be modest because his only talent is knowing how to kill; calling the *robin* a "vilain garçon," Arlequin criticizes his roguish eyes, dainty nose, light-fingered hands, and disgusting manner, muttering that he wished he had thrown this stone into the sea; noting the appearance of his son—a skullcap, a chevalier's wig, a Capuchin's beard, a turned-up collar, colored clothing, a sword, a bundle of plumes, white stockings, and red and black breeches—Arlequin declares that, like his grandfather, Prometheus, such people perpetuate themselves without ever having slept with a girl.

A simple object or device such as a ring or wand was often sufficient to evoke the marvelous. In *La Ceinture de Venus* (1715), Lesage built his plot around a belt.[58] Fortune has given Arlequin a sack of silver to improve his bad luck, while Mezzetin receives a belt from Cupid that will make him attractive to beautiful girls. Testing their respective gifts on the same girl, Nicole, Mezzetin emerges triumphant. Off to Paris, Arlequin and Mezzetin amuse themselves by swapping the belt, both thereby attracting the same girl.

Finally, *opéra-comique* authors evoked exotic marvels by plunging their characters into utopian lands, where they defy the bounds of time and space and where social behavior contrasts with life as it was known to eighteenth-century Parisians. The setting of *Le Monde renversé* (1718) by Lesage and D'Orneval, for example, was a strange land populated by vaulting grotesque animals and oddly acting people.[59] Speculating where they might be—they have flown over the Black Sea, Constantinople, China, Egypt, and Passy—Arlequin and Pierrot land on a griffin. Their hunger is satisfied by the magical appearance of sausages, turkeys, macaroons, cheese, and wine. From two girls, Argentine and Diamantine, they learn about this upside-down world, where unfaithful husbands are imprisoned; where two rich people cannot marry each other because it would prevent equitable distribution of wealth; where philosphers are amusing merrymakers who impart their knowledge in song; where judges are incorruptible, merchants scrupulous, actors respected, seigneurs decent and modest, actresses virgins; where procureurs, whose profession is attained only after 300 years of noble lineage, are honorable, virtuous, and do not know the meaning of the word *cocu;* and females can be doctors. Near the end of this episodic farce, Arlequin and Pierrot lose the two girls to rivals in a roll of the dice, but Merlin, descending in a chariot, awards them the girls anyway and, with a wave of his wand, transforms them into upright citizens. Cleansed of gluttonous desires and Parisian iniquities, Arlequin and Pierrot celebrate their transformation and renewal in a vaudeville finale.

Le Monde renversé has most of the characteristic elements of the early *opéras-comiques*. It features acts of magic, metamorphoses, and exoticism: The *sauteurs* tumble about in their animal suits; the characters fly on a griffin over a forest populated by otherworldy creatures. Merlin alters the outcome of fate, symbolized by the role of the dice, and transforms Arlequin and Pierrot into virtuous beings. The traditional reference is made to physical needs, in this case to the hunger of the two protagonists. These were the staple ingredients of the *opéra-comique*. Audiences were given a fantasy world where magic provided happy resolutions. Yet this was all done in a way that humorously satirized both the real and the magical worlds. Descending chariots, metamorphoses, mythical beings were all conventional devices of the bastion of high culture—the Opéra. At the Comique they appealed both to the popular taste for exoticism and magic *and* the taste for derisive laughter at the world beyond the marketplace. As for the real world, the satire in *Le Monde* is too obvious to require much comment: Lesage lampooned regency morality, economic inequality, pretentious philosophers, and officials like the procurator who bought their offices in a government ridden by venality. The utopian setting doubtless enabled him to comment freely about his own society.

But if Lesage, Piron, and the other craftsmen of the Comique needed utopia, Mount Parnassus, and Baghdad for their social criticism, they required no such exotic backdrop for their derision of the grand theaters. These elite institutions waged a relentless battle to suppress the Comique, a battle that the *forains* brought to the stage and that determined the musical format of popular theater. In one of the most fascinating episodes in the social and cultural history of early modern France, the proprietors of the fair theaters used every stratagem and evasion imaginable to combat the campaign of the privileged theaters. Ridiculing their illustrious brethren was an important weapon in their arsenal.

4

The Politics of Culture:
The Struggle Against Privilege

THE DISTINCTION between popular and elite entertainment in eighteenth-century Paris hinged on the existence, prior to the creation of the Opéra-Comique, of monopolistic privilege and on the determination of the grand theaters to gouge, subvert, or eradicate the *petits spectacles*. Politics shaped the differences in cultures. The high courts, the Crown, and the police stood behind the prestigious theaters. All the *forains* had were the crowd, the monks, and their own artful cunning and will to succeed.

The Opéra, bearing the title Académie Royale de Musique, was founded as a cultural showcase of the monarchy. The privilege granted to Jean-Baptiste Lully in 1672 and to the many musical entrepreneurs who succeeded him conferred on the Opéra the exclusive right to present, for the court and the public, works whose texts were entirely sung unless Lully and his successors chose to grant or sell that right to someone else. After the success of his first opera, Lully got the crown's approval to take over from Molière's players, later the Comédie-Française, Richelieu's theater in the Palais-Royal. In 1673 a royal ordinance also reduced the number of musicians that the Molière troupe could employ from 12 instrumentalists to 6 and from 6 singers to 2. Dancers were banned from the Comédie Française in 1682. Singers were completely prohibited, and the number of instrumentalists was further reduced by order of the Crown in 1684.[1] Nevertheless, after the emergence of the Opéra-Comique in the early eighteenth century, the Comédie-Française persisted in its use of music in an attempt to remain competitive. Hiring such composers as André Campra and Jean-Joseph Mouret, the Comédie-Française presented many pieces with vaudevilles quite similar to *opéras-comiques*.[2] The *forains*, in turn, simply made fun of the grand theater's feeble

attempt to woo the crowd. In a prologue entitled *Les Comédiens corsaires*
(n.d.) Pierrot shouted:

> *Ma foi, Messieurs les Corsaires,*
> *Il est bien honteux à vous*
> *Pour rétablir vos affaires*
> *De piller gens comme nous.*[3]

The Opéra periodically attempted to curb its partner-in-privilege. In June
1716 a group of syndics who had taken over its management obtained a
ruling from the Conseil d'Etat condemning the Comédie-Française's use of
leaflets, an orchestra, and a large number of vocalists for productions of
Molière's *Le Malade imaginaire* and *La Princesse d'Elide,* restating the earlier
ordinances and limiting the number of instruments to six and vocalists to two
and forbidding dances.[4]

The Académie Royale de Musique was also concerned about encroach-
ments on its privileges by the *forains.* In 1677 the lieutenant general of police
forbade Brioché, the marionettist who performed near the Pont-Neuf and
after 1699 at Saint-Germain, from using magic on the grounds that it was
contrary to Lully's privilege. The same official in 1679 granted the acrobatic
troupe of Charles Alard the right to add a few discourses to their act, but on
condition that singing and dancing be excluded. The Académie also obtained
the suppression of a marionette show called the Troupe Royale des Pygmées.[5]
Despite some leniency toward the fair players, the Académie's monopoly
over French lyric theater was reaffirmed, and fines for violations of its
privilege were issued frequently.

Although Molière's company suffered initially from Lully's power, they,
too, later received the exclusive right to present drama in verse. As early as
1664, Molière successfully persuaded Louis XIV to close down a small
theatrical company in the fairs on whom the king had earlier conferred the
title "Troupe du Dauphin." The movement toward monopoly accelerated
when, after Molière's death in 1673, the Crown ordered the merger of his
troupe with the Marais theater. The Comédie-Française was founded in
October 1680, when Molière's former company at the Hôtel Guénégaud
merged with the actors of the Hôtel de Bourgogne. The basis of the
Comédie's persistent claims to a theatrical monopoly during the eighteenth
century rested on the royal ordinance of 21 October 1680, which gave it the
exclusive right to perform theatrical works in French. The company was also
subsidized by the Crown, for whom it performed at Versailles,
Fontainebleau, and elsewhere. It enjoyed numerous other benefits as well: the
use of the king's horses when traveling to the royal châteaux and two écus
a day for expenses when performing for the court, as well as a ration of

wine, bread, and firewood. Its only real competition in the last years of the seventeenth century came from the Italian actors who took over the Hôtel de Bourgogne with authorization by the Crown to perform Italian comedies.[6]

The Comédie-Française first exercised its monopolistic privilege in 1681 against the fair players. Posters went up at the fairs advertising La Troupe Royale du Grand Scot Romain which promised an assortment of marvels: the Great Scot would transform water into wine, milk, butter, and perfume; he would regurgitate a salad as fresh as one from the market, two plates of live fish, a bouquet of fresh flowers, live birds, 300 or 400 pieces of gold, and other assorted items. The poster also promised a rope vaulter and farces performed by an Italian troupe. Each loge seat cost one écu, but the gallery went for 20 sous and the parterre for 10.[7] The performances were held at the tennis court on the Rue Mazarine near the Comédie-Française. During the same year, another poster proclaimed the appearance at the Foire Saint-Germain of a company called La Troupe de Tous les Plaisirs, who presented new comedies, tightrope performers, and a somersault act, all for the price of 7, 15, or 30 sous.

The French players reacted angrily. They requested police action against this Great Scot, whom they accused of causing disturbances in front of their theater in the Hôtel Guénégaud. The police were requested to stop the performances and to tear down the theater. Nicolas-Gabriel de la Reynie, lieutenant general of police, issued a summons to the Scot and ordered him to stop performing. When the Scot disregarded the order, the French players got Commissaire Lemaistre to draft a statement against the Scot. Lemaistre verified that a farce was being presented at the *jeu de paume*. After an official report was filed, the Scot was ordered to rewrite his posters and to employ no more actors in his shows. He complied. The same course of action was taken against La Troupe de Tous les Plaisirs. These actions enforced the privilege of the two theatrical troupes who enjoyed royal favor, the French players at the Hôtel Guénégaud and the Italian actors at the Hôtel Bourgogne. And they were reinforced by subsequent decisions. In 1688 the French and Italian troupes succeeded in closing a theater in Saint-Germain known as Les Petits Comédiens François, and in 1690, despite his personal appeal at Versailles, Alexandre Bertrand's marionette theater was demolished by the police, and he was fined 100 livres. Bertrand had added acrobats, tightrope walkers, and a comedy performed by live actors to his dancing marionettes at Saint-Laurent.

The struggle between privileged and popular entertainments[8] came to a boil at the turn of the century after the Comédie-Italienne was expelled in 1697. The Comédie-Italienne, which had obtained exemption from the musical monopoly of the Opéra, had been playing satirical French comedies with

French songs for two decades, as well as parodies of the pieces of the other theaters. It was, therefore, a thorn in the side of the Comédie-Française, which was not in the least unhappy about its departure. But it was the fair players who reaped the benefit from the Italians' expulsion. Bertrand and others began appropriating the pieces given by the Comédie-Italienne, which formed a ready-made repertoire.[9] Bertrand even rented the Hôtel de Bourgogne shortly after the Italians left, and he began giving acrobatic shows that included excerpts from the Comédie-Italienne pieces. He lasted only a week, however. The Hôtel was closed on command of the Crown, but Bertrand and Charles Alard, the son of a bathkeeper and one of the best acrobats and mimes of the period, took their players back to the fairs. They figured they could hide behind the old franchises of the fairs. Their productions, a blend of tightrope walking, singing, and farce, challenged the privileges of the Comédie-Française and the Académie Royale de Musique, which mounted a campaign of repression against the fair entertainers. Passive resistance and clever evasions were the best weapons against power and privilege. Conflicting jurisdictions and slow legal procedures also helped the *forains* to frustrate the elite theaters, but the assertions of monopolistic privilege were not abated.

The troupes of Charles Alard and Maurice Bertrand dodged police rulings against their use of music, dance, and farce in 1699 and 1700 by appealing the lieutenant general's prohibitions to the Parlement of Paris.[10] The *forains* enjoyed mounting success with fair crowds, but in June 1703 the Parlement upheld the police and fined the fair actors, who were ordered not to produce long, written pieces. Presenting detached fragments of plays to elude the authorities, the fair troupes managed to stall by appealing twice more to the Parlement in 1703 and 1704.

In February 1706, however, the Comédie-Française sent new petitions and reports to the police, who subsequently ordered Bertrand, his associate Christophe Selle, and the widow Maurice, whose husband Maurice Von der Beck had been one of the outstanding acrobats of the fairs until his death in 1699, to stop all dialogues in their shows and to desist from presenting any piece that would be "contrary to the rules of propriety and decency."[11] Each entrepreneur was assessed a fine of 300 livres to be paid to the Comédie-Française plus an additional 20 livres to the king. Future offenses would result in the demolition of their theaters. Less than a month later, new orders stipulated that 6,000 livres be paid in damages, that the previous fines be paid, and that the theaters be destroyed.

This time the popular entertainers turned to Jacob Du Frénoy, the collector of revenues for the abbey of Saint-Germain, to whom the *forains* paid rent, arguing that the judgements against them were injurious to the interests of Cardinal d'Estrées, abbot of the monastery and proprietor of the land where their shows were given. The cardinal, in turn, drew yet another court into the affair by petitioning the Grand Conseil to subpoena the French actors. The *forains* also dispatched their own petition. In the words of one historian, "the mitre joins the trampoline" to plead for justice.[12] The Grand Conseil responded favorably. It issued a subpoena to the French players in March 1706 and ruled that the whole matter must be thrashed out under its jurisdiction. The magistrates of the Parlement, angry that their jurisdiction had been infringed, promptly discharged the French actors from the subpoena. On 15 June 1706 the Parlement ordered that all appeals be made to it.[13] Early in July, Bertrand received a summons from the Parlement demanding payment of his fines plus 300 livres for costs. He was threatened with imprisonment.

The jurisdictional squabbles enabled the *forains* to continue playing,[14] but in due time the Parlement reached a final verdict and reasserted its authority. On 22 February 1707 the high court nullified the appeals of the *forains,* restored the fines and costs previously levied, and forbade dialogue in the productions. The wiley *forains,* however, concocted a clever subterfuge that enraged the Comédie-Française: One performer spoke in monologue while the others mimed their replies. The *forains* also achieved the effect of a dialogue by having one actor deliver his lines, then retreat quickly to the wings as another actor rushed out to reply. The *forains* incorporated dances and songs into these clever monologues, one of which, Fuzelier's *Arlequin écolier ignorant, ou Scaramouche pédant scrupuleux,* first performed in February 1707, had a run of five consecutive seasons. Neither the police nor the Parlement had specifically outlawed music in their productions. Finally, the *forains* resorted to what were called *pièces à jargon:* They achieved a dialogue of sorts by having one of the actors speak in a way that could not be strictly construed as French prose.

The courts continued to haggle and to hear conflicting testimony while the popular and elite theaters battered each other with accusatory memoirs. The fair players even tried a clever ploy to win the goodwill of the magistrates: they offered to contribute more than one sixth of their annual profits (the amount paid by the privileged theaters) to the hospitals for the care of the poor if the Parlement would allow them to continue performing.[15] Their offer was rejected. Perhaps more important, Alard and the widow Maurice negotiated early in 1708 with the director of the Académie Royale de Musique, Pierre Guyenet, for permission to employ instrumentalists, singers, and dancers and also to use scenery. Their action was a hedge against any proceedings that might be instituted against them by the Comédie-Française. The growing resolution of the magistrates to support the Comédie-Française against their rivals and the pact that the *forains* made with the opéra were perhaps the most decisive factors in establishing the future character of the popular theater. Prior to these events, the pieces of Alard and Maurice consisted mainly of dialogues, monologues, and mime; thereafter, they relied more and more on vaudeville airs.

In the ensuing years, the *forains* continued to sustain the assault of privilege: the police ordered the enforcement of an *arrêt* of 2 January 1709, upholding the previous orders of the Parlement, fining the *forains* 1,000 livres, and threatening the destruction of their theaters. In fact, in February 1709 the French players did tear up one of the theaters at Saint-Germain, smashing the scenery and the benches in the parquet. Although the Grand Conseil intervened and ordered the French players to pay damages, the Comédie took the whole matter to a higher level—the Conseil privé of the king—which upheld the Parlement.

By 1710 it was clear to all concerned that power lay with privilege. The popular entertainers of the fair had used clever stratagems to dodge the restrictions imposed on them. They had converted monologues into dialogues by miming, shuffling actors about, and speaking softly; they had moved their shows to the protective wings of the fairs, whose proprietors were churchmen; they had taken their cause to the Grand Conseil, which had supported them against the Parlement. The jurisdictional disputes enabled the *forains* to continue performing to capacity crowds. Nevertheless they had violated the privilege accorded to the French players by the Crown. Yet for the Comédie-Française, it was not just a question of upholding their rights. The French players were irritated by the public's enthusiasm for these marketplace farces. They were frustrated by declining audiences. From its founding in 1680 until the turn of the century, the Comédie-Française had had large audiences. It drew an average of 140,000 paying spectators a year between 1680 and 1715, hitting a peak of nearly 168,000 in the 1700–1701 season.[16] But from 1701 to 1712 there was a steady decline in audience size. The count was 114,000 in the season of 1709–1710. After a brief recovery toward the end of Louis XIV's reign, the decline resumed and worsened, falling below 100,000 seven times prior to mid-century. The actors of the Comédie-Française complained of having to close their theater for want of an audience, attributing this to the competition of the fair theaters. In his *Lettres historiques sur tous les spectacles de Paris* (1719), Nicolas Boindin stated that "for some time we see the Comédie-Française absolutely deserted."[17] Thus, the trends during these formative years of popular theater were bleak for the Comédie-Française, and that helps to explain its aggravation and its persistent struggle in the years to come. But, for the time being, they had won, or so it appeared.

The struggle now, however, took on a new dimension: the Académie Royale de Musique became a participant in the disputes because the fair entertainers had used music and dance much more extensively in their productions as the pressure from the Comédie-Française mounted. In 1708 the debt-ridden Opéra negotiated an arrangement with Charles Alard and the widow Maurice enabling them to use music.[18] The Comédie objected on the grounds that the Opéra was exceeding the terms of its privilege, and early in 1710, taking advantage of the widow Maurice's death, it successfully pressured Pierre Guyenet into canceling the agreement with Alard.

Once more, however, the popular entertainers displayed their ingenuity. Alard's actors mimed their roles on the stage while the lines that they would have spoken were written in large letters on scrolls that the actors carried in their pockets and held up for the audience to see, thus enabling those in the crowd who were literate to follow the action. These pieces soon became musical comedies, however, as authors began writing the texts in verses that were sung to the melodies of well-known vaudevilles. Mingling with the audience, the *forains* sang the airs to the newly composed verses that were unfurled on scrolls or placards. Moreover, the *forains* began distributing printed copies of the couplets to the crowd. In 1712 they also used two children dressed as cupids to unfurl the placards, which were held in the air by poles or suspended from the flies (*cintres*) over the stage. These techniques enabled the actors to move around more freely and the audience to see better. Since the tunes were familiar, the actors easily got the crowd to sing as a chorus while watching the animated pantomime on the stage and reading the verses on the placards or printed sheets. The *forains* also used a small orchestra to play the airs.[19]

The structural unity and dramatic substance of these *pièces en écriteaux* were practically nonexistent. They relied on bacchanals, grotesque ballets, gesticulation, and buffoonery, leaning on the appeal of visual spectacle and vaudeville.[20] Nevertheless, to the consternation of the French players, the fair crowds loved the *pièces en écriteaux,* probably in part because the *forains* brought their embattled struggle with the Comédie-Française to the audience's attention, winning its sympathy and support by ridiculing the exalted adversary. For example, in *Le Retour d'Arlequin à la foire* (1712), described as a "divertissement à la muette," Thalie, muse of comedy and protectress of the *forains,* complains that the *Romains* (the Comédie-Française) have abolished laughter.[21] Touched by the problem, Jupiter charges Momus, the god of gaiety, to take an old Arlequin and his comrades to Paris, where, despite the regulation of silence, they will attract the public's interest. Armed with *écriteaux,* Arlequin and Pierrot on horseback chase the *Romains* from their stage. Assured by Thalie that he will be avenged by attracting crowds and that he can entertain without speech, Arlequin does gyrations, grimaces, contortions, and dances; and he banters with Pierrot about the plight of the Comédie. The *forains* thus used the traditional horseplay of the *sauteurs,* popular vaudeville tunes, placards, and ridicule of the grand theater in order to survive. The mocking imitation of the *Romains,* which the fair players soon discovered delighted the crowd, the grimacing, and the buffoonery were especially important in the *pièces en écriteaux,* as in other fair shows, because they provided a return to childhood. Along with taunting gibberish, gesticulation, and buffoonery, they are the common denominators of children's laughter.[22] The taste for slapstick and visual parody at the fairs—and masks too—is doubtless a throwback to childhood.

It is also significant that in another of these pieces, *Ecriteaux des festes Parisiennes* (1712), it is Carnival that comes to the rescue of the *forains.*[23] Descending from the skies in a saucepan, accompanied by two pastrycooks, one on a stove, the other riding a horse, Carnival and his friends have been summoned to the fair by Arlequin and Scaramouche who are eating heartily to rattle their kettles and pans in a mighty stramash of mockery. Two of the French players, presumably the butt of the derision, arrive with a fatted ox as Carnival bids the *sauteurs* to perform and the masked dancers to sing. The piece reminds us that the *opéra-comique* of the fairs was conceived in medieval charivari and the Feast of Fools. As the persiflage of childhood play is reawakened in the grimacing buffoonery of the *forains,* the life cycle of carnival begins again. Rendered speechless, the fools of the fair strike up their songs and shindy. They are born again through carnival. They will feast and celebrate physical endurance, and they will ridicule dignity, order, and privilege.

The success of the *pièces en écriteaux* sent the French players rushing to the Châtelet to get the *commissaire* to verify what the *forains* were doing in order that they might be stopped. In 1711 the *commissaire* confirmed that Alard used an orchestra of eight musicians and that several costumed actors performed mute while appropriate songs were displayed to the crowd. His report stated that the placards gave his actors a means of expressing themselves "in very nearly the same way they would have with the faculty of speech."[24] Similar reports were filed against Laplace, Dolet, and others. The wrangling continued for a few years, but in the end the power of the Opéra, which needed the income from the *forains,* proved greater than that of the Comédie-Française.

Guyenet died bankrupt in 1712. A group of syndics to whom he was in debt took over the Opéra, and in October 1713 they negotiated an arrangement with two new entrepreneurs of the fair *spectacles,* Madame Gaultier de Saint-Edme and Dame Baron. Dame Baron was the daughter of the widow Maurice, the widow of an actor of the Comédie-Française, Etienne Baron, and the wife of Chartier de Beaulne, a *commissaire.* These two enterprising ladies agreed to work together while maintaining their separate *spectacles,* which they referred to for the first time in 1713 as *opéra-comiques.* They had no difficulty working out a financial deal with the syndics similar to the one concluded in 1708 with Charles Alard, who died in 1711 from a wound sustained during a somersault. Jean-Baptiste Constantini, known as Octave since the days he had worked for the Comédie-Italienne in Paris, took over Alard's troupe. He had returned to Paris after the Italians' explusion in 1697 and had secured a lucrative job as inspector of the barriers of Paris. Dolet, Bertrand, and Laplace also formed a company, but they had no agreement with the Opéra. These *spectacles* all used vaudevilles and displayed the verses to the audience either by means of scrolls or large placards suspended from the flies. In 1712 Madame de Saint-Edme hired the successful dramatist of the Comédie-Française, Alain-René Lesage. Earning about 2,000 livres for each fair, Lesage wrote around 90 plays for the *forains* between 1712 and 1738.[25] The *spectacles* of Dame Baron (known after her second marriage as Dame de Beaulne) and Madame de Saint-Edme were publicly designated *opéras-comiques* when Beaulne got permission from the Opéra to use this term on 26 December 1714. They were identified in the fairs by the names of the well-known actors who starred in the two shows: Baxter and Saurin for Beaulne's and Dominique (Pierre-Françoise Biancolelli) for Saint-Edme's.[26]

The term *opéra-comique* designated both the theaters and the comic genre that mixed spoken dialogue and pantomime with songs and dances. The genre was conceived from the beginning as a *spectacle* that would comically ridicule opera and serious theater generally. Built on the spirit of biting satire and jest characteristic of the vaudeville, it was a genre tailored to the critical banter of the marketplace. In a discourse to the crowd delivered before the performance of *Le Temple du destin* at Saint-Laurent in 1715, the actor Saurin blamed the imperfection of the genre on the constrictions of the vaudeville, but he added that "if playful performances entertain you, if shows low and vulgar disgust you, that is your taste, sirs; it is our job to adapt to you and that is what we propose."[27] Putting the coarse raillery of the streets onto the stage and lampooning the established theater as an elite bastion of repression was the Comique's formula for success. The popularity of the fair shows resulted from the public's sympathy with the *pièces en écriteaux*, which the campaign of the Comédie-Française had caused the *forains* to contrive and which proved more appealing than the old farces in prose had been.

Still, the *forains* might not have survived had it not been for the Opéra's bankruptcy, which enabled them to dodge the restrictions of the Comédie by using singing and dancing.[28] The French players were helpless when the regency upheld the Opéra's right to authorize music in other *spectacles*. On 23 December 1715, Jérôme Phélypeaux Pontchartrain, minister of the Maison du Roi, noting that the ordinances against fair troupes "have not until now been able to hold them in the confines of their estates," ordered *sauteurs* and ropedancers not to augment their shows with comic scenes "under whatever pretext" on penalty of a 1,000-livre fine.[29] The lieutenant general of police and the prévôt of Paris were ordered to enforce the edict. But three days later, Pontchartrain specifically authorized a new contract with one *spectacle,* and on 6 January 1716 Dame de Beaulne signed such a document giving her the right to have singing and dancing in return for the sum of 25,000 livres. A year later, Madame de Beaulne agreed to increase the payment to 35,000 livres in return for an exclusive 15-year guarantee to present *spectacles* with songs, dances, and symphonies under the name Opéra-Comique. The arrangement with Saint-Edme was dissolved.[30] Saint-Edme's troupe, like the others at the fairs, had no recourse but to return to tumbling, ropedancing, and *pièces en écriteaux* without music. The battle against privilege was now fought among the *forains* themselves as well as with the elite theaters.

The problems of Beaulne and the other *forains* were far from over. In 1716 the regent welcomed the Comédie-Italienne back to Paris. It enjoyed privileged status and the right to use music. The Comédie-Française, mired in a 300,000 livre debt in 1718,[31] complained angrily of the infringement of its privilege by both the *forains* and the Opéra. In July 1718 the regent annulled the compact between Beaulne and the Opéra, and in the fall he ordered that all shows be closed at the conclusion of the fair except the ropedancers and the marionettes.[32] Accepting defeat, Madame de Beaulne went to Louisiana, where her husband got the position of general procurator of the colony. She returned to Paris after his death a few years later and had to accept employment as an usher. The *forains,* meanwhile, reacted by explaining their plight to the public in several pieces presented before the Saint-Laurent fair closed.[33]

With hilarious scorn Lesage and Fuzelier let the *forains* fight it out with the two comedies in their prologue, *La Querelle des théâtres.*[34] The first Comédie rebuffs La Foire's welcoming embrace, wailing

> *Mes yeux sont étonnés du monde que je vois*
> *Pourquoi faut-il, hélas! qu'il ne soit pas chez moi.*

"You are angry to see well-bred people here," sings La Foire. "When Parisians come to the Opéra-Comique, you accuse them of bad taste, yet they seem reasonable to you when they attend your theater." The anger of the two comedies intensifies when the Opéra, "the traitor," approaches: "It is he, cursed fair, who has snatched you back from the obscurity where I made you return." Depicted ludicrously, the Opéra dances in, singing an air from *Les Fêtes de Thalie* about the carnal knowledge of 15-year-old girls. The comedies wrestle him to the floor, but the Opéra rises with laughter when the *Romains* vow to pillage and smash everything in the fairs. A sword fight ensues, during which the comedies shriek

> *Détruisons tous les forains*
> *Auteurs de notre indigence;*
> *De nos propres mains*
> *Tuons cette engeance.*

But with the Opéra's help, the *forains* are victorious. The piece created such a sensation that, despite the order abolishing the Opéra-Comique at the fair's closing, the regent's wife ordered the *forains* to present it at the Palais-Royal in October, along with Lesage and D'Orneval's farewell to the fair, *Les Funerailles de la foire.*[35] In the latter work *la foire* dies in the Opéra's arms.

These sallies against the grand theaters may have endeared the *forains* to the public, but they did not, of course, alter the regent's ruling. The Saint-Laurent fair of 1718 did indeed witness the death of the Comique. Privilege had won, but what the government and the French players did not seem to realize was that the fair players would not give up, nor would the public. In bringing the struggle to the stage, the *forains* had found a means of rallying the crowd even if live actors could not speak, sing, or mime. At Saint-Germain in 1719, Fuzelier and D'Orneval used marionettes in a parody of Lully's opera *Atys* entitled *La Grand'mère amoureuse.* Prior to the performance, Polichinelle delivered this harangue to the crowd:

Monseigneur the public, since the plays from France and Italy, masculine, feminine, and neuter, assume the burden of haranguing you, do not take it badly that Polichinelle, following the example of the big dogs, comes to piss against the walls of your attention and to flood them with the torrent of his eloquence. If I present myself to you as the orator of the marionettes, it is not for some plums; it is for the purpose of telling you that you should pardon us for displaying a second parody of *Atys* in our little boutique; here is the reason for it: the fine wits meet; *ergo*, the author of the Comédie-Italienne and the one of the marionettes should meet. As for the rest, Monseigneur the public, do not count on finding here the gracious execution of our friend Arlequin; you would reckon without your host. Just imagine that we are the oldest privileged ones, the naughtiest rascals of the fair; imagine finally that we have the right in our pieces not to have common sense; that we have the right to stuff them with nonsense, odds and ends, moonshine; you will see in a moment the exactitude with which we uphold our rights. Good evening, Monseigneur the public; you would have had a prettier harangue, if I were more adept. When you will have made me richer, I will make the haranguer of our very honored neighbor the Comédie-Française work for me, and I will pronounce to you my rhetoric with the tone of Anna and an ornamental sound like a trumpet. Come then in a crowd; I will open my doors for you, if you open your pockets to me.[36]

The *commissaires'* accounts indicate that the *forains* resorted to their old dodges in 1719 and 1720.[37] Fuzelier also attributed the *forains'* ability to elude the orders against them to the regent's tolerance.[38] That became apparent in 1721, when a royal ordinance sanctioned a new contract between the Opéra and the Opéra-Comique, headed by Marc-Antoine Lalauze. Thus, the *forains* returned in late July with *Le Rappel de la foire à la vie* by Lesage and D'Orneval. The Opéra and the Comédie-Française may have acceded to the revival because they needed the *forains* as competition for the Italians in the fair.[39] It is also significant that the ordinance upholding the new agreement permitting the Comique to reopen stipulated the sums to be paid to the hospitals: "A sixth franc of the total of the receipt will be deducted for the benefit of the said hospital, 150 livres for the costs of each performance, and on the balance the ninth in support of the poor of the Hôtel-Dieu. . . ."[40]

The Comique celebrated the reopening in *Le Rappel*. Opéra, consoling the mournful *forains,* promises to go to Hell in order to capture the fair from Pluto.[41] Pluto's court and the mighty guardian dog Cerberus are put to sleep with music from a new opera, and Opéra welcomes La Foire and her actors, though asking them for money. The two comedies feign pleasure at the return of La Foire, who is greeted warmly by Monsieur le Public sprouting different heads. A heated argument then ensues: the Comédie-Italienne accuses Public of being too indulgent toward La Foire, making her insolent and rushing to see her bad pieces. Yet the Comédie-Italienne offers to give vaudeville pieces if that is what Public wants. Though Public agrees with La Foire that each should stick to his own craft, La Foire, to the chagrin of the Comédie Française, welcomes Italienne as a companion to the fair.

Lesage and D'Orneval have obviously referred to the Comédie-Italienne's effort to succeed in the marketplace. When the Italian players failed to draw crowds even after they began holding balls after the performances, Lesage could not refrain from poking fun at them. In *Le Régiment de la Calote* (1721), Comédie-Italienne sings thus:

> *Nous avons pour plaire aux yeux*
> *Fait grande dépense*
> *Croyant qu'on n'aime en ces lieux*
> *Que vaine apparence:*
> *Mais le trait original,*
> *C'est d'imaginer un Bal*
> *Dans la ca, ca, ca,*
> *Dans la ni, ni, ni,*
> *Dans la cu, cu, cu,*
> *Dans la ca, dans la ni, dans la cu,*
> *Dans la canicule;*
> *Chose ridicule!*[42]

The Italians absorbed the blow although their shows were not successful. Consequently, they pressured the regent to revoke the privilege of the fair players. At the conclusion of the Saint-Laurent fair in 1721, the regent again ordered the *forains* to restrict themselves to tightropes and marionettes. Only Francisque Molin was exempt. Molin, who had friends in high places, received permission to give pieces with one spoken part. He adroitly hired the talented, audacious Burgundian poet Alexis Piron, who devised his ingenious monologue, *Arlequin Deucalion,* which circumvented the 1721 *arrêt* while staying technically within the restrictions imposed on Molin.[43] It must have infuriated the Comédie-Française that after Francisque's privilege was annulled, he could come up so quickly and cunningly with a piece that captivated the crowds, made a mockery of the eminent poets and their privileged theater, and took a swipe at *le monde* as well.

Using the Burgundian patois he knew so well, Piron also cut loose at the privileged theaters in a three-act *opéra-comique* for marionettes against which the prohibitions on speech and song did not apply produced by Francisque in 1722.[44] Arriving at Olympus and finding all the gods asleep, Momus orders Morphée, the god of dreams, to take his boredom to the French theaters:

> *Si tu veux verser tes pavots,*
> *Vas sur les théâtres de France!*
> *Y-avance! Y-avance! Y-avance!*
> *Vas y regner en mon absence.*

The muse of comedy asks each of the gods why he sleeps. Jupiter blames the Opéra, where in a recent production the machine transporting him to earth failed to work:

> *Ce coquin là m'assassine:*
> *Au diable soit sa machine!*
> *J'ai mal encore à l'échine,*
> *Tant elle me cahota*

When awakened, Mars leaps up, swinging his sword wildly in the air:

> *Ah, cadedis! où sont-ils?*
> *Cape de bious! que jé lez ebentre!*
> *Qui bibe!*
> *Ah, messieurs excusez! jé rébois.*

Momus and the gods play a game: Each mimes an occupation for the others to guess. Momus cries, and Apollo guesses correctly that he is a comedian of the Comédie-Française. Apollo struts majestically, swishing his hips, beating a tin cup with the heel of his shoe, declaiming through his nose. Mars mistakes him for the Mercury of the Comédie-Française, but Momus knows that he is an Italian comedian. Usually spared in these productions, the Opéra also fell victim to Piron's pen. Asked if he likes operatic singing, Momus responds:

> *Mais j'aime mieux le carillon,*
> *De la Samaritaine,*
> *Dondaine, dondaine,*
> *Que tout le faux bourdon*
> *De Melpomène.*

Apollo and Momus discuss Thalie's absence in Italy, where she wishes to speak all alone and she alone wishes to speak. No matter, Apollo declares, there is another muse—La Foire—who, like Cupid, is pretty, gay, charming, and humorous. The daughter of Bacchus and Venus, La Foire is mute and lives like a fish because the jealous Thalie cut out her tongue—to everyone's sorrow. Addressing La Foire, Jupiter sings the final vaudeville:

> *Vos grandes soeurs ont bien tort,*
> *De vous mépriser si fort:*
> *Chez Melpomène l'on soupire,*
> *Lire, lire, lire.*
> *Et chez Thalie on s'endort,*
> *La Foire seule fait rire.*

Molin and Piron kept the Comique alive with their marionette and jargon pieces, enabling Lesage, Fuzelier, and D'Orneval to stage a defiant comeback in 1722 and Antoine de La Place to risk using live actors in 1724. In July, Maurice Honoré, the candlemaker for the Paris theaters and collector of money for the Hôtel-Dieu, obtained the privilege of the Comique. He and his successor, the playwright Florimond-Claude Boizard Pontau, set new records for attendance at the Comique. Pontau's troupe continued to be harassed by the Comédie-Française, which in 1731 got the Parlement to limit the Comique to child actors performing in mime. This backfired, however. The children caused such a sensation that the king invited them to Versailles, evidently the first time that a fair troupe had performed at Versailles for the king.[45] Despite large audiences, however, Pontau had financial problems. He found it difficult to pay the annual fee of 15,000 livres stipulated in his contract with Louis-Armand-Eugène de Thuret, formerly captain of the Regiment of Picardie, who directed the Opéra from 1733 to 1744. In addition, the *quart des pauvres* cost him several thousand livres a year. Pontau also paid his performers more than his predecessors. In the early years of the Comique,

Bertrand and other directors paid the actors 20 sous a day plus supper when they performed.[46] These meager salaries obliged the *forains* to take on additional work. Men were singing and dancing teachers, painters, and carpenters; women were dressmakers and washed clothes. But Pontau paid his actors and dancers annual wages of between 600 and 1,000 livres while violinists earned 30 sous per day, or over 1,000 livres a year.[47] Fuzelier and Lesage earned 2,000 livres per fair, and under Pontau they received 50 livres every day that one of their pieces was performed. In 1739, Pontau paid 12,232 livres to his actors, dancers, and musicians; 1,600 for rental of his theater; 3,458 livres as his contribution to the poor; and 15,000 to the Opéra. There is no record of the amount he took in, but his debt to the Opéra, which took the largest portion of his revenue, was over 53,000 livres. There were rumors that year (1739) at the Café Procope that Pontau had fled to Holland with the funds of the Comique and that the Opéra would take over the theater.[48]

In fact, in March 1743, Thuret took possession of Pontau's loge and sold the privilege to Jean Monnet, an author and actor, on the terms of a six-year lease at 15,000 livres annual rent.[49] Monnet was a major innovator. Supported by two financiers, he redecorated the theater at Saint-Germain and purchased new costumes and decorations by François Boucher. He hired the celebrated comedian Pierre-Louis Dubus, called Préville, from Rouen to direct a company of 24 actors and actresses. He enlarged the orchestra to 18 musicians, hired Rameau's nephew as conductor,[50] and gathered a corps of 14 dancers directed by Jean-George Noverre, who years later sponsored major reforms in ballet at the Opéra. And he gave Charles Favart a commission of 2,000 livres a year plus author's rights for new pieces and made him the manager of the Comique.[51] Favart's duties included reworking some of the old pieces, advising young authors, and directing rehearsals. Monnet recruited better musicians and paid them more than previous directors had. In 1744 his conductors (Blaise at Saint-Germain and Boismortier at Saint-Laurent) each received 400 livres, an increase of 200 livres over the amount Pontau had paid. The first violinist was paid 400 livres. The new musicians in the orchestra included six violinists earning between 150 and 400 livres, 3 cellists at 300, 200, and 150, a contrabass at 300, 2 hunting horns at 300 and 150 livres, 2 flutists at 200 and 150, and 2 bassoons who were paid 200 livres each. A music copier was paid 100 livres. Monnet spent a total of 4,100 livres on the orchestra, an increase from Pontau of 750 livres. His 12 actors and 12 actresses were paid a total of 10,600 livres, up from 5,900 under Pontau, who had used fewer performers. The ballet corps got 4,150. The total cost of the 2 fairs under Monnet was 28,779 livres.[52]

Monnet was too bold and too successful. The French and Italian theaters were deserted in 1744, while the last performance at Saint-Germain by Monnet's troupe was overflowing despite a special charge of six livres for every seat. The Comédie-Française got the Crown to forbid spoken passages in the *opéras-comiques* in 1744.

In the meantime, François Berger, the former receiver general of finance of Dauphiné and a protégé of the comte de Maurepas, replaced Thuret as the director of the Opéra. Berger took the position that the *opéras-comiques* were actually musical dramas because the texts were rendered vocally. The pieces were, therefore, similar to, and competitive with, those of the Opéra. Berger persuaded the Crown to make the Opéra-Comique the property of the Opéra, expel Monnet from the fairs, and nullify all deals made with Thuret.[53] Thus, despite Monnet's lease, Berger ousted him without indemnity. Hiring Favart for 4,000 livres a year, Berger then took over the proprietorship of the Comique himself in 1744. All Monnet could salvage was the sale to Berger of the decorations from the Saint-Laurent theater for a sum of 4,733 livres. These effects included Pegasus made from paper and twigs, for which he got 61 livres. At the urging of the duc de Villeroi, Monnet then went to Lyons to become the director of its opera.

The Comédie-Française and the Comédie-Italienne lost no time in mounting a new attack, demanding that the Opéra-Comique be suppressed. The two theaters were supported by the anonymous authors of several letters published in 1745. One attributed the Comique's success to the frivolity of the age, the stupidity of the public, and the loose morals of the female entertainers.[54] It is probable that these public letters were only an accompaniment to an act of suppression already decided upon. The politics of privilege determined the Comique's fate. In June 1745 the Conseil d'Etat ordered its suspension.

The long struggle between popular and privileged theaters, a struggle in which the *forains* had to cope not only with the harassment of the Comédie-Française but also with the magistrates of the Parlement and the Crown, led to one curious consequence. Whereas early in the century the *forain* directors and actors acted in concert against their enemies, they became divided when the Académie Royale de Musique awarded the exclusive privilege of the Comique to one of the directors. Though the privilege passed through several hands before being given to Monnet, the arrangement with the Opéra, and through it the Crown, turned the Opéra-Comique into a privileged theater. The other *forains* had to return to acrobatics, marionettes, and *pièces en écriteaux*.

Perhaps the most important result of the struggle with the Comédie-Française was the creation of a new form of lyric theater. The constant pressure of the Comédie against the performance of spoken dialogues, indeed against anything resembling a play, forced the *forains* to turn to vaudevilles and mime. Singing and dancing became the hallmark of the fair shows when the Opéra sold them the right to use music. The struggle also led to the

Comique's realization that the most important weapon they had was pithy satirization of the enemy. Derisive laughter had always been endogenous in the marketplace. In the absence of any support from the courts and help from the Opéra only for a price, the Comique hoisted the battle against privilege to the *tréteaux*, where ridicule of the grand theaters became as unrelenting as their efforts to suppress the *forains*. The conditions of combat reinforced the tradition of marketplace mockery. Thus, separation between popular and elite theatrical entertainment was rooted in the politics of privilege.

II

THE CHAMPS-ELYSEES,
THE BOULEVARDS,
AND THE PALAIS-ROYAL

5

Time of Triumph, Time of Loss

THE MIDDLE DECADES of the eighteenth century were an important transitional period in the history of Parisian theatrical entertainment.[1] The Opéra-Comique was revived in 1752 with the blessing of the Crown and entered the most critical decade of its history. Its musical and dramatic materials were completely reshaped by a new generation of composers and writers, who turned it into a serious theater that Lesage would not have recognized. The long struggle against privilege came to a thundering halt in 1762, when the Opéra-Comique was absorbed by the Comédie-Italienne. The theater of the people left the fairs. The transformation of *opéra-comique* was a musical-dramatic affair of enormous magnitude; its assimilation by the Italians seemed the crowning victory of ancien régime privilege. From one perspective, this transformation appears to be a progressive development consistent with the perception the philosophes had of their age. Under the guiding genius of people such as Michel-Jean Sedaine and André Danican Philidor, the theater of the streets was purged of vulgarity, buffoonery, and vaudeville airs. It became a vehicle of moral didacticism and serious social commentary. But from another perspective, the transformation and assimilation seem to constitute a great popular loss, the theft of a *forain* show, the murder of marketplace humor, the *embourgeoisement* of taste.

The ban on the Opéra-Comique was lifted by the Crown in December 1751 mainly because its suppression had not attracted audiences back to the privileged theaters, and the Opéra needed the revenue it could derive from selling the privilege to operate, as had been true in the time of Lesage. For all its monopoly over French musical life, its subvention by the Crown, which was first given in 1744 in the amount of 45,000 livres, and its many fiefs, including the Concert Spirituel, which paid the Opéra 6,000 livres a year for the right to give instrumental concerts at Easter time, the Opéra was a financial disaster.[2] The Crown turned over the Opéra to the city of Paris in 1749 with the Marquis d'Argenson, minister of the king's household, acting as its royal supervisor. The city, in turn, appointed directors to administer the Opéra.[3] But its financial difficulties did not diminish. The Bureau de Ville was delighted when the Crown gave the green light to the Opéra-Comique. In 1751 the Opéra's debt was 1,132,972 livres, 2 deniers. This was an increase of 752,192 livres since 1704.[4] Welcomed back from London, Jean Monnet agreed to a six-year lease of the Comique beginning January 1, 1752, at a rental of 12,000 livres for each of the first three years and 15,000 annually thereafter.[5]

The talented director worked feverishly to scrape together a troupe that could open at Saint-Germain in 30 days. Like his predecessors in the embattled years, he cleverly used a prologue at the first performance on 3 February 1752 to ingratiate himself and his company with the crowd.[6] Helped by Pierrot, Opéra-Comique hobbles back to the fair to the welcoming cries of the actors and actresses who sing

> *Le public ne se plaît qu'où vous êtes*
> *L'ennui préside où l'on ne vous voit pas.*

Pierrot tells Opéra-Comique that he has lost many fine performers to the Opéra and that the Comédie-Italienne has stolen many of his couplets and ballets. Pierrot believes that he can succeed, as in the past, with a few *flons flons,* but Opéra-Comique insists that the public will no longer tolerate a mere rebus; it demands good taste. To the vaudeville air "On fait ce qu'on peut," Mademoiselle Rosaline then sang this *compliment:*

> *Messieurs, songez, je vous supplie,*
> *Vous qui nous aimâtes toujours,*
> *Que notre rapel à la vie*
> *Remonte au plus à trente jours;*
> *Usez donc pour nous de clémence,*
> *Nos acteurs y comptent beaucoup*
> *On n'est pas maître tout d'un coup,*
> *Vous savez que, quand on commence,*
>   *On fait ce qu'on peut,*
>   *Et non pas ce qu'on veut.*

Monnet brought to the new Comique considerable administrative expertise and experience, an eye for talent, and the financial support of six silent partners. From Pontau's creditors he obtained the theater at Saint-Germain, which was refurbished, and he spent 45,000 livres to build a new theater at Saint-Laurent, which most of his contemporaries regarded as the most elegant, comfortable, and acoustically excellent in the capital.[7] The architect was Roland le Virloys, and François Boucher executed the designs for the ceiling and the decorations. Its dimensions were 100 feet by 48 feet. Far surpassing any of the earlier *salles* at the fairs, the stage of Monnet's theater had a depth of 40 feet. The six loges on each side of the hall were about two metres wide. Semicircular amphitheaters were built at the rear of the second and third stories, while the main floor was entirely given over to the parterre.[8]

While in London, Monnet studied the theaters of Drury Lane and Covent Garden, and he learned a great deal about stagecraft from David Garrick —lessons that he applied at the Comique. He was also adept at attracting excellent writers, musicians, decorators, and actors, including several former Comique players who had gone to the provinces. His company included 7 actors, 8 actresses, 21 male dancers, 14 female dancers, a 19-piece orchestra, a conductor and a music master, 11 decorators, and various costume designers and ticket takers.[9] He introduced Jean-Joseph Vadé, who became the master of the *poissarde* genre, to the Comique, and he brought back Charles Favart, who had already broken new ground before the suppression in 1745 and who was now at the peak of his career.[10]

Monnet was also a more effective disciplinarian than his predecessors. He actively enforced a group of regulations issued by the Crown governing the Comique. Actors and actresses were ordered to be in costume at times designated in advance; attendance at rehearsals was mandatory; actresses were forbidden to have anyone in their dressing rooms except hairdressers and "persons necessary for their preparation."[11] Performers, especially females, were confined to the stage, the wings, and the loge nearest the orchestra and could remain in the theater after performing only if "they behaved modestly and did not wander about." Drunkenness was forbidden. Fines of six livres were levied for each infraction of the rules, and the money was given to the neediest persons in the company. Monnet's enforcement of these regulations probably did alter the traditionally free decorum in the theater and conceivably helped to improve the quality of performances.

Monnet's administration was marked by immediate success. The receipts for his first three-month season at the splendid Saint-Laurent theater reached an all-time high of 133,000 livres.[12] Many contemporary observers commented on the popularity of his shows. The *Almanach des spectacles* (1756) wrote of "the general acclaim of a prodigious and always enthusiastic crowd of spectators."[13] D'Argenson recommended that the Comique replace the deserted Comédie Italienne and that Monnet take over the direction of the Opéra so that it, too, might succeed.[14]

But in his zeal to make the Opéra-Comique an illustrious theater, Monnet spent beyond his means, especially for ballets and scenery. The crowds were large and the proceeds substantial, but they were not sufficient to pay for the expenses of his *spectacle*. Therefore in 1757, Monnet sold the three remaining years of his contract with the Opéra for the substantial sum of 83,000 livres, which he used to pay his debts and to establish an annuity, to a group that included Favart, serving as artistic director at an annual salary of 4,000 livres plus one twelfth of the profits; Julien Corby (or Corbie), the husband of a chambermaid of the duchesse de Choiseul and the negotiator of the contract; Moët (or Moëtte), the son of a bookseller who took charge of the administration; J. B. Dehesse (or Deshesses), an actor at the Comédie-Italienne who was the ballet director; and Coste de Champeron, a councillor for the Parlement of Paris.[15] The new proprietorship was ratified by the directors of the Opéra in January 1758, and the associates agreed to pay the Opéra 20,000 livres for the first three years and 22,000 for three additional years.

During and after his tenure at the Comique, Monnet was lionized by just about everyone interested in the theatrical world. The nature of this praise provides some inkling of the significant changes that took place in mid-century, and even more important, of the perception people had of the Comique's tranformation. The *Almanach des spectacles* summarized the situation rather well. Monnet, it insisted, had been forced to compromise his high standards because of the traditions of the fair theater, but at the same time he improved the tone of *opéras-comiques,* making it possible for his successors to purge the theater of indecency and for ladies to attend without embarrassment:

> M. Monnet incontestably has the honor of having torn down the *tréteaux;* he was the first to give the form of a regular theater to this *spectacle;* but not daring to jump suddenly over the enormous gap that existed between the burlesque and often obscene genre that its location and its spectators themselves seemed to demand, and the enjoyable and light genre that seeks out and attracts the proper people, he felt constrained to allow at this theater from time to time buffoonery, coarse gaiety, and occasionally a strong expression.[16]

La Harpe, Grimm, the Abbé de La Porte, Fréron, and many other writers of the time echoed this opinion, accentuating the positive achievements of Monnet from their points of view. François-Antoine Chevrier declared that the Comique had been justifiably criticized in the past for indecency, but that, thanks to Monnet and Favart, it had become "a respectable entertainment that attracts all Paris. . . ." The Comique had become "reconciled with the fair sex" because "obscenity was banished from it and one heard only gentle equivocations linked more to the genre than to the author's mind. . . ."[17] Respectability through a loftier tone—that was the perception of Monnet's achievement and of that of his immediate successors. Marketplace vulgarity was a thing of the past, and the Opéra-Comique could look forward to an accepted position in polite society.

In all probability, Monnet was given too much personal credit for changes that had actually begun before his arrival on the scene and continued even more swiftly after his departure. But that is a less important issue than the transformation of *opéra-comique* itself. What had changed? Who was responsible? Aside from Monnet, what musical and dramatic factors led street *spectacle* to the brink of respectability?

The changes had begun with Charles Favart, the son of a pastrycook, who cut the old Comique loose from its moorings.[18] Of the five main ingredients of the genre (see Chapter 3), Favart virtually eliminated three: the marvelous, foolish buffoon characters, and the struggle against privilege. He substantially modified another—physical humor and sexual innuendo. But although Favart was receptive to the musical changes in the 1750s, he remained steadfastly loyal to the musical linchpin of *opéra-comique*, the vaudeville.

Favart owed his knowledge and enthusiasm for vaudevilles to his father, who often took him to the Opéra-Comique and who wrote songs and couplets for vaudeville tunes: "My father had a lively spirit and an open gaiety; he made songs easily; he fit moral principles and other precepts that he wanted to instill in me on vaudeville airs: I retained them easily in singing with him."[19] Favart took over the family bakery in Paris when his father died in 1730, but he also began writing vaudeville couplets in the style of Panard for Bienfait's marionettes. His successful comedy in vaudevilles *Les Deux jumelles* attracted the attention of a wealthy *fermier-général*, who introduced him to polite society and encouraged him to follow a career at Pontau's Opéra-Comique. Although he wrote a number of texts set to vaudevilles for this theater between 1735 and 1741, Favart attached little importance to them and did not sign or publish any until *La Chercheuse d'esprit* in 1741. This work, a parody of Lully's opera *Thésée*, established Favart's brilliance in selecting vaudevilles exactly appropriate to express the situation, character, or mood of his text. He used 70 different vaudevilles in *La Chercheuse,* a work that enjoyed a record-breaking 200 consecutive performances at the Comique.

Favart read music himself and understood vocal ranges, but, more importantly, he was extraordinarily knowledgeable about the storehouse of vaudevilles available in his time, and he was more astute in picking and varying them than any writer in his century. He was very clever in selecting a *timbre*—the original phrase designating a vaudeville tune—whose words could express the social position or personality of the character singing the tune. On hearing the vaudeville airs, eighteenth-century audiences could usually recall the *timbre* and therefore understand why it was a phrase relevant to the situation. For example, in *La Chercheuse,* when Medea complains of her husband's coldness, he repies with a vaudeville whose *timbre* is "c'est une autre affaire."[20] Favart should not be credited, however, with greater subtlety than he possessed: He often used the *timbre* in his verse so that the audience could not fail to recognize his cleverness.

His genius at selecting vaudevilles made the Comique more of a musical theater than it had ever been because Favart almost eliminated prose and declaimed verse in his texts. Nearly everything was set to vaudeville airs, even dialogues. The ban imposed on speaking in 1744 by the Comédie-Française accounts in part for this, of course, but even before that Favart had already begun to accentuate the vaudevilles over spoken passages. Moreover, under Favart a trend was established in which newer vaudevilles began to be favored over the old songs. Supposedly more emotionally forceful, the new vaudevilles were usually airs that their composers derived from operatic pieces and ballets. Most were longer (50 or 60 measures) than the old vaudevilles, which seldom exceeded 25 measures. Their rhythms were swifter, and their textures were lighter. And writers began to employ a more elegant, poetic style and a more sophisticated tone, with references to nightingales, the scent of flowers, cool winds, and sky.

Remaining firmly committed to the old songs, Favart nevertheless welcomed and encouraged the new ones as he did the more sweeping musical changes of the 1750s. When Italian influences began to invade France, Favart saw in them possibilities for the enrichment of the vaudeville tradition. He managed to work within both the old and new styles. In other respects, however, he was less wedded to the retention of tradition. He abandoned the tangled imbroglios, the disguises and mistaken identities, the acrobatics, obscenities, and buffoonery that had characterized the Comique from the beginning. Magical transformations, genies, apparitions, and superhuman feats were also discarded. Seeking to prove that an *opéra-comique* need not be licentious or impossibly bizarre, Favart selected as a favorite theme the first blush of love of a simple, naive villager. His characters were peasant folk, innocent of the vanity, ambition, and jealousy of the real world. These village ingenues were content with the charming rusticity of country life though they were often tempted by aristocratic materialism and hypocrisy.

In *Ninette à la cour* (1756), for example, Favart's naturally virtuous heroine loves a simple village youth, Colas, but she is also attracted to a passing seigneur, Prince Astolphe, who lures her with descriptions of the good life and lofty demeanor of his court. Astolphe's gallant ways evoke jealousy in the rough-hewn Colas, whose offensiveness drives Ninette into accepting the prince's offer to share his fortune. Her virtue and simplicity are tested by Astolphe's wealth and apparent dignity, but, predictably, she soon discovers that he is capricious and corrupt, and, rebelling against the wealth and snobbish etiquette of his court, she happily returns to the bumpkin.

The "lesson" of *Ninette,* as of others of Favart's pieces, was as obvious to eighteenth-century audiences as it is today: Happiness lies in the simple, natural life, a humble village existence uncorrupted by the world of wealth, manners, and hypocrisy. His Ninettes, Bastiens, Zirphiles, and Colins were not ambitious for the status and riches of wealthy lords, as Arlequin and Isabelle had often been. Awakening from childhood to an awareness of their senses, they had no knowledge of the world, no fears and suspicions; they built relationships on spontaneous affection and retained their innocence as they confronted life. Such characters were certainly not real; they were, in fact, less real than Lesage's doctor, the defecating Gilles, and Arlequin as the king of Serendib. Favart's characters were, to say the least, sentimentalized peasants living in a pretty, idyllic world. The Goncourt brothers compared it to that of the painter François Boucher:

> Just as Boucher's shepherdesses move in a countryside where the sheep have pink ribbons round their necks and the white doves flutter against a pale-blue sky, so Favart's Bastiennes were never seen in any French field, and the country-side . . . suggests a Boucher rather than Longus and both rather than Nature.[21]

One wonders how Favart's depictions of sweet, innocent young lovers so lacking in a spirit of derision could have appealed to the raucous crowds at the fairs. Favart discarded so many of the techniques, characters, and material of the old Comique that one is left guessing about the appeal of his works. But that they were appealing is undeniable. Attendance was heavy. At the final performance of *Acajou* in 1744, for example, one observer wrote that the crowd was so large that

> the barrier that separated the orchestra from the parterre broke. In order to repair it, they tried to get everyone who filled the parterre out of the hall, but in vain. People seated on the stage went down there in order to make room for new spectators, who completely filled up the stage. In this confusion it was impossible to refund the money of those who were forced to leave. Several made threats. Six of the most obstreperous were arrested. M. Monet [sic] conducted himself during this incident with great discretion. He got those who had been turned over to the Corps-de-Garde released. He treated the discontented to a harangue, half amusing, half touching, which conciliated everyone. Never had a performance been so lucrative. All the seats were at 6 livres; and the theater was so full that only one actor at a time could appear. There was no symphony, no ballets; nothing could be heard, not even the *compliment.* People applauded very much; and everyone left satisfied; less, however, than the entrepreneur.[22]

It seems likely that the most important reason for the success of Favart's pieces was their sensuality. He used sexual equivocation, which fair crowds had always loved, while removing its traditional crudeness. In *Le Génie de l'Opéra-Comique,* Equivoque sings

> *En tenant des propos d'amour,*
> *Iris badinoit l'autre jour*
> *Avec Damon sur la fougère;*
> *Un serpent caché sous les fleurs*
> *Sortit et piqua la bergère:*
> *Pour un plaisir mille douleurs.*[23]

In *Les Ensorcelés* a blacksmith ponders what gives women pleasure:

> *Toujours danser,*
> *Se trémousser*
> *V'là l'plaisir des filles.*
> *Des violons*
> *Et des chansons,*
> *Propos joyeux*
> *Et petits jeux,*
> *Bouquets, ribans, et des garçons bons drilles,*
> *V'là l'd'sir*
> *Des filles,*
> *V'là l'plaisir.*[24]

Martin Cooper is quite right in his observation that the basic interest here was still the same—"the comedy and absurdities introduced into human existence by the sexual element in human nature."[25]

But there was much more to Favart's use of sex than equivocation. His naive ingenues awakening to the sensations of new love were alluring because they had the natural openness of youth yet were physically mature. His female heroines were just 14 or 15 years old. It must have titillated audiences, as it still does, to see vulnerable young girls filled with desire, yet innocent and natural.

Like Piron in *La Rose,* Favart developed entire *opéra-comique* plots around sexual themes and images. That his first major triumph at the Comique, *La Chercheuse d'esprit,* was such a work is perhaps an indication of the nature of Favart's appeal.[26] The entire piece concerns Nicette's search for *esprit,* which her mother, Madame Madré, angry that she will not marry the wealthy procurator and royal notary, Monsieur Subtil, sends her off to find. An intellectual, Monsieur Narquois, offers her one type of esprit— "seasoned reason" derived from reading books on law, philosophy, and rhetoric—but he is unable to provide the natural esprit commanded by her mother. Other encounters finally lead Nicette to Alain, who is as ignorant of esprit as the young girl. In his search for esprit, Alain is nearly seduced by Madame Madré, but in the end he and Nicette find esprit together in the fields as they strip a bouquet of wild flowers.

Favart took great pride in this kind of sentimental sensuality, which he and subsequent writers regarded as a progressive leap away from *forain* vulgarity and slapstick. He later blamed the "excessively free gaiety and the bad taste for equivocations" that prevailed in the Comique's early days on the corruption of the regency, a period "of intoxication and giddiness when the system of [John] Law, by confusing all the estates by fortunes quickly made and little deserved, brought with it inevitably the corruption of taste and morals."[27] Lesage, Piron, and others initiated some reforms, he avowed, but they stopped short out of the conviction "that a cynical liberty constituted the genre of the opéra-comique and must be its distinctive characteristic." Time was required for change. "Only by imperceptible degrees" (and, Favart assured his correspondent, by his own efforts) was the Comique made "worthy of upright people." Like Monnet, Favart probably took and was given too much credit for the changes at the Comique. Though remaining faithful to vaudevilles, he had set the fair theater on a new course. But he did not foresee the major musical change of the 1750s—the abandonment of vaudevilles in favor of original scores incorporating Italian musical elements.

The impetus for this change came from the successful performances in Paris in 1752 and 1753 of comic opera bouffes by an Italian troupe.[28] Opera bouffes were used in eighteenth-century Italy (they began about 1715) as intermezzi or interludes between acts of a longer, serious opera, though by the 1740s they were being performed as separate pieces. Unlike *opéras-comiques,* these pieces were for the most part originally composed; they were sung throughout in ariettes and recitatives without spoken passages. The most striking stylistic traits of the Italian intermezzi were melodic clarity and simplicity, very rapid tempi, sharp accents, repetitions of short motifs, and a juxtaposition of chromatic progressions with wide, arching leaps in the melody. These works gave prominence to the bass voice. They were also characterized, as Donald J. Grout has pointed out, "by the absolute fidelity of music to text; the singing seems to be simply a highly flexible, sensitive, melodic declamation of the words, preserving and heightening every detail that might contribute to the comic effect."[29]

The great popularity that works such as Giovanni Pergolesi's *La Serva Padrona* (first performed in Naples in 1733) enjoyed is partly explained by the fact that French opera audiences had already become accustomed to large doses of Italian musical procedures, especially in a new genre known as the *opéra-ballet;* the taste for *divertissements,* usually danced *spectacles,* was very strong at the Opéra.[30] The existence of a parallel musical comedy—*opéra-comique*—and the mounting enthusiasm for Italian music and *divertissements* thus helped the Italians to succeed as they had been unable to do when they first introduced intermezzi to Paris in 1729. Many of the opera bouffes with recitatives replaced by spoken prose were translated into French. They were performed mainly at the Comédie-Italienne, where their popularity was even greater than the original productions at the Opéra. Describing the reception of *La Servante Maîtresse* (*La Serva Padrona*), Joseph de La Porte wrote: "The public rushed there in a drove. The prodigious number of performances [190] that this drama had, the roar with which it was supported, announces an approaching revolution in our music. In spite of prejudice, Pergolesi's ariettes were sung at the court and in the city. . . ."[31]

Public interest in the Italian works also stemmed from the controversy they aroused among philosophes and others known as the Querelle des Bouffons. In taking up the cause of Italian music out of motives of both taste and ideology, the philosophes insisted on comparing opera bouffes not with the musical theater of the fairs but with the lyric tragedies and ballets of the French Opéra.[32] In a sense this was understandable because it was opera that the philosophes wanted to reform, and the first performance of *La Serva* in 1752 was given at the Opéra between acts of Lully's *Acis et Galathée*. The stylistic contrast was striking. "The heavy garment of the many-voiced counterpoint is exchanged for the airy and transparent dress of homophony."[33] Ironically, however, it was at the Opéra-Comique that the Italian influence would operate, not at the Opéra, which soon turned its back on Italian intermezzi and obtained the expulsion of the Italian troupe in 1754.

The philosophes affirmed the overwhelming superiority of Italian music. Leading the pack, Rousseau argued that language determines the character of vocal music and that since the prosody of the French language lacks clarity, it cannot generate good melodies and rhythms. As a result, French composers must resort to complex harmonies and thick counterpoint that is devoid of melody, offensive to the ear, and a return to barbarism. By contrast, Italian vocal music, because of the language, is simple, animated, expressive, and melodious. Rousseau even denied the possibility of composing airs in the Italian style with French words because of the mute syllables, nasal sounds, and the indefinite prosodic quantity of the syllables.[34]

As the torrent of pamphlets for and against Italian opera bouffes poured down on Paris, Jean Monnet, who favored French music in the dispute, used Rousseau's charge to splash mud in the faces of the Italian partisans. Monnet declared that he was searching for a worthy Italian composer to do the score of a new lyric comedy by Jean-Joseph Vadé. Monnet produced the opera bouffe, *Les Troqueurs,* based on a story by La Fontaine, at Saint-Laurent on 30 July 1753. It was presumably an Italian composition. Only after *Les Troqueurs* won the acclaim of the public, especially the Italian faction, did the wily Monnet reveal that the score had really been composed by a Frenchman,

Charles Dauvergne.[35] Monnet later wrote:

> It was necessary to anticipate the cabal of the *bouffons;* the fanatics of Italian music, persuaded that the French had no music, would not have failed to wreck my project. Along with the other two [Vadé and Dauvergne], we would keep the secret; then in order to put the enemies that I was ready for on to a false scent, I spread around the story that I had sent some words to Vienna to an Italian musician who knew French and who wanted very much to apply his talent to the language. This false news rushed through the entire city. . . .
>
> The piece was then performed, and although performed and sung by actors who did not know music, it was generally applauded.
>
> The *bouffonistes,* convinced that this music had been composed in Vienna by an Italian, came to compliment me on the acquisition I had made of this good author, and confirmed once more the great superiority of Italian music over ours. As delighted by their sincerity as by the successful deception that I had pulled on them, I presented M. Dauvergne to them as the real Orpheus from Vienna.[36]

Monnet and Dauvergne had proved that a Frenchman could compose successful original music for an Italian opera bouffe sung in the French language—if, indeed, that needed to be proved. But influence of the Italian intermezzi and of the Querelle des Bouffons was far more consequential for the musical development of the Comique than Monnet's clever prank. At first the French were content simply to translate the Italian pieces. Soon, however, French writers began to parody Italian ariettes in their newly composed texts. Favart lifted ariettes from Vincenzo Legrenzio Ciampi's intermezzo *Bertoldo in Corte* for use in *Ninette à la cour.* Finally, by the end of the decade, *opéras-comiques* with original music in the Italian style were performed at the fair theaters. Scarcely realizing what they were witnessing, Monnet and Favart beheld two revolutionary changes: the waning of the vaudeville in favor of new music in the Italian style and a tremendous upsurge in the importance of composers. Favart's *Ninette* marked a transition between *opéra-comique* in vaudevilles and *opéra-comique* in ariettes; it was a transition from works where the poet played the leading role both in writing the text and in selecting the vaudevilles to those where the composer's role was at least equal, if not superior, to that of the poet. Favart's *Ninette* became known as Duni's *Ninette* after Egidio Romoaldo Duni rewrote the score for a performance at the court of Parma in 1756, where French influences were strong.[37] A few years after *Ninette,* the *Almanach des muses,* reflecting contemporary opinion, declared that the poem is only a kind of outline for the musician: "It is for the music to develop what the words should only indicate."[38]

It was the Italian ariettes that formed the basis of the revolution in *opéra-comique*—those simple, melodic airs on which the philosophes bestowed the magic word *natural.* Ariettes were short, lyrical pieces with flexible, diverse rhythms. Most were composed in stanzas, and many were in the popular form of the canzonet, with its characteristically light textures, short verses often of no more than four syllables, and melodic strophes. Although somewhat more regular, the French adaptations of the ariettes usually retained the Italian rhythmic structure and verses of different lengths. The ariettes were very expressive, using lots of accents, clipped musical phrases, and rapid modulations. Ariettes proved enormously popular to Parisian audiences, so much so that Charles Collé wrote in 1764 of "the epidemic fury for the music of ariettes that has swept three fourths of the public."[39]

A new generation of composers, including Duni, the French composers Pierre-Alexandre Monsigny and François-André-Danican Philidor, and the Belgian André Grétry, embraced the Italian style warmly, gradually shedding vaudevilles and severing the ties with the old Comique. They were aided and abetted by a flock of new writers, including Michel-Jean Sedaine, Jean-François Marmontel, and Louis Anseaume, who were just as adamant about reforming the dramatic content of *opéras-comiques*. These writers built on the reforms of Favart but went far beyond him in creating a serious lyric drama infused with pathos, bourgeois morality, and social criticism.

The pivotal work in the Comique's transformation was *Le Peintre amoureux de son modèle* by Duni and Anseaume, first performed at Saint-Laurent on 26 July 1757. Monnet, who was dubious about Duni's ability as an Italian to handle French prosody, later asserted that the work "ended by fixing French taste for this music."[40] The work was comprised mainly of ariettes, but it is difficult to tell who was at the helm in this piece because Duni actually used music he had previously composed for *Il Pittore inamorato,* and Anseaume had already demonstrated his ability in earlier works to parody Italian music. The plot concerns the loves of an old painter, Alberti, and his apprentice, Zerlin, for Alberti's model, Laurette.[41] In love with Zerlin, Laurette rejects Alberti's affection. Finally recognizing the love that exists between the two young people, the old artist unites them and marries his former governess. This undistinguished tale bears little resemblance to the *opéras-comiques* of Lesage or Favart. Not only are the physical humor, satire, and magic absent, but Anseaume also dispensed with sexual equivocation and imagery in what was a dull but serious dramatic work. It was very successful and remained in the Comique repertoire for several years. Duni, who stayed on in Paris and composed 20 more *opéras-comiques,* took the occasion of *Le Peintre's* success to lambast Rousseau. In the preface to the published score he wrote:

> While in Paris, an author struggling to prove that the language that is spoken there is not made to be set to music has written *Le Devin du village;* there has never been such a pleasant inconsistency! As for myself, an Italian living in

Parma, I set only French words to music; and I have come here to pay tribute
to the language that has furnished me with melody, feelings, and images.[42]

Although Monsigny established a reputation as a fine melodist in his debut
at the Comique in 1759, his *Les Aveux indiscrets* was overshadowed in the
1759 season by the new work of Philidor and Sedaine, *Blaise le savetier*. They
had collaborated on *Le Diable à quatre* in 1756, which mixed vaudevilles,
parodies, and the new ariettes, and both had already launched promising
careers, but this work catapulted them to fame. Born in Dreux in 1726,
Philidor came from a family of accomplished musicians.[43] His father had
played fife, bassoon, crumhorn, oboe, and marine trumpet in the band of the
king's Grande Ecurie. As a page of the royal chapel, young Philidor was
entitled to music lessons, and he learned harmony from no less an eminent
composer than André Campra. He was soon able to earn a living in Paris by
teaching and copying music. Philidor's great passion, however, was not music
but chess. As a child he demonstrated an extraordinary talent for this game,
so much so that by age 18 he was able to earn a living at it. In 1745 he went
on tour, playing in Holland, Germany, and England, and in 1748, with the
financial support of the duke of Cumberland, he wrote an analysis of chess
that was published the following year.

In 1754, Philidor was lured back to Paris from London and back to a
musical career only by the persuasiveness of Denis Diderot, who wrote him
a beautiful letter arguing that chess was no replacement for music.[44] Having
heard Handel's music in London, Philidor was anxious to try his hand at this
style of composition. He wrote several motets à la Handel, but when he failed
to secure a position as a court musician, he turned to lyric theater. A more
imaginative composer than Duni, Philidor introduced such new forms to
opéra-comique as unaccompanied quartets and orchestrally accompanied
recitatives. Unlike the melodist Monsigny, Philidor worked with varied
harmonies and was much more attuned to the importance of orchestral and
choral music.

Born in Paris in 1719, Michel-Jean Sedaine was a stonecutter by trade like
his father.[45] A student at the Collège des Quatre Nations, where D'Alembert
was one of his classmates, Sedaine was exposed to the singers, showmen, and
acrobats who performed nearby on the Pont-Neuf. He later attended the
Opéra-Comique regularly, met Favart and Vadé, and began writing songs. In
1748, Nicolas Le Conte, a criminal lieutenant at the Châtelet, after hearing
Sedaine sing, took him into his household and supported his quest for a
career in lyric theater. Preoccupied like Favart with the problem of selecting
vaudevilles that were perfectly coordinated with the sentiment and cadence
of the text, Sedaine published *Poésies fugitives* (his first publication), which
included several vaudevilles with original texts. But Sedaine soon tired of

vaudevilles and grew anxious to apply his dramatic ideas to new music. Collaboration with Philidor seemed the perfect answer.

Blaise le savetier, based on La Fontaine's *Conte d'une chose,* was an enormous success, having an initial run in 1759 of 68 performances.[46] It was a modern *opéra-comique* in nearly every respect. Few of the old vaudevilles were incorporated into Philidor's score.[47] Ensembles were used extensively, even a quintet, and orchestral coloring helped to express the moods and emotions of the drama. The text throughout was closely coordinated with the music, pushing the composer to the forefront of the production. The drama dealt with the efforts of Blaise and his wife, Blaisine, to fend off a bailiff, Monsieur Pince, who was in love with Blaisine and who came to confiscate their furniture because the cobbler could not pay his debts. Sedaine injected humor into the tale in a scene in which Pince hid in an armoire as Blaise and his wife feigned a jealous argument. The work concluded when Pince's wife discovered her unfaithful and vexed husband in the armoire.

Philidor and Sedaine continued their successful collaboration at Saint-Germain in 1761 with *Le Jardinier et son seigneur,* the last piece in which they used well-known tunes. The vaudeville finale pronounced this moral: The simple country life of a family is everything; grandeur is nothing. The year 1761 marked the end of Sedaine's partnership with Philidor for 14 years. Anxious to work with other composers and impatient with Philidor's slowness, Sedaine began an association with Monsigny that lasted 16 years. Most writers then and now consider their first work, *On ne s'avise jamais de tout* (Saint-Laurent, 1761), to be a landmark in the history of *opéra-comique.*

The farcical elements that still crept into works such as *Blaise* were entirely eliminated in *On ne s'avise.* There is no equivocation or vulgarity. The heroine, Lise, is not a coquette, but a naive virgin who departs from a convent only to be locked up by the governess of her guardian, Monsieur Tué, who wants to marry Lise for her money. Dorval, an *honnête homme,* loves Lise for her goodness, wisdom, and beauty; but he is foiled at every turn by Tué and the governess, Marguerite. Disguised as a prisoner, Dorval manages to pry Lise loose for a few moments from the hawkish governess by giving her a purse with a louis d'or inside, a deception justified by Dorval's good character and honorable intentions. Sedaine, in whose works disguises replaced the marvelous, also used the prisoner's garb to reveal Tué's lack of charitableness: Begged by Dorval for relief from his poverty and misery, Tué throws him a liärd and kicks him out of the house. Almost the only comic relief in the piece is provided by a book of instructions on guarding Lise with lists of potions to instill virtue and forbidden items such as paper, pen, and "des haha" such as coiffures, corsets, and kerchiefs. In the final scene Dorval denounces Tué to the *commissaire* as a scoundrel lusting after wealth. When he and Lise profess their love, saying that only death will separate them, the *commissaire* obliges Tué to consent to their marriage, pointing out that Dorval is wealthy and from a good family. Marguerite sings:

> *Vous qui croyez que des tendres esclandres*
> *Un registre peut être l'ecueil,*
> *Ah! croyez-moi, brûlez votre recueil;*
> *Et faites-en, faites-en des cendres.*
> > *Contre un sexe enchanteur*
> > > *Et flatteur*
> > *Dont les charmes,*
> > *Dont les armes*
> > *Sont surs de leurs coups,*
> > *Vainement on subtilise:*
> > > *On ne s'avise*
> > *Jamais de tout.*[48]

On ne s'avise was a full-fledged lyric drama with an accent on sentimentality. The tie with the vaudeville past was cut. Monsigny's freshly composed love ariettes formed a melodious accompaniment to Sedaine's carefully organized, unified plot. The spoken passages had a sophistication and dramatic tone that evoked few memories of the fair *tréteaux*. The work would have been unrecognizable to the founders of the popular lyric theater.

The new directions taken by Comique composers and dramatists were extended in the years to come. Sedaine was full of himself in 1762, calling his new work, *Le Roi et le fermier,* a new genre, and boastfully labelling it a "comedie en trois actes mêlée de morceaux de musique." For him, Monsigny's music was the incidental element. The novelty lay in the serious, didactic theme of the drama, which he borrowed from a tale by the English playwright Robert Dodsley. Sedaine wrote: "Never has a theatrical scene opened so completely to the poet a broader scope to explain useful truths without failing in the profound veneration with which he should be filled. . . ."[49] By "useful truths" Sedaine really meant his own Rousseauist social philosophy. *Le Roi et le fermier* and *Le Jardinier* attributed the virtues of courage, generosity, and fidelity to the peasantry, and depicted the aristocracy as being morally corrupt.

Sedaine and Monsigny continued to develop social themes with moral lessons in subsequent works such as *Le Déserteur* (1769), which was the first work Sedaine called a lyric drama. Written in 1766, just after the success of Beaumarchais' *Le Philosophe sans le savoir, Le Deserteur* was conceivably influenced by that work and by the dramatic ideas of both Diderot and Shakespeare.[50] Moreover, in it Monsigny seemed to illustrate Diderot's notions of the dramatic resources of music in *Le Neveu de Rameau*. His airs reinforced the range of emotions in the text. Indeed, borrowing a technique used in serious opera, Monsigny composed the climactic moment of despair at the end of the first act as an orchestrally accompanied recitative. The piece enjoyed great success. The *Mémoires secrets* reported with irritation that "today all of Paris rushed to the *Déserteur* with the alacrity or rather the fervor that people have for the dear *opéra-comique*."[51]

Although Sedaine, Grétry, Marmontel, and others carried the reforms at the Comique even further in later years, the new generation of composers and writers had already totally transformed the old fair theater by the late 1760s.[52] Virtually nothing of the old Comique remained: Arlequins, vaudevilles, derisive satires, equivocations, marvels, vulgarities, physical stunts, appeals to the crowd for support—all had been banished from *opéras-comiques*. Sedaine and his colleagues had "elevated" the Comique to the status of a serious theater for the presentation of didactic lyric dramas infused with the cult of *sensibilité* and laced with social criticism. Some scholars see the new Comique as a participant in the deeper, more sweeping changes taking place in French society as part of the mounting opposition to the society and culture of the ancien régime.[53] In such judgments, however, the scholar has the benefit of hindsight. Sedaine's social criticism was, after all, pretty tame stuff, whether by necessity or intent. But if his aim was neither to crush the Opéra nor to incite revolutionary desires, he and the others were changing popular lyric theater according to the vogue of "enlightened" opinion. Donald Grout, as usual, is on the right track when he writes: "The 'advanced' ideas of the day, the currently fashionably criticism of the social order, the doctrines of Rousseau and the other Encyclopedists, were reflected, though in a harmless enough fashion, in these works."[54]

What did Parisian society make of the musical and dramatic revolution at the Opéra-Comique? How did people respond to the passing of the vaudeville tradition and to Sedaine's celebration of sentimentalized bourgeois morality? Two figures—Favart and Vadé—indicate the attitudes of the traditional craftsmen of the Comique. Having already initiated important changes in his pre-1752 works, Favart was not unhappy to see the drama become more sophisticated. On the other hand, he might have been expected as the consummate vaudevillian of the age to resist the invasion of the Italian musical style. His attitude, however, was that ariettes could exist side by side with vaudevilles even in the same piece; that the two styles would enrich *opéra-comique*. They would provide variety. It did not occur to Favart or Monnet that the Comique could exist without its fundamental resource—the vaudeville air—or that the ariette would rapidly become so popular that vaudevilles would become superfluous remnants of the past to be discarded by the new poets and musicians and relegated to the boulevards.

Jean-Joseph Vadé's response to the new situation was quite different. Whereas Favart made his peace with the new lyric theater of the 1750s and

1760s, Vadé went his own independent way, one that not only preserved vaudevilles but also breathed renewal, however short-lived, into the market-place character of fair theater. Born in Ham in Picardy in 1720, Vadé pursued a career in Soissons, Laon, and elsewhere as a financial controller before coming to Paris in 1746, where his friends obtained a post for him in the Bureau du Vingtième.[55] In his spare time he wrote facetious songs, madrigals, epigrams, and fables, which circulated in manuscript in the Parisian cafés. His good friend Charles Collé wrote: "His manner is to depict flower sellers and fishwives quarreling; and he uses in this style all the base words that they speak to each other realistically in a natural way."[56] Vadé went to work for Monnet at the Comique in 1752, writing parodies, fables, and, of course, the opera bouffe *Les Troqueurs* in 1753. But in 1755 at Saint-Germain he cap-tivated the crowd with his first lyric comedy in the *poissard* genre, *Jérome et Fanchonnette.* Two years later he died of a hemorrhaged abscess. His passing was the veritable death knell of lyric farce at the Comique.

Originally meaning one who was smeared with tar or slime such as a fishmonger (derived from *poix,* i.e., pitch), *poissardes* came to mean harangu-ing fishwives and, more broadly, Seine boatmen, innkeepers, fair merchants, ragpickers, water porters, fruit peddlers, charcoal dealers, menders, the food sellers of Les Halles, and inhabitants of particular parts of Paris such as the fish market along the Seine and of the old faubourgs of Montmartre and Les Porcherons.[57] Eventually, *les poissards* simply meant the *bas peuple* of Paris and their street banter. *Poissard* dialect had been used in the seventeenth century in some vaudevilles, in pieces of the Comédie-Italienne, and the marionette shows. In the eighteenth century, Carolet used it in plays. On the stage, its most extensive use was in *parades,* both those of the fairs and of the private theaters of nobles and magistrates, written by Anne-Claude de Tubières, Comte de Caylus (perhaps the true creator of the genre), Charles Collé, Thomas-Simon Gueullette, François-Auguste Paradis de Moncrif, and Barthélemy-Cristophe Fagan. Collé later wrote: "But these spicy scenes in which they were given, the free gaiety that is put into them, the filth expressed even in their vicious, raw pronunciation caused gales of unre-strained belly laughter among all the seigneurs of the court, who were not quite in the habit of being gross and of seeing such free pranks in the king's house even though they were intimate with the deceased Louis XV."[58]

Aside from *parades,* however, *poissarderie* was rare in the *opéras-comiques,* Lesage, Favart, and others preferring Burgundians, Gascons, and other provincials, along with peasants, to Parisian characters and dialect. These authors' depictions were vague and sentimentalized, however, because they did not really know anything about peasant life and were not trying to be realistic. Alexis Piron was more familiar with provincial speech and manner-isms, and his works for the Comique showed it. When Carolet, Piron, and even Favart began to use *poissarderie* in the theater (not just in *parades*), they were almost forced into more realistic depictions because they were not playing to peasants but to the *poissards* themselves. A. P. Moore correctly suggests that the *poissard* "was part of Parisian life, which a Parisian audience could control; its representation had to be convincing or it might have been whistled off the boards."[59] It was in this spirit that Favart attempted to re-create the people and speech of les Halles in *La Fête de Saint-Cloud* (1741).

Still, Favart did not know these people much better than he did the peasantry. But Vadé did. He went to the markets and mingled with the beef porters, oyster sellers, and fishwives. On Sundays he frequented the *guinguettes* in Les Porcherons to the northeast of the city, where workers drank and sang in the company of disguised aristocrats. As a result, Vadé's "somewhat rough and ready, but forceful and spontaneous pictures of the lower classes con-trasted with the more sugared and *précieux,* sentimental and 'popular' characters of Favart. . . . With Caylus, he is one of the early realists who copied natural and simple people with a scrupulous exactness, although with a tinge of sympathetic satire."[60] Vadé's characters were also vastly different from those Sedaine introduced. Straining to make Sedaine a realist, Louise Parkinson Arnoldson put it this way: "The exaggerated realism of Vadé became in his [Sedaine's] work a painting, not of the people gross in language and manners, but of the little folk, engaging, humble, naive or artful, who surround us."[61] One scene of dialogue from Vadé's *Les Racoleurs* (1756) indicates how colorfully Vadé captured marketplace dialect.

SAUMON:
On m'a dit comm'ça qu'un monsieux m'demande: où c'qu'il est donc, c'mon-sieux? Je n'en vois non plus que d'sus ma main, parlez donc, la Ramée, est-ce-ty vous qui pernez c'te prétesse-la?

LA RAMÉE:
Oui, la maman: c'est moi, la paix, espliquons-nous lullement. T'nez, la mère Saumon, vous avez tort de n'pas donner Manezelle Javotte, vote fille, à monsieux la Brèche, non Sargent; c'est brave homme, quand j'vous l'dis.

SAUMON:
Quand j'vous dis et quand j'vous douze, moi, qu'vot Sargent n'y touchera pas, entendez-vous? Parqué, j'vous trouve encore bien cocasse de m'déranger d'ma marchandise pour si peu.

Reactions to Vadé and his genre *poissard* were mostly positive. His employer Monnet was more enthusiastic about Vadé than any member of his Comique troupe, and he hinted that Vadé's death, which Monnet linked to the waning of the vaudeville, contributed to his own departure: "One could even add that the vaudeville, this child of freedom and national gaiety, died with this unaffected poet, from the same epidemic that always saps the great French music."[62] The genre *poissard,* which some "overly refined critics seemed to scorn," made audiences laugh, Monnet insisted, despite themselves. Both philosophe and antiphilosophe also lauded Vadé. Elie Catherine Fréron praised him highly, but so did Jean le Rond D'Alembert, who declared that the "genre *poissard* immortalized the name Vadé to the extent that *la basse populace* furnished him the model of it, and *cette bonne compagnie,* who consider themselves the faithful guardian of good taste, paid him the honor of amusing themselves with it."[63] Even the stodgy *Mercure de France* wrote this about *Jérome et Fanchonnette:* "This trifle was universally applauded and deserves to be. It has brought back to this theater the foolish gaiety that suits it. It arouses bursts of laughter. . . . It has been a long time since people genuinely laughed at any *spectacle.* . . . We are obliged to Vadé for having given us a *pastorale* that is not a '*moutonnade.*'"[64] The *Mercure* echoed a view held by many in Parisian society: that there was a dramatic genre and a taste public traditionally and aesthetically appropriate for each of the Parisian theaters and that they should not take over each other's material (except for parody) or public. Vadé has no intention of emulating the Opéra, the *Mercure* observed. "He has taken the tone suitable to the theater for which he works."

It is evident that the *Mercure* was not just complimenting Vadé. It was rapping the Opéra for having recently presented opera bouffes and the Opéra-Comique for moving off in an untraditional and threatening musical-dramatic direction, casting aside the crudeness of Vadé and the early Comique writers. And that was the most significant issue of the 1750s and early 1760s. Vadé was a flash in the pan. He had many followers as a vaudevillian and *poissardiste*—Fleury de l'Ecluse, André-Charles Cailleau, Toussaint-Gaspard Taconet, and Charles-Jacob Guillemain—but they all worked for the boulevard theaters, not the Comique. *La Serva Padrona* had already made an impact on French music, and Sedaine and Philidor had already made their debuts at the Comique when Vadé died in 1757. Favart accepted the changes at the Comique while Vadé's uniquely independent course proved to be an aberration. Thus, Vadé aside, what was the reaction to the Comique's transformation from marketplace farce to serious lyric drama?

There is no way of telling what *le bas peuple* thought. Their taste for the vaudevilles and vulgarity of the old Comique is well documented. It is also a fact that Comique crowds remained large as the *spectacle* changed profoundly. But can we be sure that it was the same audience? If the pieces of Lesage and Piron were aimed at the lower ranks, and they were, those of Sedaine and Philidor seem not to have been.

The attitudes of literary folk are better known, and they were favorable for the most part. The philosophes were the most positive spokespersons for what they perceived as progressive reforms at the Comique. They had been either indifferent or hostile to the old Comique, but having campaigned vigorously for Italian music during the Querelle, they felt vindicated by the musical revolution at the Comique. Moreover, Diderot had considerable influence on Sedaine, especially after 1761.[65] And Grimm was as harsh in his criticism of the old *opéras-comiques*, especially the vaudevilles, as he was effusive about the new Comique. His only criticism of *Le Maréchal* by Philidor and François-Antoine Quétant was that it included some vaudevilles, "this detestable remnant of the old Opéra-Comique."[66] In 1764, when vaudevilles were virtually defunct at the Comique, the baron took a parting shot at them:

> This genre was no less odious to people of taste than to those who hold that public decency counts for something. If the latter were indignant at being constantly subjected to stupidities, obscene or satirical allusions, [and] filthy equivocations, the others were no less shocked to hear dialogue in vaudevilles and in couplets without any musical accompaniment.[67]

By contrast, he praised ariettes and the achievements of Monsigny, Philidor, and Grétry. At first uncertain about Sedaine, Grimm changed his attitude to one of unabashed encomium: "This man really has talent; he is the only poet in 60 years who brings to mind Molière's comedy."[68] A year later, following *Le Roi et le fermier,* Grimm said of Sedaine: "His pieces are full of truth, of simplicity, and of truly comic strokes. If an Italian poet, having the simplicity and skill, ever took it into his head to translate them . . . these pieces would furnish charm and delight for all of Europe."[69]

One of the greatest disappointments in Grimm's life was Sedaine's failure to carry the revolution he had been so instrumental in causing at the Comique to the Opéra. He tried, at least, with *Aline, Reine de Golconde* in 1766. Though it was a box-office success, the critics panned the work severely, and Grimm blamed Sedaine and Monsigny for having wished "to conform in every respect to the protocol of the French Opéra."[70] Other philosophes shared Grimm's unhappiness at the failure to achieve reform of the Opéra.

Most journalists of the time joined the philosophes' chorus of acclaim for the new Comique. Joseph de La Porte, in *L'Observateur littéraire,* stated that many had believed that the Comique would decline with Monnet's departure. He happily reported that this had not happened: "The attention, taste, activity, unity, and good understanding of the directors, all combine for the general good; clever poets, great musicians, celebrated ballet masters, select actors, excellent orchestra, everything tends to justify the renewal of ardor that has set in again for this theater and that promises for the future even more brilliant successes."[71] The *Almanach des spectacles* offered the same verdict:

The year 1761 must be marked among the glorious epochs of the Opéra-Comique. The large number of new pieces that have been successful, the extraordinary crowds of spectators especially during the fair Saint-Laurent, the performance of *On ne s'avise jamais de tout* at the court theater are all events that confer honor equally on the actors and the directors of this *spectacle*.[72]

The *Almanach des muses* was also fairly consistent in its praise of the Comique, stating in 1765 after the performance of *Rose et Colas* (Monsigny and Sedaine) that if every *opéra-comique* were a "masterpiece" like this one, "the genre would have more partisans among people of taste."[73] It did not escape the *Almanach's* notice, moreover, that after 1762 *opéras-comiques* were performed at court with increasing regularity.

The Opéra-Comique opened at Saint-Germain on 31 January 1761 with a *compliment* in the form of a prologue, *Courte et bonne,* in which Carnival, bored and disgusted by the effeminate bearing of the new Opéra-Comique, summons the ghost of the old theater to sing vaudevilles, examine subjects appropriate for the Comique, and question two machinists about the presentation of marvels. Both *L'Avant-coureur* and *L'Observateur littéraire* came down hard on the piece. Contending that it was full of "old hackneyed, worn-out riddles," *L'Avant-coureur* asserted that the sarcastic vaudeville couplets were distasteful to the audience.[74] *L'Observateur* pointed to the obvious contrast between the stale prologue and the brilliant new productions of the Comique. Noting that the title had had to be changed "out of modesty," La Porte insisted that the adverse reaction to the vaudevilles was evidence that public taste had changed.[75] These remarks may tell us less about changing taste, however, than they do about the compulsion of philosophe and journalist alike to condemn vaudevilles in their zeal to applaud the musical and dramatic transformation of *opéra-comique*. As the Comique changed, the fate of vaudevilles became a burning issue. Those approving the change—and they appear to have been the majority among the literary public —always associated vaudevilles with indecency and vulgarity. The partisans of the ariette viewed the vaudeville as an odious survival of the dark age of the popular theater. It was downright Gothic.

Nevertheless, the vaudeville had its defenders and the new Comique its critics among the literati of Paris. No doubt, the most interesting critic was Elie Catherine Fréron, whose periodical, *L'Année littéraire,* fired broadsides at the philosophes. In a review of Sedaine's *Oeuvres dramatiques,* Fréron took up Collé's complaint about the composer's domination of the new genre.[76] He lamented the passing of the simple vaudeville tunes in favor of the somber lyric dramas of Sedaine with their frivolous ariettes. Yet, while appearing to favor the old farces, Fréron attacked Sedaine for increasing the public's taste for vulgarities. Molière, Corneille, and Racine are deserted at the Comédie-Française because it requires taste and delicacy to appreciate a well-written play whereas the Comique caters to the "common brood of spectators." Where, asked Fréron, were the censors when Madame Simon's daughter in *Le Jardinier* said, "Que dans l'instant je te frotte," and "La beauté n'est qu'un fétu?" Whatever good ideas Sedaine might have had in *Le Roi,* Fréron insisted, were lost by the need to show off the ariettes. Fréron concluded that Sedaine had "prostituted his talents to a genre too little worthy of occupying them."

One of the sharpest critics of the changes at the Comique was Claude-Joseph Dorat, who lambasted the wailing, tearful seriousness of the *opéra-comique,* where everyone bawls, laments, and has convulsions. He charged that the pieces were given for intellectuals, who were to be pitied for wanting "to enslave the games of the imagination to geometric calculations, interrogating their mind in order to find out if their soul should be moved and promising themselves sensation only when it is authorized by a syllogism."[77] Simon-Nicolas-Henri Linguet, in his *Annales politiques, civiles et littéraires,* also blamed the intellectual elite, especially Marmontel, for the "philosophical torpor" and the useless "scraps of morality" that had seized the popular lyric stage. Linguet, like Fréron, lamented the passing of the vaudeville: "These light and malicious vaudevilles of the fair, which have caused such ridiculous and odious persecutions, were made for the character of the nation; people did not argue about the music; they did not foist lugubrious dramas on any theater; they were not philosophers; but people did laugh; they sang; they were French."[78]

The most sarcastic criticism in the press came from the authors of *Le Redoteur,* who maintained that women never hear *opéras-comiques* without experiencing "redoubled palpitations, excessive heart pangs, even total suffocations."[79] The ariettes from *Le Déserteur* cause "absolute disgust that is accompanied by a violent migraine." The vapors, which, the authors exclaimed, have become so common, "are the direct effect of the melancholy humor that gaiety attenuated but that dramas and a multitude of somber writings have restored."

Finally, Alexandre du Coudray, one of the keenest observers of the Parisian scene, blamed the popularity of funereal *opéras-comiques* laden with mournful exclamations and vague morality on the "crêpe de l'Anglomanie."[80] The English have inflicted their need for gloominess on a traditionally joyful people. Du Coudray accepted the rage for ariettes, but he appealed for the retention of vaudevilles and the old episodic comedies. They were born in France and are part of the naturally gay spirit of the French people, he argued. "They should please you, oh joyous Parisian, all the more because you are the father of this genre and of the gay and malicious vaudeville that is the soul of this *spectacle.*"[81]

Far harsher, more powerful voices than these were heard, however, voices not really of protest against the musical and dramatic revolution at the Comique but of the jealous ambition seeking to take command of it. The newfound popularity of the Comique opened the old wounds of the privileged theaters. The Comédie-Française was irritated, but the most aggrieved party was the Comédie-Italienne, which was performing opera bouffes and French and Italian plays to half-empty houses in their theater on the Rue Mauconseil. Charles Favart, who worked for the Italians for several years, declared that the Opéra-Comique had "absolutely crushed all the other spectacles."[82] Edmond-Jean-François Barbier confirmed this view, writing that the "*opéra-comique* injured greatly the other *spectacles* of Paris, especially the Comédie-Italienne."[83] The Comédie had a deficit of 400,000 livres in 1760.[84]

The Comédie, which enjoyed Crown support and the official title of *comédiens du roi,* appealed to the king, calling for the suppression of the Opéra-Comique and charging it with performing indecent works. In a turgid *Mémoire* published in 1761, the actors posed as the defenders of morality and decency against a theater dedicated to perversion and the corruption of good tast.[85] Yet, while venting their outrage and contempt for the fair theater, the Italian players advocated taking it over. They pointed out that they had called earlier for a merger of the theaters in order to end the awful state of affairs but that their appeal had only stimulated greater public attendance at the Opéra-Comique. The actors complained that even though they offered better plays and better performers, they could not meet their expenses. The harm done to the three great *spectacles* has reached such a point, they charged, that when the merger was first suggested, the three were deserted whereas at the Opéra-Comique "one was smothered in the throng of spectators three hours before the start of the pieces. . . ." Even the censor appointed by the police to evaluate the fair *spectacles* (the Abbé Chevrier) was extremely lenient, they declared, treating the *forains* almost as if they were a privileged theater. Worst of all, the Italian players insisted, the *forains* were luring *le monde* to their indecent shows: "The proper people, who were formerly ignorant of trivial and coarse language, are obliged to throw themselves into it today in order to follow the torrent that sweeps them into the booth of *Blaise le savetier* to see if it has spirit, jargon, and repugnance whereas our more beautiful pieces are deserted." The Opéra, which has also been ruined, the actors asserted, should realize that the small pittance it derives from the Comique is not worth the pretensions and bad taste that must be endured by everyone. Moreover, the *Mémoire* charged the Comique with selling out to foreign culture: "Foreigners, whose masters we should be, are going to become our models, and we will be on the verge of barbarism if people do not concern themselves very seriously with restoring taste through the sacrifice of a *spectacle* absolutely devoid of anything." Finally, promising to purify the Comique, the Comédie-Italienne offered to absorb it and pay the cost involved if the king would allow it and if he would terminate the *quart des pauvres*. The authors pointed out that when the merger was made, they would be able to play these pieces for the court "bien épurés."

The Comédie also dispatched memoirs to the first gentlemen of the king's chamber, begging them to look at the great discrepancy between the proceeds of the privileged theaters and those of the Comique and insisting that the merger was favored by all "good patriots."[86] The Comédie guaranteed the reimbursement of Corby and a pension for Monnet, promised to destroy the theater at Saint-Laurent so that no other *spectacle* could use it, and refused to indemnify the Opéra. As for the personnel of the Opéra-Comique, the memoirs suggested that they go to the provinces. The authors insisted that they had all the actors they needed to present *opéras-comiques* at the Comédie-Italienne and that keeping the Comique performers would only lead to dissension. Finally, the Comédie recommended that a moratorium be placed on *opéras-comiques* so the public could forget the actors. Comique productions should be reserved for the summer because it is "a dead season."[87]

Reminiscent of the attacks of the Comédie-Française earlier in the century, these memoirs reek of the bitter jealousy of the Comédie-Italienne and of its irritation, as a privileged theater enjoying Crown subsidization, that it had to suffer the competition of the popular entertainers. This motive clearly predominates in the memoirs though the Comédie cloaked its intentions in a cape of morality, good taste, patriotism, and tradition. Its real aim was to suppress its rivals and take over the profitable production of *opéras-comiques,* leaving the *forains* to fend for themselves. But the Comédie needed the Crown's approval and assistance to carry out the crime, and it had to indemnify the directors of the Comique.

Negotiations began in the fall of 1761 and continued until January 1762. The outcome seemed uncertain. Favart's *Mémoires* indicate his mounting apprehension, beginning as early as June 1761. "The Opéra-Comique has had such a brilliant success at the last fair," he wrote, "that it has aroused the jealousy of the other *spectacles*."[88] Favart thought it was possible that the Comique would be absorbed by the Opéra, leading to an odd double bill such as *Armide* (Lully) and *Blaise le savetier*. A few days later he reported that "the court and the city are in the greatest fermentation; all the orders of the state from the princes of the princes [*sic*] to the lowly populace are waiting for a great event; interest in foreign affairs seems to disappear in the face of a greater interest. What is the issue? *Parturient montes, nascetur ridiculus mus;* it is our little *opéra-comique* that captures the general attention."[89] In December he wrote: "People are awaiting the union of the Opéra-Comique with the Comedie-Italienne."[90] Favart noted that the Opéra wanted to absorb it and the Comédie-Française wanted to destroy it because it makes people "abandon Rodogune and Cinna for some bagatelles," but that a takeover by the Comédie-Italienne was favored by the first gentlemen. Favart was angry that Corby was advocating the position of the Comédie-Italienne, thus abandoning his associates. He predicted that Corby, "the creature of the minister," would get a life pension of 6,000 livres whereas the others would get nothing. He indicated, however, that people flattered him with assurances that he would receive a pension "for having been the creator of this bad genre."

The Opéra-Comique had some defenders, including one surprising dignitary, the archbishop of Paris. Testifying before the Conseil des Dépêches, the archbishop supported the retention of the fair actors on the grounds that their contribution to the poor was needed.[91] He was supported by the general procurator and the hospital administrators. On 25 December 1761, Favart wrote: "His Majesty was quite astonished that a prince of the church become the advocate of the histrions whom he excommunicated."[92] A few days later, Favart seemed to believe the merger would not occur. He wrote sarcastically: "Thanks to our holy archbishop, whose apostolic hand has the power to bind and to unbind, the Opéra-Comique, excommunicated and blessed at the same time, will remain in the same state and, what is more, under the protection of His Eminence; the matter is decided."[93]

Other voices of protest were also heard. Officials of the city of Paris, in whose charge the Opéra had been placed in 1749, fearful no doubt that the Opéra would be deprived of its remunerative grip on the Comique if the latter were delivered to the Comédie-Italienne, protested vigorously in a *Mémoire* dated 24 December 1761.[94]

The Crown settled the issue, however, by turning it over to the first gentlemen, who asked Papillon de la Ferté, the intendant of the menus plaisirs of the Crown, to take a hand in the administration of the Comédie-Française and the Comédie-Italienne.[95] Papillon wrote: "M.M., the Premiers Gentilhommes, desirous of seeing order restored in the *spectacles* and knowing through their own experience that this was impossible if the comedians were not constantly supervised, decided to engage the intendants des menus, who until then were involved only in the *spectacles* of the court, to undertake to follow those of Paris."[96] Papillon used his new power broadly in an effort to increase the receipts of the Comédie-Italienne. He embarked on a two-year reform plan, which probably was aimed from the outset (1760) at a merger with the Comique.[97] He dealt swiftly with the complaints of the actors and pensioners, hired several new performers, made additions to the repertoire, facilitated the payment of a portion of the Comédie's debt, and installed loges at the Hôtel de Bourgogne similar to those of the Comédie-Française, which were rented by the prince de Conti and other notables.

His work bore fruit early in 1762. In January the intendant proposed to the duc d'Aumont, one of the first gentlemen, that the Opéra-Comique be leased to the Comédie-Italienne and that a treaty be made between the Comédie and the Opéra.[98] The old Opéra-Comique was dissolved on 29 January 1762 by the first gentlemen, and the merger, as it was called, between the Comédie and the Comique was realized on February 3, when the "new" theater presented *La Nouvelle Troupe* by Voisenon and Anseaume, *Blaise le savetier,* and *On ne s'avise jamais de tout.* The merger stipulated that the Comique's repertoire and five of its actors—Messieurs Laruette, Audinot, Clairval, and Mademoiselles Dechamps and Nessel—be taken over by the Comédie-Italienne.[99] Most of the others joined provincial troupes. The combined company comprised 12 actors, 9 actresses, 9 principal dancers, 28 male and female extras, a 22-piece orchestra, 23 employees, and a council of 7.[100] Although Favart and his associates were not to receive pensions, the intendant and the first gentlemen ordered that the Comédie reimburse them in amounts ranging from 7,000 to 14,000 livres, totaling 54,000 livres. As for the Opéra, the Comédie simply assumed the five years remaining on Monnet's lease with the stipulation that the Opéra continue to receive 30,000 livres annually. The amount was later lowered to 20,000. Corby, Monnet's successor, relinquished the theaters at the fairs and all their effects to the Comédie, which, in turn, promised the Opéra to honor all of Corby's contracts.[101]

What authority and interest lay behind the termination of the most popular attraction of the Parisian fairs? Who really dictated the merger? The moralistic diatribes of the Italian troupe certainly were not sufficiently compelling to achieve it. Not even the intendant or the first gentlemen could have brought about the union of the two theaters on their own authority. The real source of the merger was the final and absolute seat of power—the Crown. *Le Nouveau spectateur* remarked cryptically that "the born Superiors of the theaters ordered the merger of the Opéra-Comique with the Comédie-Italienne. In a city with so many idle people, it is necessary to multiply entertainments so the people will kill time in a harmless way."[102] There may have been some truth in *Le Nouveau's* explanation of the Crown's motive, but of greater importance was the Crown's interest in elevating the status of the Opéra-Comique. Their productions were in vogue. They were considered to be "too important for the fairs."[103] The Crown wanted to bring them to court on a regular basis, yet *opéras-comiques* were not deemed sufficiently dignified to be royal entertainments, and, perhaps more important, the actors did not belong to a royally privileged theater. As a result, when *opéras-comiques* were occasionally brought to court, they were performed by Opéra singers who were not adept at working in that genre.[104] If the fair players were absorbed by the Comédie-Italienne and elevated thereby to the dignity of *comédiens du roi,* then they would acquire respectability and could perform regularly at court. In addition, they would have a permanent theater in Paris all year long, except for Holy Week. Performing in a proper theater also would enable the queen and members of the court to attend without embarrassment.[105] Having gained the necessary respectability, the Comique did, in fact, appear at court in November 1762, performing *Blaise* and *On ne s'avise jamais*. It was not long before the players were making a weekly trek to court. Marie Antoinette became so enamored of their fare that she began playing some of the roles.[106]

The merger was an enormous success at first, propelling the Comédie-Italienne into the catbird's seat of the Parisian theatrical world. Receipts totaled 3,274 livres on the first night alone and continued to average over 2,000 livres a day. The receipt for February and March was 131,523 livres.[107] After attending the first performance on February 3, Bachaumont declared:

> Never before have the Italians been besieged by a crowd like the one today. It was a fury without parallel: waves of curious people succeeded each other and spilled out into the nearby streets; the opening of the Opéra-Comique at their theater drew this prodigious concourse. Everything has been sold out for several days up to the *paradis*.[108]

André-Guillaume Contant d'Orville called the opening day "the most celebrated day ever in the annals of the theater."[109] The loges were rented a week in advance, and on the morning of the first performance, he observed the streets near the theater were "jammed with an extraordinary throng of guards and people who came to get hold of tickets that could not be secured in advance."

Bachaumont and others hoped the vogue would be short-lived. The *Nouvelles à la main*, calling *opéras-comiques* "the current madness," was confident that the theater's success would be fleeting because many people felt these pieces lost much of their charm by being played at the Comédie-Italienne.[110] Even Favart noted that the audience found the fair actors to be rather "shabby" on the Italian stage, and he warned that Audinot and Deschamps might be dismissed at Easter. Contant d'Orville's remarks are the most revealing. After the first few performances, he noted, the same public who applauded *Blaise* at the Comique recoiled from it and seemed to hold tacitly that there was a certain "tone of decency and nobility for each theater" that is not transferable.[111] Contant assured his readers that this "tacit convention is real." The Italians now perform pieces that are better left to the "*parades* of the tumblers"; "what is charming at the fairs" is out of place at the Comédie-Italienne.

The success of the Comédie, thus, was disturbing to some because it upset the conventional separation of taste publics and theatrical genres. It was disturbing to people such as Bachaumont, who regarded themselves as the guardians of good taste because it threatened to undermine the public's appreciation of classical theater at the Comédie-Française and the tradition of *tragédie-lyrique* at the Opéra. Bachaumont's fears were justified, for the Comédie-Française did suffer, and those who believed *opéras-comiques* would be a passing fancy were disappointed. The records of the Comédie-Française, in fact, reveal that between 1750 and 1774 only one play drew an audience of 25,000 over the course of 27 performances. In 1763 the Comédie-Italienne took in a record-breaking 700,000 livres, and it remained the most popular theater in Paris for several years.[112]

Who was the victor in the merger of 1762? From one perspective, the Opéra-Comique seemed to have won or gained ground. The Comédie-Française had failed to eradicate it. The merger guaranteed employment for some of the popular entertainers and ensured the continuation of *opéras-comiques*. It gave the actors legal sanction and privileged status as *comédiens du roi*. They now had a permanent theater—the Hôtel de Bourgogne—and could perform all year independent of the fair seasons. By 1780 the first gentlemen and other officials were referring to the theater as the Opéra-Comique, indicating an apparent victory for the *forains* over the troupe that had taken them over in 1762. Moreover, the Comédie stopped performing French plays in 1769 and Italian plays in 1779 because they drew so poorly in comparison with *opéras-comiques*. In 1783 the Comédie moved into a new theater called the Salle Favart, designed by M. Heurtier, inspector general of the king's buildings, and by M. le Camus, architect of the duc de Choiseul, and located on the duke's property, the spot where the Salle Favart still stands.[113] The theater looked onto the boulevard that took its name, Boulevard des Italiens, from the troupe though the entrance was in the opposite side so that the rear of the theater faced the boulevard. Some contemporary writers believed the actors did not wish to be identified in any way with the street entertainers who populated the boulevards. For example, J. A. Dulaure, one of the principal commentators on Parisian street life in the 1780s, asserted that the Comédie-Italienne was fearful of being assimilated by the boulevard shows. Houses were even built at the rear of the theater, he observed, in order to hide the prestigious theater from this "defamed promenade." The fear of being dishonored "resembles the pride of newly ennobled persons."[114] In any case, the Comique had shaken off its past. It was completely unlike its old self.

Viewed from another perspective, the merger of the two theaters was injurious to the Comique. Only a handful of the actors was hired; the rest had to seek jobs elsewhere. Nessel and Audinot left in May. The Opéra-Comique lost its independence, falling under the control of the Italian troupe and the administrative authority of the first gentlemen and the intendant. Even Baron Grimm, certainly no friend of the old Comique, noted that the merger "has not been approved by the public, which would prefer to see this *spectacle* under the authority of Messieurs the First Gentlemen of the Chamber. People are justifiably afraid that the taste of the public will be consulted less in the future; it would be fair to allow it at least to be the master of its entertainments."[115] Above all, the Comique had lost the setting of the fairs, which had done so much to determine the popular character of the genre and its audience. There was, of course, nothing in the union itself that entailed changes of genre or repertoire. But removing the Comique from the raucous fair environment probably accelerated the movement toward abandoning vaudevilles in favor of ariettes and increasing the dramatic seriousness of the productions. It is interesting that by 1777 a performer named Bigotine felt obliged to apologize to the *Journal de Paris* for including *tours du drapeau* in his performance as Arlequin at the Comédie; he vowed to discontinue these stunts, which the *Journal* insisted were not acceptable at the theater of Goldoni and Sedaine.[116]

But the greatest loss was suffered by the fairs and their diverse clientele. However they felt about the merger, most writers of the time sensed that the loss of the Comique doomed the fairs. The Abbé Chevrier called it "a mortal blow."[117] Barbier wrote: "If this merger lasts a long time, one can see that it will totally destroy the fairs Saint-Germain and Saint-Laurent."[118] Ironically, the fair Saint-Germain was destroyed by fire in March 1762—everything except the *salle* of the old Comique. It was rebuilt, but Barbier and others were correct: The merger doomed the lyric theater of the fairs. That great propagandist of popular entertainment, Jean-Baptiste Nougaret, penned its obituary:

> *Où la musique agréable éclatante,*
> *Faisoit goûter une joie innocente;*
> *Cet Opéra que gouvernoit Momus,*
> *Qui le croiroit? O ciel! n'existe plus;*
> *Par un arrêt, plein de rigueur extrême,*
> *On le força de s'immoler lui-même.*[119]

The lyric theater that emerged from all these changes of the 1750s and 1760s, however, cannot be called "popular" entertainment if the standards of the early eighteenth century are invoked. Not only had the Comique lost the marketplace and moved into the status of a privileged theater, but the genre itself had become radically transformed. Gluck's alleged revolution at the Opéra was less a departure from the tradition of Lully and Quinault than were Grétry and Marmontel from Lesage and Gillier. No one now denies that the lachrymose dramas of Sedaine and the robust ensembles of Philidor have more substance than the frivolous pastiches of D'Orneval. But in abandoning the vulgar banter of Arlequin, the episodes of street life, the folklike vaudeville airs known to all, and the caustic thrusts at privileged culture, the Opéra-Comique ceased to be a popular theater. Had the taste of Parisians improved, as the philosophes liked to believe, or was the new Comique aimed at a different public? Was there no longer a public or a home for the acrobats, mimes, marionettes, and vaudevillians who had launched the popular theater?

6

Entrepreneurial Dilemmas: The Case of the Fair Saint-Ovide and the Champs-Elysées

THE DEPARTURE of the Opéra-Comique from the two venerable fairs of Saint-Germain and Saint-Laurent in 1762 began a decline of the fairs that was never fully arrested. Far from spelling a general recession in popular entertainment, however, this decline helped to stimulate its spread into other parts of Paris, where new kinds of *spectacles* flourished alongside the traditional fair shows. Two such locations were the Place Louis-le-Grand (Place Vendôme) and the Place Louis XV (Place de la Concorde), which successively became the home of the Saint-Ovide fair. The extant documentation on this fair, richer than on the others, affords a close-up view of the management of fairs and the problems of their merchants.

The fair's beginnings were unusual. In 1662 the pope's Corsican guard insulted the duc de Créqui, who was the French ambassador to the Vatican. In reparation, Pope Alexander VII gave the duke the remains of Saint Ovide discovered in the catacombs, which Créqui, in turn, gave to the Capuchins, whose quarters bordered the Place Louis-le-Grand. The saint's annual fête attracted crowds that drew merchants and entertainers to the fair.[1]

The fair did not come into vogue until the 1760s, when it ran from August 14 until September 15. Its surge in popularity was such that the *Almanach parisien* reported in 1765 that Saint-Ovide was "no longer confined to the common people" because persons "of distinction" began attending.[2] The equestrian statue of the Sun King in the center of the Place Louis-le-Grand was surrounded by the boutiques of jewelers; dressmakers; bakers; grocers; hardware dealers; handkerchief merchants; turners; linen cloth makers; and lemonade, beer, and wine merchants. The hottest-selling items in 1762 were wax figures of Jesuits expelled that year from France.[3] In 1766, 23 different

entertainments were listed at the fair, including marionette and optical
shows, a billiard parlor, a sea monster, and a Passion play. The most important theaters of the boulevards, notably, Jean-Baptiste Nicolet's Grand
Danseurs de Corde (see Chapter 7), went to the fair. Nicolet's popularity was
so great that people nearly suffocated, asccording to one observer, trying to
get into his "miserable hovel."[4] In addition to Nicolet, a Monsieur Gaudon,
a *danseur de corde* and comedian, opened a theater at Saint-Ovide.

The most unusual entertainment at Saint-Ovide was the café of Monsieur
Valindin, which opened in 1771. There a group of blind musicians gave violin
concerts (one played a string bass) and took turns singing *vaudevilles*, each
followed by a choral refrain.[5] Music scores and candles were placed in front
of them, which, of course, they could not see. Wearing a red robe, pointed
wooden shoes, and a helmet that sprouted donkey ears, their conductor
straddled a stuffed peacock and was perched on a high platform to the side
of the musicians. Fusiliers had to be stationed at the entrance to the café to
restrain the crowds trying to get in. The vogue of this bizarre *concert des
aveugles* was so great that other café proprietors imitated Valindin.[6]

At the so-called café of the nymphs, a musical group adorned with
coiffures said to be in the Greek style sang couplets and ariettes. Nymphs and
fancy coiffeurs were fashionable. The *Mémoires secrets* declared:

> The police, always attentive especially in these disastrous times, anxious to
> supply the people with nourishment for their curiosity and a distraction from
> their misery, have conceived a new *spectacle* to entertain them, all the more
> enjoyable since it costs nothing. For a long time at the stalls of the print
> merchants, people saw some very original caricatures on our lofty coiffures, for
> both women and men, called *à la Monte au ciel*. These figures have materialized
> in a café of the fair Saint-Ovide, these strange figures of both sexes remaining all
> evening as a prey to the stares of the multitude who never tire of examining them
> and laughing at them. The whole business is accompanied by analogous music
> and very obscene songs that should be intolerable even to the ears of a nation so
> very little prudish as it is, but which gives its partiality to the so-called license of
> the fairs. This farce attracts an enormous crowd.[7]

The café was arranged like a theater and featured a troupe of chubby nymphs
who sang suspended on a cloud over the stage. In their midst a young girl
made up as cupid exhibited herself in some fashion. At the Café Champêtre,
one could hear an orchestra of shepherds playing in the center of a grotto
made of shells. Their instruments were decorated with tinsel.

The arrangements that the more than 180 merchants of Saint-Ovide made
with a variety of workers, entrepreneurs and officials were characteristic of
fair enterprises generally in eighteenth-century Paris.[8] The merchants dealt
first of all with an architect-entrepreneur, in this case, one Duchesne, who by

11. Concert by blind musicians at the Café des Aveugles at the Saint-Ovide fair in 1771. (BN photograph C 20864, or Qb 1771. See also MC, Topo, p.c. 38c.)

12. The Saint-Ovide fair on the Place Louis-le-Grand (Place Vendôme). (BN CE 70 C44330. See also Qb 1777, T 10, number 9631 or Va 234 and 234a.) The inverted writing is the result of a vue d'optique process.

a contract authorized in 1763 by Lieutenant General of Police Antoine-Raymond-Jean-Gualbert-Gabriel de Sartine and Commissaire Girard agreed to build 129 loges on the Place for the period of the fair and to put them up again the following year in return for 34 livres rent per loge. This was the innocent beginning of an angry relationship between the shopkeepers and the proprietor revolving around such problems as the contracts, financial burdens, and jurisdictional dilemmas.

When Duchesne refused to pay the fire fighters who put out a fire in the stall of a joiner in October 1763, the merchants claimed that he had not fulfilled his contractual obligations to guarantee the safety of the booths. They accused him of despotic practices. Monsieur Gaudon's theater was left half built; the framework consisted only of rafters, according to the *commissaire*'s assistant, which made it unsafe for the public. It was still in the same condition the following year, when demolition and reconstruction were recommended. More seriously, at the 1764 fair, Duchesne, using wood from the Saint-Germain booths, proposed to build 25 additonal ones that were much smaller than the originals, yet the price was increased to 70 livres a loge. Insisting that this violated their original contract with the proprietor, the merchants asked Commissaire Girard to permit them to negotiate with another entrepreneur named Aigon. Commissaire Girard was favorable to the merchants' appeal and informed the lieutenant general that Duchesne's plans were " ridiculous" and his price excessive. He supported the merchants' request to hire Aigon to build loges like the original ones. This arrangement was approved, and Aigon built 129 booths for the 1765 fair. It was a rare instance of the *commissaire*'s taking the merchants' side.

Although Duchesne was the proprietor of the loges, it was the merchants' responsibility to engage the commodities and services of a variety of suppliers and workers. They contracted with barrel makers, locksmiths, sweepers, and the Parisian Guard. The tables that follow for 1764 and 1765 show the cost of these contracts.

A

A glassmaker for 150 lanterns 14 to 15 inches high, equipped with iron wires, shutters and sockets at 55 sous per lantern	412.12
Cleaning the lanterns	30.
Locks	237.13
Rental of 15 barrels	10.
Filling the barrels with water	36.
The Parisian Guard	403.15
Supplementary Guard	1088.
Procureur of the Parlement	274.17
Fire fighters	43.4
Sweepers	36.
The *commissaire*	240.
The *commissaire*'s clerk	72.

B

Amount due from 1764	74.
A wooden chest for storage of candles	10.
365 livres of lantern candles at 9 sous a livre, plus 24 sous to carry the candles	165.9
24 livres of ordinary candles	53.10
21.5 livres a day for 17 days for the Guard plus 15 for the sentinel posted from 2 until 5 A.M.	378.5
Fire fighters	40.16
Glassmaker for one-fourth payment of the lanterns	130.
Rent of barrels and reimbursement for 1 lost	13.
Lighting the lanterns, sweeping, and filling the barrels	40.
The *commissaire*	240.
The *commissaire*'s clerk	48.

These were some of the typical annual expenses of the fair merchants. But it was not uncommon, as in 1765, for them to have additional legal and related expenses, such as those arising from their battle with Duchesne in

1764. These included the following:

To an avocat for consultation about Aigon's new loges	36.
Mémoires sent to the lieutenant general replying to those of Duchesne	15.
Clerk of the court of the Châtelet	6.
Other *avocats* for assistance in the appeal of the Châtelet ruling	48.
Secretary of the reporter of the fair for preparation of extracts refuting Duchesne sent to the procureur	168.
Refreshments at the Châtelet hearing	18.

The combined expenditures for goods, services, and fees related to the arbitration of the merchants' confrontation with Duchesne amounted to 1,790 livres, 8 sous, 3 deniers. This exceeded the total receipt of that year's fair, which was 1,716.7.3. In 1765 the receipt was 1,049 livres, 114 livres less than the costs, which ran 1,193 livres. The merchants were in the red in 1766 and 1767.

Despite the precarious financial condition of the Saint-Ovide merchants, officials of the crown and of the city conceived plans for a much larger enterprise involving not only the construction of a *place* with an equestrian statue of Louis XV and the relocation of the fair to this spot but also the development of the Champs-Elysées. The Champs was an alluvial plain for the most part, stretching from the Tuileries to the hills of Chaillot. An order by the Conseil d'Etat in 1667 enabled André Le Nôtre to cover it with elm trees in a quincuncial arrangement and to trace an avenue leading to the Rond Point in a direction established by the axis of the main lane of the Tuileries.[9] Colbert bought several pieces of land for the king along the Champs, and a guard was established to keep watch in the area. Nevertheless, the Champs was not much frequented in the early eighteenth century except at Easter, when there was a promenade to the Abbaye de Longchamp, and in late August, when Parisians thronged to the fair of Bezons, which always culminated in a grand procession from the Etoile back to Paris. The Etoile, a terreplein elevated about 100 degrees above the level of the place Louis XV, was used mainly as a gathering place for hunting parties.[10]

In 1754, however, two events occurred that greatly affected the future of the Champs-Elysées. Louis XV purchased the *hôtel* and gardens of Louis Henri de la Tour-d'Auvergne, comte d'Evreux, located in the increasingly fashionable Saint-Honoré quarter and flanking the Champs. He gave them to La Pompadour, which increased the coming and going of the elite in the area. A few years later, her brother the marquis de Marigny, the king's superintendant of buildings, commenced new plantings of trees and grass, dug trenches to catch the rain water, smoothed the avenue, and extended the Champs-Elysées to the Etoile. He also laid out the Allée des Veuves (now the

Avenue Montaigne) extending from the Rond Point to the river, so named because mourning widows who were not expected to appear at public promenades went there for fresh air and relaxation.[11] In the meantime, the city bought several properties and houses in the vicinity and began to commit itself to developing the Champs as an area of promenade and entertainment. A restaurant opened on the Champs known as Au Jardin du Roy. Theaters were built on both sides of the Avenue Marigny. Sellers of lemonade, beer, wine, and tea were drawn to the Champs. A palm reader set up shop near a *boule* field. Horses pulled *guinguettes* erected on carts along the avenue. Public coaches called "carabas" took people from the Place Louis XV to Versailles. Oddly shaped vehicles such as the "wisklett de chasse" carried celebrated actresses of the Opéra and Comédie-Italienne along the Champs. A certain Sieur Balp held horse races there.[12] At the Pont Royal one could take a boat ride on the river for 5 sous. The police gave an entrepreneur permission to operate a carousel on the Champs but did so reluctantly on the grounds that "this sort of play usually attracts in the area around it a populace who can only make respectable people increasingly shun this side of the promenade."[13] A casino opened near the grill of the Champs, where for 24 livres one could buy a book of 30 tickets with the right of free entrance for a lady companion.[14] Rustic balls were held there. The Champs was even outfitted with open-air chamber pots for the public's convenience.

It was also in 1754 that the Crown and the city decided to build the long-anticipated equestrian statue and *place* commemorating Louis XV at the extremity of the Tuileries gardens, which would mark a grand entrance to the Champs. *Lettres patentes* authorizing them were issued on 21 June 1757 although the designs were not completed until 1763.[15] The architect Jacques-Ange Gabriel was authorized to design the Place by the Bureau de Ville and the procurator of the king in June 1758. His plan was for a parallelogram 250 meters long and 174 meters wide. Edme Bouchardon sculpted the statue, which depicted the king as a Roman crowned with laurels. It became a cynosure of popular scorn and was regularly covered with epigrams and grafiti.[16]

The city was expected to raise the money to build the *place*, but it was obliged to delay the construction because of the cost of the war and the "circumstances of the times."[17] City officials had to ask the king for an annuity of 500,000 livres for construction, which Louis authorized.[18] The costs of constructing this *place*, where Louis XIII had once hunted falcons and a Roman aqueduct had once carried waters from the hills of Chaillot to the Palais-Royal, were enormous. The machine used to transport and erect the statue alone cost 20,000 livres.

Inaugurated in a ceremony sponsored by the city on 20 June 1765, the *place* served as an elegant doorway to the newly cultivated Champs-Elysées,

13. Place Louis XV. (MC. Topo, p.c. 127.)

flanked by Gabriel's two handsome palaces and the gardens of private *hôtels* to the north, graced with a fountain adjacent to quarters for guards and firemen at the southeastern angle, and connected to the Tuileries gardens above the surrounding trenches by the Pont-Tournant. Coaches crossed these trenches on arched bridges. Walkers, however, had to pass over planks, which led to so many accidents that the comte d'Angivilliers, director general of buildings, ordered a more secure passageway with posts to prevent the intrusion of coaches. Still the area was hazardous for pedestrians because of the ditches and coaches and because the western side was muddy in winter and dusty in summer. The *place* was not paved until 1776.[19]

How dangerous the *place* was became sadly apparent on the occasion of a fête sponsored by the city on 30 May 1770 to celebrate the marriage of the Dauphin to Marie-Antoinette.[20] A special fair to run nine days from May 15 was installed on the boulevards from the Porte Saint-Antoine to the Porte Saint-Honoré. City officials appealed to Parisians to light the facades of their houses and close their shops on the day of the nuptial benediction. Food and wine were to be distributed in all quarters of Paris on May 30. The Place Louis XV was cleaned, and two large illuminated pavilions were erected on it. Hired by the city to mount a mammoth fireworks display, one of the Ruggieri brothers constructed a temple of marriage with a large colonnade placed against the statue as the principal decoration of the show. The temple was surrounded by a parapet with dolphins at each angle emitting pools of fire. The facades of the temple were rigged to gush flaming cascades. The palace was topped with a pyramid culminating in a globe. Not far from the statue Ruggieri set up a building to house additional fireworks. He planned to set off a brilliant bouquet from this building as the climactic moment of the display.

During the show, a rocket fell into the reserve building, discharging the bouquet prematurely and panicking the horde of spectators. One of the unfilled trenches was located at a point congested by pedestrains and carriages. The press of the frightened crowd proved too great to be contained. Many people stumbled, and others began pushing and screaming, causing several persons to fall into the ditch during the crush. The melee could not be halted until a reinforcement of the Watch arrived, but by then several people had perished, and many lay injured. Calling it more like a spectacle of "a besieged city than a marriage fête," the *Mémoires secrets* reported that 133 bodies were taken to the cemetery of the Madeleine. Siméon-Prosper Hardy described the scene as follows. There was "such a prodigious number of carriages that the crowd was extremely maltreated. Dead bodies were collected that filled 11 cars, and they were at first taken to the cemetery of the parish of the Madeleine, faubourg Saint-Honoré, in order to expose them afterward in the street so that they could identified."[21] Unclaimed persons were buried in the parish cemetery. The dead included three knights of the Order of Saint-Louis, several clerics, and some pregnant women.

A few days later it was learned that the Dauphin had sent 2,000 écus to Lieutenant General Sartine with this accompanying letter: "I have learned of the misfortune that happened in Paris on my occasion. I am moved (*pénétré*) by it. I have received what the king sends me every month for my small pleasure; I can only dispose of that; I am sending it to you: help the most unfortunate."[212] The Dauphine and the princes of the blood also contributed, and the *fermiers-généraux* gave 5,000 livres. The clergy of the Grands-Augustins gave Sartine 10,000 livres for the families of the deceased.

The Parlement of Paris subsequently blamed the incident on inadequate police control whereas the *Gazette de France* charged that the commander of the Guard was playing vingt-et-un at the time of the accident and that the crowded carriage route was not supervised. Rumors began spreading in the days following the incident that the number killed was much larger than originally believed. Hardy noted a police report listing 367 dead, and a bulletin circulated publicly fixing the number at 688: 5 monks, 2 abbés, 22 "personnes distinguées," 155 bourgeois, 424 "menu peuple," and 80 "noyés."[23] Concluding that the matter had gotten out of hand, the lieutenant general of police sent a letter to the parish priests of the city certifying that 132 people had been killed on the Place Louis XV. He asked for their help in dispelling the rumors: "If it is impossible to diminish the general sorrow, at least one should try to destroy the impression that these lists have caused. . . ."[24] Hardy observed that the public still believed the real number was 688.

The terrible accident of 1770 was a fateful inauguration for the future Place de la Concorde. The authorities were determined, however, to turn the *place* and the Champs into the new pleasure land of Paris. In cooperation with a group of anonymous private investors, royal and city officials decided to construct a grandiose pleasure palace known as the Colisée at the Rond Point. An *arrêt* issued on 26 June 1769 by the Conseil du Roi authorized this gargantuan structure where various kinds of *spectacles* were to be presented. Its opening was to coincide with the festivities surrounding the Dauphin's marriage, but it was not ready until May 1771. In the meantime city and Crown officials decided to move the Saint-Ovide fair to the Place Louis XV as a means of attracting crowds to the nearby Colisée and the Champs.[25] A *Mémoire* to the lieutenant general of police, apparently written by Audinot, a director of one of the *spectacles* at the fair, referred to the relocation of the fair as an event to which "the minister appears to extend some favor," where merchants are forced to go.[26] Saint-Ovide opened on the Place Louis XV in the summer of 1771, dovetailing nicely with the inauguration of the Colisée.

Government officials not only hoped to lure crowds from the boulevards but also wanted to avert some of the problems that had plagued the fair at its former location and to establish rules and procedures pertaining to its operation. The city prévôt, Claude-Henri Bernard, chevalier de Boulainvilliers, and Lieutenant General Sartine issued the first set of articles governing the fair on 22 February 1771. Its annual opening was set for 14 August and the closing for 15 September. The articles prohibited merchants and colporteurs from selling their wares on the Place Vendôme and in the environs of the Place Louis XV. Each booth, 11 square feet in size, was assessed 18 livres to pay for the costs of security, cleaning, and lighting and for the honoraria, costs, and salaries of workers and officials. The funds were to be turned over to Commissaire Trudon. Merchants and entrepreneurs of *spectacles* were obliged to sweep in front of their loges every day and to keep a barrel of water on hand to guard against fire. Lighted heaters or stoves were prohibited at night, as were wood fires at all times. Goods were not to be laid out in front of boutiques. A board of four syndics was established to administer the fair on behalf of the merchants. They were to have free entry to the *spectacles*. Every year the syndics were to select two or three merchants who, in turn, had the sole authority to choose a new syndic to replace one of the four. Only "solvent persons and of good morals" should be chosen.

A second set of articles was issued by Sartine on 22 July 1773 containing three new rules: Entrepreneurs were ordered to build solid loges and a properly covered guardhouse; all booths were to close one hour after the *spectacles*; merchants were prohibited from "encumbering the public way."[27]

Because the stipulations of this ordinance were limited in scope, designed to address immediate problems rather than long-range policy and because they did not put an end to the confrontations among fair groups, the lieutenant general issued a more comprehensive ordinance in August 1775. It charged the syndics with the job of maintaining order, paying the costs of the fair, representing the merchants, and conciliating their interests. The merchants were decalared accountable to the syndics. The ordinances speci-fied that the expenses of each merchant should be the basis for determining assessments. The number of syndics was set at four, two to be elected every year in May by a plurality vote in an assembly of all the merchants presided over by the new *commissaire*, Sirebeau. Three of the syndics should deal in merchandise; the fourth should be a merchant of edible products. The two oldest syndics were obliged to retire every year. A final article seemed to contradict one of the principles stated at the outset of the ordinance by basing the annual charges for security, cleanliness, lighting, honoraria, and services on the size of the boutiques and salles. The sum of 40 sous was specified for each foot of frontage. Payments were to go to Sirebeau, one half at the opening of the fair and the rest after the first 15 days. The *commissaire* then remitted this sum to the syndics, enabling them to pay the bills.

The accounts indicate that during its years on the Place Louis XV the fair Saint-Ovide either broke even or had a surplus. The 1771 fair, which was prolonged until 23 October, showed an exact balance of costs and receipts. The merchants paid the syndics 3,456 livres 5 sous; the entrepreneurs of *spectacles* (20 were listed), limonadiers, and food dealers paid 1,124 livres 10 sous, for a total of 4,580 livres 15 sous. The same sum was reached when payments for posters, lanterns, the Guard, fire pumps, the *commissaire*'s fee, watering the *place*, and other services were totaled. The 1772 ledger showed the syndics' receipts at 4,949 livres and expenditures at 4,881 livres 19 sous, and in 1773 the receipts rose to 7,378.1 and expenses 7,377.17. The break-down of costs was as follows:

Guard	2502.19
Fire fighters	190.16
Watering	520.
Upkeep of lanterns, repairs, and storage	200.
Candles	795.12
Earthwork	260.
Lantern illumination	72.
To Aigon for prolongation of the fair at 3 livres per loge	429.
To Aigon for supplemental posts	28.

Construction and furnishing of a Chambre Syndicale	100.
Rental of carriages for the affairs of the fair	84.
Purchase of eyebolts, nails, linchpins, papers, and other furnishings and salaries of daily workers	49.4
Letters and commissions	20.
Drinks for the workers	30.
Ordinary candles	133.
The assistants of the lieutenant general	36.
Gratuity to the sergeant of the Guard	24.
Inspector of police for the *place*	24.
Honorarium to Commissaire Trudon	450.
To Trudon for "some outlays"	3.
The *commissaire*'s clerk	60.
Illuminations at the four visits of the royal family	1126.
Honoraria to the four syndics	240.
Total	7377.17

The accounts for 1774 showed a balance of receipts and costs at 6,018 livres 4 sous each. 149 loges covering a terrain of 18,000 feet were in use that year, and the merchants' share of the costs was 2,682 livres plus 1,272.10 for 15 days' prolongation. It is noteworthy that at this fair the *spectacles* occupied 21,000 feet of space and paid 1,493.14 plus 570 for the prolongation. The syndics observed that it was the comedians and the *limonadiers* who sought the fair's extension. In 1775 the fair had a surplus: The receipt was 8,484.13 livres; the expenses, 8,309.8. The receipt on the 150 boutiques at 38 livres 10 sous each for 1776 was 5,775 livres. The wine and food merchants and *spectacles* paid an additional 1,941 livres, and there was a surplus of 175.5 from the previous year, making the total receipt for 1776 7,891 livres 5 sous.

Neither the ordinances governing the fair nor the financial records, however, indicate the angry disputes that raged among fair people during the Place Louis XV years. There was a four-cornered management of the fair in these years: the overall supervision of Commissaire Claude Robin Trudon and his successors, who had to approve all contracts and who held the civil jurisdiction and police authority; the proprietor, Jean Aigon, who built the booths; a group of four syndics who provided the capital, collected rents, hired workers, and took over the general financial management of the fair; the merchants and entertainers. Other parties closely involved were the Parisian Guard and the lieutenant general of police. Quarreling and conflicting interests characterized the relationships of these individuals and groups from the outset.

Prior to the opening of the fair on 14 August 1771, the Guard clashed with the syndics over matters of security.[28] The Guard succeeded in getting the lieutenant general to order the syndics to have the terrain of the *place* smoothed in order to prevent vehicular accidents and in getting Aigon to build a guardhouse for 36 men next to the statue of the king. But its demand that the fair close at midnight to preserve "decency and good order mainly in the neighborhood of the Champs-Elysées, which offers to libertines and people of bad intentions a refuge that they can abuse" was opposed by the syndics on the grounds that it would eliminate Nicolet's last show of the evening, hurting his and the *limonadiers'* profits. The sharpest disagreement came over the number and placement of guardsmen at the fair. The Guard insisted that 30 fusiliers, an officer, and sergeant be on duty every day, with additional sentinels and corporals at the boutique entrances, the Pont-Tournant, the statue, the quai entrance, the opening to the Champs-Elysées, and in front of the guardhouse—22 in all at a fee of 20 sous per fuselier and 22 for corporals. They also called for a 9-man night watch at 2 livres 10 sous each. The Guard stipulated that the merchants would pay half of these costs and the *spectacles* the other half. The syndics argued that so many guards were unnecessary and asked that they be reduced.

Another grievance against the Guard was their negligence in controlling traffic. The syndics informed the *commissaire* that coachmen parked in front of boutiques while their masters strolled in the fair; others pulled up in front of the booths simply to watch the crowd or let their horses rest, often for more than an hour. Arguing that this impeded business, the syndics reasoned that it was pointless to pay so many guardsmen if they could not keep the traffic moving.

Disputes over the Guard raged for several years until the *commissaire* fixed their number and salary in 1776. He called for 1 officer at 12 livres a day, an adjutant at 4.10, 3 corporals at 1.7 each, and 22 fuseliers at 1.5 each. An additional corporal and 2 fuseliers were to remain in the fair until 4:30 A.M., each receiving 2 sous, and a corporal and 4 guardsmen at 1 sou each were ordered for the time between dawn and the opening of the fair. The total cost of the Guard was 50 livres.

The relationship between the merchants and Jean Aigon was as difficult as that with Duchesne when the fair was on the Place Vendôme. The merchants' contract of 4 June 1771 called for Aigon to build 150 loges on Louis XV (only 138 were built and 4 were not occupied in 1771), each 11 feet wide, 11 feet deep, with galleries of 8 feet. These booths were to have floorboards and sliding shutters with vents. New wood was specified for the structures, and Aigon was to repair weather damage, disassemble the booths each year, and rebuild them the following year. The merchants agreed to pay 54 livres in 3 installments per booth per year, not including prolongations.

The complaints against Aigon began in August 1773, when several merchants sent a report to the assembly of syndics charging that Aigon had not fullfilled his obligations. One complained that several rafters in his boutique were broken, leaving gaping holes in the roof. He claimed that much of his merchandise had gotten wet and that he had had to make the repairs himself. Another pointed to the bad condition of the compartments of his booth and insufficient boarding on his shutters. Joining a chorus of protest, Nicolet, director of the Grands Danseurs de Corde, declared that all the planks of the facade of his *salle* were loose and that he had been unable to get Aigon to repair them. He also noted Aigon's failure to install a drain, with the result that water had damaged many of his effects. Another merchant protested having to spend the night in his loge because rotten wood prevented him from closing the door securely. The syndics and the *commissaire*, who made inspections of the booths, received complaints from over two thirds of the fair merchants, most charging that the planks were rotten, cracked, or uneven, causing property damage and creating dangerous hazards.

The syndics also had their gripes with Aigon arising out of squabbles over locations at the fair. All the merchants wanted to be as close to the *spectacles* as possible because that was where the crowds were. As Commissaire Trudon put it in a *mémoire* to Sartine: "It is inevitable that the public would go to find them [the theaters] even if they were in the trenches." The problem was that the design of the fair put all the *spectacles* on the same side in 1771 and 1772. Merchants on the opposite side complained angrily about their emplacement and the hazards caused by the press of carriages. Deciding that the fair should be redesigned in a circular layout, the lieutenant general authorized Aigon to confer directly with Louis-Gabriel Moreau, the city architect, about the plan. Aigon then began allocating locations to the merchants, which drew the ire of the syndics, who objected that this gave Aigon too much authority and intruded on their prerogatives. They referred to the authoritarian tactics of Duchesne and the merchants' victory over him. They insisted that Aigon was only a worker carrying out police orders and that the merchants were the true proprietors of the fair. Having appropriated the authority of renting the booths himself, Aigon forced the merchants to bribe him in order to get a good location. The syndics appealed to the lieutenant general to empower the *commissaire* to supervise the assignment of booths. They were successful.

But the fracas over locations did not die when the fair was eventually redesigned in 1776.[29] The new plan called for a circle of 52 booths around the equestrian statue and 91 booths along avenues coming into the fair. The syndics protested that this greatly reduced the number of booths in the center of the fair while increasing those on the side streets, which had always been difficult to rent. They predicted that booths separated from the main circular body of the fair and from the *spectacles* would lie vacant. They also complained that space had been allocated for only 4 cafés rather than the former number of 18 or 20. To compensate for the reductions in favorable locations, the syndics proposed increasing the size of the booths, allowing merchants to sell more than one product, reducing the width of the rue Royale coming into the fair to close the gap between the avenue booths and the main enclosure of the fair, and constructing a cordon of oval boutiques around the grill of the statue to correspond to the oval shape of the enclosure. The latter change enabled them to increase the number of boutiques at the center and reduce those on the avenue, restoring space for cafés and small *spectacles*. The bureau objected to narrowing the avenues on the grounds that it would impede the circulation of traffic, but it agreed to the cordon provided the booths were low and of equal height. Most irritating to the syndics, the city insisted on dictating and enforcing the redesign of the *place*.

The reconstruction of Saint-Ovide did not avert disputes of all types among fair personnel and officials. The *commissaire* was deluged with *mémoires* from the syndics, the *spectacle* proprietors, and the chief officer of the Guard. They clashed over when the honorarium to the officer had been first established, whether cabarets and cafés should be classified as *spectacles*, and whether the officer of the Guard was authorized to be an inspector of the *spectacles* and to collect a special fee for that service. The syndics complained about merchants renting their boutiques to other merchants without permission. The syndics reasoned that if such abuses were tolerated, "one would no longer know those who frequented the fair, and unqualified people could be brought in, even people of evil life."[30] Uncontrolled subletting, they argued, was prejudicial to merchants who had waited a long time to get a place in the fair. The merchants countered that the syndics were preoccupied with their jurisdictional authority and not with the interests of the merchants.

These disputes reached a climax over the selection and membership of the syndicate. The merchants of edible products charged that, contrary to the practice followed at the fairs of Saint-Germain and Saint-Laurent, they lacked representation on the syndicate. Several abuses stemmed from this "reprehensible monopoly . . . contrary to equity and equality": some merchants used their booths for more than one trade; consumable products were sold freely at the fairs by colporteurs without fair concessions; those engaged in *commerce de bouche* had to pay 3 livres per foot of boutique frontage whereas other merchants, who had covered loges with colonnades, decorations, and candles, paid only 30 sous. Contending that it had been understood when Saint-Ovide opened in 1771 that colporteurs would be banned from the fair, that all boutiques would pay 18 livres for 11 feet of frontage, and that the syndics would act to establish order and economy, the food and drink merchants charged that "disorder and waste" had reigned on the Place Louis XV because the *merciers* had appropriated the syndicate. Such discrimination was unlawful, the food dealers argued, because "each citizen is equal in relationship to the sovereign and public order."[31] But because only one type of merchant was elected syndic, colporteurs boldly hawked wine, liquors, eau-de-vie, pastry, and meat at Saint-Ovide without sharing the costs of the fair. Moreover, the *spectacles* and food merchants paid a dispro-portionately high percentage of the costs: In 1774 the food merchants occupied 543 feet of frontage out of a total of 1,693 feet. They paid 4 livres 12 sous a foot whereas the merchandise dealers paid 33 sous. In violation of the flat sum of 18 livres per 11 feet of frontage, the *merciers* extracted more money from the food dealers; this was unknown to the *commissaire* because the syndics presented their accounts already made out, thus concealing their fraud. Their accounts are always carefully balanced, the food merchants charged, to create the appearance of equity, and there was no audit to see if the receipts were phony. The food merchants also questioned the amounts reported for lantern candles; earthworks; watering; and the honoraria cover-ing the costs of letters, commissions, paper, tips, carriages, and cockades.

Not long after these charges were filed in March 1775, the four syndics, Mignot, Ciriez, Meunier, and Lepelletier, replied. They attributed the cause of the grievances to the sale of wine by beer dealers, a practice legally exercised through *lettres de regrat*. The syndics held that they were not empowered to prevent a merchant from selling one thing rather than another. As for outsiders selling edible products, the syndics argued that it would be unheard of for those frequenting the fair to be denied the freedom to sell food. On the other hand, the syndics noted that they had backed up two food dealers who stopped a Monsieur Mazange, who had no boutique in the fair, from selling wine on the *place* until Mazange produced a letter from Sartine authorizing his sales. They also observed that none of the restaurant keepers of the fair had ever been prevented from carrying his food and wine through the fair.

On the issue of discrepancies over the amounts paid by different types of merchants, the syndics asserted that the merchants, occupying 149 loges at 11 square feet of land totaling 18,000 feet, paid 4,200 livres; the *traiteurs* and *spectacles*, however, held 21,000 feet and contributed only 2,100 livres despite the fact that they took in 20 times more than the merchants. After collecting modest amounts for several years from the *traiteurs*, amounts incommen-surate with the *traiteurs'* space and profits, the syndics admitted to having raised the amount assessed the food merchants. The syndics promised that because of the complaints they would reduce the tax, but they insisted on assessing each merchant, whether of food or merchandise, on the basis of the amount of land he occupied. Those who held more would pay more. Denying the allegation that they falsified the accounts, the syndics noted that their records were kept in a carton for the inspection of all and that the *com-missaire* verified their receipts.

Finally, the syndics addressed the principal complaint of the *traiteurs*—that they were not represented on the syndicate. Citing the one-time election of a *limonadier* at Saint-Germain 60 years earlier, the syndics denied that *traiteurs* were always represented on the boards of the two old fairs. Proof that the syndics of Saint-Ovide did look out for the interests of food merchants was provided by the Mazange and other similar cases. Abuses and disputes, they continued, were really the province of the Guards, not the syndics. Moreover, it was understood that the syndics should be selected from among "the most notable" merchants, who would be replaced at the annual election by "solvent people and of good morals." The syndics noted in conclusion that only a few *traiteurs* had signed the complaint, the others either being unable to write or unaware of the document. That the syndics, representing the merchandise dealers, viewed themselves as an elite morally, financially, and intellectually is clearly revealed in their defense.

But the affair was not over. The principal author of the *mémoire* of the *traiteurs*, a man named André, arranged an assembly of merchants, which met in the syndics' quarters in the presence of the *commissaire* in October 1775, where he angrily denounced the syndicate. All the charges were repeated, and representation on the board was demanded. The syndics, in turn, denounced this assembly to the lieutenant general, accusing André of calling them rogues and cheats and of seeking to gain a seat in the syndicate. They demanded that the police condemn his insolence before it led to attacks by others. André was subsequently reprimanded, and Commissaire Sirebeau informed the lieutenant general on 6 October 1775 that the claims of the syndics were well founded.

Although the *spectacle* directors shared common interests with the merchants and especially with the *limonadiers* and café proprietors, they were less vocal in their complaints against the proprietor of the loges and the syndics. The syndics did, of course, defend them against the special taxes imposed by the officer of the Guards for inspection of the *spectacles*. One problem touched them deeply, however: the law that they turn over over one fourth of their proceeds to the hospitals for the support of the poor. First imposed by the Crown on the Opéra and the Comédie-Française on a regular basis in 1699, the tax was soon extended to the fair theaters. The annual amounts were collected by commissioners employed by the hospitals.

On several occasions the theater directors unsuccessfully protested the exactions and sought reductions in them, but no appeal was more urgent, even threatening, than that of Nicolas-Médard Audinot, who brought his Ambigu-Comique from the boulevard to Saint-Ovide in 1774. Under great pressure from the fair merchants and the police, Nicolet and others had already moved to the fair, and Audinot was obliged to follow in their footsteps. His troupe at this point included 14 musicians, 16 female and 20 male actors, and 26 employees. To compensate these theater directors for the costs of moving and establishing their shows at the fair, the police suggested that the *quart des pauvres* taken from them on the boulevards be waived at Saint-Ovide. But it was not, causing howls of protest from the entrepreneurs of the fair, who in 1774 called the exaction unjust and cruel, and from Audinot in a long *mémoire* to the *commissaire* in 1775.[32]

Referring to the lieutenant general's assurances that the tax for the poor would not have to be paid at the fair, Audinot's *mémoire* pointed to the unusual plight of his company: Most *spectacles* could make a profit by giving two performances an evening, but because his troupe was comprised of children who were not robust enough to withstand two shows, he was unable to do so, and the anticipated abolition of the tax for poor relief had not been issued. Audinot attributed the latter to "outrageous reports" to Lieutenant General Le Noir about his profits. The one fourth earmarked for the poor did not constitute profit, he argued. It represented money paid to the workers and players of his troupe: "This receipt, is it not the bread of a troupe of unfortunate children who have no way to live except by the miserable *tréteaux*?" Offering to relinquish his own earnings for the sake of his young performers, Audinot posed a bold challenge:

What would be said of a government in which one would proclaim as free a fair that since its inauguration actually enjoyed this privilege, in which a large number of merchants would be forced to go to this fair at considerable expense, in which one would then ruthlessly fleece these same merchants by taking from them not a fourth of their profits but a fourth of their total sale without regard to what the merchandise cost them, without regard for their travel and instal- lation costs?

He concluded that "no law of the prince either authorizes or permits such an act of violence." His strong appeal fell on deaf ears.

The Saint-Ovide fair was supported during its brief residence on the Place Louis XV not only by the police, the *commissaire* of the Châtelet, and the prévôt of the city of Paris, but also by the Crown. Members of the royal family visited it several times. In 1773, for example, the Dauphin was there on 2 September, the comte and comtesse de Provence on 6 September, Mesdames de France on 8 September, and the Dauphin and Dauphine again on 13 September. These royal visits were a financial hardship for the mer- chants, who had to pay for special illuminations. The visits in 1773 cost them 6 livres each, but since several merchants could not afford the cost, the syndics had to kick in an additional 288 livres.

The interesting aspect of these special fêtes for royalty is that they were initiated by the syndics rather than by the police or the city. The fêtes were necessary, according to Mignot, one of the syndics, in order to call the princes' attention to the luster of the Saint-Ovide fair. The syndics were determined to impress the royal family because they believed it would enable them to make the fair a permanent event. Mignot told his colleagues on 1 September 1773 that despite the "state of splendor" that Saint-Ovide shared with no other fair of the realm, "there are risks from year to year that it would be abolished."[33] He, therefore, proposed exploiting the royal visits, justifying the heavy costs of the illuminations in the process, by getting the Dauphin and Dauphine to request *lettres patentes* from the king guaranteeing the fair in perpetuity. In a strange qualifying remark, Mignot said the Crown should be assured that the fair is for the Parisian merchants "to the exclusion of the *forains* and people without virtue." It is hard to believe that the syndic meant by *forains* the entertainers of the fair because it would not have survived without them as the police well understood. Yet *forains* was the customary term used to designate the theatrical people and showmen of the fairs. In any case, the syndics took steps to obtain the lieutenant general's support for their project and to get him to force the merchants to contribute to the expenses. The syndics got his and the *commissaire*'s approval, gave the orders for the illuminations at an assembly of the fair merchants at the Chambre Syndicale on 4 September, and sent petitions to both the Dauphin and the king requesting *lettres patentes*. They also asked the minister for Paris, the duc de la Vrillière, for his support. But for unrevealed reasons, the Crown decided not to guarantee the fair's future. Possibly the public's coolness toward the Champs-Elysées convinced the Crown, the police, and the minister that the Saint-Ovide fair was expendable.

The history and fate of the Champs-Elysées and especially of the Colisée paralleled that of the Saint-Ovide fair. There is no doubt that from the very outset the Colisée was an affair of state. Indeed, it was launched in 1769 by the secrétaire d'Etat of the maison du roi, who was entrusted with its overall supervision and determined to make it a success.[34] The decision to build this entertainment palace had been made by the Crown after deliberation by several ministerial committees, who viewed it as "a monument of the luxury, the grandeur, and the opulence of the nation."[35] The prévôt of Paris and the lieutenant general of police also had a hand in its management and were charged by the Crown to use it for public celebrations. The city pledged 50,000 livres toward its construction.

Open on a regular basis every Wednesday and Saturday, the Colisée was meant to be an expanded version of the Waux-Halls of the boulevard, the Saint-Germain fair, and the Vauxhall in London. It was intended as a shrine of public entertainment for the presentation of pyrrhic *spectacles*, nautical fêtes, pantomime shows, concerts, and balls. Only productions deemed competitive with those of the two Comédies and the Opéra were forbidden. The directors of the Colisée were former heads of the Opéra-Comique: Julien Corby, now in the household staff of the duc de Choiseul, and Jean Monnet.

The manager, Duchesne, had built the loges for the Saint-Ovide fair on the Place Louis-le-Grand. But given the size and opulence of the Colisée, the key people in this enterprise were the entrepreneurs who put up the money and who remained forever anonymous because, according to Pidansat de Mairobert, they were "so ashamed of their foolish enterprise."[36]

The original capital investment was estimated at 720,000 livres, but the figure quickly rose to 2 1/2 million. Before the structure was finished, the investing proprietors of the Colisée were 1 1/2 million livres in arrears. The interest on this at 5 percent constituted a rent of 90,000 livres, which, along with 20,000 required annually for pensions and gratuities, 3,000 for the cost of each performance, and 180,000 to replenish the capital investment, amounted to an annual outlay of around 200,000 livres.[37] They had to stop work on several occasions in order to seek new subscribers. The proprietors apparently realized at least as early at 1770 the risks they were taking, but they were reassured by the Crown, which sensed "the advantages and pleasure for the public of these voluptuous establishments" and granted them "every possible means to attract *les amateurs refroidis*."[38]

Moreover, the comte de Saint-Florentin, the minister in charge of Paris, beat off attempts by the Comédie-Française to block the Colisée. He also forced Torré to close his Waux-Hall on the boulevard for a time, and when the latter reopened, his poster stated that it was with "the permission of the entrepreneur of the Colysée and with the agreement of M. le Comte de St. Florentin."[39] The authorities also suddenly began cutting all the trees on the boulevards under the pretext of improving the appearance of the area, but actually, in Bachaumont's view, "to force the public, deprived of every other pleasure, to proceed in droves to the Colysée, which has been made an affair of state and whose cost, one is assured today, the government is paying."[40] Calling the whole enterprise "madness," Bachaumont believed the receipts would never be as large as the operating costs and that the proprietors would regret their investment.[41] Early in 1771 the proprietors felt the financial crunch severely and stopped all construction. The Colisée opened in May 1771 though there were still sections of the structure that had not been finished.

When Bachaumont's prediction about the construction and performance costs proved accurate, the entrepreneur-proprietors and their creditors began hurling accusatory *mémoires* at each other, and legal proceedings were instituted. The proprietors insisted that they be indemnified for more than 38,000 livres in rents that had not been paid and for construction delays by workers. They also sought liberation from the annual 20,000 livre sum they had to pay the Opéra and from the amounts demanded by the *fermiers-généraux*. They appealed to the city and the Crown to discharge their debts. The creditors, in turn, appealed to Lieutenant General Sartine for support, and a commission to judge the disputes headed by Sartine was appointed by the Conseil d'Etat.[42] In the meantime, the Colisée was closed (some thought permanently) in May 1773, and Torré was allowed to reopen his Waux-Hall. But the government was not ready to give up. Whether it paid the proprietors' bills is not known, but the Colisée sprang to life again in 1774. In that year, despite the loss of two months because of Louis XV's death, the Colisée earned its largest profits to date. Still, the 227 creditors, who had formed a syndicate in December 1773, continued to complain about overdue payments.

In size and profusion, the Colisée was the most grandiose structure Parisians had ever seen, The Conseil d'Etat entrusted the project to Le Camus de Mézière, architect of the duc de Choiseul, who presumably was inspired by the circus of Vespasian. Requiring three years to complete, the Colisée was designed as a circle 300 feet in diameter within an octagon.[43] A rotunda or ballroom 80 feet high with a radius of 60 feet was built at the center of the circle, surrounded by a concentric circle of galleries and fluted Corinthian columns. These were surmounted by 16 gilded caryatids, which appeared to support the cupola. A lantern 34 feet in diameter in the center of the cupola lighted the rotunda with 81 chandeliers. The galleries were decorated with blue, tucked drapes studded with rosettes. The balconies between the caryatids had green drapes fringed in gold and contained 16 bays with crimson drapes. The coverings that hung from the balconies were supported by 32 Ionic columns and 16 pilasters. There were niches with statues, marble inlay, and a ceiling painted with flying cupids. A space was left at the southeast and southwest sides for 3 galleries and peristyles. Crowds could pass directly from the rotunda to an oval basin, or *cirque*, holding 6 feet of water, and then through a peristyle and 5 grand arcades. A colonnade, additional galleries in 3 tiers, and an upper terrace, all seating a total of 3,000 people, looked onto the basin. An esplanade off the basin could accommodate an overflow of 5,000. Four cafés were installed near large circular rooms to the northeast and northwest of the rotunda. The structure was fronted by a huge iron grill and two small buildings, one a guardhouse and the other for a ticket booth. Several terraces and gardens formed wings off the main building.

On performance evenings, the Champs glittered with lights from the Place Louis XV to the Rond-Point, and from the high terrace of the Colisée one could see the *hôtels* of the faubourg Saint-Honoré, the Tuileries and the Cours-la-Reine, and across the river the Palais-Bourbon and the Invalides. In addition to the cafés and boutiques, the regular entertainments of the Colisée included balls in the rotunda featuring two 30-piece orchestras, a joust with musical accompaniment in the basin, fireworks, and concerts.[44]

The first special attraction at the Colisée was musical: Mademoiselle

Le Maure, a celebrated soprano at the Opéra, came out of retirement in July 1771 to innaugurate a long series of concerts. The directors also experimented with special effects by having violins echo her vocal phrases from a perch high up in the amphitheater. The Colisée also catered to people's curiosity about mechanical contraptions, in this case, new, unusual musical instruments. In 1773, for example, an organist named Joinville performed on a cembal' organo or "clavecin organisé" of his own invention.[45] Made of wooden pipes, it was designed in such a way that the player could strengthen or soften the sound without removing his hands from the keyboard. On another occasion, a German clavecin teacher named Milchmeyer played his "Concert Méchanique" at the Colisée. The machine tooted a concerto for two flutes and piano.[46]

The directors of the Colisée were willing to try just about anything in order to attract the public. On one occasion they sponsored a fireworks competition among three of Paris' top pyrotechnists.[47] A lottery was also held.[48] The winning ticket, drawn from a mechanical sphere, paid 20,000 livres. In 1772 cockfights were presented with birds brought from England, but the show was an utter failure.[49] Evidently, the cocks could not be held on the table set up for the fight. They ran under the skirts of the female clientele, causing general consternation and demands for refunds.[50] A repeat match was held a few days later, but the two cocks killed each other. Equally unsuccessful was a man walking on water by means of a cork jacket.[51] In 1774 the directors brought in a well-known horseman named Hyam, who did somersaults, leaps, and other gymnastic stunts on his racing horses.[52]

The most intriguing experiment at the Colisée was an art exhibition held in 1776. The brainchild of the manager, Duchesne, who notified the curés of Paris that the exhibit would not contain impious art, the salon housing the exhibit was installed above the vestibule of the main entrance.[53] Duchesne's intention was to give unknown artists a chance to display their works. Over 200 paintings, sculptures, engravings, and designs were listed in the catalog. Prizes were given for the best works: 2,800 livres for historical tableaux, 800 for statues at least 30 inches tall made from baked earth, and 300 for engraved plates. On a more regular basis, the Colisée relied on pantomime *spectacles*. Trying to make them as spectacular as possible, the directors focused on themes from Greek mythology, such as Zeus giving life to the ravishing, diabolical virgin Pandora and the Titans' furious assault of Olympus.[54] To enhance the antique flavor of these pageants, the directors added their version of the Olympic Games—men racing on four parallel tracks with a garland of flowers atop a column awaiting the victor, followed by a fireworks display depicting the Temple of Venus.[55]

Fireworks were always the main attraction at the Colisée. They have had a venerable history and a virtually timeless appeal since their invention two thousand years ago by the Chinese. Some societies worshiped fire; others made it a symbol of their ruler. Since antiquty fire has been used in festivals such as a the Feast Day of Saint John. As a universal symbol of joy, fire and fireworks were and are especially appropriate for public celebrations because they can be seen and enjoyed by everyone. Italian pyrotechnists introduced fireworks in France, where they quickly became associated with royal pageantry, especially at the court of Louis XIV. In 1730, Giovanni Niccolo Servandoni commemorated the birth of the Dauphin with a fireworks show on the Seine. The Ruggieri brothers from Bologna brought their spectacular arsenal of fireworks to Paris a few years later. They gave performances for the court and the city of Paris.[56] Louis XV was so impressed that he attached three of the brothers, Petronio, Pietro, and Antonio, to his menus plaisirs. Another brother, Gaetano, went to the court of George II. It was not long before fireworks became a major entertainment for Parisians. After seeing a fireworks display on the Seine in 1741, D'Argenson declared that whereas previously fireworks had been reserved for the grandest occasions, they were now a regular, profitable enterprise for pyrotechnists, who rented out chairs and scaffolds as at the Opéra.[57] Servandoni and the Ruggieri also used fireworks in public theaters, initially at the Comédie-Italienne. In 1776 the Ruggieri obtained permission from the king to open a huge garden on the rue Saint-Lazare in the Porcherons quarter, where they produced *spectacles pyriques* with dramatic themes bearing such titles as "Le Combat Magique" and "Les Forges de Vulcain." They also ran the Waux-Hall at Saint-Germain, and they became the principal pyrotechnists, along with Torré, of the Colisée.

The universal, timeless appeal of fireworks, whether in pagan rituals or royal pageantry, Bastille Day celebrations or presidential inaugurations, must be attributed to the myriad of images and emotions they arouse in spectators. Their dazzling effects inspire reverie in some, terror in others. Appearing to be alive and unpredictable, they can plant in the imagination the ideas and sensations of violence, passion, luxury, and hell. In the hands of the Ruggieri and of Torré, pyrotechnics became a marvelous art. Producing crackling explosions and sprays of bubbling fire, they were able to evoke specific images of dragons, shooting stars, erupting volcanoes, and glittering palaces.

The pyrotechnists attained the maximum impact of their art at the Colisée because it was uniquely equipped to combine fireworks with aquatic shows and funambulism, thus enhancing the illusions and enchantment that fireworks aroused. On occasion, however, the awesome marvel of pyrotechnics and funambulism could turn into a scene of real terror, as in August 1773. The Colisée's poster proclaimed that a celebrated stuntman from the fairs known as le beau Dupuis "would make a grand ascent on the tightrope and would climb to the top of a magnificent decoration depicting in fire of diverse colors the splendid portal of the church of Nôtre-Dame."[58] Military music and Bengal lights accompanied the *spectacle*. As thousands looked on, an explosion announced the fireworks from the cupola at the top of the rotunda, and Dupuis appeared at the bottom of a cable that sloped upward from the base of one side of the wall to the peak of the fireworks framework. The snakes, rockets, and wheels broke into flame. Dressed in a white satin costume and brandishing torches in both hands, Dupuis made his ascent to the top of the cable where he was silhouetted like an apparition against the radiant flames. As he began his descent, someone in the crowd shouted that the rope was loosening. In the confusion that followed, a person dressed as a pyrotechnist began turning the cylinder around which the cable was wound. Disaster followed. The crowd screamed as the cable sagged. Dupuis tottered, then fell 50 feet to the tiles below. Ordinarily, the basin into which he fell was full of water for the jousting, but it had been drained because the water had become fetid. Doctors tried to attend to his internal bleeding and broken bones at a nearby café, but Dupuis fell into a coma and died. It is not known who the apparent pyrotechnist was or whether his actions were accidental. A judge later ruled that it was murder.

As with the Waux-Hall at Saint-Germain and the Redoute Chinoise at Saint-Laurent, one wonders who went to the Colisée. The *Almanach parisien* declared that it attracted "the most fashionable people of the capital," and George-Louis Lerouge, the king's ordinance supervisor, stated that it "brought together princes, the great of the realm, foreigners of the first rank, the nobility, the wealthy, and the bourgeoisie."[59] The marquise de Langeac, one of the foremost patrons of the Colisée, took the ladies of the court on a tour of it on opening night (23 May 1771).[60] In 1776 the queen, Monsieur, the comte d'Artois, and Madame Elizabeth de France left a performance of *Coriolan* at the Comédie-Française to attend the Colisée.[61] Seated in a special box built in the vestibule with a view onto the basin, the queen watched a fireworks show specially arranged by Duchesne (who had been notified in advance of the royal visit), featuring a Chinese cascade and the Temple of Mars. The Queen's party then toured the gallery of the rotunda, where they were entertained by a children's dance troupe. Dressed in costumes "appropriate to characterize the Nation," the dancers "gathered together in galant postures," laid garlands of flowers at the queen's feet, and placed a crown of myrtle and roses on her head. Mademoiselle Joly sang the vaudeville air "Je sens pour aimable Lisette."

There is no doubt that *le monde* frequented this garish pleasure dome during its brief vogue. But the entrance fee of 30 sous put it within the financial reach of the bourgeoisie, if not of workers. Many observers commented on the mixed social composition of the crowd. Alexandre du

Coudray noted that it was curious "to see *le bas peuple* and the man of title" mingle at the Colisée.[62] Another observer declared that the remarkable thing about the Colisée "is the forgetting of wealth, dignities, ranks, distinctions. This charming equality carries all of us back to the delights of the golden age and gives rise to thousands of courtesies, attentions, considerations, kindnesses, good manners of men toward the fair sex. . . ."[63] Simon-Nicolas-Henri Linguet believed that the price seemed tailored to the bourgeoisie although he noted caustically in 1777 *le monde's* apprehension about being seen with their inferiors. The bourgeoisie, on the other hand, were afraid of being "humiliated" by the "showy scandals that seem necessary to enliven our fêtes."[64] It is possible that in their effort to create popular entertainment on the Champs Elysées, the directors, proprietors, and officials were not sure what audience they really wanted to attract. Although fireworks, when well executed, appealed to all Parisians, operatic concerts and balls seemed to be aimed at the elite; and aquatic jousts, formerly a river attraction, were accociated with *le bas peuple*. Mercier blamed the failure of the Colisée on this confusion: "This was not at all the rendezvous of the people; the interior had nothing entertaining enough; boredom hovered under the vaults. For whom was it built? Was it for *les grands* or for the bourgeoisie? For *les grands*? It was not voluptuous enough. For the bourgeoisie? There were no popular pleasures."[65]

But it may be that the proprietors wanted to obtain a mixed public from the very outset. The fairs had always been marketplaces where social integration took place. Although no one planned it that way, that was their nature. It is possible that those responsible for the Colisée wanted to duplicate that social mix. At least one observer, who remained anonymous, believed the primary value of the Waux-Halls in general and the Colisée in particular was that they brought together the rich, the great, and the poor like large rivers and little streams joining "the sea of the world."[66] Since the majority of people were never able to afford the entertainments of the rich, he asserted, "these two portions of the public are always separated, like two enemy peoples who out of hatred appropriate another language, totally different manners, styles, customs." Torré's Waux-Hall forged a reunion in miniature, and that—"each person seeking to join himself to the whole" —was what the *spectacles* are all about. "Each class of this public is ennobled, and all seem to comprise no more than one. . . ." The real appeal, he insisted, was not the individual performers or shows, but "the *spectacles* of society." The author viewed the Colisée as a real sign of progress because it could hold so many more people and was located in a commodious avenue with tickets at modest prices. Whereas at the Opéra or the Comédie-Française, the honest bourgeois was segregated in the second or third boxes from the countess in the first, at the Colisée there was at least the appearance of equality. He concluded:

> Let us give much grandeur to the places reserved for public *spectacles*; the seats will become less expensive, more within the reach of everyone; and the rich person and the one who is not will feel together, will enjoy themselves reciprocally. The inequaltity of ranks, always humiliating to the lower classes, will disappear; the idea of good fortune will replace envy, and Humanity will be as happy as it can be.[67]

Certainly, these were inflated, optimistic sentiments, but they suggest that as popular entertainment spread in the city and as the government became involved with *spectacles* beyond the level of privileged theaters and official fêtes, the idea of the public *spectacle* as a forum for social integration as well as a distraction from hard economic and political realities was growing.

For all that, the Colisée still had more detractors than boosters, and the government eventually had to concede that it was a mistake. Some of its critics disparaged specific entertainments. Pidansat de Mairobert grumbled that the jousts were presented in "a kind of tub or muddy pool that offers neither the expanse nor the sport nor the perspective necessary in such *spectacles*."[68] Mercier was even harsher: "After having seen tumblers fall into filthy, muddy water, one would walk in a vast solitude under the badly painted galeries to the sound of baroque music."[69] Bachaumont, who carefully followed each step in the development of the Colisée, complained that a show billed as a "fête Chinoise" was canceled without reason and replaced by "a carnival farce worthy at the very most of a marionette *spectacle*, and the public did not deserve to be fleeced because one paid double to see . . . Savoyards dressed in paper, *gourgandines* clothed as queens and princesses, a shabby procession, everything that the most disgusting *mascarade* can offer."[70] Bachaumont also suggested that the Colisée functioned as a brothel. Noting that this "Parthenon" was announced in Rétif de la Bretonne's *Pornograph*, a work approved by the government, he observed that in the interior of the building there were "a multitude of rooms and cells that one foresees can be suitable only for amorous tête-à-têtes."[71]

The most persistent general criticism of the Colisée was that the government was trying to contrive entertainments for the people; that the official world was intruding on free choice, imposing its setting and its taste on a stubborn, indifferent population. Mercier wrote: "The administrators of our pleasures have certainly gone to great pains to give them to us: they wish to compose our amusements instead of letting us create them; and every effort of imagination that they make for us, only ends in denying us liberty, gaiety."[72] Bachaumont declared that the "determined will of the minister to use the most extraordinary means to force Paris in some way to turn toward this place" made people laugh at him for wanting "to restrict them even in their pleasures and deprive them of what they relish the most."[73] The *Courier d'Avignon* put the matter quite simply: "An enlightened magistrate cannot impede citizens in the choice of their entertainments. . . ."[74]

None of the government records reveals why city and Crown officials were so zealously committed to the Colisée, why "political views were joined to the establishment of the Colisée."[75] Conceivably officials were among the investors, who were never publicly identified. No doubt, officials were motivated by a desire to keep a restless population occupied with "harmless diversions," a phrase used often by the police during these years. Yet there is no explanation for their determination to move the entertainment scene from the vibrant boulevards to La Pompadour's backyard. The best guess of contemporary writers, who expressed bewilderment over the government's intentions, was that the Colisée, along with the Champs and the Place Louis XV, were seen as a monument to the king's *gloire*. In addition, Bachaumont attributed the Crown's interest to a fear that the English would mock the French if they were unable to mount an enterprise comparable to the London Vauxhall.[76]

Whatever their motives, official efforts to manufacture a *palais du spectacle* failed. The more the secrétaire d'Etat used his influence "to force idlers to change their direction," Pidansat wrote, the more deserted the Colisée became.[77] The costs of construction and operation far exceeded the proprietors' expectations, and their debts continued to mount while the government took no action to bail them out despite all its assurances.

In desperation, Duchesne, who had tried every means available to him to attract crowds, wrote a long letter to the *Journal du théâtre* in September 1776 attempting to prove the financial viability and value of his *spectacle*.[78] He constantly compared the Colisée to Torré's Waux-Hall, which suggests that he and his official backers realized that the boulevards provided the main competition and that the government had probably already decided it was losing the struggle. Duchesne contrasted the spaciousness of the Colisée to Torré's little *spectacle* sandwiched between other buildings. Attributing the Waux-Hall's popularity solely to the vogue of the boulevard, Duchesne pointed out that the bourgeoisie found it unpleasant because of the crowded street and the packed seating. He declared rather cryptically that "the bourgeois, free but shy, is excluded by certain considerations and cautions of reputation, of fortune, which do not permit the appearance of certain liaisons, which, without really existing, would seem to him and would be noxious." The Colisée, Duchesne insisted, avoided these inconveniences because it was "susceptible to the coming together . . . of the great and the small." The great "find there what they were looking for at the Waux-Hall and even more"; the small go there "without fear of being noticed, and everyone disappears into the crowd at will." Imagine, Duchesne wrote, a bourgeois seeking to obtain a few hours of relaxation for his family: "does he bring them to the Waux-Hall? Luxury, seen too close by, and the comparison that he cannot escape, will humiliate him; if he goes to the Colisée . . . he escapes to what he wants. What other pleasure can he take that would be no more expensive than this one? And this is also actually the reason why the Colisée has more spectators than the Waux-Hall." It may be significant that Duchesne used the argument of the social integration of "the great and the small" in a letter he must have known would be read by government officials.

Duchesne's other concern was to prove the financial viability of the Colisée vis-à-vis the Waux-Hall. He noted that whereas the Waux-Hall took in 60,818 livres 16 sous in 44 performances in 1773, the Colisée, sequestered most of the year by the Conseil d'Etat, earned 30,239 livres 16 sous in 9 performances. The comparative expenses for the same period were 12,004 livres 1 sou, 8 deniers for the Waux-Hall and 2,515 livres, 16 sous, 6 deniers for the Colisée. Duchesne concluded that if the Colisée had been able to open 44 times, it would have spent over 1,000 livres less than the Waux-Hall. The manager supplied similar figures for 1774 and 1775. He confidently predicted an annual profit of 30,000 to 40,000 livres in future years.

Finally, Duchesne made several recommendations: that the Waux-Hall be closed; that the fee paid to the Opéra (20,000 livres) be terminated on the grounds that the Colisée's entertainments had been restricted; that, unable to pay its creditors, the Colisée be treated as a debtor deserving help; and that the Opéra perform an act or two from its repertoire every Thursday at the Colisée, the two *spectacles* sharing the profits.

Although the government turned a deaf ear to these proposals, Duchesne pushed on with his enterprise. His art exhibition in 1776 had been a success, and in early 1777 he announced that a new display would be mounted. The government's attitude now began to become apparent. In June the comte d'Angivillier stopped the exhibition.[79] An *arrêt* of the Conseil d'Etat dated 30 August 1777 ordered the termination of all art exhibitions and lotteries at the Colisée.[80] The authorites gave no reason for their action, and everyone at the time seemed baffled by it.[81] But the *arrêt* went even further. It stipulated that the Colisée was not to give fêtes or *spectacles* of any kind without the permission of the lieutenant general. Furthermore, it requested the names, professions, and residences of all the proprietors, along with the amounts each had invested in the enterprise. Failure to comply would result in the closing of the Colisée. Thus, the Colisée was confined solely to fireworks.[82] These punitive measures still did not deter Duchesne, probably because fireworks had always been the Colisée's mainstay. It is, therefore, ironic that fire consumed whatever hopes the backers of the Colisée had for its future.

On 22 September 1777, shortly after midnight, fire destroyed 27 boutiques, 2 cafés, and 2 *spectacles* of the Saint-Ovide fair in less than 15 minutes. Audinot's theater was spared.[83] Only the young daughter of a confectioner in whose loge the fire began was injured, but the losses in merchandise were sorely felt. One jeweler reportedly lost 100,000 livres worth of goods. The cause of the fire was attributed to a candle left burning in a sweetshop by a servant who left the establishment to attend Nicolet's *spectacle*. It did not help matters that the fire fighters' pumps were in poor condition. People speculated, according to Charles Favart, that Audinot's theater did not burn because he was an actor, automatically excommunicated, who, therefore, was a sorcerer. Joined by Nicolet, Audinot turned over the proceeds from his show for two days to the merchants. But this sum of 4,604 livres scarcely made a dent in the losses, which the syndics estimated at 433,512 livres. Whether the police, as one source suggests, decided prior to the fire to suppress the fair "because of the inconveniences that it causes" and the fact that it was prejudicial to the corps of merchants of Paris is uncertain, but Saint-Ovide was not rebuilt after the fire.[84]

At that point, Duchesne must have realized the Colisée was doomed. He did announce a sale of season tickets for 1778 in October 1777, hoping for a subscription of 4,000 people, but the Colisée never opened again. It was officially closed by an *arrêt* of the Conseil on 9 March 1779. The *arrêt* cited the disputes among the proprietors, creditors, and workers and the bad condition of the building.

Despite all the money pumped into it, the whole enterprise of the Champs-Elysées was not successful as a recreation area. Evidently, the terrain remained forbidding even after the improvements made by Marigny. During Louis XVI's reign, the marquis de Villette referred to the Champs as "a torrid or glacial zone, a field of mud and dust on a rough and uneven terrain that dislocates the most solid coaches, breaks the back of the most robust horses, and destroys the unfortunate pedestrian who ventures into these regions and nourishes the extravagant idea of going on foot as far as the forest."[85] Moreover, the location west of the city made it inaccessible for many Parisians although that alone can not explain its failure because the fairs of Saint-Germain and Saint-Laurent were also rather remote. The discontent of the merchants and performers at the Saint-Ovide fair and the failure of the Colisée to meet the expectations of Crown and city officials and to reward its investors with profits dealt a severe blow to the Champs. In addition, the *honnête homme* was apparently discouraged from going to the Champs, according to Gilleron, custodian of the Etoile, because "prostitutes and beggars . . . abound there every day."[86] Gilleron explained that the girls attracted the French and Swiss guards, who took them to nearby cabarets to get drunk. On returning to the avenue, always dark at night, they started fights, disturbing decent people; "upright citizens, frightened and complaining about the lack of security, find themselves on these promenades like the many beggars who are also there and who for the most part are men of very bad appearance." Frédéric, the chief guard of the Champs who sent daily reports to the police, wrote in 1788 of having to stop an abbé accompanying a female Negro at 8 P.M. Although the abbé insisted he was hearing her confession, Frédéric told him "not to repeat the offense of confessing his penitents at night under the trees."[87] The police received other complaints about criminals, drunken coachmen, dueling, and schoolboys playing *jeu de barres*. Little effort was made to control the situation, however, after Saint-Ovide and the Colisée closed. *Le monde* shunned the Champs. The bourgeoisie were uncomfortable there. For *le bas peuple*, the Champs was remote and aristocractic. The equestrian statue of Louis XV on the Place remained an object of popular scorn.

The real cause of the demise of the fair and of the Champs probably lies in the fact that the boulevards had already captured the public and continued to prosper, and the Palais-Royal burst into the entertainment life of the city in the 1780s. The Champs, the Colisée, the Place Louis XV, and the relocation of Saint-Ovide were the creations of officialdom. Their hope was to devise recreation for the elite and the bourgeoisie as well as for *le bas peuple*, but they learned that the atmosphere of the marketplace could not be contrived. The whole area reeked of an officially concocted culture, an attempt to lacquer a deeply divided society with a veneer of equality. Certainly, the enterprise was a sign that popular culture had broken the confinement of the old fairs, that it was being embraced by *le monde*.

7

Streets of the People

THOMAS ROUSSEAU characterized the Parisian boulevards as odious, infected thoroughfares of sin frequented by impudent libertines, nymphs of the chorus, spangled scoundrels, and corrupt recruiting sergeants, places where people were pushed, tripped, battered, and thrust into orgiastic dissipation, where innocent girls learned prostitution and young men lost all sense of decency, reason, and propriety and ended up contracting "le mal Amériquain."[1] Others, however, believed that these beautiful lanes lined with sparkling cafés and sprightly *spectacles* displayed the magnificence of the capital city.[2] Certainly, they were the greatest show in pre-Revolutionary Paris, the center of a renaissance of marketplace culture.

The boulevards were formed in the sixteenth century when François I extended the wall on the northern side of the Temple and had a trench dug creating ramparts, which extended from the door of the Temple to the Porte Saint-Antoine on the eastern edge of the city.[3] In 1668 the first trees were planted on the terreplein adjacent to the trenches, and in 1670 the Conseil d'Etat ordered the demolition of the wall of Philip Augustus and the extension of the boulevard westward from the rue du Temple to the Porte Saint-Martin, a gate built by Charles V more than 100 yards to the south of the gate (of the same name) constructed years later by Louis XIV. A year later, orders were given to extend the boulevards to the Porte Saint-Honoré, but the Boulevard du Temple remained the principal link in the chain until Baron Haussmann's time. By 1705 the boulevards comprised an extended avenue 100 feet wide flanked by rows of trees. Houses sprang up along the ramparts, and the gardens of the stately *hôtels* of the Marais bordered the boulevards on the inner side. Beyond the ramparts lay fields of

161

lettuce, sorrel, mushrooms, and artichokes; and to the north, the windmills of Montmartre.

By the eighteenth century the boulevards had become a real thoroughfare linking one side of Paris to the other and an increasingly popular place to promenade. Working to make them attractive and clean, the *prévôts des marchands* had the pedestrian lanes sanded and the main avenue watered every day in summer. In the 1780s the bastions and counterscarps were destroyed, the trenches were filled, the land was leveled, and the central thoroughfare was paved. The city began installing streetlamps in 1781, and the side lanes were outfitted with stone benches and chairs. In the meantime, a second set of boulevards extending from the barrier of the Invalides to the Hôpital Général fronting the Seine was completed in the early 1760s, creating a veritable ring around Paris.[4] Although a few *spectacles* were installed there, the new boulevards never achieved the popularity of the old ones.

The boulevards offered a variegated spectacle. There was glamour: Diamond-clad courtesans and countesses, indistinguishable to onlookers, wended their way under the trees in decorous coaches. There was filth: The clogged lanes were often turned into miniature dust bowls or muddy ravines, and the unwary stroller was doused with urine and feces hurled from upper-story windows. There was music: an unremitting blare of chanting, drumming, and tooting. The bells and cymbals of the clowns fought for attention against the squalls of merchants selling cocoa, apple turnovers, orgeat, and barley sugar. Insults streaked the air like summer lightning. There were thievery, brawling, and prostitution. On 11 July 1767, Louis Joron, *commissaire* of the quarter of the Temple (1765–1770), reported that Jean-Baptiste Le Vasseur, a coachman employed by Dame Costé, proprietor of new carriages on the Pont-aux-Choux, had charged Dame Gaillardot, a seller of fruit and tisane on the boulevard, and her cousin, a turner, with insulting and assaulting his wife and her friends.[5] After calling Le Vasseur's pregnant wife a "bitch," Dame Gaillardot allegedly jumped on her and beat her while the cousin kicked her several times in the stomach causing a miscarriage. Following an incident a month later, when Dame Gaillardot smacked Sieur Badaule and his wife with a broom handle and threatened to burn down their house on the rue Vieille-du-Temple, Joron sent the habitually drunk woman to jail.

The *commissaires* also had to listen to complaints from jealous husbands. When Pierre Gabriel Liedet, who operated a billiard hall on the Boulevard du Temple, accused one of his regular patrons, a mason named Brissart, of forming a liaison with his wife, Joron wrote that the pair had become so overtly intimate that "several times they caused a scandal in the billiard hall with regard to the players and spectators."[6]

Prostitution occupied the *commissaires*' attention more than any other problem. Soliciting on the boulevards was common, and there were several brothels in the area that the lieutenant general often obliged the *commissaires* to search.[7] Prositutes were often rounded up in their dens, in the cafés, or in front of the *spectacles*. They were whisked to the *commissaire*, where their heads were shaved, and then taken to the Salpetrière.

People gathered on the boulevards ostensibly to promenade or to attend the *petits spectacles*, but really to ogle each other, shout at the grimacers and stuntmen on the *tréteaux*, get drunk, and feel the physical press of unsegregated human flesh, as on the Paris métro at rush hour today. For some, the shoving and elbowing was disagreeable. A young law student from Leyden wrote in disgust:

> At the end of two hours we felt harassed, black and blue, and choked by the dust that we had swallowed. We deplored the empire of fashion that swept away reason and comfort, and we promised each other never to return to breathe the suffocating air charged with pestilential fumes. The noise of the charlatans had made us deaf and dried out the palate: our sense of smell was swollen by the suffocating vapors, and of all our senses the only free one remaining was touch.[8]

Everyone came to what Benjamin Franklin called the club of the Quatre Nations.[9] Bejeweled ladies mingled with ragged street urchins. *Petits-maîtres* showed off their mistresses and luxurious carriages.[10] Old men sat on the benches along the shady lanes telling strollers the latest gossip about the boulevard entertainers or engaging them in games of chess, dominoes, or pegtop.[11] Hester Thrale from England was struck by the numerous shop-keepers who brought their families to the boulevards. The shopkeeper, she declared, belied the traditional image of the "the fawning Parisian, the supple Gaul. . . . He lives as well as he wishes, he goes to the Boulevards every Night, treats his Wife with Lemonade, and holds up his Babies by Turns to see Harlequin or hear the Jokes of Merry Andrew."[12] Marquises and lackeys, young pages and financiers, *robins* and tramps, all were engaged by the giddy gallimaufry of sights, sounds and aromas. Mercier spoke of the boulevards as the place "most open to every estate."[13] The complete social integration of this marketplace was evoked vividly by Pierre Jean Baptiste Nougaret:

> Do you hear the sharp, little voice of the impatient marquise blending with the awful swearing of a porter addressing Hell and Paradise? Everything in this moving tableau of *Vis-à-vis, Berlines, Désobligeantes, Cabriolets, Carrosses, Remises, Fiacres, Charettes* seems bizarre, peculiar, ludicrous. See in the glass carriage the ugly woman of title with her rouge, her diamonds, the paste shining on her face whereas the *roturière* just to the side in a simple dress is brilliantly fresh and plump. Look at this wealthy canon sunken into his cushions dreaming of nothing while the old magistrate in an antique berline reads some petition.[14]

Enticed by the pungent smell of new wine, the sight of swishing skirts and bare bosoms, artisans, merchants, and coachmen flocked to the cafés, where they drank eau-de-vie, ratafia, and scalded beer; played cards or billiards; and listened to the Savoyard girls play their hurdy-gurdies.[15] The singers who strolled in from the streets always dangled cups at café patrons in hope of hearing the sound of a clinking sou. Yet a penniless person could sit in the café until 11 P.M. listening to the music freely without being told to leave. "His ear will enjoy more than his stomach, and the symphony will take the place of supper. Every café owner makes *a free gift* of his stove, his chairs, and his orchestra to an infinite number of people who whether out of laziness or leisure vegetate in absolute idleness."[16] "Habit confirms this inactive life," Mercier contined, "and one sees clearly in wandering through the cafés how many men there are who are horrified by work and for whom the days are a boring length. In this inertia they all seem to serve as a prelude to the calm of death and to cherish rest even more than life. When they expire, these people do not seem to die but to cease only going to the café."

The Café Turc, the largest on the boulevards, with decor suited to its name, enticed the high-steppers into its long, illuminated garden separated by a wall from the avenue. Decked out with arbors and summerhouses, it was famous for its ice cream.[17] The Alexandre, visited frequently by the police, was the turf of streetwalkers and homosexuals. On one occasion a singer named Hélène incited a brawl at the Alexandre, principally among artisans and *officiers*.[18] More than 30 people were involved; 4 were killed and several wounded. Hélène was sent to the Salpetrière, where she was charged with drunkenness; the others were arrested. The *Gazette noire* wrote that "infamies, horrors take place in this café that it is useless or, rather, that it would be too filthy to mention."[19]

The boulevard *traiteurs* usually served their food and drink in large halls, with smaller rooms on the sides reserved for lovers. The unwary customer of these haunts often wound up paying for three or four times the number of bottles of wine he had drunk since his bill was calculated by the number of bottles under his table, and many were pitched there by habitués.[20] The *traiteurs* catered to male patrons who had picked up girls on the street and to hurdy-gurdy players. "At the orgies, made up of girls and young libertines already surfeited by the excess of pleasure, these female hurdy-gurdy players sought to arouse their senses with lascivious songs, which they accompanied with very expressive gestures, and were often spectators of the effect that the role they are playing produces on the gathering."[21] On the air of "Du prévôt des marchands," they sang:

> *Déchargez votre pot au lait,*
> *La laitière charmante,*

14. Promenade on the boulevards. The scene shows Fanchon playing the hurdy-gurdy in front of a café. Engraved by Augustin de Saint-Aubin. Courtesy of the Musée des Arts Décoratifs (hereafter AD). (Number 330. See also Bn Réserve, Ef32 and CE Qb1770, Va 292, vol. 3.)

> *Et si la danse vous plaît,*
> *Que le plaisir vous tente,*
> *J'ai mon violon tout prêt*
> *Qui vous rendra contente.*[22]

The popularity of the boulevards also owed a lot to a beautiful girl named Fanchon, who befriended seigneur and singer, servant and soldier.[23] Known by all, she became a character in plays, novels, and *opéras-comiques*. She can also be seen in engravings of the boulevards. Born in Paris in 1737, Fanchon Chemin played Savoyard folk tunes on a hurdy-gurdy and sang vaudevilles by Piron and Collé to the delight of the crowds in the cabarets and along the street. Her notoriety increased when Lieutenant General Sartine ordered her to appear before the *commissaire* in 1763 and instructed her to behave with greater decency. Fanchon read the police inspector's letter publicly in the cafés. On 28 February 1767 she was incarcerated for 12 days for bad conduct and disturbing the peace. She promptly resumed her colorful career on the boulevards, however, and became such a legend that many other hurdy-gurdy players later used her name.[24] Fanchon, who married a fair merchant when she was 18 years old and raised four children, earned so much money at her trade that she was able to buy a splendid *hôtel*.

15. Costume of a cobbler. Late seventeenth century. (BN photograph 51–B7789.)

Aside from the cafés, gambling dens, brothels, and the parade of humanity, people were attracted to the boulevards by acrobatic buffoons performing on open-air *tréteaux*, carnival barkers displaying curious animals, giants, mechanical devices, *farceurs* who regaled the crowd from balconies with lewd slapstick, and a colorful array of hucksters such as the tisane peddler with his heron-feathered cap, a tin fountain on his back and two silver goblets chained to his belt, who shouted, "à la fraîche, qui veut boire?"[25] Charging 3 deniers for a few sips (he jerked the cup away quickly by the chain), he drained his portable kettle 12 to 15 times along the trek up the boulevards, earning up to 7 livres a day.[26] His clients were bemused by the witticisms, roulades, and popular rebuses that flowed from his lips as steadily as the liquid from his fountain.

The little theaters that sprang up in the 1760s and 1770s were, however, the principal attraction on the boulevards. Indeed, the grand fair tradition of farce and fantasy enjoyed its most exuberant hour in the boulevard theaters on the eve of the Revolution. Judging from the great success of these theaters, the taste for acrobatics, buffoonery, vaudevilles, and satire had not abated.[27] The *Almanach parisien's* comment that "*le beau monde* relished it [Nicolet's *spectacle*] and frequents it every day" was reiterated constantly in the press.[28] Moreover, ticket prices at such *spectacles* as the Ambigu-Comique and the Théâtre des Associés were fixed by the police in a range from 6 to 24 sous so that the general public could afford to attend, thus preventing "the dangerous consequences of idleness" and, many hoped, discouraging "la bonne compagnie" from going to a "cheap" show.[29] The earliest of these theaters, Les Grands Danseurs de Corde, exemplifies the nature of popular entertainment in pre-Revolutionary Paris. An analysis of its repertoire may help to clarify the meaning of popular culture.

Founded by Jean-Baptiste Nicolet (1726–1796)), who had taken over his father's marionette show in 1759, Les Grands Danseurs were a troupe of acrobats, dancers, actors, and musicians who performed in a wooden theater built in 1764 on the Boulevard du Temple.[30] Because the location of his theater was virtually a swamp, Nicolet had to dry out the pools of water in the street and fill in the muddy holes so that people could get into his show.[31]

Determined to restrict the Grands Danseurs to pantomime, the Comédie-Italienne complained angrily to the police and the first gentlemen of the chamber, who supervised the Italians and Comédie-Française, against Nicolet and other boulevard entertainers for doing pieces in verse, prose, and ariettes, for which the Italian players were obliged to pay the Opéra 20,000 livres annually.[32] Their campaign, which began at least as early as 1764, prompted this remark by Baron Grimm: "If one did not know our passion for exclusive privileges, one would have difficulty believing that the three *spectacles* of Paris, the Opéra, the Comédie-Française, and the Comédie-

16. Engravings seller. Engraved by G. N. Cochin fils. Courtesy of the Bibliothèque de l'Arsenal (hereafter BA). (Estampes 202, number 11.)

17. Les Petits Hollandois and acrobats of Nicolet's Grands Danseurs.
(BO, Cirque 1 (10).)

Italienne, have united against a miserable player of farces of the boulevard called Nicolet in order to prevent him from performing spoken pieces and to reduce him to pantomime."[33] The complaints resulted in a police ordinance issued on 20 April 1769 ordering Nicolet to present nothing resembling the fare of the privileged theaters. He was to confine his show to tightrope acts, pantomimes, marionettes, and *parades*. Pieces with vaudevilles and dialogue were explicitly forbidden. The orchestra was limited to 6 violins, and again a ceiling of 24 sous was placed on tickets. The artful producer responded by mocking the privileged players, which delighted his audiences, and by presenting spectacularly staged pantomimes.[34] It galled the Opéra when the Grands Danseurs staged a "heroic and burlesque pantomime" called *L'Enlèvement d'Europe*, which prompted the author of the *Mémories secrets* to declare that Nicolet's theater "is today the rival of the lyric theater and surpasses it in a very well-devised and very precise play of machines, in the magnificence of the decorations, the good taste of the costumes, the pomp of the spectacle, the number of actors, and finally by a performance of admirable perfection."[35] The Opéra tried to stop the presentation, but the lieutenant general refused on the grounds that it was just for Nicolet to be compensated for his expenditures on the production.

Although Nicolet succeeded in making pantomime a popular attraction, he was eventually able to elude the restrictions placed on the Grands Danseurs, making his *spectacle* a mixture of genres. The poster advertising his show for 20 August 1785 provides a typical representation of his fare:

> La Troupe des Grands Danseurs du Roi will present today, Thursday 1 September 1785 the fourth performance of Roi Lu, parody of Roi Lear, tragi-comedy: [*Les*] *sauteurs* will do the leaps of the carp, the eel, the bear and the lion; performing Deux Figaro, Sieur Ribié will play the role of the father and Sieur Mayeur that of the son; for the third time [*Con*] *tentement passe richesses*, proverb; Sieur Fonpré will play the role of Sans-Quartier; *l'Heureux désespoir, la Taverne enchantée, Un voleur qui vole l'autre*, pantomime with machines in five acts, very comical, with a new *divertissement*. Between acts the balance of the ladder, the little allemand, the Basque, and so on will be given. [One] will begin with *Arlequin soldat déserteur*, pantomime with machines in three acts without interval.[36]

Nicolet used many playwrights, but his favorite was Toussaint-Gaspard Taconet, whom Grimm dubbed "the Molière of the boulevard theater."[37] Taconet wrote over 50 parodies, farces, and *parades* for the Grands Danseurs and was celebrated for his portrayal of market people. Like his father, Taconet was a carpenter and was originally employed in that capacity by the Comédie-Française before becoming an actor with the Opéra-Comique.[38] He returned to carpentry after the 1762 merger of the Opéra-Comique and the Comédie-Italienne, but when the boulevard theaters appeared, he joined Nicolet's troupe as an actor and playwright. He learned how to render realistic performances of drunks, gossips, and bunglers by associating with such types in the cabarets of the boulevards, La Cortille and Les Porcherons. In works such as *Les Ecosseuses de la Halle* (produced at Nicolet's theater in May 1767)), Taconet reproduced the *poissard* slang and insulting banter of the pea shellers of the market. He depicted café proprietors, musicians, wine merchants, dancers of the boulevard, and Nicolet's theater in a play with vaudevilles entitled *Les Foux des boulevards*.[39] Nicolet's rival, Audinot, and the actresses Deschamps, Arnout, and Rosaline were represented in *Le Compliment sans compliment* (1761), the celebrated café proprietor Ramponeau in *La Mariée de la Courtille, ou Arlequin Ramponeau* (1760), and Vadé in *L'Ombre de Vadé*. Taconet's personal performances in *parades* on the outside balcony of Nicolet's theater drew crowds of 20,000 on Sundays, including ladies of high birth, who stopped their carriages to watch, and penniless tramps who jostled their betters. He even got away with satirizing an inept *commissaire*, Rochebrune. The latter protested to Lieutenant General Sartine, but the production continued.[40]

Many of Nicolet's performers, especially the acrobats, became stars of the

Parisian entertainment world. Le Petit Diable, a funambulist, became an overnight sensation when he executed a dance with eggs tied to his feet. He also did balancing acts on planks and chairs and walked a tightrope wearing wooden shoes on an inclined rope.[41] He attracted the attention of the comte d'Artois, who hired the Diable to teach him the art of funambulism, establishing a vogue at court.[42] Le Beau Dupuis, a funambulist who later fell to his death, was celebrated for his somersaults over a burning plank, leaps over a racing horse, and springboard vaults over a pyramid of 12 men.[43] An abandoned child like many of the popular entertainers, Dupuis won the court's approbation after a performance at Choisy-le-Roi in 1772. The king was so impressed by Nicolet's troupe that he gave them the title of Spectacle des Grands Danseurs et Sauteurs du Roi.

Alexandre-Placide Bussart, who wrote pantomimes with what might be called acrobatic choreography for Nicolet, was often featured in the advertisements of the Grands Danseurs, which called attention to his "leap over a ribbon strung six feet in the air, flips from one side of the theater to the other, and a rope dance swinging a flag bearing the arms of France."[44] A Polish acrobat did a balancing act on a chariot rolling on an iron wire.[45] The illustrious equilibrist Joseph Brunn pushed a child in a wheelbarrow along an iron wire.[46] Mr. and Mrs. Storkinfeld danced the Hungarian onion in high boots and spurs.[47] Nicolet's eight Spanish tumblers and dancers performed carrying wooden batons two feet long and wearing sonorous buckles strapped to their wrists.[48] During the contredanses, they unleashed a shower of baton blows, twisting their arms in every direction. The dance was executed in such a way that the batons struck the wrist buckles in perfect cadence without injuring the dancers.

One of Nicolet's star performers was a monkey named Turcot, who not only performed on the tightrope but also as a character in *parades* on the balcony over the entrance to Nicolet's theater. He became famous for his parody of the celebrated actor Molet, whose maladies he mimicked wearing a nightcap and slippers.[49] A stanza from a popular song of the time commemorated his mimicry:

> *L'animal, un peu libertin,*
> *Tombe malade un beau matin,*
> *Voilà tout Paris dans la peine:*
> *On crut voir la mort de Turenne,*
> *Ce n'était pourtant que Molet*
> *Ou le singe de Nicolet.*[50]

In an age bathed in an ocean of criticism, Nicolet's performers and his shows had their share of shrill detractors. Mayeur de Saint-Paul found his players to be as unbridled on the streets as the rest of the boisterous boulevard crowd.

> If one did not know these people to be Nicolet's *danseurs de corde*, one would think he was in the woods in the midst of assassins when one encounters them on the boulevards. Pantaloons, long frock coats, a large cloak, uneven hat, curled-up hair in a braid, a fat, knotty stick in hand, that is the attire of these gentlemen; to insult everyone, to injure whomever they must, to create an uproar at the places of all the wine merchants of the rampart, to get drunk with scoundrels, that is their conduct.[51]

Rétif de la Bretonne was the most abrasive critic of Nicolet's show and his audience. He called the *spectacle* "a monstrous heap of things that astonish, . . . a chaos that the spirit can not unravel and that is only appropriate to divert this species of spectators who only see mechanically and who understand nothing."[52] Contending that Nicolet's gross farces were "appropriate to a certain class of citizens," Rétif, nonetheless, was concerned that Nicolet was making too great an impression on artisans. His criticisms were echoed by Alexandre Du Coudray, who accused Nicolet of perpetuating "bad taste, the obscene genre, . . . and shameful morals," and by Louis Gachet, who castigated the dances of "men disguised as women who execute some roulades and turns" that "have offended urban spectators."[53] But the critics could not stifle the mounting popularity of the boulevard shows. Bachaumont, who claimed Nicolet had earned over 100,000 écus by 1769, wrote of the "public ardor" for Nicolet. "Women of the greatest distinction," he declared, "are infatuated with his indecent *parades*."[54]

Were the perceptions of Rétif, Du Coudray, and others that Nicolet's *spectacles* were obscene and immoral accurate? Thirty-eight pieces have been selected at random from the years 1763 to 1789. They give us a picture of Nicolet's repertoire. Although not every year is represented (the largest number sampled for any single year was 3), there are gaps of no more than two years in this sample. Twenty-eight of the plays exist only in manuscript, and 27 are anonymous. The 9 identifiable authors include Dorville, Taconet, Fagnier, Mayeur de Saint-Paul, Pleinchesne, Vadé, Arnould, Beaunoir, and Dorvigny.

Although the type of genre is indicated for 32 productions, there does not appear to have been much variation in Nicolet's repertoire over the years. Ten are designated farces, or some variation such as *farce bouffonne* and *ambigu farce*; eight bear the label of comedy; seven were *parades*; six were called pantomimes, or some variation such as *ballet pantomime melé de dialogue*, *pantomime avec vaudevilles*, and *pantomime arlequinade*. One piece was designated an *opéra-comique*. Like the early fair entertainers, the Grands Danseurs relied heavily on visual communication through slapstick, stunts, gesture, and dance, but most productions had dialogue and song as well. Rustic places and enchanted isles were the favored settings (13 pieces); others included boutiques, cafés, shops, châteaus, and the streets.

Sorting out the characters depicted on Nicolet's stage with special attention to their occupations presents many problems. In several instances, the character's socioeconomic status is not indicated and is impossible to guess. It is not always possible to distinguish between artisans and merchants or between apprentices and employees. A special category of people with service jobs could be established to separate them from other types of workers although the former greatly outnumber the latter. Traditional *opéra-comique* characters such as Arlequin, Colombine, Gilles, Colin, and Isabelle, who appeared in more plays (14) than any other type of character, are presented sometimes just as themselves whereas in other productions they have designated occupational roles. It is necessary to establish a miscellaneous category that includes characters who appear frequently as well as ones who appear only once or twice. This diverse group includes coquettes, foreigners, slaves, corsairs, virgins, lechers, and thieves.

Despite these problems, the characters in Nicolet's plays can be analyzed. The largest category was nobles, who appeared in 14 of the 38 productions examined. Sometimes they were lampooned, especially when identified as Gascons or when they used their wealth and rank to press an unwilling girl into marriage. More often, however, they are treated sympathetically, often acting as beneficient arbiters in village imbroglios. Artisans, including millers, forgers, wigmakers, tailors, cobblers, and pastry chefs, figured in 12 of the 38 pieces. The same number of plays depicted people in the arts and letters and in the professions, such as doctors, judges, and teachers. Twelve productions also featured workers—woodcutters, washerwomen, chimney sweeps, fishwives, stable keepers, café waiters, gardeners, and peasants. Along with nobles, characters from these three categories were, thus, the ones most frequently used by the playwrights whom Nicolet employed.

In descending order of frequency, servants including lackeys and valets appeared in 11 plays. Three character types were each presented in 9 pieces: officials (bailiffs, *commissaires*, tax assessors and collectors, process servers); merchants (florists, perfume sellers, café proprietors, ribbon sellers); and gods, demons, ogres, fairies, and magicians. Soldiers and clerks were each depicted in five plays, and abbés and apprentices each in two. Several plays included many characters of the same type such as servants and merchants.

What observations can be drawn from these data? First, the characters familiar to fair audiences in the early part of the century reappeared on stage at the Grands Danseurs. They had simply migrated from the Opéra-Comique to the boulevards. Secondly, though the folk of the Parisian streets, the village bumpkins, the *garçons* and *coquettes*, and the Arlequins were as numerous as ever, there was a noticeable decline in the frequency of super-human creatures from the early fair shows to the boulevard *spectacles*. Some plays were still set in exotic, utopian lands, and magic still played a role in boulevard theater, but fewer productions involved these elements than in the early years of marketplace theater. Thirdly, although nobles figured in more of Nicolet's pieces than any other character type, when workers, apprentices, clerks, and servants are grouped together, *le bas peuple* emerge as the prepon-derant group on Nicolet's stage. Adding artisans and petty merchants further swells the ranks. Moreover, workers, artisans, merchants, clerks, and ser-vants were always treated sympathetically, if humorously, whereas mockery and derision were usually reserved for officials and professionals. Boulevard theater still pitted the cultural world of ordinary people against an establish-ment of wealth and power.

Did the thematic material of these plays also reveal the celebration of marketplace culture? More than half (20) of the plays examined revolved around ridicule of established society and of a range of recognizable social types, forming the largest thematic category of the productions.[55] A procur-ator was the principal victim of derision in La Bourbonnaise (1719).[56] Two plays entitled *L'Avant-souper* (1770 and 1774) mocked the life-style of the urban aristocrat, especially the cheeky, fast-living sons of robe and sword aristocrats who, roving from loge to loge, made a spectacle of themselves in the theaters.[57] A lecherous tutor was the object of scorn in *Le Bal masqué* (1775), as was a fat, boorish Gascon marquis in *Arlequin amant et valet* (n.d.); both were favorite boulevard characters.[58] *L'Apoticaire ou la nupce grivoise* (1768) mocked a master apothecary called Anodin.[59] He was caned by a coal merchant, a wigmaker, a young girl, and a bourgeoise for prescribing drugs that killed members of their families. *Arlequin aux fêtes flamandes* (1767) pitted a seigneur, his friend Valère, and his valet Arlequin against a vindictive bailiff who forbade dancing in a village because one of the peasant women refused to let her daughter marry him.[60]

In *L'Avantageux puni* (1786), the target was a penniless, city-dwelling marquis seeking to marry a baron's daughter for her money.[61] His plan was to get her dowry, then leave her to her parents and return to Paris. A simple villager, Dinval, who loved Julie, the baron's daughter, argued his moral beliefs with the marquis, who called honor a chimera, reason a foolish mask, virtue a meaningless title, and fidelity a useless word used by the elderly. The play also depicted the contrast between the marquis, who turned the baron's grounds into an English garden and made love to his wife, and the coarse baron who rose at sunup, protected his peasants, treated women honorably, cultivated the earth, and gave assistance to the unfortunate. The marquis described his life-style in these lines:

Do you wish to be admired? . . . you show yourself at promenades, or heap ridicule on someone; you arrive at the *spectacle* and make a big noise to attract attention; you enter all the loges, even though you have nothing to say; you remain only long enough to display a new suit: you appear in the foyer, speak your view on the new opera, whether you have seen it or not; then you encounter a friend on the staircase, the crowd surrounds you, you tell your secrets loudly, you recall an affair or invent one, you pull out your watch, call your lackeys, are impatient at their slowness, you leave the friend or call him back to ask if he saw the baroness, you announce some charming retreat where you saw her, where, to put it better, you trick the stylish beauties, you relate the story of two or three well-known girls; if there is nothing to tell about them, you invent some scandalous anecdote about them. . . . Then you arrange a supper with a few dancers, charming society! Not spiritual, but playful, ravishing for only two hours. You eat; you leave these ladies, you go to the academy, you play, lose, fret, you fight sometimes, you wound or are wounded, it is the same thing, you go home, you sleep late, you get up at noon, and the next day you start all over again. That is the charming life of which you provincials have not the least idea.

Enraged by the marquis' attitude toward women, Dinval reasoned that if rich aristocrats did not seduce females with gifts and promises about the future, all, regardless of class, would be honorable. Dinval, of course, wins Julie, a victory of the nobility of virtuous character over urban aristocratic pretension, hypocrisy, and vice.

These sketches of pieces of Nicolet's repertoire reveal that characters drawn from the upper social ranks—the urban aristocracy, professional people, and especially officials—were all fair targets of the derisive mockery of the boulevard theater. So were merchants and artisans, who are often difficult to tell apart. Poets and musicians were usually depicted as ridiculous and pretentious, fawning over their aristocratic patrons. Intellectuals were always either pedants or charlatans. A distinction was made between the hardworking, well-meaning country seigneur and the dissipated, immoral dandy of the city. Officials of the Crown were never portrayed, but the boulevard writers showed no mercy toward tax men, procurators, and bailiffs. They were corrupt, unjust, mercenary, and lecherous. It was evident what kinds of people, behavior, and values boulevard audiences wanted to see lampooned. Behind the stereotypes lay the people of the real world whom the people of the streets had to accommodate and serve. The distinctions of rank on the boulevard stage were real. On the stage, however, the villains always lost. Nicolet's theater was rife with duped nobles and imprisoned officials, providing the fantasy of victory for the virtuous little people.

Who were the heroes? The last play mentioned above, *L'Avantageux puni*, points to a second thematic category that identifies the heroes: the idea that actual distinctions of rank are artificial; that true nobility arises from virtuous behavior; and that happiness stems from ordinary domestic existence, hard work, honesty, and fidelity. Sixteen of the 38 plays examined involve that theme.

In *Arlequin récompensé ou la justice des dieux* (n.d.), a sharp contrast is drawn between a wealthy seigneur, Damelas, and an impoverished shepherd, Arlequin, who is denied the hand of Damelas' daughter.[62] Seeking to verify the humanity of men, Jupiter and Mercury descend to earth dressed as indigents. Requesting shelter at Damelas' residence, they are turned away by his servant Pierrot because his master does not "receive people of their kind." After Damelas slams the door on the disguised gods, the generous Arlequin welcomes them at his humble cabin, where they sleep on an earthen floor. That night Damelas recognizes his mistake when the gods appear to him in luminous garb in a dream, but it is too late: Jupiter and Mercury destroy Damelas' house with a thunderclap and transform Arlequin's hut into a palace. Arlequin's generous nature has not changed, however; he tosses the palace keys to Damelas, taking as his sole prize the seigneur's daughter.

Beaunoir's *Jeannette* (1781) recounts the misfortunes of two servants who are mistreated by their employers and abused by a *commissaire*.[63] A clerk proclaims the moral of the play in the final lines: "Is this servant a slave or a citizen? All tasks in society are respected and balanced; the more the servant has duties to fulfill toward his master, the more he acquires rights to his master's kindness, from which it follows that the master should never mistreat him." A rich iron merchant from Limoges, who is depicted as a boorish clod, insults the workers in a village inn in *Le Quiproquo* (1780).[64] When one tries to help him with his bag, the merchant screams: "Learn, animal, that I am neither a foreigner nor a fool. I am Léonard, Master of Forges from Uzerche in Limousin. I have one of my *garçons* to serve me; hence, I do not need to pay a rascal who is useless. Give me a room and after that, go to the devil." The merchant, who unsuccessfully tries to force his affections on a girl from the village, is contrasted sharply with a soldier staying at the inn who is of mediocre rank and fortune, but an honest man with a "good heart."

Most of *Arlequin déserteur dans les isles* is a nonsensical farce about the adventures of Arlequin and his companion Thibaut on an island ruled by a queen and populated by sensual girls and cold, lazy men.[65] The piece has an interesting denouement, however, and some striking lines about work as a symbol of nobility. Thibaut sings:

> *Après de moi que l'laboureur*
> *est noble autant comm'son seigneur.*
> *La terre est mère de tous les hommes,*
> *le laboureur est d'tous les rangs,*

> *et l'on a vu des gentilshommes*
> *labourer eux-mêmes leurs champs.*

Arlequin endorses the principle of social equality, and in the end he and Thibaut win over the queen, who obliges all the inhabitants to work in the useful arts.

The nobility of work and the simple life were graphically set forth in *Arlequin fendeur* (1777).[66] Robert, a farmer, ties Arlequin, a servant, to a tree to be eaten by wild animals because he has dared to woo Colombine, whom Robert has promised to Pierrot, a miller. Woodcutters rescue Arlequin, however, and take him to their camp, where his potential as a woodsman is tested by the master and his cousins. Cousin Hermite instructs Arlequin in the code of the workers: They help each other and the less fortunate. They subsist on black bread and water. "Drink this cup of water; it is the drink given us by nature. He who will be content with this nourishment will be the richest and happiest of men because he will never know poverty." After teaching Arlequin how to cut wood, the hermit initiates him into the fraternity of cutters, whose motto is "work and humanity." In the final act, Arlequin and the woodsmen save Robert from thieves, and Arlequin disdainfully refuses Robert's money as a reward.

Finally, in *Le Père Duchesne, ou la mauvaise habitude* (1789), Dorvigny contrived a genuinely humorous portrait of a gruff, ill-mannered, warmhearted stove setter named Duchesne who cleans the chimneys of a marquis' château.[67] The marquise's chambermaid, Lucille, loves the coarse Duchesne, but fears he will prove offensive to her noble employers, whose consent to marriage they must obtain. Duchesne refuses to alter his manner on the grounds that affecting polish would make him like everyone else. In the interview, Duchesne's rival, Gilotin, the marquis' valet, affects politeness as Lucille pokes her lover every time he lapses into salty language, much to the marquis' amusement. Duchesne gets quite carried away when asked to talk about his career as a seaman, which included firing a canon:

> Tout aussitôt pan! pan! patapan! pan! v'là notre artillerie qui fait un feu d'enfer! et le Triomphant dans le beau milieu de la fumée et du sabat! . . . Et notre Capitaine qu'était un b . . . un *b* . . . un brave homme intrépide tout-a-fait qui était en avant en chemise le pistolet à la main; et qui nous criait à pleine tête . . . *Allons sacr* . . . allons enfant! *f* . . . feu babord! . . . *F* . . .feu tribord. Tombez moi dessus *ces b* . . . ah! *mille nom d' un triple!* Ah! *f* . . . .

The marquise shouts that Duchesne is mad, and Gilotin is convinced he has won when the marquis rebukes Duchesne for not respecting their condition. Infuriated, the cursing chimney sweep protests that he would rather lose than be a fop; that he must be himself and use his own language. In the final scene,

Duchesne apologizes to the marquise but loses his temper at Gilotin, calling him a bastard and an imbecile. The marquis and his wife agree to the marriage, however, on the grounds that his trade never enabled him to learn good manners and "it is better to be brusque and kind than polite and bad-hearted."

Sexuality in various forms constitutes the third major category of thematic material in Nicolet's plays. Eighteen of his productions deal with adultery, promiscuity, seduction, abduction, loss of virginity, prostitution, debauchery, and lechery or a combination of these. Usually, these matters form part of a satire on the morality and frivolous amusements of *le monde*. In *Les Aventures du Gascon aux boulevards* (n.d.), for example, the chevalier de Rapigac recounts his adventures to Blaisac, a renter of chairs, among effeminate *petits-maîtres* and amorous abbés in the salons and *spectacles*.[68] Realizing that rich married women who do not have lovers are "du mauvais ton," the penniless marquis takes up with a lady named Lucinde de Mont-fardée, who accompanies him to the boulevards and feigns great wealth. He soon learns, however, that she is a cobbler's daughter and that she has gone off to a house of ill-repute with two horsemen. It is perhaps worth noting that the only portion of this play that was censored is a scene involving the theft of Rapigac's watch. He complains to a sergeant, who advises him to imitate the thief because "it is the adventure of the boulevards."

La Bourbonnaise (1769) concerns the abduction by an abbé of an inn-keeper's daughter from Vichy and her instruction in Paris in the art of coquetry by a prostitute named Mademoiselle Des Usages.[69] In *La Colique* a lecherous old teacher named Cassandre tries to trick his young pupil, Isabelle, into marrying him by convincing her that marriage is the only cure for her vapors.[70] Feigning colic, Isabelle dupes Cassandre into summoning the village surgeon with whom she elopes. Finally, in *Colinette ou la vigne d'amour*, Amour gives Colin a magic vine, which will enable him to seduce Colinette: "If the first arrow with which love is aroused causes a few tears, pleasure will soon dry them," Rosette assures Colinette, who fears that the vine will be bitter, that the second taste is delicious. Colinette's mother, Simone, warns her that if she tastes a single grape from the vine, she will lose her "basket" (*panier*) and will not be able to face the villagers. Encouraged by Amour, Colinette cuts the vine with Colin's pruning knife and enjoys the "innocent pleasure" of love.

Several of the plays included in this sample satirize life on the boulevards and Parisian fads. *Le Bal de Passy* mocks intellectuals who admire the English, and *La Tante dupée* makes fun of the French taste for gallantry. The rage of ballooning that struck Paris in 1783 after the first manned ascent in the Tuileries gardens is the subject of *Arlequin volant* and of many other boulevard productions. The popularity of waux-halls and of lotteries is the thematic material of *Le Wauxhall des Porcherons ou la lotterie. L'Avant-souper* and other pieces satirize the aristocracy's enjoyment of after-theater suppers. *Arlequin amant et valet* contains references to seduction in the gardens of the Palais-Royal, the most popular spot in Paris in the late 1780s. The Opéra is ridiculed in *Arlequin au diable,* and *filles d'opéra* figure in some productions. *Le Fou par amour* even treats the still popular belief in the medicinal power of music. The scant attention, however, to competition among the Parisian theaters and the persistence of privilege is striking when compared to the early decades of the Opéra-Comique. Only three plays of those sampled refer to theatrical matters. It is also noteworthy that there was a decline in the marvelous, a staple ingredient in early *opéra-comiques.* Only eight plays involved magic, utopias, gods, or sorcery.

Only ten of the plays in manuscript in this sample showed evidence of the censor's pen, and none of the material eliminated changed the plays in a substantive way. The most heavily censored play was *Le Bal de Passy* (1767), which was evidently held up for two years before being performed in 1769. In addition to eradicating the words *beszée* and *Roi,* the censors eliminated a long passage in which an author, M. de Rimedure, attacks the playwrights, actors, and dramatic taste of the day. Doubtless the censors recognized and protected well-known authors. Sections were also cut in which Rimedure was criticized for copying everything bad and nothing good about the English character, a country gentleman said he bowed only to the king, and two boutique girls talked about being ravaged by a lecher, becoming prostitutes, and seducing a procurator's clerk.

Love's complaint that he is no longer welcome at court was scratched out of *Colinette ou la vigne d'amour,* a seduction scene was eliminated in *Arlequin volant,* and passages dealing with the authenticity of a noble title and mockery of a judge were deleted from *Le Voyage de Figaro.* A widow's comment about her husband's being a good lover was eliminated from *Les Scènes de l'amour sont de tout âge* (1772): "Je vous assure qu'il remplissoit bien les devoirs marital et surtout de la manière que je l'aimois."[72]

In *Le Voyage de Scaramouche et d'Arlequin,* Crébillon cut a passage in which a doctor, after hearing Scaramouche say that he liked sex after eating, declares that nothing is more unnatural. The word *pillé* used by a girl in the play was scratched, and when Arlequin tells the girl he wants to make love, Crébillon changed the phrase to "to please you."[73] "Quelques filles de hazard" was deleted from *Arlequin aux fêtes flamandes,* as well as a bailiff's line about girls wanting to please him: "Elles se précipiteront sous moi."[74] Finally, all the concluding vaudeville couplets in *L'Ecole villageoise* are inked out and are unreadable.

From this we can conclude that the lieutenant general of police or the censor selected from the Comédie-Française or the Comédie-Italienne cut two kinds of passages: sexually suggestive words or expressions and pejorative references to royalty or to high-ranking nobles, officials, and authors. There was no consistency in the first type of censorship. The plays abound in sexual innuendo, most of which the censor passed. In addition, the actors were probably quite explicit in their visual posturing. Nor was much consistency maintained in the second type of censorship. Nobles and officials were mocked and ridiculed with great regularity in Nicolet's productions. It seems likely that the censors recognized specific individuals in the few instances where they eliminated passages.

No doubt, censorship was lax because the police had no desire to stifle a form of entertainment that kept the public diverted. Furthermore, the censors from the great theaters were primarily interested in preventing the boulevard troupes from presenting or imitating the classical repertoire. They wanted Nicolet's shows to be episodic and vulgar on the mistaken assumption that this would deter *le monde* from attending them. Finally, the dramatists who wrote for the Grands Danseurs were quite aware of the kinds of material that the censors objected to. It is probable, therefore, that they exercised self-censorship.

Nicolet's principal rival on the Boulevard du Temple was Nicolas-Médard Audinot, who received permission from Lieutenant General Sartine in 1768 to open a *spectacle*.[75] Audinot was born in 1732, the son of a singer in the cathedral chapter in the town of Bourmont in Lorraine. He learned music from his father but went to Paris at an early age to become his brother's apprentice in barbering and wigmaking. In 1756 he was employed as a musician in the duc de Gramont's household. His brother's clients got him a job at the Opéra-Comique in 1758, where he proved such a success as a writer, composer, and actor that the Comédie-Italienne retained him after the merger in 1762. Baron Grimm wrote at the time that Audinot "is without contradiction the greatest comedian that there is in Europe."[76] His *opéra-comique Le Tonnelier* became a staple of the Italian repertoire. In 1763 he joined a private theatrical company formed by the prince de Conti that gave performances at Conti's château on the Île-Adam. Following a brief, successful return to the Comédie-Italienne in 1764, where he was a hit in *Blaise le savetier*, he resigned for good because he was given only secondary roles, many of his plays were rejected, and the theater would not hire his daughter, Eulalie.[77]

After a brief term in 1767 as the director of a *spectacle* at Versailles, Audinot launched a marionette show at the Saint-Germain fair, where he gained his revenge on the Italians by presenting each puppet as a performer of the privileged theater. He brought his marionettes to the boulevard in 1769. Renting some land owned by Nicolet at the angle of the present Boulevard Voltaire and the Avenue de la République, he built a rather strange-looking theater with Gothic vaults and columns.[78] The police soon permitted him to substitute child performers for puppets. Ranging in age from 6 to 17, these youths (29 in all) played the familiar roles of Arlequin, the abbé, the pedant, the soldier, and the peasant; and they, too, were taught to mock the Italian players. Audinot put this play on words on his curtain: "*Sicut infantes audi nos.*"[79] Partisans of the Ambigu defended Audinot's use of children on the grounds that his theater served as a school for players who one day might join the the Comédie-Française.[80] Although the lieutenant general of police believed that children were not robust enough to endure the strain of working at the Ambigu, his reservations were not sufficiently strong to impel him to stop the show or to prevent him from ordering Audinot to take his *spectacle* to the Saint-Ovide fair.[81] Nor did he act to stop Audinot from abusing the children and treating the actresses as his personal harem.[82]

The Ambigu-Comique, as Audinot dubbed his *spectacle* in 1774, was such an immediate success that the privileged players moved quickly to circumscribe it. The Opéra forbade song, dance, and an orchestra; the Comédie-Française ruled out declamation; and the Comédie-Italienne denied Audinot the use of vaudevilles and ariettes. Audinot fell back, therefore, on pantomime plays, a genre in which he and his troupe attained great skill and that captivated the theater public. Simon-Nicolas-Henri Linguet regarded Audinot's mime as superior to the ballet at the Opéra by the celebrated Noverre and declared: "He has realized with child actors, whose talents were due to him alone, an aspect of the incredible things that the ancients tell us about *Mimes* and that we regard as absurd tales; he has drawn tears, evoked terror, admiration; he has produced all the effects that often fail at the great theaters and in the best pieces."[83] Gradually, of course, Audinot introduced spoken comedies and music despite the protests of the privileged theaters.

The Ambigu-Comique owed its great popularity in the early months of its existence to the clerks of the Parlement of Paris and the Châtelet who came there in droves. Ticket prices of 12 and 24 sous made the Ambigu as accessible to the lower ranks of society as Nicolet's Danseurs.[84] Moreover, ladies of the court also began coming regularly to the Ambigu. Bachaumont lamented that the crowd of libertines, loose women, and idlers at the Ambigu had attracted people of higher station: "This society has drawn another sort. Women of the court, who in this capacity think they are above all prejudice, have not disdained to appear there, and this theater is the rage of the day. It is even more frequented than Nicolet in the time of his monkey."[85] In 1772, Madame du Barry invited Audinot's troupe to perform for the king at Choisy-le-Roi, and the prince de Soubise brought them to Saint-Ouen. The triple bill on both occasions was *La Guinguette* by Pleinchesne, *Il n'y a plus d'enfants* by Nougaret, and *Le Chat-botté* by Arnould. Thus even a show of the lowest rank was deemed fit for a king. Audinot was permitted to state on his posters that his troupe had performed at court.

The name Audinot chose for his theater was most appropriate. It was so named, according to one observer, because "a mixture of *opéras-comiques*, farces, and pantomimes are presented there and because its nature is ambiguous."[86] His dramatic farce was varied. Genres were mixed. During an evening at the Ambigu, one witnessed a farrago of gesture, spectacle, parody, dance, satire, song, burlesque, and banter. Audinot had no alternative in following this inventive, if episodic, sort of entertainment because the censors, Préville for the Comédie-Française and Dehesse for the Comédie-Italienne, altered his pieces and those written for his theater by François-Mussot Arnould, Roger-Timothée-Regnarde de Pleinchesne, Jean-Julien Renout, Pierre Jean Baptiste Nougaret, and others.[87] Unconcerned about the morality of Audinot's productions, the censors sought only to ensure that they bore no resemblance to works in their repertoire and that they had no dramatic unity, coherence, style, or logic. When they spotted a good piece, they either suppressed it or made "pitiless cuts."[88] In other words, as was the case with Nicolet, censorship was a device to keep theatrical cultures separate, and, it was hoped, to segregate taste publics.

Using censorship in this way angered many theatergoers of the time. Mercier complained that because the privileged players insist that only they have the right to perform "reasonable pieces" and are upheld by the authorities, "the people are condemned to hear only the expression of licentiousness and foolishness."[89] The censors, he charged, make themselves the arbiters of public morality, denying moral standards to the very people "who have the greatest need to receive some salutary instruction."[90] For Mercier, thus, and for many contemporaries, freedom from censorship would upgrade the people's theater. It would enable it to be "reasonable" and instructive, which is what many defenders of boulevard theater wanted it to become. Making the pieces of Audinot and Nicolet edifying and instructive would be the final justificaton of a theater for the *menu peuple*. But it would break a cultural barrier defended by the grand theaters and upheld by the high courts of justice.

Faced with censorship and the invocation of privilege, Audinot made the most of his situation. He relied on the vogue of spectacular pantomime productions, and he took advantage of his apparent influence with highly placed persons (Campardon refers to "high protections")[91] to incorporate speech, music, and dance, however episodically used, in his pieces. In fact, Audinot discovered that censorship worked to his advantage: "he was astonished to see that on leaving the hands of the mutilator, his pieces were only made better and were more relished by the public."[92] One observer attributed this to the fact that the appeal of obscene gesticulation and equivocation was enhanced by being executed by innocent children.[93]

A careful analysis of Audinot's repertoire is impossible because so many of the works were pantomimes and not many of the instructions for these or the texts of works in prose or verse survive. A general impression of his pieces can be derived, however, from the texts that do remain, descriptions of his pieces by contemporaries, and the lists of titles and genres in newspapers and almanacs.

The pantomimes, Audinot's speciality, were usually staged in spectacular fashion, making full use of ballet, music, stage effects, and occasional insertions of dialogue and song. The subject matter ran the spectrum from allegory, fable, and history to farce and parody. Audinot, along with Noverre at the Opéra, seemed to Parisian audiences to be reviving a lost art of antiquity, one full of marvelous invention. An English observer perhaps captured the enthusiasm best:

> Nevertheless, it is not necessary to imagine that a *ballet pantomime* in France resembles anything like our *divertissements* of this genre in which an Arlequin, a *pantalon*, a Frenchman, and a clown are charged with making the spectators laugh, except when the decorations provoke the applause of the public. The French *ballet pantomime* consists neither in the enchantments produced by Arlequin's magic wand, nor in the grotesque postures, bizarre positions and lascivious cadences of the dance. The drama is simple, regular, and moving. The action, though mute, is animated and perfectly intelligible in each of its feats, as variable as they are. In this genre of *spectacle* which Noverre first introduced on the French stage, but which had been cultivated successfully in Rome by Bathyllus and Pylade, feelings are expressed as much by the dance step as by looks; each posture rouses the attention of the spectator, takes possession of his soul, enflames him to the point of indignation or moves him to tenderness and pity. Such is the power of the pantomime dancer over the passions that people of refined taste and exquisite sensibility prefer this genre of *divertissement* to the most moving scenes of the tragic muse.[94]

The pantomines at the Ambigu are so difficult to classify that one has the impression that either Audinot or the newspapers simply made up short genre-characterizations for these works, all of which were variations on a theme. The *Journal de Paris*, for example, referred to *Le prince noir et blanc* as a "pantomime à spectacle, mélée de dialogue, féerie en deux actes."[95] *L'Empirique* was descibed as a "pièce épisodique en un acte avec un divertissement pantomime."[96] The *Journal* called *Des Rapsodies ou Arlequin cochon de lait* a "pantomime with machines *pour rire* in which a menagerie of live animals of several species, a giant, and a devil will appear, all interspersed with dialogues, mascarades, and divertissements."[97] One piece, a pantomime mixed with dialogue called *Le Géant désarmé par l'amour*, featured a real giant, 7 feet 2 inches tall. The role of Love was played by a child 3 feet, 1 inch.[98]

Most of Audinot's early pantomimes were farces. The one he chose for the king to see at Choisy-le-Roi—*Le Chat-botté*—will suffice to suggest their character. Although there was no dialogue in Arnould's pantomime, the author published a program outlining the plot. When three peasants living in a hamlet in a wheat field decide to share their goods, the oldest receives a mill; the second, an ass; and the youngest, Guillot, a puss-in-boots.[99] Despite the cat's affection, the young peasant is unhappy with his share until the cat proves his worth. When Puss delivers a letter from Guillot to Lise, the seigneur's daughter, two thieves appear, one leading an ass, the other carrying a braided coat. They rob the seigneur. The cat disrupts the theft, however, by putting a thistle under the ass's tail, causing the animal to buck wildly, break his halter, and run into the woods. Forgetting their booty, the thieves chase the ass, but the cat leads them astray. In the meantime, Guillot arrives at the seigneur's house dressed in the braided coat. Puss-in-Boots announces him. Reapers and woodcutters gather for a festive dance before leaving for the hunt. While strolling through the countryside, the seigneur, Lise, and Guillot find themselves in the peasants' hamlet, where Puss-in-Boots chases a mouse up a tree. A fairy emerges from the tree thanking the cat for setting her free, and, on Puss's request, she erects a château on the spot for the cat's master, who takes Lise's hand in marriage. As the fairy serves a banquet and the peasants dance, Puss-in-Boots, mounted on the thieves' ass, executes a dance to express his joy at Guillot's good fortune.

Performed over two hundred times and revived several times, Audinot's three-act pantomime, *Dorothée*, was doubtless the most popular work ever produced at the Ambigu-Comique.[100] Produced a decade after *Le Chat-botté*, this pantomime was a serious piece, bereft of the buffoonery that marked Audinot's earlier productions. In the first act of *Dorothée*, the apparently unwed heroine, who has a child by her lover Trémouille, rebuffs the advances of the mayor of Milan. Jealous of her lover and furious at Dorothée, the mayor threatens her with legal action and summons archers to drag her off to jail. The second act finds Dorothée chained to a stone bench beneath a pillar in a dungeon. The mayor threatens to put the girl to death unless she will submit to him, which she refuses to do. The act ends tearfully as her child, who has come to console her and to plead for her life, is pried from his mother's arms. Act three takes place in a public square where a placard announces that Dorothée will be thrown onto a funeral pyre unless she is saved by a brave knight. As the officers of the court and guardsmen arrive, Dunois, a knight, rushes to defend Dorothée, who shows him a small portrait of Trémouille, vowing her eternal fidelity to him. Recognizing her lover as his best friend, Dunois swears to avenge the outrage the innocent girl has suffered and to defend his friend's honor. In a fierce combat Dunois slays the chief of the guards and his troops, but he is impaled on the stake in the process. As he and Dorothée are about to be burned, Trémouille rushes in to save them. The mayor lunges at Trémouille with a dagger, but he hurtles into the flames as the lovers are reunited.

In addition to melodramatic pantomimes like *Dorothée* and burlesque pantomimes like *Le Chat-botté*, Audinot presented comedies, some in pantomime, satirizing the social fads of the day, and parodies of well-known operas and dramas. The swirl of controversy in the press during the 1770s over Gluck's so-called reform operas was delightfully satirized at the Ambigu.[101] Nearly everyone in Paris, it seemed, suddenly became an authority on opera and joined the partisans of Gluck or his Italian rival Piccini. In Audinot's play *La Musicomanie* (1779), which became one of the most popular pieces in this repertoire, the central characters are a German music master, Baron de Steinbak, and his student, Double-Croche, who, to please his master, must learn to play the violin, flute, organ, bassoon, double bass, oboe, kettledrum, clarinet, clavecin, hunting horn, hurdy-gurdy, and fife.[102] The baron vents his wrath on Léandre (who wants to become his lackey in order to seduce his daughter, Isabelle) because the only thing he can play is a comb. When the baron scolds Isabelle for not practicing the clavecin enough, her maid defends the girl by informing the baron that Isabelle has the coiffure of Iphigénie, the shoes of Olympiade, and the collar of Armide—all, of course, the subjects of operas. When the baron returns in anger from a concert complaining about the obscure style, the bad taste, and the loud whistles of the audience, Anodin, an apothecary, prepares a remedy that will make his ears less sensitive to the piercing sounds of modern music. Claiming that he has the original harmony, that of the pestles, in his boutique, Anodin sings a song he has composed:

> *Petit lait pour Mademoiselle;*
> *Un clistère pour son papa;*
> *Sirop d'orgeat pour Isabelle;*
> *Sirop d'opium pour son papa;*
> *Un demi lock pour Euphrosine,*
> *Pour Isabelle un lock entier,*
> > *Pour purifier*
> > *Pour fortifier*
> *Son petit coeur at sa poitrine.*
> *Rhubarbe et casse pour les gens.*
> *Total quatre-vingt quinze francs.*

Mocking Piccini, Audinot introduces an Italian musician named Vacarmini who promises the baron that he will carry out the necessary revolution in

France by using music to " paint the passions" to the point that the French will be made "to spit blood" and that he will depict all the battles of Alexander in his operas, the history of France in his *opéras-comiques*, and the *Encyclopédie* in his vaudevilles. The only plot in *La Musicomanie* is Léandre's attempt to learn music from Double-Croche in order to secure a position in the baron's household so he can seduce Isabelle. Léandre finally succeeds when he proposes that the baron found a school in which children will be trained in music from the cradle; they will sing but never speak. The baron gives his daughter to Léandre in order to produce children for the school, and the baron's student marries Isabelle's maid, Euphrosine, to enrich the school with little double-croches (semiquavers).

Many observers of the Parisian theatrical scene began to notice in the mid-1780s a change in Audinot's repertoire from satire and burlesque to more serious pieces with moral messages. Their perception was correct. In Gabiot de Salins' *Esope aux boulevards* (1784), for example, Esope, representing wisdom, uses fables to disabuse a misanthropist of his cynicism about human nature.[103] Lucas, Esope explains, cultivated a tree with just one peach on it. Although the rest of the tree was ugly and useless, the single peach made it worth caring for; in time there would be others. Defects must be tolerated for virtue to exist.

Audinot's own play *Le Porte-feuille* (1785) best demonstrates the change at the Ambigu.[104] Rosalie has found a portfolio containing 50,000 écus in a carriage, which her friend, Sophie, tells her will enable her to become esteemed in society. Rosalie, however, insists that she must find the person to whom the money belongs despite the fact that her landlord is pressing her for the rent. After taking the portfolio to the *commissaire*, Rosalie returns home to meet her lover, Dorly, who has run away from his tyrannical father, Dormon, taking a valuable jewel case with him. Dormon arrives with the *commissaire*, demanding that the house be searched for his jewel case and complaining that he has lost 50,000 écus. Trying unsuccesssfully to persuade Dormon that there are honest people in the world, the *commissaire* finally gives Dormon the portfolio and tells him of Rosalie's honesty while Dorly emerges with the jewel case.

Even the author of the once critical *Mémoires secrets*, who earlier called the Ambigu a "school of licentiousness,"[105] was persuaded that Audinot had really changed his ways, turning boulevard theater into a school of instruction: "Before him, upright people dared not go there [to the boulevard theaters]; they were reserved for the rabble, girls of the streets, libertines: buffoonery, indecency, debauchery held forth there. Little by little, he [Audinot] has raised his to a more upright tone. His colleagues are piqued with emulation, and the boulevard has almost become the school of good morals, whereas the other theaters are degraded."[106] A philanthropist named

Monthyon also congratualted Audinot for elevating his subject matter:

> You have come to understand that a theater like yours exerts a pernicious or salutary influence on the inferior classes of society. It is not in showing Polichinelle drunk and arousing laughter at this drunkenness that drive the people from the dirty route of the cabaret, so I sincerely congratulate you for having substituted for this character and others no less obscene, real, natural characters. Call attention to beautiful examples of courage and virtue, brand energetically all vices, and you will purify the morals of the people.[107]

The *Journal général* commented that "the trivialities and coarse, indecent jokes" that traditionally characterized the Ambigu had been replaced by moral dramas that taught lessons in virtue.[108] A letter to the *Journal de Paris* in 1784 lauded Audinot for eliminating equivocations and showing respect for morals.[109] With reference to Gabiot de Salins' play *L'Astrologue favorable*, performed at the Ambigu on 10 December 1784, the *Affiches annonces* remarked that if everyone followed the example of the Ambigu, the people would be given "models of virtue and wisdom that will make their amusements more profitable."[110]

Such commentary did not please the privileged theaters. They had observed with dismay the popularity of Audinot's pantomimes. No amount of mutilation could obliterate the appeal of his *spectacle*. They sensed that the gap between popular and classical theater was closing. They did not sit idly by, however. Late in 1771, following the enormous success of a parody of the opera *Alceste*, the directors of the three major theaters of Paris succeeded in getting an *arrêt* from the Conseil d'Etat that reduced Audinot to four musicians, outlawed song and dance, and officially ranked the Ambigu as a *spectacle* of the last class.[111] This order provoked such a furor on the boulevards that the authorities granted Audinot the right to make a deal with the Opéra whereby he could have singing and dancing in return for an annual payment of 12,000 livres.[112] The Opéra, however, was still not satisfied. The director sent a *Mémoire* to the secrétaire d'Etat in 1776 protesting the competition of the boulevard shows and recent augmentations in the size of Nicolet's and Audinot's orchestras. One observer declared: "It is believed that the minister of Paris will strip these *spectacles* of everything that can interest people of taste in order to leave only those things that would satisfy the *menu peuple*."[113] The aim, in short, was to keep cultural worlds separate and unequal and, it was hoped, taste publics as well. The authorities did not act, but in 1777 they did order Audinot to halt performances of *La Belle au bois dormant*, a popular work, on Tuesdays and Fridays, days of operatic performances.[114]

The Comédie-Française also registered complaints with the Conseil d'Etat. In 1778 it charged that the Opéra was intruding on its privilege because its productions of *Iphigénie* and *Andromaque* were nothing more than Racine's plays set to music, and it demanded that the Parlement of Paris prevent Nicolet and Audinot from presenting "continuous pieces, embellished with brilliant decorations and machines."[115] The Comédie also requested that, as the boulevard theaters existed for the people, they be limited to a maximum of 12 sous a ticket. In its lengthy *Mémoire* to the Parlement the Comédie-Française reviewed all the rulings of the seventeenth and eighteenth centuries defining their privilege and limiting the *forains* to simple *parades, danses de corde*, and pantomime in an effort to prove that the original assumption behind their privilege—that theatrical competition weakens theater by dividing its resources—was still valid.[116] They argued that their traditional rights had steadily eroded since the early 1760s with Nicolet's move to the boulevards, Audinot's switch from marionettes to child actors, the boulevard directors' disregard for the prohibitions against song and speech, the expansion of their troupes, and Nicolet's performance of genuine comedies and grand *spectacles*. All this, the French comedians concluded, had led to a loss of taste, prostitution of talent, and the public's desertion of the classical theater.

Audinot and Nicolet ignored this latest outburst by the Comédie, but the directors of another *spectacle*, the Variétés-Amusantes, responded on behalf of all the boulevard theaters in July 1785. Their argument was threefold: (1) Louis XIV's action in 1680 was not intended to be a permanent theatrical policy; (2) holding the privilege of the boulevard *spectacles*, the Opéra had legally authorized the establishment of popular theaters; (3) theatrical competition was healthy and stimulated progress in the arts. So the battle raged, but there was very little the three privileged theaters could do to blunt the appeal of both the Ambigu and the Grands Danseurs. Both troupes grew in size. By 1780, Nicolet employed 20 instrumentalists; 60 dancers; 30 actors; and several tumblers, equilibrists, and jugglers who amused the crowd at intermission.[117] Throughout the 1760s and 1770s, the response of Audinot and Nicolet to the complaints of the privileged theaters and the police ordinances officially restricting their fare (proof itself that the rulings were ineffective) was always mockery.

It seems rather evident that Audinot and Nicolet knew that they had little to fear from the authorities who reiterated restrictions but did not enforce them. Bachaumont was doubtless correct in his belief that the police favored entertainments for the people all over the city so that "the populace of every quarter could have their fill and relax pleasurably from their labors. . . ."[118] Another observer declared: "Make a nation laugh, put before it some *divertissements* of its own taste, and you will never have to fear its discontent."[119] The comte de Saint-Florentin echoed the official attitude best when he declared that "spectacles for the people are necessary, the system of Louis

XIV has changed."[120] Indeed, after Audinot's players had performed for the king at Choisy-le-Roi, Louis XV was dubbed "le bien-aimé des forains,"[121]

Evidently, the government's policy of encouraging popular entertainment and winking at the violations of the privileges of the Comédie-Française and Comédie-Italienne was reinforced by the aristocracy's taste for the fare of *le bas peuple*. Keeping ticket prices low did not discourage *le monde* from going to the boulevards, as the privileged theaters had hoped. People are deluded, Baron Grimm wrote, in believing "that in sorting out in this way the people of society from the common people, one will make going there [to the Grands Danseurs] distasteful to well-bred people and that one will draw them back to be bored at the Comédie-Française and the Opéra."[122] All the accounts of Parisian life stress the gathering of highborn and lowborn on the boulevards, the social mixture of theater audiences, and the enormous popularity and success of the Grands Danseurs, the Ambigu-Comique, and other shows. They may have been aimed at *le bas peuple*, but everyone came. The Dauphin and the comte and comtesse of Provence appeared on the boulevard in June 1773, and in 1775 a fête was held at Versailles that re-created the atmosphere of the boulevards. A replica of Nicolet's theater was built for the production of two *opéras-comiques*. Performers from the Opéra presented Boutellier's *Alain et Rosette*, a *pastorale* from the repertory of the Grands Danseurs. Nougaret gloated, "It is indeed singular that a *spectacle* that certain persons affect to scorn has the glory of having furnished a piece from its repertoire to the first theater of France."[123]

The Parisian press is perhaps the best indicator of the extent to which the barrier between theatrical cultures was being breached in the 1780s. In the early 1770s Parisian periodicals routinely listed only the programs of the privileged theaters.[124] In its first year (1777), the *Journal de Paris* provided résumés of plots, commentaries on productions, and letters to the editor. Popular *spectacles* were categorized separately under the rubric "Boulevard," and in 1777 only Nicolet's show was listed and without commentary.[125] Even after other shows began to appear in the press by 1779, they were carefully distinguished from the prominently featured grand *spectacles* by means of a heavy bar, a space, or a different rubric. But by the 1780s the *Journal de Paris* provided the bill of fare for all the principal boulevard attractions. The *Almanach des muses* was moving in a similar direction: In 1779 it began a column entitled "Pièces des Boulevards," listing the programs of the Grands Danseurs. The number of pieces mentioned grew from 2 in 1782 to 21 in 1784. Moreover, in 1785 both the *Journal de Paris* and the *Annonces et avis divers* lifted the Variétés-Amusantes out of its subordinate place and listed it just below the three grand *spectacles*, thus creating a tripartite division of theaters. The *Annonces* later completed the obliteration of the old hierarchical separation by deleting the lines between theaters.

Even changes in censorship in the 1780s reveal the approaching end of distinctions between theatrical cultures. It became evident to the censors that in plays such as *L'Avantageux puni* (1786) at Nicolet's theater the bawdy buffoonery of earlier days was replaced by more serious material containing moral lessons. In celebrating fidelity, generosity, kindness, and the dignity of labor, Nicolet and Audinot were endowing their pieces with social utility and tearing down the walls separating popular from elite entertainment. Therefore, instead of striking offensive phrases or passages, the censors of the two comedies began appropriating entire plays from the boulevard theaters for presentation on their own stages. The Comédie-Française took Dorvigny's *Les Noces Houzardes*, and the Comédie-Italienne took over from the Variétés-Amusantes, Beaunoir's *Fanfan et Colas*, a work that Grimm characterized as morally instructive.[126]

But for all their defiance of the politics of privilege, their success at winning a broad-based public, and their avoidance of censorship and repression, Audinot, Nicolet, and other boulevard entertainers were finally obliged to bow to the power of the first theater of France. In the 1770s annual deficits at the Opéra were running over 100,000 livres despite changes of administration, the success of Gluck's operas, and crown subsidies. Determined to keep this hallowed institution of royal culture afloat, the Conseil d'Etat in July 1784 turned over all the boulevard theaters to the Opéra. The edict stipulated that the king "wished to reduce the number of *spectacles*, which until now have been authorized only as *spectacles forains*, by subjecting them to the privilege exercised by the Académie Royale de Musique. . . ."[127] The edict, which was really aimed more at revenue than reduction, gave the Opéra sovereignty over the popular *spectacles*. It could lease its privilege to whomever it chose under its own price and conditions. The Comédie-Italienne paid the Opéra 40,000 livres a year; Nicolet was assessed 24,000. Both, of course, had long paid subsidies to the Opéra, so there was no real change of policy for them although both were hurt financially by the action. Audinot, however, felt the sting of the Opéra's new power when the Ambigu was jerked abruptly from him by Gaillard, a singer at the Comédie-Italienne, and Dorfeuille, a theater director in Bordeaux, who simply offered to pay the Opéra more. In addition, everyone else had to pay his tribute: Monsieur Nicoud gave 6 livres a year for the right to entertain the crowd with his monkey; Monsieur Albini paid 1 livre for his crocodile; Monsieur Marigny was assessed 2 sous a day by the Opéra for his dwarf exhibition.[128] Clearly, it was in the Opéra's interest to encourage an increase in the number of popular shows, not to reduce them as the edict suggested. Indeed, the Opéra's earnings from the popular *spectacles* rose from just over 40,000 livres in 1784 to well over 150,000 in 1788.[129]

But the decree did not make the Opéra solvent. It succeeded only in inciting the wrath of the boulevard, stirring up internecine conflict among the popular theaters, and infuriating the other two privileged theaters. The decree was like a death rattle of the ancien régime. The Crown had no solution to the plight of its musical showcase other than resorting to the politics of privilege of the absolute state and penalizing the popular entertainment world that was beginning of engulf Paris. Indeed, the great irony of the 1784 decree is that it led to an explosion of popular entertainment and to a further closing of the elite/popular cultural gap with the opening of the Palais-Royal to the *forains*.

As for Audinot, his fortures plummeted when he lost the Ambigu to the directors of the Variétés-Amusantes. He was shocked by the sudden decision of the Opéra, with which he had signed a treaty on 1 May 1780 agreeing to pay 12 livres for each nightly performance. In addition, in August 1784, Audinot had agreed to up the ante to one tenth of the receipt of each performance. The inspector general of the Opéra had terminated pacts which Audinot regarded as binding and permanent.[130] The Opéra, however, interpreted the July decree as a permit to negotiate with anyone, and the prestigious lyric theater found the deal offered by Gaillard and Dorfeuille (40,000 for the Variétés and 30,000 for the Ambigu) more lucrative than that of Audinot. Complaining that Audinot was already in arrears in his payments, the Opéra, backed up by orders from Baron Breteuil, secretary of state for the royal household, and charged with supervision of the Opéra, even got Commissioner Vanglenne of the Châtelet to station a sentinel at the door of the Ambigu during the latter half of December 1784 for the purpose of seizing the money owed the Opéra.[131]

Audinot gave his farewell at the Ambigu on 31 December 1784, appearing before a tearful audience after a performance of the proverb *La Fin couronne l'oeuvre, ou les adieux*.[132] He then took over a *spectacle* kown as the Comédiens de Bois de Boulogne, established in the Ranelagh dance hall in 1778 by August-Louis-Bertin de Blagny, a *trésorier-général*. This theater, also featuring child performers, presented works in verse and prose with vaudevilles and dances.[133]

Audinot, however, continued protesting to the Conseil d'Etat and the Châtelet his loss of the Ambigu.[134] In a review of the dispute in 1780 for the Conseil, Armand-Thomas Hue de Miromesnil, keeper of the seals, strongly upheld Audinot, and the proprietor was eventually victorious.[135] In October 1785, Audinot, who had formed an association with Arnould, returned in triumph to the boulevard when Gaillard and Dorfeuille relinquished the Ambigu to him.[136] He remained until his retirement in 1795. Gaillard and Dorfeuille devoted themselves to another legal struggle to gain definitive control of the Variétés-Amusantes, which they intended to take to the Palais-Royal.

The great success that Audinot and Nicolet enjoyed induced others to start theatrical *spectacles* on the boulevards. Two of Nicolet's former employees, Nicolas Vienne and Louis-Gabriel Sallé, formed the Théâtre des Associés in 1774.[137] Badly pock-marked, Vienne turned his grotesque appearance to advantage by learning how to grimace, a much admired street art in the eighteenth century. Known as Beauvisage, he did his grimaces for the crowd standing on a stool in front of the Grands Danseurs. In 1774, Vienne and the actor Sallé built a wooden hut on the boulevard, where they, like Audinot, began with marionettes and then switched to live actors. Their varied repertoire included some of the old *opéra-comiques* and even bits of the classics, usually with disguised titles and performed humorously, such as *Le Cid*, *Zaire*, *Andromaque*, and *Tartuffe*. One observer wrote:

> Another theater attracts to the tragedy the artisan who wants to gape and the man of taste who pretends to be amused. A band of unfortunates, the most miserable people who would ever groan on the planks of a village barn, execute dramatic performances of all genres. Here an actress in an astonishing costume, such that she could be carried in Thespis' chariot, begins in this way the tragedy of *Zaire*:
> "Je ne m'attendais pas, jeune et belle Zaire. . . ."
> They are called the *Associés*; sometimes they play the same piece for an entire month: the title of the piece is written very simply in chalk on the door.[138]

Charging just 6 sous for admission, the Théâtre des Associés was frequented by fishwives, coal merchants, stagehands, and peddlers; and it became a notorious hangout for lecherous old men and boulevard prostitutes who plied their trade in the loges, which prompted the police to halt evening performances.[139] Financially, the theater was a success. Mayeur declared: "Even though this hovel was occupied only by boot cleaners and girls from the boulevard, by apple peddlers and hawkers of scandal sheets, the Associés takes in every year nearly 2,000 écus, after expenses, as the archbishop forced them, like Nicolet and Audinot, to give one fourth of their receipts to the poor every Sunday and Thursday."[140] The police closed down the Associés completely in 1777 but reopened it four years later. Lieutenant General Lenoir was honored in a song sung by one of the comedians in the role of a fishwife:

> *Les rubans qui j'aimons le mieux*
> *Pour nous parer, sont d'rubans bleus,*
> *Si Jérôm veut me plaire,*
> *Si Jérôm veut m'avoir,*
> *Je voulons qu'il préfère*
> *Les noirs . . . Vive Lenoir.*[141]

Another of the new *spectacles* was the Théâtre des Elèves de l'Opéra, run by an opera dancer named Abraham and a provincial actor named Tessier. They opened their theater on the Boulevard du Temple opposite the Rue Charlot in January 1779. The elaborate building had six fluted columns and a peristyle surmounting a bas-relief depicting Cupid in a chariot.[142] Three tiers of loges graced the interior. Its pearl gray walls were spangled with gold ornaments. Hercules at the foot of Omphale was represented in a painting on the ceiling, and statues of Dance and Music flanked the stage. The Elèves was ostensibly intended as a school to train young dancers for the Opéra, and, as a result, the troupe performed mainly ballets and pantomime *spectacles*.[143] Despite its early success, the Théâtre des Elèves lost money, and Abraham and Tessier leased the theater to a certain Parisau for 100 louis in 1780. Parisau got into difficulty, however, for not paying his creditors and for presenting comedies by various authors under his own name.[144] He was eventually arrested, and the Théâtre was closed by a royal ordinance in September 1780.

The Variétés-Amusantes was, without doubt, the most important of the newer boulevard theaters.[145] It was founded by an actor of the old Opéra-Comique, Louis L'Ecluze de Thilloy, who had become a dentist after the Comique was closed in 1745. The police, who were anxious to revive the fair Saint-Laurent, gave L'Ecluze permission to open a theater there in 1778. Using a company of 13 actors, L'Ecluze had as his first production a one-act comedy, *Les Talismans*, coupled with Vadé's *La Pipe cassée*.[146] He charged 3 livres for the first loges, 20 sous for the second, and 12 for the parterre. When the fair closed, L'Ecluze moved into a dance hall on the boulevard. Construction had also begun on a new theater at the angle of the Rue Lancry and the Rue Bondy near the Boulevard Saint-Martin. L'Ecluze could not meet the costs of his theater, however, and before it was ready for occupancy in April 1779, he fled into the Temple to avoid his creditors, whom he owed 44,822 livres.[147]

The secrétaire d'Etat then awarded the concession of the new boulevard *spectacle* for a 15-year period to two opera dancers, Louis-Joseph Hamoir and François-Duval Malter, and their accociate, a charcoal merchant named Mercier. They borrowed 45,000 livres in order to pay L'Ecluze's debts. They also paid L'Ecluze a pension of 4,000 livres.[148] Taking in between 1,600 and 1,700 livres a day, the Variétés-Amusantes was a success among all groups of people: "Not only do the people flock there in crowds, but [also] the city and the court. People of the highest rank dote on it; grave magistrates and bishops go there in grilled boxes; the ministers have gone, the comte de Maurepas especially, a great amateur of the farce."[149]

But when fire destroyed the theater of the Opéra in 1780, a provisional theater was hastily constructed on the Boulevard Saint-Martin for the royal company, which began performing there in October 1781. Unhappy to be cheek by jowl with the popular players, the Opéra persuaded Lieutenant General Lenoir to close the Variétés. As compensation, Malter and Hamoir were allowed to rent the Théâtre des Elèves on a nine-year lease. They each agreed not to take more than 1,000 livres a year as personal earnings until the lease was paid. They were also authorized to sell the theater on the Rue de Bondy. When the Opéra later got proprietary control of all the boulevard *spectacles*, it awarded the Variétes in September 1784 to Gaillard and Dorfeuille. Malter and Hamoir, thus, suffered the same fate as Audinot, and like him they fought back. The Conseil d'Etat was flooded with charges of violations of the law and demands for compensation.[150]

The central issue in this tempestuous dispute in which the crown gave its beleaguered academy of music absolute control over the popular entertainment world was that of proprietary rights or, more precisely, usufruct. These rights were clearly spelled out in a letter by Malter to Baron Breteuil in January 1785.[151] Recognizing that the king alone could accord a privilege for a *spectacle*, Malter declared that the conditions for the proprietorship of that *spectacle* were then customarily established by the police acting on orders from the secrétaire d'Etat. This well-established procedure had been followed in 1779 establishing the proprietorship of Malter and Hamoir and setting forth their obligations to l'Ecluze. It was understood on trust in the word of the king and his minister that this proprietorship would last the customary 15 years, and all the money spent on the theaters and their effects were based on that understanding. Therefore, Malter contended, when the Opéra received the privilege of the *spectacles forains* in July 1784, he and his associates should have been regarded as the proprietors of the privilege of the Variétés, holding it as usufruct. Having been deprived of it, they should be indemnified. In a statement with revolutionary overtones, Malter concluded:

The laws that are the most important to enforce in all governments and principally in a monarchical government are those of property; it is essential to the general good order as to the well-being of each individual, that each person preserve what belongs to him. Moreover, through all of its history, properties have been regarded in France as sacred; his Majesty himself, though invested with sovereign authority, imposed on himself the obligation to respect them and indeed to protect them when they are attacked. These fundamental principles of every wise and enlightened government are rediscovered in all ordinances dictated by legislative wisdom. It is not at all favor nor gratitude nor concessions emanating from royal beneficence, which preserves, if not explicitly, at least implicitly, the rights of others.

Surely, Malter declared, in issuing the July *arrêt*, the king did not intend to assume the power of according a privilege that would result in the denial of proprietary rights.

Malter went to some lengths in his letter to indicate that he was not contesting the Crown's right to award a privilege to the Opéra or even the Opéra's right to give the lease to Gaillard and Dorfeuille. The Opéra had acted properly by making provision in the lease for the new proprietors to indemnify the old proprietors, honor the contracts with the actors, and pay for theaters and effects. His complaint was against Gaillard and Dorfeuille for not complying with the lease and, therefore, violating the laws of property and the will of the king, his minister, the lieutenant general, and the Opéra. Unquestionably, the main concern of Malter and Hamoir was their financial loss, but none of Malter's circumlocution could obscure the primary issue: the arbitrary denial of proprietary rights by royal use of privilege.

The repertoire of the Variétés, at least in its early years, is best exemplified by one piece—Louis Dorvigny's *Janot, ou les battus paient l'amende*—the most popular play of the eighteenth century. First performed on 11 June 1779, this *comédie-proverbe*, a theatrical form borrowed from the private theaters, revolved around the blundering foibles of a simpleton, Janot, a character who had appeared in a play at least as early as the sixteenth century and was virtually lifted from folklore.[152] Dorvigny made him convincingly naive and sympathetic, and through his rendering of *janotismes*, or absurd speech inversions, the actor Maurice-François Rochet, known as Volange, achieved fame in the role.

In the opening scenes of the play, Janot, whom Monsieur and Madame Ragot have sent to buy lamb and wine for their dinner, calls to his beloved Suzon from the street beneath her window to throw him the key to the front door so that he might enter and embrace her.[153] Hearing Janot, Simon, Suzon's father, dumps the contents of a chamber pot on him. Janot believes Suzon has committed the vile deed. When Janot relates his misadvanture to Dodinet, who moves from side to side to avoid the foul odor, his friend advises him to complain to the *commissaire*, who will see to it that he gets financial compensation. But Janot soon learns from the *commissaire*'s clerk that he must pay to register a complaint. Although only 24 sous are required, the clerk piles on additional fees in order to pry from the foolish Janot the 6 livres he was given to buy food for the Ragots. Believing that Janot has squandered the money in a cabaret, Ragot fires his employee and refuses to pay his back wages. Alone and hungry, Janot laments his misfortune:

A déjeuner! en attendant faudrait souper, et je n'ai pas le sou, et Je ne connois personne de connoissance encore. La nuit comme ça si c'étoit le matin, y a des Auberges, on va se mettre à table, on boit, on mange, et ne faut pas d'argent pour ça . . . dans les Cabarets on ne paie qu'en sortant; moi je ne sortirois pas . . . je tombe de sommeil, si y passoit queuque fiacre sur la place, je dormirois une coupe d'heures dans la carosse . . . ou si j'avions tant seulement un petit fagot pour me réchauffer, au coin d'une borne-là, de trois sous et demi! . . . Jarni, je ne sais ce qui me tourmente le plus; si c'est le froid, si c'est la faim; je crois que c'est le sommeil, . . . ou plutôt c'est la colère! . . . mordienne! je suis enragé après ste Mamselle Suzon, qu'est cause de ça; faut que je m'en venge . . . j'y vas casser ses vitres; quiens, attrape! pan, encore une! . . . ça me réchauffera. Pan, va toujours.[154]

In the course of his lament, Janot throws some stones, which break a cobbler's windowpane. Kicked by the angry cobbler and hauled off by the Watch, Janot is ordered by the *commissaire* to pay a fine, but, unable to do so because he has given the only money he had to the *commissaire*'s clerk, Janot is thrown in jail. The hapless Janot mutters: "It is always the beaten who pay the fine."

Les Battus created a sensation. The author of the *Mémoires secrets* called it "the rage of the moment."[155] By August 1779, the play had been performed over one hundred times, and by October over two hundred times.[156] Grimm reported that the crowds at the 112th performance were so large that not even two loges had been sold for the first performance of Voltaire's *Rome sauvée* at the Comédie-Française.[157] In July 1780, Métra observed that *Les Battus* had been performed over one thousand times.[158] Unable to go to the Variétés for reasons of propriety, the king and queen invited L'Ecluze to present *Les Battus* at Versailles in September 1779. Many critics were, of course, appalled that the production of a ridiculous farce at a boulevard theater could achieve such success. *L'Année littéraire*, for example, declared: "What will our successors say when they read in the history of our theaters that *Les Battus paient l'amende* has had over two hundred performances in the course of one year; also, these fools have already found a crowd of imitators; there is not a single schoolboy today who does not aspire to be seen acting on these *bastard stages*."[159] *Les Battus* was parodied at all the popular theaters. The Variétés itself followed it with *Janot et Dodinet rivaux* and *Le Mariage de Janot*.[160] The Grands Danseurs offered *Jeannette ou les battus ne paient pas toujours l'amende*, which had 49 performances in 1781.[161] *Les Battus* was a personal triumph for the heretofore obscure Volange. He was welcomed in the salons. Porcelain busts of him came into fashion. Songs, engravings, and verses with Volange as the hero were hawked in the streets, and the actor was the talk of the cafés: "It is Jeanomanie on one side, Jeannotisme on the other."[162] When Volange had a mild cold in December 1779, the street in front of his residence was reportedly lined with the carriages of solicitous ladies and gentlemen of high rank.[163] Admitting that he was embarrassed to discuss the matter, Grimm nonetheless wrote: "The object of such vigorous enthusiasm, the idol of such rare and sustrained admiration, the man in short who can be called at this time the man of the nation is a certain M. Janot, who plays, it must be admitted, with the greatest realism the role of a fool who is sprayed from a window like Don Japhet from Armenia."[164]

Volange demanded higher wages from L'Ecluze, whose profits from the show enabled him to discharge 200,000 livres in debts. When L'Ecluze refused, Volange accepted a job at the Comédie-Italienne. The author of the *Mémoires secrets* declared that Janot's debut at the Italienne on 22 February 1780 marked a unique epoch in theatrical history because whereas other actors had enthusiastic fans, Janot "dragged along with him all the rabble of the boulevards and the fair. These bandits, furious to see their idol carried off, seemed to want to recover him and bring him back to the *tréteaux*. They beset the doors and the box office; they filled the street."[165] Two police squads had to block off the street in order to prevent people from being crushed by horses and carriages. Scalpers reportedly sold tickets for 36 livres.[166] Inside the corridors were jammed with people, the musicians were surrounded, and the tumultuous parterre had to be cleared. Cabals formed, including people from the Variétes demanding their hero's return, the French comedians who wanted Volange to fail, the Italians who had swallowed their pride but were still irritated to have a *forain* in their midst, and female admirers of the actor. The *Journal de Paris* divided the audience into three categories: those "seduced by . . . the astonishing reputation" of Volange at the Variétés and who believed he was competent to do other roles; those who were convinced that in moving to the Comédie-Italienne from the boulevards, Volange would show that he was totally lacking in talent; and those who after observing carefully would conclude that Volange was talented in playing roles "analogous to his means, to his habits," such as a fool, a valet, or a brute, but that "he could not execute the role of the *doux monde*."[167] The *Journal* left no doubt which camp it had joined. Disassociating itself from "the fracas of the parterre," the *Journal* wrote that Volange had "a heavy bearing, a raucous voice . . . no nuance, no finesse," making him fit for the part of a drunken peasant.[168] Volange did have a successful debut in *Les Trois frères jumeaux Vénitiens* by Colalto, but in the ensuing weeks his popularity tumbled as quickly as it had risen. But the end of the year he had returned to the Variétés.[169] Evidently, the Italians were glad to be rid of this invader from the boulevards, whose presence tarnished their prestige. But his return to the Variétés was as triumphant as his debut in *Les Battus*.[170]

The bustling ambiance of the boulevards and the success of the Ambigu, the Grands Danseurs, and other theaters quickly attracted a throng of entertainers, both old and new, to the scene. Entertainment exploded like a star in the firmament on the Parisian boulevards.

From the fairs came acrobats, freaks, marionettists, menageries, ventriloquists, machinists, and *cabinets de physique*. Madame Vigée Lebrun reported that her six-year-old daughter found the Fantoccini Français so lifelike that she believed the puppets to be real.[171] The Fantoccini performed every day different three-act pieces with songs and ballets with such titles as *Néron, Empereur des Romains avec Arlequin, son bouffon, exécuteur de ses ordres.*[172] A Portuguese octogenarian executed his ventriloquism by carrying on a dialogue with an *automate* that emitted the voice of a three-year-old.[173] His chief competitor was a grocer named Saint-Gilles, who allegedly convinced a doctor that he lodged an evil spirit that had to be exorcised.[174]

In the boulevard menageries, elephants shared the scene with a siren from the Atlantic, a steer with three eyes and three horns, a four-foot wild man, a Turkish horse who solved arithmetic problems, and a sea monster with the body of a wolf. The boulevards even provided the eighteenth-century version of a shooting gallery. Installed in 1775, this attraction, known as the Modèle d'un théâtre de chasse, enabled the crowd to fire crossbows at live rabbits and game birds mounted on pieces of cardboard painted with hunting scenes.[175] Freaks included an Algerian giant, 6 feet 8 inches tall; a female albino Negro; and a 42-year-old dwarf from the Indies, who stood 27 inches high.[176] A fat cat posed as a ferocious tiger at one menagerie.[177] Conjurers performed their tricks whenever they could attract a few people, who paid as little as two sous.[178] They made cards, peas, money, and balls disappear and often performed with small animals.

Although mechanical contraptions had lost the vogue they enjoyed at the fairs, they still could be found on the boulevards. Sieur Perrin presented his Automates et Tours d'Adresse every day at 6:00 P.M. at the theater of the Elèves de l'Opéra, and Sieur J.-M. Missel, billed as the empress of Russia's former machinist, had a cabinet featuring "hydraulic machines," whereby he simulated tempests at sea by using candles and jets of water. His *spectacle*, located next to the Café Turc, cost 24 and 12 sous.[179] In his *spectacle méchanique*, Monsieur Rabiqueau, an *avocat* who insisted that his show was a school of physics, mathematics, and mechanics where the secrets of nature would be revealed along with miraculous illusions, represented the planets with lights and mirrors, conducted electrical experiments, displayed a mechanical red-legged partridge, and performed a miniature pageant depicting a legendary magical tree inhabited by fairies. By boulevard standards, Rabiqueau's prices were steep: The best seats cost three livres; others were priced at one livre, four sous.[180] He also gave a course in experimental physics at the Hôtel de Carignan on the rue Bailleul. At the Nouveau Spectacle de Physique the mountebank-entrepreneur unlocked a sealed chest without touching it, allegedly by the force of his will. His Negro *automate* indicated the time of concealed clocks, and in a final act he magically extinguished the candles on a chandelier from distances of 30 and 60 feet. There were many such cabinets on the boulevards with optical, mechanical, and electrical shows; some entertainers were playing with real science, which they understood imperfectly; others were charlatans. The author of *L'Année littéraire* wrote: "Never has the public taste for experimental physics been more general nor more widespread than today."[181]

The public was especially enamored of the musical devices in the cabinets. For example, a mechanical instrument called an archicorde was played every afternoon on the rue de Saintonge near the boulevard. Imitating the sounds of a violin, a bass, a clavecin, a harp, and a guitar, the archicorde could produce the sound of an entire orchestra.[182] Along the boulevard itself, ambulatory musicians made up in ingenuity what they lacked in technology. Crowds enjoyed following one-man bands, such as the fellow who played a violin with his hands while, with a bow attached to his foot, he produced a continuous buzz from a bass extended from his torso.[183] The crowd threw money at a man with no feet who rode a horse up the street singing and fiddling. Mercier, who deplored the incessant cacophony of the boulevard, declared:

> Whenever there is some discontent among the people, the police double the music of the streets, and it is prolonged two hours later than usual. When the ferment increases, ambulatory music is let alone in the intersections; the drum resounds from morning to night; gunshots on one side, clarinets on the other, soldiers mounting the guard around the palace, singers raising their voices to the roof-tops, that is how one appeases the spirits, by the most singular contrasts; the gambling dens that had been closed are reopened; a little more license is conceded to girls; the *parades* of the boulevards are lengthened, and people who sing, who play freely, who see new prostitutes, forget guns, pay no attention to them any longer, and, thoroughly giddy, dream only about the enjoyment of the moment.[184]

The *cabinets de physique* featuring optics, a favorite entertainment of the fairs, also found their way to the boulevards, where a society increasingly enamored of science, but not yet clearly distinguishing it from magic, was attracted to them. A German named Zaller used glass and mirrors to contrive the illusion of fireworks in his *cabinet optique*. In 1776 he featured an optical pageant simulating the entry of Pope Pius V at the Vatican. Monsieur Bernard, who charged 24 sous for a seat and 2 sous to stand, created illusions of palaces going up in flames by means of lanterns placed behind transparent curtains. Sieur Noel promised that he would reveal a fluid, neither magnetized nor electrified, that would make it possible for people to communicate at a distance.[185] *Ombres Chinoises* were brought to the boulevards by Jean Marquais in 1772.[186] In 1775, Sieur Ambroise opened his Théâtre des Récéations de la Chine, promising an *ombres* show with moving ghosts, sea machines, a flaming sunrise, and other marvels.[187]

As they had done at the fairs, Savoyard girls followed the crowds to the boulevards with magic lanterns strapped to their backs, announcing themselves with hand organs. Peering into these boxes equipped with pieces of glass, candles, and painted lenses, spectators viewed scenes of London, Constantinople and Peking; the battle of Fontenoy; and sea combats with cannon smoke for as little as six deniers.[188]

The boulevards even sported at least one cabinet where water witching was performed by a peasant from Provence. Using a device called a hydroscope, he vowed to discern which of two brass vases covered with marble slabs contained water.[189] The water-filled vase was, in fact, marked. His ruse was exposed when a member of the audience secretly filled both vases.

The prince of the boulevard magicians was Nicolas-Philippe Ledru, known as Comus (god of feasts, lovers, and debauchery), who achieved fame at his Expériences Physiques et Mathématiques on the Boulevard du Temple, in which he featured catoptrics, prestidigitation, fortune-telling, mind reading, vanishing, and phantasmagoria.[190] Comus began as a mere sleight-of-hand trickster. His expertise as a conjurer was so extraordinary that the duc de Chartres asked for lessons and was reported to have spent six hours at a time learning Comus' art.[191] After he met and learned about scientific instruments from Edward Nairne and Jesse Ramsden in England, however, Comus grew more serious about his scientific showmanship. In April 1777 he conducted experiments on the decomposition of light without glasses or prisms for Joseph II, in Paris disguised as Count Falkenstein. In 1781, Louix XVI commissioned him to build scientific instruments and to execute meteorological maps for the navy. The king dubbed him professor of physics of the children of france. The Faculty of Medicine verified Comus' success in using electricty to combat nervous disorders and epileptic seizures in 1783 at his cabinet on the boulevard.[192] In 1784, Louis XVI conferred on Comus the title of physician of the king and the Faculty of Medicine of Paris. His writings were published in the Abbé Rosier's periodical, *Observations sur le physique*. Cited in scientific publications for his research on the effects of electricity on plants and animals, the human brain and nerves, Comus became an authority on the medical uses of electricity, especially in the treatment of epilepsy. His crowning achievement was the establishment of a clinic on the rue des Rosiers for the collective electrical treatment of epileptics. Encouraged by the duc d'Orléans and sanctioned by Lieutenant General Lenoir and Dr. Philip, dean of the Faculty of Medicine, Comus and his son administered electrical treatments twice a day plus monthly purgings. They also treated women afflicted with amenorrhea. Reports suggested that Comus' electroshock therapy was successful, and he received praise from such notables as Cardinal de Rohan, the duchesse de Villeroi, and the vicomte de Bussy. With government backing, he treated for no remuneration as many as 60 people at a time. His clinic eventually became too small when he began treating other ailments such as hemiplegia, aphasia, and neuralgia, so the king gave him land near the convent of the Célestins (angle of the rue du Petit-Musc), which was secularized in 1776. For Baron Grimm, Comus formed a notable contrast to the occult practices of Pierre Mesmer. He did, indeed, make the leap from boulevard conjurer to serious therapist. Yet he did not abandon his cabinet on the boulevards, where Nougaret credited him with dispelling the popular belief in sorcery and the supernatural.

Comus had three specialities at the boulevard cabinet. First were his experiments with the "universal fluid," which were wide-ranging: He submitted the powder of a diamond to electrical discharges in order to distinguish a Mogul from a Brazilian gem; he demonstrated the different motions of electricity by applying it to loadstone and glass; he attempted to compress ether and gold; he tried to revive dead and paralyzed people with electrical charges; he transmitted electric shocks through a circle of people in such a way that some felt them while others did not; he tried to apply electricity to "the annual economy"; he demonstrated the analogy between electricity and "the principal motor of the nerves"; and he disproved the hypothesis that electricity can alter light bodies.[193]

Secondly, Comus transmitted thoughts from one person to another separated by a curtain or a room. Denis Diderot, who did not share Grimm's enthusiasm, wrote to Sophie Volland: "Comus is a charlatan from the ramparts who twists the mind of all our physicians; his secret consists of establishing communication between two people from one room to another without the discernible assistance of any intermediary agent."[194] Thirdly, Comus featured optical shows, especially phantasmagoria. Using lanterns, he achieved the illusion of luminous phantoms or specters jumping out at an audience seated in a dark room. The effect was obtained by beaming shafts of reflected light onto small images printed on a cloth. The object or phantom appeared very small and distant, then became larger and suddenly ominous.[195] Thus, Comus, whose cabinet attracted "the most brilliant society," formed a curious bridge between popular and academic science, between *spectacle* and laboratory.[196]

"Entrez, entrez, messieurs, venez voir le grand couvert; entrez, c'est tout comme à Versailles." Such was the cry of the barker beckoning to the boulevard crowd to enter the cabinet of Sieur Curtius, whose popularity equaled that of Comus.[197] For just two sous the public could see an enchanting variety of wax figures, in some cases remarkably lifelike busts, in others whole assemblies of illustrious or notorious characters.

Parisians had long been used to seeing wax figures.[198] They were displayed in crêches or scenes of the Passion on the Pont-Neuf and the Hôtel-Dieu. Moreover, early in the eighteenth century, Antione Benoit (d. 1717) attracted people to his *cabinet* at the fairs, where he featured wax portraits of courtesans, and Mademoiselle Biberon displayed anatomical wax figures modeled on cadavers in her *cabinet* at the Estrapade.

The German Curtius (Creutz) was, however, the age's most illustrious wax artist, specializing in models of the celebrites of the time: Rousseau, Voltaire, Linguet, the comte d'Estaing, Mesmer, and Cagliostro among others. His most famous work was a portrayal of the royal family and the emperor Joseph II seated at a table laden with food called "Le Grand Couvert." It formed a humorous contrast to his "Caverne des Grands Voleurs," a room filled with notorious villains. Although Curtius maintained a permanent collection, he changed many of his figures as they passed from fashion. His most striking scenes included a portrayal of the queen preparing for bed and a representation of the grand cascade at Saint-Cloud.[199] One of his more curious portraits was of Frederick II wearing his own clothes. The wax figure reportedly astonished spectators not only because of its close resemblance to the Prussian monarch but also because of the great simplicity of the dress.[200] Beside the figure, Curtius placed three uniforms belonging to Frederick, two of which were extremely tattered.

Despite the low cost of admission, Curtius was able to attract enough patrons to earn as much as 100 écus on a good day.[201] Testimonials to his art were effusive. Mayeur de Saint-Paul, who viciously deprecated nearly all the boulevard folk, wrote: "A crowd of the curious and of amateurs continuously fills the interior of this salon, and it is with just reason. The arts appear there in all their brilliance, and the magnificience that reigns there serves only as an accessory to the superior talents of this consummate artist."[202] Mayeur added that Curtius would have been mistaken for a magician in a less enlightened century. Yet, although the public is not fooled, "it is no less seduced by the appeal of the marvelous."[203]

If Comus and Curtius catered to all social levels of the heterogenous crowd on the boulevard, the Italian pyrotechnist Torré seemed to aim his *spectacle* more at the elite, or at least that can be inferred from the comparatively high cost of seats.[204] Torré was the proprietor of the summer Waux-Hall built in 1764 on the Boulevard Saint-Martin prior to its counterparts, the winter Waux-Hall at the Saint-Germain fair and the Colisée on the Champs-Elysées.[205] Called a "man of genius and brilliant imagination," Torré built a large rotunda decorated like a ballroom with mirrors reflecting the light and surrounded by a gallery with columns, pilasters, paintings, gilding, and draperies.[206] Beyond the rotunda, set up as an amphitheater and equipped with loges backed by cafés and boutiques, lay a garden where illuminations were held.[207]

Almost from the outset, Torré was besieged by problems and attacked by rivals. In August 1765 fire destroyed his storage house, setting off explosions audible all over Paris and killing five men and wounding several others.[208] In September 1768, Torré added *tréteaux* and an apron to the front of his stage, where actors and actresses performed *parades* with Italian ariettes, which elicited strenuous complaints from the buffoons and farceurs of the other *spectacles* that Torré was violating their "ancient right."[209] They took him to court, charging that his show was a menace to public order. He lost the case, and the Waux-Hall closed in 1768.[210] Unable to pay his debts, Torré was allowed to give public balls at the Waux-Hall. He opened four cafés depicting different parts of the world, and merchants hurried to occupy the boutiques. The author of the *Mémoires secrets* wrote: "Novelty is a great attraction in this country, and the French . . . will no doubt proceed there, where the elegant decorations, a brilliant illumination, an excellent symphony, and the most gallant women ought to gather together in order to charm the senses of the spectators."[211]

Torré continued to be plagued, however, by critics and rivals. In 1769 the Comédie-Française and the Comédie-Italienne submitted a *mémoire* protesting the establishment of all *waux-halls*. The duc de Richelieu, one of the first gentlemen of the chamber, and Papillon de la Ferté, the intendant of the menus plaisirs, supported them and succeeded in getting the comte de Saint Florentin to suppress Torré's Waux-Hall, although in Papillon's view the minister was disinclined to close all such estabishments.[212] Nevertheless, Torré reopened the Waux-Hall in June 1770 with the minister's permission.[213] Still, Torré's troubles continued. In 1776 the archbishop of Paris complained to the government that Torré's show continued through Lent whereas other *spectacles* were closed. He succeeded in closing the Waux-Hall on Sunday, causing a demonstration against the city authorities in the form of two long rows of carriages full of shouting patrons stretching from the Boulevard Montmartre to the Porte Saint-Antoine.[214]

Torré's problems continued in the 1770s, when the manager of the Colisée complained about the competition and charged that the small size and cramped space of Torré's boulevard location would deter the very people who provide such establishments with a secure source of revenue "the less brilliant bourgeoisie."[215] He outlined a list of costs and proceeds for 1773, 1774, and 1775 in order to show that the Colisée was three quarters more profitable than the Waux-Hall. The manager attempted to prove that even if the Colisée did not exist, the Waux-Hall would fail for the very reasons that occasioned its initial success: The boulevards had become a grand thoroughfare in which the Waux-Hall was wedged in among large buildings; its smallness had turned it into a species of parade "that suits only a certain class of men and women who look for each other there . . . [excluding] the timid bourgeoisie . . . ."[216] Even the appearance of having "certain liaisons" risked the reputations of the bourgeoisie at the Waux-Hall. Torré held the ace, however: The Colisée owed the Opéra 20,000 livres, it was deeply in debt, and the government had decided to scuttle it.

In addition to public dancing, Torré featured quadrilles and traditional dances performed by students of both sexes and simulated tournements in which French knights fought with lances for their ladies.[217] One such exercise featured a German quadrille with an English dance called the "lorempepe."[218] Fireworks with pyric globes, bouquets, and Chinese spears with war music were held regularly.[219] There were balls and rustic games in the garden, including a swing, a merry-go-round, and a tall, greased pole from the top of which dangled sausages and ham. The slick pole did not deter patrons from trying to grab the choicest piece of meat, and at the end of the evening the "gourmand hero" was acclaimed with brouhaha.[220] The swing evidently attracted a great deal of attention. François Cognel wrote that "girls assumed a freer bearing there than elsewhere, and the swing game allows more distracting licences for the spectator. . . ."[221] Public baths were installed in the Waux-Hall in 1789.[222] On one occasion a watchmaker named Digne displayed a mechanism in the garden that facilitated the ascension, banking, turning, and guiding of a balloon. Thirty sous were charged for performances.[223] Indeed, the garden was frequently used for aerostatic demonstrations and scientific sideshows.[224]

Torré's great speciality, however, was *spectacles pyriques*, radiant tableaux combining fireworks, dance, and music. They were loosely organized around some central theme and bore such titles as *La Bataille d'Antioche ou Gargamelle vaincu, Le Camp de Mars*, and *Fête allégorique à la gloire du roi*.[225] His *tour de force* was a "pyri-pantomime" called *Les Forges de Vulcain sous le Mont Etna* produced at the Waux-Hall in 1766. Vulcan was a very important god in Roman mythology.[226] Volcanus, protector of Rome's foundations and associated with Maia the Earth Mother, was the oldest Latin deity, antedating Jupiter. He was believed to have impregnated a young maiden with a spark from a fire. Proving his paternity by surrounding a crowd of doubters with a ring of fire, the new Vulcan became the god of the thunderbolt and the sun with the power to halt the destruction of fire and to instill the warmth of life. Also considered the first god of the Tiber and the divinity of the hearth, Vulcan had an altar in the forum, where he was feted twice every August. His attributes were a hammer, tongs, and an anvil.

Vulcan's exploits were perfect subject matter for Torré's pyric *spectacles*. Emerging from his palace at the rear of a cave, Vulcan appeared with the Cyclops in the interior of the mountain. Venus descended, asking for arms for Aeneus, the Trojan prince who fought the Greeks in the siege of Troy and whose marriage to the daughter of Latinus established the tradition of Rome's Trojan origins. The forging of these weapons enabled Torré to explode spectacular fireworks. In the view of at least one observer, his subject was perfectly analogous to the genre.[227]

Although the Waux-Hall was fairly expensive by boulevard standards, some found it reasonably priced and discerned political utility in it. An unidentified foreign visitor wrote:

> People have not reflected enough perhaps on the political side of the *spectacles* of a city such as the capital. The Wauxhall is a pastime that suits every estate, peope of all ages, and, so to speak, all personalities. It is a place of assembly where one is seated, where one changes places, where one promenades, where one chats, where one is entertained by the variety of things, and where the men are not held to any particular dress.

> Such a *spectacle*, I say, is the sort that seems to me to be suited the most to occupied men and to idle persons of a very great city.[228]

Another anonymous observer defended the Waux-Hall against charges of immorality and carried the argument for its utility even further.[229] Reasoning that since Roman times fêtes such as waux-halls represented the concept a nation had of its opulence, the author contended that national fêtes had been replaced by princely ones and that, because the state authorizes only individuals to give entertainments, the nation's taste has been split by differences in the cost of tickets. Rich and humble have been separated. Different taste publics will create enemies in society. The humble public that laughs, he contended, must be rejoined to the rich who are bored. Torré's Waux-Hall was the microcosm of this reunion, each person seeking to be reunited to the whole. Because it cost less to enter than the one at the fair, it brought together all ranks and estates. The real *spectacle* is not the artists but society itself.

Although the summer Waux-Hall and other *spectacles* of this type were welcomed by Parisians, some contemporaries scorned them. Nicholas-Joseph Sélis spoke of Torré's show as a terrible place "from which it is impossible to leave chaste."[230] He complained especially about the swings in the garden where "public women balance themselves in positions conforming to their intentions." The criticism of Nougaret and Rétif de la Bretonne was more social and aesthetic than moral. Claiming that the principal pleasure of the Waux-Hall is seeing oneself, they deplored the fact that the public preferred pure spectacle to the arts and music.[231]

In 1780 the summer Waux-Hall closed for reasons that are not clear. It was subsequently destroyed. The minister in charge of Paris stated only that the Colisée and the Waux-Hall were allowed to fall although he revealed that he was under pressure from the archbishop of Paris and the first president of the Parlement. His own attitudes were ambivalent, but it is clear that he saw the need for popular entertainments. Although holding that the number of little *spectacles* should not be increased and was already probably too large, he declared that "in a time in which the taste for the *spectacle* has become so general that in nearly every class of citizens *théâtres particuliers* are erected and *la comédie en société* is played, it would perhaps be very inconvenient to suppress all the little *spectacles* allowing only the opera and two comedies to remain."[232] He went on to add that he had not personally authorized any of the present *spectacles*, that he forbade new ones from opening, and that he would probably revoke his predecessor's sanction of the Elèves and the Variétés were it not for the great losses that would be suffered by builders, workers, and creditors. But once again the minister's tone changed. He admitted that at one time the little *spectacles* distracted many workers, but he attributed that to the dances allowed in the cabarets. Two things are clear from his statements: He had to address and to appear to agree with the influential critics of popular entertainment, and he understood its utility.

The minister's convictions were evident when a new summer Waux-Hall was built in 1785 on the Boulevard du Temple near the barrier.[233] Designed by the architects of the Redoute Chinoise, it was an oval dance salon 72 feet long surrounded by Ionic columns. The gallery above was lined with mirrors and arabesques. In addition to a garden for fêtes, the new Waux-Hall was equipped with a café in the basement built like an ancient ruin. The main entertainment consisted of dancing, illuminations, contredances performed by children, and fêtes. Prices were steep: 2 livres, 8 sous for the parterre and the *paradis*; 4 livres for the second loges; 7 livres, 10 sous for the first loges and amphitheater; and 10 livres, 10 sous for the balconies.

There is no way to tell if the summer Waux-Hall attacted the same mixed audience that attended the other boulevard *spectacles*. For the most part, the sources are mute on the subject. The prices suggest, however, that it was intended for the elite. It generated controversy involving aesthetic, social, and moral issues; and it stirred up opposition from the privileged theaters, the proprietors of other similar *spectacles*, the archbishop, and the Parlement; but the Waux-Hall had the support of the king's minister and the city officials, who despite their apparent concern over the proliferation of entertainments in Paris, found it a useful distraction for a restless populace. As with other Parisian *spectacles*, it appealed to the human fascination with glittering light and fire and offered a forum for sexual playfulness in a socially acceptable setting.

The success of the summer Waux-Hall established a vogue in the city for entertainments in settings of controlled rusticity. The Ruggieri brothers from Bologna, Torré's main competitors in pyrotechnics, opened a *jardin* as early as 1766 on the rue Saint-Lazare in the Porcherons quarter.[234] From a covered gallery 100 feet long, the public watched fireworks, pantomime tableaux like "La Descente d'Orphée" and "Thésée délivré par Hercule," and lyric panto-mimes such as "Le Combat, la mort, les funérailles et le réveil de Malborough." The Ruggieri added a drill team and horse racing in 1774, and in 1786 they sent up hydrogen balloons from the garden. They also hoisted a huge transparent winged horse (Pegasus) and rider that flew in the wind and

an eight-foot nymph coiffed in a balloon and dressed in a transparent robe.[235]
The *Journal de Paris* commended the marvels of mythological creatures
flying through the air and suggested that this kind of illusion "could be
brought to our grand *spectacles.*"[236] It is interesting to note that Ruggieri
staged an occasional balloon flight for the benefit of the poor. One such was
scheduled for 8 March 1789. The *Journal de Paris* regarded the use of
balloons to earn money to aid "a class of unfortunate people who do not feel
the prompt effects of the revival of jobs and industry" as highly commend-
able.[237]

Equally fashionable was the garden of Monsieur Ranelagh in the Bois de
Boulogne near the Château de la Muette, established in 1774. There he
presented fireworks, concerts, masked balls, comedies, and balloon launch-
ings. He charged one livre, four sous.[238] On at least one occasion the
Ranelagh property served as the scene of a royal entertainment. On the
occasion of the birth of two children of the Spanish ruling family, the ducs
de Crillon and de Mahon rented Ranelagh's theater and café and set up tents
and galleries in the gardens.[239] Ministers, foreign princes, ambassadors, and
dignitaries from court and city were fêted with an illumination, a concert, a
dramatic pantomime about the friendship of France and Spain, fireworks,
rustic dances, military music, a ball, a supper in a *féerie* setting, and the
ascension of a hydrogen globe with the following verse written across it:

> *Vive Charles, vive Louise*
> *De cette nuit c'est la devise:*
> *Que leurs noms volent dans les airs,*
> *Ils embelliront l'univers.*

The balloon fell 12 hours later on the Madrid in the Bois.

A troup called the Jeunes Comédiens also performed musical plays in the
Bois. Young children gave pieces based on the tales of Sauvigny with music
by Philidor.[240] They even presented Grétry's *Le Tableau parlant* and Beaumarchais' *Le Barbier de Seville.*[241]

A Cirque Royal on the Boulevard du Luxembourg offered music and
dances in a rotunda and a tilting game, a May pole, military music, and
fireworks in the adjacent garden.[242] Closely resembling Torré's pyric *spectacles*, Sieur Varinière, the pyrotechnician, featured displays depicting *Le
Temple de la bienfaisance à la gloire du roi* and a combat of salamanders in
which the fire was carried by electricity.[243] Tickets cost 30 sous.

Finally, a waux-hall called the Pantheon was opened on the rue de
Chartres near the Palais-Royal in 1785, intended to house the balls no longer
presented by the Opéra after its transference to the Porte Saint-Martin and
to replace the winter Waux-Hall, which had been demolished in 1785.[244]

Prices ran 40 sous for the parterre, 3 livres for the second loges, and 6 livres for the first.

Gardens without commercial entertainments of the boulevard sort included the Jardin Royal, with the royal botanical collection and a labyrinth; the Jardin de l'Arsenal on the city rampart; the Jardin de l'Enfant beside the Louvre with a terrace overlooking the river; the Jardin de Soubise in the Marais adjacent to the *hôtel*; the Jardin du Temple in the Temple; and, of course, the gardens of the Tuileries and Luxembourg.[245] The last two were often used for balloon ascensions. A noted *avocat* of the Parlement of Paris pointed out the great utility of such gardens for a city as large as Paris.[246] They enabled people to breath pure air, to exercise, and to enjoy nature and the beautiful women who strolled beneath the trees. Watching them too closely, however, drew crowds that embarrassed the women and drove them off. The *avocat* also warned against the public gardens becoming places of prostitution: "Night often lends its veil to mercenary loves; errant beauties provide easy conquests" despite the many ordinances designed to prevent these liaisons. Undoubtedly his perception was accurate. The police, for example, observed in the Luxembourg "a large number of these women [*de mauvaise vie*] who hang out there and prostitute themselves publicly."[247] In May 1741 six women were arrested for soliciting as prostitutes in the Luxembourg.[248] Mercier, on the other hand, found the Luxembourg gardens to be a calm, philosophical place where the bourgeois could send his chaste daughters and mothers could walk without embarrassement.[249] Old people, studious young men, hardworking fathers, and clerics all gathered there. Mercier's opinion of the Tuileries, however, was just the opposite.[250] He described a parade of fat procurators, indolent abbés, indifferent dowagers, officers on leave, idle libertines, and brooding, well-dressed prostitutes waiting for someone to buy them dinner—all forcing the honest bourgeois of the garden to turn their heads away or to flee. Although the police were usually not on hand as they were at the Luxembourg, a detachment from the Invalides patrolled the Tuileries, trying to keep out servants and undesirables. On the fête day of Saint-Louis, however, the Tuileries garden was open in the evening to everyone and was turned into "a grand charivari." A throng of 200,000 gave the garden a "confusion of estates, of persons, and of physiognomies. . . ."

Gardens were, therefore, very much in fashion in eighteenth-century Paris. Some were simply for strolling and ogling, but others, following the great success of Torré's summer Waux-Hall on the boulevard, were commercial *spectacles* featuring fireworks, illuminations, dances, music, and mime. Elsewhere on the boulevards, another new entertainment was born: the first version of what we would recognize as a circus. Called the Amphithéâtre Anglois and located on the rue du Faubourg du Temple, this show was the creation of an Englishman named Astley.[251] Born in Newcastle in 1742, Astley was a horseman in the army who established an amphitheater in London in 1770. He first came to Paris in 1774 as a participant in a riding exhibition sponsored by a horseman of the King of Sardinia. With his son he subsequently launched his amphitheater on the boulevards in 1782. Previous engagements obliged him to return to England in August 1782, much to the dismay of the boulevard audiences, whom he placated by giving an extra show each day. He returned to Paris a year later.[252]

The covered amphitheater, 64 feet in diameter, had the appearance of a garden with a racetrack surrounded by two rows of loges. It was outfitted with 16 slender columns and 2,000 lamps and heated by several stoves. Performances were given every day at 6:00 P.M., except Wednesday and Saturday. Prices ranged from 3 livres for first loges and 1 livre, 10 sous for second loges to 12 sous for the parterre.[253]

Astley kept his patrons diverted with a variety of entertainments, including *ombres Chinoises*, fireworks, an orchestra, clowns, acrobats, funambulists, a Chinese promenade, and feats of strength by his horsemen. These were mere accompaniments, however, to the main show—displays of horsemanship and equestrian tricks.[254] Announcements in the press referred to races, a minuet for two horses, a grand procession of horses in different postures, and a combat between an English tailor and his horse. Astley danced on galloping horses. It seems apparent from the accounts that he and his troupe were very skillful. They were joined in 1783 by the Italian Antonio Franconi, who established a dynasty of circus performers.[255] On 25 April 1786, Astley's troupe performed at Versailles for the king, queen, and an assembly of 600 people.[256]

Not far from Astley's Amphithéatre there was a much less sophisticated animal show, which was quite accessible to boulevard crowds. Run by a man named Leleu, the Combat du Taureau, as it was called, was located on the road from Pantin above the Hôpital Saint-Louis.[257] Unlike Astley's circus, animal fights had a long history in the city, probably going back to the Middle Ages. In 1645 the regency authorized an unspecified place for them in Paris.[258] In the early eighteenth century they were located at the Gate of Sèvres, where in addition to the fights, bear grease to grow hair and eyebrows and to cure rheumatism was sold.[259] For a while the lieutenant general of police stopped the combats, but by mid-century they had resumed.[260]

Leleu presented fights between bears and between deer and bulls (after the latter had been bled in order to weaken them). He tried to hold Spanish-style bullfights with toreadors and announced the appearance of Antoine Marco from Valencia in the press, but the police halted this attraction.[261] He also staged boar hunts, deer races, and stunts by a Corsican horse.

The fights that really attracted the crowds—people screamed to see them

18. Animal fight. (AD, number 257, b.3.)

—were those between dogs or between bulldogs and other animals, including bears, asses (the *peccata*), wild boars, leopards, lions, mandrills, muzzled wolves, tigers, and bulls. The bears were made to appear as exotic as possible; one was described as the big white bear from Siberia, another as the cruel bear from Poland, and another as the bear from the Pyrenees. The dogs were supplied by Leleu or occasionally by spectators. These were always fights to the death. A poster going back to 1713 stated the following:

> You are notified that one prepares for Sunday, 8 October 1713, a fight to the death of a bull that is sufficiently large and beautiful to provide pleasure, as is everything that follows, which will be well executed. First: several brave dogs will stand firmly up to several entirely different nations and battle all those which present themselves. The first clash will be given at once at four o'clock exactly against the mongrel nation; the second against that of the bears; the third against that of the wolves; the fourth against that of the bulls, the fifth against that of the badgers; the sixth against that of the cheetahs; the seventh will be the general fight where the big chief will lose his life. The end will be a dog who will be raised in the air in the midst of a grand fireworks which will be extraordinary.[262]

Arrows outfitted with petards were shot into the bulls, tearing up their flesh and weakening them before the pack of dogs was turned loose on them. In the *peccata*, an ass was driven crazy by the dogs' assaults before being killed. Its feeble attempts to bite the dogs elicted shouts and laughter from the crowd, which consisted both of *le bas peuple* and ladies of the highest social rank. Alexandre Du Coudray was shocked by the bloody spectacle of an old bull, weak from hunger, horns sawed off, tormented by flaming darts and torn apart by 12 dogs, but even more by the throng of people of both sexes, all ages and professions, "la bonne compagnie," screaming "the dogs, the dogs."[263] Admission to the combat at Sèvres, which was probably comparable to Leleu's amphitheater, was 3 livres for first loges; 2 livres, 8 sous for second; 1 livre, 10 sous for the amphitheater; and 15 sous for the parterre.[264]

Performances always ended when the victorious bulldogs were hoisted in the air in a ritual called the "enlèvement d'un bouledogue anglois," after which the dogs jumped through flaming hoops. The crowd delighted in seeing the bulldogs win the combats, which may have symbolically represented to them the struggle between civilization and barbarity. Performances climaxed with fireworks and a "Hourvari recréatif."

In addition to the Combat du Taureau, another *spectacle* near the boulevards much favored by Parisians was aquatic shows. Held in an enclosure on the Seine dedicated to Neptune and known as the Rapée (where the quai is today), the usual show featured seamen from Ecole de Navigation battling each other with lances on boats.[265] These combats were accompanied by tugs-of-war, running at the ring on water slides, challenges of various sorts among bargemen, and fireworks. One of the principal recreations was the Mat de Cocagne. A piece of round wood, usually the mast of a vessel, was mounted horizontally or vertically. If vertical, it was sunk solidly into the ground or the riverbed. The pole was made slippery by rubbing soap or grease on it. A prize at the top of the pole awaited the seaman able to climb it. If horizontal, the pole was set on an incline, supported at both extremities. Combatants had to move the entire length of the pole to get the prize. Most of them fell into the water.

Loges, rows of seats, and a platform were provided for the public on the land and on boats with tickets for 40, 30, 24, and 12 sous. The entire presentation was dressed in the garb of a *spectacle*, as Neptune emerged from the hollows of a rock on one side of the Rapée, and Vulcan with his Cyclops forged weapons on the other side. The seamen's boats were painted to represent different parts of the universe. Winners were crowned by a goddess who sprang from the depths of the water.

On occasion, patrons of the Rapée were treated to something special. In 1785, for example, a Spaniard walked on the water. This attraction occurred scarcely two years after a watchmaker from Lyons announced that he would race across the Seine under the Pont-Neuf at the speed of a horse. The *Journal de Paris* raised a large subscription for the charlatan, whose boasts were believed because the balloon flights of 1783 and 1784 made most Parisians believe that science made everything possible. The watchmaker failed to appear and was later dispatched to the Bastille. The Spaniard at the Rapée, however, walked across the river wearing wooden shoes.[266] Moving very slowly and laboriously, he had difficulty keeping his balance, but, as the author of the *Correspondance littéraire* remarked, "he had reason to believe that Saint Peter himself could not have done better, perhaps with no more grace nor with more assurance."[267] After 15 or 20 minutes on the water, the Spaniard left his shoes in a floating box in order to hide his trick from the public. The trick was that his shoes were really a two-part boat. Nevertheless, the author of the *Correspondance* admired the Spaniard's good balance, which he likened to that of a funambulist.

Although they bore little relation to aquatic spectacles, public baths also captured the fancy of eighteenth-century Parisians. Many such establishments were indoors on the streets of Paris (Luc-Vincent Thiéry counted seven in Paris by 1784, each costing three sous)[268] and copper bathtubs could be rented for eight sous a day, but Parisians preferred bathing in the river in summer at the Rapée or at several other locations on the Seine. These baths consisted of boats covered with an awning near which were sunk 20 posts 12 fathoms long and 2 wide.[269] The boat and the posts were also covered with awnings and enclosed by planks. Bathers paid three sous plus an extra sou for a towel. The baths of men and women were separated, but the *Journal du citoyen* stressed "the gathering of people of all estates who abound there in very hot weather."[270] Four baths, one on the river bank near the Place Maubert, another opposite it on the Ile de la Cité, and two near the Pont-Marie, were reserved for women. Two large posters on the Pont-Marie proclaimed: "Bains des dames publiques et particulières."[271] Rétif de la Bretonne called this poster an example of scandalous ignorance whose perpetrators should be punished. Women who wanted more privacy could hire Seine boatmen who would ferry them for 30 sous an hour further up the river, set up a small area in the water consisting of four posts and an awning, and teach them to swim.

By the 1780s one of the favorite public baths was the Bains Chinois at the Pont de la Tournelle beside the Île Saint-Louis.[272] The proprietor, Sieur Turquin, enjoyed the approval of the Royal Faculty of Medicine. For 24 sous one could rent one of 22 cabinets, each with a key, built on a barge in such a way that the river provided every person with a three-foot bath, and no one got his neighbor's water. Men and women were separated by a gallery. Finally, there were the baths and fumigations of one Sieur Albert in a marble reservoir equipped with a unique ascending, descending, and lateral shower that enabled one to dispense with a syringe because the spray was continuous.[273] Mercier wrote that a person sits on a pierced seat as the water "penetrates four inches into your anus and sprays the intestines gently, surely, for a long time, and abundantly."[274] Hot baths cost 24 sous without towels.

19. Jean Ramponeau. Engraved by Maré. Verse: on the air "Allons chez Ramponeau":

> *Chantons d'un ton burlesque*
> *La fameux Ramponeau:*
> *Sa figure grotesque*
> *Egaye le cerveau*
> *Le voilà Ramponeau*
> *Admirez qu'il est beau!*
>
> *Tout Paris court en foule*
> *Etrangers et badaux*
> *On se bat on se roule,*
> *Comme de vrais nigauds.*
> *Pour chanter Ramponeau*
> *Boire du vin nouveau.*

(BN CE photograph 56B162661. See also MC. Topo, p.c. 150H.)

20. Interior of Ramponeau's café showing the crowd and wall graffiti, including Mr. Good Humor with Mademoiselle Camargo. (BN CE photograph 56C116.19.)

Just beyond the boulevards only a short walk away lay the route from Belleville, where a jolly fellow named Jean Ramponeau operated the most celebrated *guinguette* in Paris, Le Tambour Royal. Born in Argenteuil, Ramponeau inherited from his uncle, a sacristan, a house at the Courtille, which he turned into a cabaret.[275] It was a perfect location because it lay just beyond the gate to the city, enabling Ramponeau to avoid paying taxes on his wine. As a result, he charged his patrons only 3 1/2 sous for a pint.

The most widely known feature of the raucous Tambour was the graffiti and caricatures that covered the walls. Among them were the patron goose of the Parisian cafés and Mr. Good Humor cavorting with Mademoiselle Camargo, once the most celebrated dancers at the Opéra. Ramponeau's waiters wore multicolored bonnets shaped like sugarloaves. The garrulous proprietor contributed to the festive atmosphere. Red-faced and bloated, fat-bellied, jug in hand, decked out in a three-cornered hat, he roamed among his habitués. "This was for them the living and popular incarnation of the god of wine."[276]

Better known than Buffon and Voltaire, according to Mercier, Ramponeau and his cabaret were celebrated in poetry, plays, songs, and engravings.[277] The boulevard writer and actor Taconet wrote a play (an *ambigu* with songs and dances) about Ramponeau entitled *La Mariée de la Courtille, ou Arlequin Ramponeau*. Performed by Nicolet's troupe, the scene depicted a wedding celebration in the Tambour. As the genial proprietor escorted two female merchants of the boulevards to his "cabinet des cocus," where an abbé awaited them, the wedding party celebrated the quality of Ramponeau's wine, concluding with a couplet to the vaudeville air "V'là c'que c'est d'aller aux bois":

> Divertissions-nous à gogo,
> V'là c'que c'est que Ramponeau,
> Pour y vuider plus d'un tonneau,
> Un chacun s'empresse,
> Et chez lui sans cesse
> De Rebauteure c'est un troupeau,
> V'là c'que c'est que Ramponeau.[278]

His renown was such that a new word appeared in the Parisian vocabulary —*ramponer*, meaning either to drink in a *guinguette* or to become inebriated.[279]

Ramponeau's notoriety owed a lot to his involvement in a trial. The proprietor signed a contract in 1760 with one of his customers, a theater director named Gaudon; but two days before he was to appear on stage in a piece written for him, Ramponeau abrogated the contract, claiming in a notarized declaration that his Christian conscience prevented him from taking up a career that the church condemned.[280] It is probable, however, that Ramponeau's real reason was fear of losing his popularity. A few days before he was to appear on Gaudon's stage, he had performed in a private theater at Versailles, where he was poorly received.

The celebrated Lawyer Elie de Beaumont defended Gaudon at the trial. Voltaire turned the trial into a hilarious satire. In his rollicking eulogy of cabarets, Voltaire pointed out that Rousseau approved of them and that if they did not exist, girls who would otherwise languish in sterility would become fertile and produce children useful to the church and the state.[281]

In a poem about Ramponeau, F. L. Herme de La Mothe suggested the Tambour's clientele:

> Des femmes et d'enfants quelle affreuse cohue
> Je vois en se heurtant déboucher de la rue!
> Grands Dieux! Que d'embarras! Que de cabriolets!
> Que d'abbés; de Coureurs; de Robins; de Valets!
> Etourdi par les cris, le bruit et les injures,
> Je traverse au milieu de six rangs de voitures,
> Pour demander quel est ce Spectacle nouveau:
> J'entends crier: Entrez, c'est ici Ramponeau,
> Monseigneur; Ramponeau: voyons: entrez mon Prince.[282]

The Tambour was the favorite hangout of boulevard actors and writers, all friends of Ramponeau; but it was also frequented by laborers, ambulant musicians, used-clothes sellers, guardsmen, procurators, tax officials, countesses, intendants, and fishmongers—in short by people of all occupations and social groups. Although they were often treated roughly, the gentlemen of the court accompanied by their ladies costumed in gray dresses were unabashed to appear at the Tambour. Curses pierced the air as rapidly as the soup bowls flew against the walls, and the aristocratic ladies rubbed shoulders with scullery maids and sluts. "By mutual understanding the ranks intermingled. . . . Poor and rich, noble and wretch sit down at the table side by side chatting, drinking, singing without constraint as without jealousy. Equality was not born yesterday. Pleasure invented it and consecrated it before institutions."[283]

These last remarks doubtless convey the real social importance of the boulevards and their entertainments. As the salons of the seventeenth century virtually eliminated the separation between robe and sword and blurred that between bourgeois and aristocrat, the boulevards cracked the social stratification separating the highborn and lowborn.[284] In the streets, cafés, and *petits spectacles*, all the ranks mingled openly and freely. Certainly, it was not an equality of wealth, occupation, or education; but it was one of pleasure, of taste. The culture of the people's marketplace—the streets—engulfed nearly the whole city by 1780. Aristocrats and bourgeois, like apprentices, fishmongers, and lackeys, thronged to Nicolet, to Astley, to Comus, and to Ramponeau. Those who mocked the official world were joined by those who were being mocked. The marquis marveled at feats of magic and science; he delighted in the mute *spectacles* of Audinot; he was dazzled by the equilibrists and amused by the salty *parades*, just like the tavern boy at his elbow. The taste of *le bas peuple* spread through the ranks of *le monde*, creating one society and one culture, a counterculture to the officially sanctioned world of court and city. These socially unsegregated lanes of leisure generated their own freewheeling material and moral nutrients that, despite the increasingly moralistic content of the plays, was still based on humorous satire of the traditional order.

The final triumph of this counterculture was the conquest by the ever-swelling volume of popular entertainments of Cardinal Richelieu's once elegant garden in the center of royalist Paris.

8

The Convergence of Popular and Elite Culture: The Palais-Royal

IT IS A LONG WAY from the *tréteaux* of the fairs to the arcades of the Palais-Royal, but that is where popular culture journeyed in eighteenth-century Paris. Looking onto the Louvre and the Tuileries, designed to shut out the city as Henri IV's Place Royale was earlier constructed to admit the Parisian world, Richelieu's garden became the heartland of popular pleasure in the few years preceding the Revolution. Once the home of the young Louis XIV and his mother, this regal garden symbolized the conquest of aristocratic Paris by the marketplace culture of the boulevards and fairs.

The Palais-Royal had become the property of the Orléans family in the reign of Louis XIV when the king gave it and its dependencies to his brother, Philippe, along with the right of future ducs d'Orléans to make whatever alterations they desired.[1] In the 1750s and 1760s many changes were made in the palace by the architects Constant d'Ivry, Jean-Michel Moreau, and Henri Piètre, especially after the fire at the Opéra in 1763. In 1776 the duc d'Orléans turned the palace over to his son, Louis-Philippe-Joseph, the duc de Chartres, and to Chartres' wife, Marie-Françoise de Bourbon. On December 1780, five years before his death, the duc d'Orléans ceded the proprietorship of the palace to the duc de Chartres, whose apartments were connected directly to his loges at the Opéra. The cessions were approved by the Conseil d'Etat, and the duc de Chartres, by virtue of Louis XIV's original gift, was free to change and to build as he wished as long as he did not exclude the public from the garden. The Conseil's decree ordered Chartres to raise the necessary funds prior to the alterations. The property was worth over three million livres, but the duc d'Orléans and his son were always short of money. Because of this, given the considerable speculation in property and building

21. Garden of the Palais-Royal. Engraved by Saint-Varin, 1786.
(MC. Topo, p.c. 32A–D.)

going on in this period, the duc de Chartres was persuaded (by the marquis Ducrest) to exploit the Palais-Royal. The only way to make the changes in the palace that he wished and to profit from the garden and the new constructions planned around it seemed to be to lease part of his domain, obliging his tenants to pay for much of the work and to conform to the plans of his architect Victor Louis.[2]

The *lettres patentes* of 7 June 1781 authorizing the whole venture granted Chartres the right to alienate several hundred shallow feet of the garden of the Palais-Royal and to work it up following Victor Louis' plans. Chartres was obliged to use the proceeds from the leases for the improvements in the palace itself. If these sums did not equal the cost of work on the palace, Chartres could not charge them to the Crown. Surplus funds were to be restored to the appanage. Chartres resented the last clause because he sought to improve his financial condition by the enterprise. He accepted it, however, because he believed that the most important gain at this juncture was obtaining royal approval for his venture.

The garden of the Palais-Royal, which became the center of attention, was altered in 1730; for the first time since Richelieu the cardinal's two basins were replaced by one central one with a fountain. Grassy parterres surrounded by elm trees pruned in ball shape separated the basin from the palace. A quincunx of linden trees extended from the basin northward to the rue des Petits-Champs. A grand alley of chestnut trees paralleling the rue de Richelieu ran the entire length of the garden. In this alley stood the "arbre de Cracovie," where writers, news criers, and storytellers gathered.[3]

Until the duc de Chartres turned them into a popular fair, the gardens of the Palais-Royal were a tranquil setting for strollers.[4] They attracted financiers, musketeers, judges, dukes, women of the court, writers, and doctors.[5] In short, the crowd was elegant. The women came in their finest gowns, often arranging nightly trysts in the dark shadow of the trees.

Following the desires of Chartres, Victor Louis' plans called for the construction at the southern end of the garden of an extension of the palace and on the other three sides of the rectangle an assembly of houses that would block the old houses from view to be decorated in such a way as to appear a direct and necessary dependency of the palace. A covered and continuous promenade was to be erected in front of the houses that would expand into peristyles under the new palace. Louis designed a simple, uniformly decorated facade with fluted pilasters over 40 feet high stretching from the base to the top of the structure. Arcades formed the public promenade, each equipped with a chandelier.[6] The ground floor and mezzanine of each of the 60 pavilions were to be occupied by boutiques. The first floor would extend

22. The tree of Cracovie where writers assembled. (MC. Topo, p.c. 33A–E.)

to the top of the capitals; the second would include garlands and corbels; the upper stories would be crowned by a mansard roof partially concealing a balustrade lined with vases at equal intervals. Louis planned to use the same architectural order for the new palace as he did for the pavilions; columns, however, replaced pilasters. The principal promenade of the new palace was to be supported by six rows of Doric columns equal in height to the galleries along the garden. The colonnade of the old palace was to remain.

When news first spread of Chartres' plans "to convert his garden into a sort of fair or a privileged enclosure," the magistrates, seigneurs, and financiers who inhabited the area and regarded the garden as theirs became infuriated.[7] They protested to the duc d'Orléans in several *mémoires* and sent a deputation on 6 April 1781 to the palace. Chartres greeted them unceremoniously in his shorts and bathrobe. The author of the *Mémoires secrets* shared their outrage: "One cannot see without a kind of scorn a great, very rich prince display a cupidity so sordid and reject any feeling of justice and commiseration."[8] The proprietors also went to the king and soon afterward launched legal proceedings, charging that Chartres had violated the will of Cardinal Richelieu and was not legally the real proprietor of the palace.

In the meantime, the public, fearful that the garden would lose its ambience, became increasingly concerned. A smear campaign against Chartres was waged in pamphlets, engravings, songs, and placards. There were demonstrations against him in the theaters, and he was jeered in public. Siméon-Prosper Hardy reported that the duc was booed when he walked across the garden and that he caused a brouhaha when he appeared on a balcony of the palace.[9] Considering that Louis XIV had given the palace to his brother and heirs with the right to make alterations and that each one of the successive ducs d'Orléans had modified the palace with no public outcry, the uproar was amazing.

Chartres withstood the abuse very well. Once Victor Louis' plans were drawn up and he had obtained the king's permission to change the garden through *lettres patentes* registered in June, Chartres tried to persuade the public that his alterations were felicitous. A pamphlet entitled *Exposé des changements au Palais-Royal* was published and distributed widely on his order in July 1781, explaining the changes and appealing for support. It spoke eloquently of the compensation for the loss of the grand alley of the garden by the public promenade under lighted arcades: "Spectacle and promenade at one and the same time for every season and every moment, this locale will provide a kind of beauty of which there is no example in Paris and will convince the public that in the plans decreed by S.A.S. it has not been forgotten for one instant."[10] Chartres also put on display Louis' original designs in an apartment in the palace. The proprietors were not placated, however, and studied the *lettres patentes* for some legal flaw.[11] Indeed, when on August 1 workers began cutting down the trees in the grand alley, writers, elegant women, and lemonade salesmen joined the proprietors in protesting the spoliation. Petitions were circulated, and placards defaming the duc appeared on the walls of the palace.[12] Chartres' plans also seemed to take a turn for the worse when the Opéra burned for the second time on 8 June 1781. Because it was an appurtenance of the palace, a reconstructed Opéra had to be fitted into Victor Louis' designs, and the duc requested the permission of Amelot, the minister for Paris, for that undertaking.[13]

While Chartres waged a vigorous battle to retain a new Opéra in the Palais-Royal—a battle that he eventually won—and to persuade the proprietors that he was not trying to injure them, work on the new garden continued.[14] The three streets enclosing the three sides of the new garden were named after the duc's sons.[15] They formed the reverse sides of his pavilions and arcades, closing off the garden, reducing it in size to 275 meters in length and 100 in width, and blocking the view of the old proprietors. The duc had the garden replanted with 30-year-old chestnut trees uninterrupted by quincunxes, making it seem longer than before. A rectangular esplanade was placed near the palace facade, and construction of the new Opéra was begun. The cost of the work was set at 3,302,250 livres and was to be finished with new pavilions ready for occupancy by 1 April 1784.

Priced at 5,750,500 livres each, the pavilions included both boutiques and upper stories, with the provision that facades be maintained in their original appearance without the addition of insignias or other marks. The lease notarized on 9 November 1781 between Chartres and Robert André Hardouin, bookseller, and his wife, Marie-Anne Margueritte Pochet, was typical of the contractual arrangements for Palais-Royal residences.[16] Established for nine years from the beginning of occupancy, the lease designated a pavilion on the terrain of the old garden parallel to the rue de Richelieu with three arcades (numbers 13, 14, and 15); three entrances to the garden; five cellars; two boutiques in front and one in the rear; two rooms on the mezzanine; an apartment consisting of a drawing room, an antechamber, a living room, a bedroom, a toilet, and clothes closet on the first floor; the same arrangement on the second floor; three small lodgings for *garçons* consisting of an alcove room and a closet on the third floor; and at the top level quarters for five servants. The Hardouins were obliged to pay Hector Hyacinthe Séguin, Chartres' treasurer, 37,500 livres in four installments. They agreed to pay 3,750 livres in advance to be applied to the last six months of the lease. They were required to furnish the residences, assume responsibility for repairs, and contribute to the upkeep of the street (rue de Montpensier) behind their residences and the provision of 14 large street lights and a small light at each of their three arcades. The lease further stipulated that they could not rent boutiques or apartments to merchants or workers lacking mastership and that they could not cede or transfer the lease without Chartres' permission.

Chartres lacked the funds to build the *corps de logis* of his palace (only the foundations were in place by 1785), and he had to raise a subscription to complete the Opéra. But by resorting to feudal law (reassessment of the annual *cens* where new building was undertaken in a city), he taxed the terrain and buildings parallel to the three old streets bordering the garden and pushed forward rapidly with the construction.[17] His precarious financial plight was greatly relieved on 18 November 1785, when the duc d'Orléans died.

Prior to the completion of the pavilions, Chartres' great commercial and cultural enterprise had, however, already come to life with the construction of the *galerie de bois*. Originally Victor Louis had planned four additional wings for the Palais-Royal and a colonnade, but when money ran out, only the foundations of the wing intended for the northern side of the *cour d'honneur*, replacing Richelieu's *galerie d'arcades*, were in place. The money for the principal *corps de logis* and the colonnade had not been raised. Although Ducrest and Louis urged the duc to pursue his plans to the end, Chartres suspended work on the palace, and late in 1783 he erected a covered wooden gallery on the foundations formed by the columns. Temporary huts for immediate rent were erected at a cost of only 49,247 livres. Thus, the infamous *galerie de bois* came into being—two covered promenades bordered by three rows of boutiques under a canopy. The gallery stretched from one wing to the other. It was decorated with porticoes, simulated drapery, and lamps. Dubbed the Camp of the Tartars, the gallery became the hangout of debauched youths, thieves, *petits-maîtres,* swindlers, prostitutes, and financiers.[18] A decent woman or a "reasonable man" could not be found amid the shoving and pushing, according to Mayeur de Saint-Paul, except after the theaters closed, when lackeys formed a line from the door to the middle of the Camp, where libertines screamed indecent propositions at the women and rude youths jeered and taunted the crowd. Completed in 1784, the Camp of the Tartars inaugurated the new Palais-Royal and the launching of a festival of popular culture cheek by jowl with the palace of a prince of the blood.

The camp itself attracted some bizarre curiosities, such as the wax figure of a nude odalisque known as "la belle Zulima," who, according to a poster, had died two hundred years before but was perfectly preserved.[19] Her hair partially covering her breasts, Zulima was stretched out on a canopy. For a few sous an onlooker could lift a small cloth draped over her lower body. The public realized that it was being tricked, but was still avid for this well-made imitation of a real person. Crowds in the camp could also observe the amazing Paul Butterbrodt, who weighed 238 kilos.[20] In one of the boutiques, a man executed conjuring tricks, and in another there was a curious *billard*

23. Paul Butterbrodt. (MC Topo, p.c. 33D. See also BN CE, Collection Hennin, T116, numbers 10092–10183.)

méchanique where a three-foot-high château was placed at the end of a long, narrow table. Customers attempted to roll a ball into a hole in the château. If they succeeded, the ball struck a spring, setting off a carillon and opening a series of doors from which little figures emerged carrying numbers. The place was frequented by women and hustlers. The sign at one booth promised something for two sous that God himself had never beheld. Inside, the spectator saw himself in a mirror as a voice spoke: "You see your likeness, what God is not able to see, because God is not similar."[21]

A cry of outrage echoed from the arcades against the profiteering merchant prince who threatened the opportunity of the pavilion boutiques to sell costly goods. The prince had rented cheap wooden huts to a crowd of "hussars." Such a throng of people and soon *spectacles,* cafés, and clubs descended on the Palais-Royal, however, that nearly everyone profited. By 1784 as the work on the pavilions and the garden neared completion, public opinion swung to the duc and his enterprise. Siméon-Prosper Hardy, that acute observer of the Parisian scene, had noted that as early as 1782 the public, observing the many entrances Chartres installed for access to the garden and the beautiful promenade he was creating had begun to grow less disdainful.[22] By 1784 the *Courier d'Avignon* told its readers that despite all the satires of the new garden, more and more people, even its critics, were returning to enjoy it.[23] Louis-Sébastien Mercier, objecting only to the claustral shape of the garden, was rhapsodic in his enthusiasm:

> This enchanted place is a small luxurious city enclosed in a large one. . . . It is called the capital of Paris. Everything can be found there. . . . A Prisoner could live there without boredom and dream of liberty only after several years. It is precisely the place that Plato would want a captive to be assigned in order to detain him without jailer and without violence, by sweet and voluntary chains. . . . Lucullus himself could not provide the pleasures with which he entertained that in our time a young prodigal relishes who, entrenched in the Palais-Royal, gathers together at his splendid table more sensations than one would have in the great days of Roman grandeur. . . .[24]

Rétif de la Bretonne went so far as to call the Palais "the brain of the capital, . . . the center of taste, the quintessence of politeness, or urbanity."[25] He urged the government to remove all *spectacles* from the quarters of work and of prostitution and to concentrate them in the Palais. Perhaps the redoubtable Mrs. Thrale from England best captured the changed mood of Parisians in these words:

> In the Evening my Husband showed me the new square called the Palais Royal, whence the Duc de Chartres took away all the fine high Trees, which having stood for Centuries, it was a Shame to touch with an Ax, and accordingly the

24. The cannon in the Palais-Royal. Photograph taken by the author in August, 1979.

people were as angry as Frenchmen can be, when the Folly was first committed. The Court had however Wit enough to convert the place into a sort of Vauxhall, with Tents, Fountains, etc., a Colonnade of Shops and Coffeehouses surrounding it on every side; and now they are all happy and contented, and *Vive le Duc de Chartres!*[26]

Many visitors to the Palais-Royal found the most interesting feature to be the little cannon on a pedastal in the basin, exactly on the meridian of Paris. Rigged with a convex glass, the cannon discharged every day at noon when struck by the sun's rays.[27] The cannon seemed to symbolize the flame of reconciliation between the duc de Chartres and the public.

What really enabled the Palais-Royal to succeed as a commercial enterprise and inadvertently as a nonpolitical experiment in social amalgamation was the advent of popular entertainment. The duc de Chartres welcomed the *spectacles* with open arms. His aim was "to attract the curious more and more to his palace by all sorts of games and recreations and public transactions."[28]

The first theater in the palais was Les Petits Comédiens de S.A.S. (Son

Altesse Sérénissime) Monseigneur le Comte de Beaujolais, originally intended for the private entertainment of Philippe d'Orléans' youngest son, but opened to the public on 23 October 1784, when the comte de Beaujolais, Chartres' brother, gave permission to two enterpreneurs, Delomel and Gardeur, to establish a public marionette show there.[29] It was located at the northwestern angle of the palais in the Galerie de Beaujolais, where the Théâtre du Palais-Royal is now. A woodturner by trade, Delomel made figurines and marionettes with faces of well-known people in his spare time. Jean-Nicolas Gardeur, whose brother, a tailor who made costumes for the puppets and lived in the same building as Delomel, made paper-mâché sculptures. Gardeur proposed an association with Delomel whereby they would start a theater using marionettes sculpted and costumed to look like actors of the Opéra and the French and Italian companies.[30] After forming a partnership, they rented the theater in the Palais-Royal for 14,000 livres annually with a three-year lease plus an extra 6,000 livres for the use of Beaujolais' name. The elongated theater had 22 loges, some grilled, spread along 2 rows, 20 benches in the parquet, and standing room. It held about eight hundred people.[31]

Delomel and Gardeur had an immediate dispute over ticket prices. Delomel believed tickets should be inexpensive: "We are a little *spectacle;* our prices should be small because our genre is addressed more to little pocketbooks than to large ones."[32] Gardeur's view, on the other hand, was that because their theater was under the protection of a prince of the blood, they should not adopt the low prices of the boulevard. Delomel finally consented to charge 3 livres for first loges, 2 for second, and 1 livre 10 sous for the main floor.

When they first began their *spectacle* in the palais, the directors worked with figures $3\frac{1}{2}$ feet high made of wood and paper. It was not long, however, before they abandoned marionettes and began using child actors between 5 and 8 years old, later 12 to 16. Their troupe grew to 20 actors, 20 actresses, several dancers, a ballet master, a machinist, a music master, and a 22-piece orchestra. A total of 113 people, including ushers and furnishers, were employed. The directors attracted such composers as Froment and Maillot from the Opéra and Philidor from the Opéra-Comique, along with the Italian composers Pompigni and Bambini. Playwrights included Dulaurens, Panard, Dorvigny, Beaunoir, Guillemain, and Thibault. The Petits Comédiens performed French and Italian musical comedies, ballets, melodramas, dramatic proverbs, and farces. The great ambiguity of the genres is revealed by the definition of a melodrama by Louis Raymond, the chief director (*instituteur*) of the *spectacle.* He called it a "comedy in which the dialogue is interrupted by little pieces of music," which "should be well-known airs such as Pont-Neufs."[33] The opening production of the Beaujolais was a prologue called *Momus,* a one-act proverb with vaudevilles entitled *Il y a commencement à tout,* and the fable of Prometheus with songs and dances.[34]

In Maillé de Marencourt's prologue with vaudevilles, an abbé, a young girl, a woman (Bel Esprit), a Gascon, and a Norman are gathered in the new garden of the Palais-Royal.[35] Bel Esprit tells the abbé how bored she was until he came like an angel from heaven, and he comments on her spirituality. They all discuss the opening of the new *spectacle* directed by Momus, god of raillery, as Venus and Minerva arrive. Determined to use his show to instruct youth by means of fables, Momus asks Minerva to help him restrain his natural gaiety and asks Venus to bring pleasure, laughter, and love to his theater. This entire scene was censored. The rest of the prologue concerns the efficacy of puppets (they can perform any genre of piece) and the use of vaudevilles with Momus promising not to incorporate wicked ones. Several couplets lampoon the great theaters, such as this one sung by the Gascon:

> *Admirons de fracas*
> *des grands airs d'opéras*
> *Cherissons l'ariette*
> *Elle est plus vive et plus guillerette.*
> *Mais je vous le répète*
> *Mon chant divertissant*
> *est cent fois plus plaisant*
> *que ce bruit important.*

When the Beaujolais began hiring child actors and performing *opéras-comiques,* the Comédie-Italienne protested loudly to the authorities, charging that their contract with the Opéra gave them the exclusive right to sing on stage. In a *mémoire* to the minister, the Comédie-Italienne spoke of the ruin the new theater would cause at the three *spectacles* established on royal authority, especially to the Italian players, whose theater was in the same vicinity and performed in the same genre.[36] The Comédie referred to its heavy costs and the unwarranted competition for an audience. In response, the Petits Comédiens resorted to an ingenious dodge harking back to the early days of the fair theaters. As the players mimed the action on stage, performers in the wings delivered the songs and spoken parts. The public was fascinated by these sung pantomimes, especially by the remarkable coordination achieved by the two sets of performers.[37] An English spectator, remarking on the perfect synchronization of the onstage and offstage performers, stated that "the illusion was so perfect that it has given rise to many wagers on the question of whether the voice did not come from persons on the stage."[38] The *Almanach musical* wrote that nearly everyone "believes at first that these are children speaking and singing," creating "the perfect illusion."[39] In his review of the first production in mime and song at the Beaujolais (Froment's *Le Vieux soldat* and *L'Amateur de musique*), Baron Grimm wrote: "The performance of it is directed with so much intelligence that without having seen it it is difficult to form an idea of the illusion it produces; the harmony of gesture and word is so accurate and so perfect that even after having been forewarned, one is still tempted to doubt that there were really two persons who shared the same role like that."[40] Only the voices of Hardy and Métra were raised in discontent. Hardy remarked that the Beaujolais was as "contrary to good morals" as other theaters of its type.[41] Métra was also moralistic, although in less than a year he was won over to the sung pantomimes.[42] All accounts indicate that the Parisian public came to the new theater in droves, which made the Italian players, soon joined by the French, all the angrier. The Comédie-Française argued that emulation, useful in the crafts, was dangerous in the arts, especially in comedy; if competition is beneficial within one theater, it is bad when it occurs between two different troupes.[43]

The child actors were reasonably well compensated. The directors signed contracts with the parents of every child. Salaries of 400 to 500 livres a year were paid to children between the ages of 5 and 9; those between 9 and 12 received 600 to 800 livres, and those between 12 and 16 got 1,000 or more livres. As these wages were higher than those of many workers, positions in the troupe were much sought after.

The Petits Comédiens became a noisy, raucous *spectacle,* where authors formed cabals to jeer at the first performances of each other's pieces and audiences constantly interrupted the players with shouts. The din grew so bad that Delomel and Gardeur had to post a sign at the door threatening the expulsion of spectators who caused demonstrations in the hall by their cheers and whistles. It did little good. When an *opéra-comique* called *La Politique à la halle* was performed, a crowd from the central market screamed at the actors and demanded that the director be thrown in the cellar. The police had to ban the piece. By the late 1780s, of course, many of the performers were no longer children. Male spectators began entering actresses' dressing rooms, and the theater became notorious as a place of debauchery. Lieutenant General Lenoir after repeated warnings dispatched a squad of police to the theater in 1788. By that time the actors were speaking and singing from the stage, the remaining children and offstage performers had been dismissed, and the directors were paying the Opéra a tribute of 833 livres a year.

The second theater at the Palais-Royal was the Variétés Amusantes. Once Gaillard and Dorfeuille had gained control of that troupe on the boulevards, Chartres took the initiative in bringing it to the Palais.[44] Although he did not sign a lease with Gaillard and Dorfeuille until February 1787, Chartres did authorize a provisional wooden theater for the use of the boulevard troupe.[45] It was constructed in 1784 in the garden of the princes (*cour d'honneur*) in the southwest part of the Palais, where the Comédie-Française is today. The theater was conveniently equipped with several grilled loges intended for important men, widows in mourning, and "everyone in whom prudence or decency inspires the desire to see without being seen."[46] Prices were steep: 3 livres for first loges; 1 livre, 10 sous for second; and 1 livre for third.

There was an immediate uproar from the French comedians, who appealed to the new minister of Paris, Baron Breteuil, in November 1784 to forbid the Variétés. They even sent a delegate to Versailles to see the minister, but he reported back that the court was too concerned about Dutch politics and other matters to grant the French players the protection they wanted.[47] The Comédie retained only its censorship rights over the new Palais-Royal theater.[48] Despite their charge that the Variétés claimed to have a theater superior to the three principal *spectacles* of the nation, the Comédie-Italienne was equally unsuccessful in stopping the Variétés.[49] It was clearly in the interest of the police and the government to encourage the growth of new *spectacles* out of motives that were "purely political."[50] Noting that the *spectacles* were more crowded than ever, the *Journal de Paris* commented that they were necessary in large cities in order to prevent "a greater evil."[51] The epidemic of spectators, according to the *Journal,* spanned all classes. When the *spectacles* closed for three weeks over Easter in 1789, the lieutenant general was extremely upset "because it had been proved to him that heads ferment more when the *spectacle* did not occupy idlers."[52]

The Variétés Amusantes was a company of 12 actors, a prompter, 10 actresses, 12 male and 13 female dancers, a ballet master, a machinist and a tailor and also the two directors.[53] With the duc in attendance, the Variétés gave its first performance, a prologue entitled *Palais du bon goût,* on 1 January 1785. With a packed house, the directors took in nearly 6,000 livres.[54]

Gaillard and Dorfeuille gradually attempted to upgrade the status of their *spectacle.* They began calling it the Théâtre des Variétés and sought approval to name it the Variétés Dramatiques in order to disassociate it from the boulevard shows.[55] The press cooperated to the extent of listing the Variétés separately from the boulevard attractions.[56] The directors tried in addition to achieve a more elevated tone in their pieces in order to be more in keeping with the august surroundings of the Palais-Royal. Observers commended the change. The *Almanach du Palais Royal,* admittedly a prejudiced source, declared:

It has left many of its farces at the boulevard that would have been out of place in the spot that it occupies and where they would not have been equally approved; and it begins to take a tone befitting *la bonne compagnie* that is inclined to frequent it. . . . Its repertoire is refined by the wise and enlightened taste of M. d'Orfeuille, man of letters, who is conscious of the need to give this *spectacle* the tone of decency. He accepts only pieces where it prevails, the appropriate means to assure this *spectacle* the favorable welcome of the public that it enjoys today.[57]

The author of the *Almanach* believed that good actors, the favorable attitude of the government, and the protection of the duc d'Orléans (Chartres) would lead to even better quality at the Variétés, culminating in a return to the era of Molière. Though not as ecstatic, the *Journal général* also took note of the fact that the Variétés became a more noble *spectacle,* abandoning the boulevard farces.[58] The author of the *Almanach forain* also chimed in. He was especially caustic in rebuking critics of the Variétés. Responding to the charge that the Palais had succumbed to the taste of the lowborn, he wrote: "It appears . . . that people prefer the gay and unaffected genre to the trivia that has occupied the stage [Comedie-Française] for far too long."[59] He insisted that the Variétés now ranked with the two grand dramatic troupes.

One should not be misled, however, by claims that the Variétés greatly upgraded its repertoire after it moved to the Palais-Royal. It simply moved in the same direction as the other little theaters on the boulevard in this period. It relied less on farce and slapstick, and its shows had greater thematic unity, panache, and often a social message; but satire and ribald humor were not abandoned.[60] The same was true of the Petits Comédiens after they switched from marionettes to live actors. In Guillemain's melodrama with ariettes, *Alexis et Rosette,* for example, Rosette, a woodcutter, is torn between her love for the poor Alexis, a farm worker, and the wealthy Colin, whom she realizes will provide for her and her mother.[61] A subplot concerns the irritation of Simon, a seigneur, at his hardworking employee, Alexis, whom Simon mistakes for a lazy libertine who squanders his money. Not realizing that Alexis has used his free time not to carouse and chase girls but to help Rosette's mother cut wood and that he has used his money to pay Rosette's debts, Simon fires him. Rosette chooses Alexis for her husband, however, because he has "a good heart." Colin gives her up gracefully, and when Simon realizes his error, he rehires Alexis, apologizes, and blesses the marriage. Although this melodrama had comic dances and some double entendres, it celebrated the virtues of the hardworking, generous, and honest country boy who triumphs over wealth and injustice. This was a common theme in the boulevard *spectacles,* at the Variétés and at the Beaujolais.

What was happening in all the little theaters was the culmination of a century-long process: The works of the *petits spectacles* and of the *grands spectacles* were becoming more alike. Much earlier in the century, the Opéra-Comique had borrowed the main tools of opera: song, dance, and the marvelous. Not long after the Opéra-Comique was founded, the Comédie-Italienne began to produce opéras-comiques while the Comédie-Française quietly had greater recourse to music in its productions. In the 1750s the

25. Café du Caveau (right) and Salon de Curtius (left). (BN CE Ef71, numbers 5 and 6 and photograph 75A30805.)

Opéra imported Italian opera bouffes with ariettes, which became the musical staple of the Opéra-Comique after 1760. The productions of the Comédie-Italienne, especially after its merger with the Comique in 1762, became much more serious. Boulevard theater revived the standard characters, vaudevilles, gymnastics, and bawdiness of the old Comique but drifted toward a more elevated genre by the 1780s. It became more mundane. The Variétés was no exception. Thus, throughout the century there was such extensive borrowing among the theaters that any distinction between popular and elite entertainment based on genre quickly collapses. Only one dimension of popular theater remained constant: the humorous, sardonic mockery of the marketplace, and, like the marvelous and the celebration of physical existence, that too was waning.

As happened on the boulevards, the establishment of theater in the Palais-Royal led to an invasion of the duc de Chartres' garden by popular entertainers of every sort. Many retained the traditional combination of fantasy and the physical. Attracting "a great concourse of curious people from every estate," Curtius brought his wax museum to the Palais.[62] His salon at Number 7 contained a balustrade that divided patrons into two groups, one paying 12 sous and the other 2. A ventriloquist performed twice daily in Curtius' salon for 24 sous.[63]

Dominique-François Séraphin opened an *ombres chinoises* at arcade 127 in September 1784 in a hall that held 150 people.[64] Séraphin, a marionettist from Lorraine, brought the *ombre* technique, which Grimm had seen at a private theater, from Italy, where he had lived for some time. Receiving permission in 1772 to establish a theater in the garden of the Hôtel Lannion at Versailles, where he performed for the royal family, he was given the right in April 1781 to call his show "Spectacle des Enfants de France." The *lettres patentes* authorizing his show, signed by the king, stated that it would contribute to the "entertainment of the children of France."[65] When he moved to the Palais-Royal with his *ombres chinoises* in 1784, the king exempted him from paying the customary fees to the Opéra. For 24 or 12 sous one could see a sequence of tableaux with dances, funambulism, animated animals, and magic acts as well as plays mixed with songs and vaudevilles. Each performance was preceded by *feux arabesques* representing tempests, cascades, the forges of Vulcan, shipwrecks, palaces, and the portraits of great men. Séraphin had a repertoire of over two hundred scenes, all shown in the light and shadow technique using seven- or eight-inch-tall paper cutouts suspended by thread or cord. A clavecin was played between scenes. Marie-Françoise Christout has written: "A middle road between phantasmagoria and the *spectacle* of marionettes, the theater of Séraphin gratified more closely the illusionism in vogue by the suppresion of every trace of manipulation."[66]

Lasting one and a half hours, Séraphin's *ombres* were shown every day at 6:00 p.m. before large audiences. All accounts indicate that his *spectacle* was an enormous success, drawing large audiences including *la bonne compagnie*. Pieces such as *La Chasse aux canards, Orphée aux enfers, Le Magicien,* and *Arlequin corsaire* were provided by Gabiot de Salins, Dorvigny, Caron, Guillemain, and others. Guillemain's *Le Pont cassé* can serve to illustrate the kind of work Séraphin presented.[67] Through the transparent curtain the audience saw silhouettes representing a bridge with a broken arch over a river with a house bearing an insignia to the right. A jolly fellow named Le Petit Gas dug at the bridge when an irritated traveler at the opposite end of the bridge asked if he could make it across. Le Petit Gas sang back at him:

> *Les canards l'ont bien passée*
> *Lire lire laire!*
> *Les canards l'ont bien passée,*
> *Lire lon pha!*

To the angry shouts that he was not a duck, Le Petit Gas shouted no, but a turkey. Le Petit Gas continued to mock the traveler, who wanted to reach the

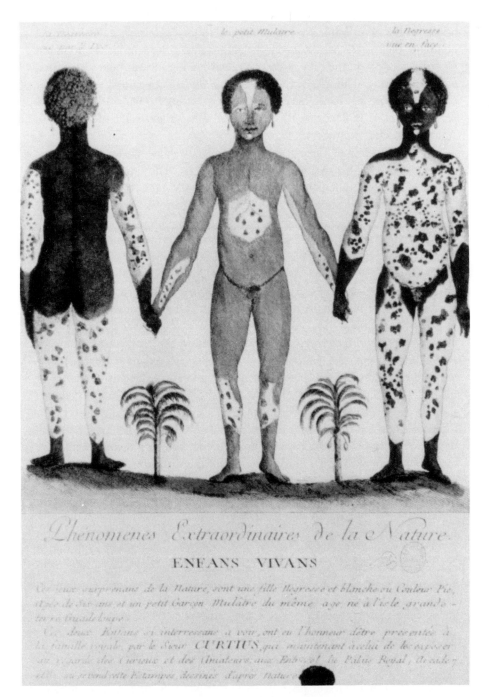

26. "Extraordinary phenomena of nature." Negroes from Guadeloupe displayed by Curtius at the Palais-Royal. (MC. Topo, p.c. 33D.)

house on the other bank, an inn belonging to Gas's master. After hailing a boatman, the traveler was stoned as he passed under the demolished arch, but he arrived safely on the other side and rewarded the furious boatman with a paltry two sous. This playlet for *ombres chinoises* concluded with a fight between the traveler using his cane and the mocking bridge worker with his pick. Evidently, audiences tended to divide between partisans of the mason and those of the bourgeois.[68]

After the Beaujolais turned to child actors, two new marionette theaters equipped with grilled loges opened in the Palais. The first, known as the Pygmées François, opened at arcade 105 in a hall that held two hundred.[69] Operated by Pierre-Siméon Caron and Jean-François Baudin, the show featured pyrotechnic displays of cascades, temples, bouquets, rockets, cones of fire, and national fêtes. The 14-inch-tall puppets performed plays with ariettes by means of offstage voices. Their repertoire included works by Anfossi and Paisiello. Tickets cost 24 and 12 sous. The other troupe, the Fantoccini Italiens, moved from the boulevard into the garden next to the Café de Foy.[70] Their fanciful three- and five-act plays, executed by two-foot tall figures, included *La Descente d'Arlequin aux enfers pour recevoir la magie, Dom Bernard du carpe, Le Bon et le mauvais génie,* and *Arlequin soldat de Catalogne, ramoneur, enfant, statue et perroquet.* Ballets featuring metamorphoses and machines were performed between acts, such as the dance of the hussar (with a flag, leaping routines, a rabbit who turned into Arlequin), the dance of a magic lantern transformed into a woman (a lantern porter who loses his limbs and from whose head a dancing girl emerges), the dance of the hunter who kills birds, the ballet of two Janots who turn into deer and are mounted by shepherd girls, and the dance of the drunkard. Mandolin solos were also played. One could pay as much as 12 livres for a private loge, but the parquet sold for 24 sous; and the second loges, for 12.

The rage for magic, illusion, and science that gripped Paris in the pre-Revolutionary years held full sway in the new arcades. For an admission price of 24 sous, Sieur Belon at number 140 displayed two astronomical machines demonstrating planetary movement every day from noon until 10:00 p.m.[71] Sieur Bontout conducted experiments in physics with mechanical devices every day at 6:30 p.m. in the theater of the Petits Comédiens, and another machinist presented a mechanical deer leading a "Cabriolet Méchanique," which turned and moved backward and forward at the command of persons seated in the vehicle.[72] For the steep price of 3 livres, one could enter Sieur Pelletier's Cabinet de Méchanique, Physique, Hydraulique at No. 44.[73] For the lesser price of 1 livre, 10 sous, Sieur Pinetti conducted experiments in physics in the theater of the Variétés Amusantes.[74] The botanist Michel Adamson had a cabinet of natural history near the Beaujolais.

27. Magic lantern. Courtesy of the Musée des Arts et Métiers,
photograph 1394.

It was inevitable that balloons would come to the Palais-Royal. Sieur Ensten from Strasbourg mounted a show at arcade 77 in which a chevalier rode an equestrian figure $9\frac{1}{2}$ feet tall but weighing only 28 ounces.[75] Another "physician" built an aerostatic machine in the shape of a ship. Pending the success of the flight of his 28-foot-long vessel, he planned to construct one four times larger.[76]

Like the boulevards, the Palais-Royal was host to an expanded range of entertainments, all welcomed warmly by Chartres. Museums and clubs were perhaps the main innovation. The Musée des Enfants, for example, was established by Sieur Tessier to instruct children.[77] Short plays with ariettes and vaudevilles presented in a salon theater provided lessons in history, geography, mythology, military drills, declamation, and science. On an adult level the Musée de Comte d'Artois was dedicated to the advance of human knowledge. A meeting place of artists, scientists, and amateurs, it was founded, under the auspices of the duc d'Orléans and later the comte d'Artois, by the aeronaut Pilâtre de Rosier, who was killed in June 1785 when attempting to cross the Channel in a balloon. Pilâtre established it originally in 1781 on the rue Sainte-Avoie as a laboratory containing instruments of physics and books on science, art, and literature and also newspapers and periodicals. He moved into the new Palais-Royal in November 1784 at the corner of the rue Saint-Honoré where the Opéra had been formerly. After Pilatre's death, when the comte d'Artois became its patron, the musée added professors of science and languages. In the evenings, readings, performances of theatrical pieces, reports of discoveries, and exhibitions of inventions were held. All males regardless of estate were admitted provided they satisfied "the formalities necessary to be admitted into any upstanding society. . . ."[78] Women gained admission only with a presentation signed by three members of the musée. The musée was an enormous success, counting over seven hundred subscribers at four louis each within a month of its opening. It kept up a steady correspondence with the academies, *collèges,* and amateurs of science; and it enjoyed the support of the Royal Observatory, the Royal Society of Medicine, and the Royal Veterinarian School.

Private clubs modeled on those in London with quarters in the Palais-Royal included one founded by the duc de Chartres, the Club des Planteurs ou Société des Colons, whose members, French or foreign, had to be property holders in America and who could not be engaged in mercenary activities; the Club Politique (activities unspecified), which barred persons under 25 years of age and foreign ministers; the Club du Salon des Arts, where men of letters, scientists, and artists paid 72 livres a year to read new books and brochures, play chess, peruse the scores of operas, symphonies, and *opéras-comiques* in a music salon, and converse; the Club Militaire for soldiers decorated with the cross of Saint-Louis, who amused themselves at a cost of 60 livres a year by playing backgammon, reading the papers, and studying maps; the Société Olympique, a group of over three hundred distinguished men and women, including three princesses of the blood, which held parties, suppers, balls, and concerts; the Société Philharmonique, an organization of musicians, against whom the members of the Musée de Comte d'Artois complained to the *commissaire* for drowning out their scientific readings with "vain and ephemeral" noise;[79] the Société du Caveau; the Club Maçonique; and the Société des Amateurs des Echecs for chess players who were military men, magistrates, and financiers.[80] These clubs were less formal than the salons of Paris. Most of the trappings of etiquette were dispensed with.[81] Relationships were simple and direct, without the gallantry of former times. Members were elected. At first suspicious of these clubs, the government decided to tolerate them probably because it found surveillance fairly easy. When the Salon des Arcades, founded by the chevalier de Changran (or Champgrand), began featuring gambling, however, the government took steps to curb the clubs. The societies were notified that all games were prohibited.[82] Only the chevaliers of Saint-Louis were exempt.

Although most of the Palais-Royal entertainments were successful, one of Chartres' pleasure palaces never went very far beyond the construction stage. In the middle of the garden where the fountain is today, he built what was called the Cirque, 13 feet deep and almost 10 above ground.[83] A gallery formed by a colonnade of 72 columns in the Ionic order surrounded the ground level and subterranean periphery of the Cirque surmounted by an upper gallery with trellises, pavilions, and a garden. A terrace with a balustrade and flowers 18 feet wide covered with rolled copper crowned the upper gallery and served as a promenade. Four forecourts, two circular ones at either end and two rectilinear ones at the laterals, were filled with running water and fountains. Porticoes in the center of these forecourts served as entrances, with two staircases descending to the galleries and arena below. A large hall with fireplaces and mirrors was built under each of the four entrances. The sanded arena was 300 feet long, 50 feet wide, and 26 feet high. A second subterranean gallery was built beneath the canals and was intended for public circulation. A subterranean route for carriages led to the arena from the buildings abutting the palace. A basin adjacent to the palace formed the southern rim of the Cirque, which was flanked by four kiosks where journals, refreshments, and pamphlets were sold.

In order to fund this enterprise, the duc opened a subscription in 1786 at shares of 20,000 and 15,000 each with an interest of 5 percent to be paid in 20 years. Subscribers were given a quarter of a loge or entrance for life. The demand for subscriptions was too large to accommodate everyone. Opinions of the new structure, however, were largely negative. Whereas Jacques-Antoine Dulaure thought that it would bring to mind "the famous gardens of Babylon," the author of the *Mémoires secrets* believed people would suffocate in the underground promenade.[84] He accused the duc of "sordid cupidity" in planning 60 boutiques and cafés for the Cirque. The *Courier d'Avignon* shared this attitude, calling the Cirque "a collection of objects of dissipation and frivolity of which there is, perhaps, no parallel."[85]

The Cirque was intended as a promenade but primarily as an amphitheater for equestrian shows and fêtes. Indeed, Astley hoped to take his *spectacle* to the Cirque. The minister of Paris, on orders from the king, however, forbade Astley from establishing his show in the Palais-Royal and ordered the duc de la Ferté to point out to the duc d'Orléans "the inconvenience that Sr. Astley's enterprise would entail and to engage him not to grant his protection to a project that would not fail to excite the liveliest and best-founded objections of all the *spectacles* of Paris."[86] With the equestrian shows forbidden, the Cirque was used for balls, games, tableaux, and fêtes, but it was quite a flop. A menagerie was located there when it burned in 1799.

The principal Palais dwellers, without whom the duc's venture probably would have failed, were the merchants.[87] They included 40 jewelers selling silver buckles, porcelain, hardware, knickknacks, and gold and silver jewelry; 2 bureaus of trust to sell items such as art objects, clocks, engravings, statues, jewelry, marble, and bronze (the proprietor took 4 percent of items valued at 300 livres, 2 percent for those at 600, 1 percent for 1,200, and $\frac{1}{2}$ percent above this figure); 3 tobacconists; 1 harquebus dealer; 3 cutlers; 4 dressmakers; 1 pill shop; 1 ink shop; 1 store for ordinary and molded candles; 1 for Chinese and other powders and portable pumps; 9 drapers who sold material for morning coats, country clothes, trousers, satin brocades and embroideries, coarse linen from Naples, percale, dimity, batiste, muslin, embroidered jackets, gold material, Pekin, Indian satins, English flannels, and jersey fabrics; several cabinetmakers; ebony and ivory dealers; 1 grocer; 9 engraving stores, 1 of which sold pictures of nudes; 1 shop selling horse and carriage equipment; 3 fan shops; 5 florists; 7 clock merchants; 8 bookstores, located mostly in the Passage du Perron or the *galérie de bois,* which sold everything from the best literature to libelous pamphlets, banned books, and scandalous works written on commission; 3 linen merchants; 10 haberdashers; 1 furniture store; 4 music merchants; 5 opticians selling barometers, thermometers, spectacles, paintings on glass, telescopes, opera glasses, and luminous phosphorous in bottles enclosed in tin boxes; 3 wallpaper shops; 6 perfumers; 4 puppet and children's game stores; 14 silk merchants; 2 painters; 1 newsstand; 18 tailors; 2 wine boutiques; a dealer in fold-up rubber raincoats; a shop selling bear grease made by savages to prevent thinning hair; 2 paper shops; 5 hat stores, 4 button shops; 2 hairdressers; and 2 bureaus of the royal lottery.

Although there were many fancy boutiques in the Palais, there were also several merchants who bought used clothing from rich people, which they displayed for sale in glass partitions whose poor light concealed their defects. They bought these goods mostly from libertines and sold them to clerks, actors, and *petits-maîtres*. None of the boutiques in the Palais was sedate; dishonesty was common. Copper was passed off as gold, *strass* for diamond. Mercier, who watched debauched people milling about amid the mountains of ribbon, gauze, flowers, boxes of rouge, and pompons, reported that the effrontery of the boutique owners was duplicated nowhere else in Paris.[88]

There were four confectioners in the Palais, one of whom, M. La Faye at number 31, also sold perfume. His confections were tantalizing, often exotic: glazed chestnuts, orange flour biscuits, apricot jam from the Auvergne, pistachios coated with chocolate, peppermint and spiced lozenges from England, and lemon vinegar lozenges. La Faye also sold African marigolds; orange and lemon tuberous root; jasmine, vanilla, and mustard perfume; anise from the Indies; candy sweetmeat boxes; syrups; ratafia; pomades; powders; toilet water; red vinegar; Strasbourg crepes; dye; liquid opiate to clean teeth; furniture oil; and "some extraordinary liqueurs that leave nothing to be desired both for suavity and salubrity." At number 219 a merchant-grocer sold pineapples, preserves, Provençal olives, Lyonnaise sausages, Bayonne ham, spiced bread from Rheims, and all sorts of cheese and wine. M. Gendron's pastry shop at number 257 specialized in potato cake from Savoy, "so light and so delicate [it] is always stomachic and antiscorbutic." The queen's crystal manufacture was located at Numbers 49 and 50; and the general storehouse of wines, at Number 99. It was considered bad form to drink French Burgundy or Champagne, so seigneurs, *petits-maîtres,* and even actors purchased the wines of Madeira, Cyprus, Malaga, and Bordeaux at the central depot.[89]

There were several itinerant peddlers in the Palais. Several sold game—pheasants, hares, partridges. Others sold fruit, lemonade, even stolen dogs.[90] Clusters of bankers, courtiers, and merchants combed the garden speculating in the stock of the Company of the Indies and the Bank of Saint-Charles. Money lenders gathered in the early afternoon to make loans at 25 percent interest. Solicitors for *avocats,* procurators, bailiffs, and clerks also tried to drum up business, and women solicited other women to provide them with a man for a fee. The most interesting of all the itinerants was a man named Benoît, dressed in the garb of a Franciscan and known as the Supérieur des Marronistes, who sold hot chestnuts. Benoît, who had special sanction from the duc to sell in the garden, realized that in order to attract crowds to his concession something bizarre was necessary.[91] Seated on his ebony throne, he shouted to the crowd:

> Sirs, I have gathered you to tell you that I have perfected my talent. I may not be the equal in eloquence of all those who occupy the lycée, the museums, the

clubs of the Palais, but I am as zealous. They stir up the air with vain words; I provide realities. They caress the ear, I delight the Palais [pun on the word *palate*] by means of an exquisite fruit. Yes, gentlemen, I offer you a healthy, substantial, succulent, pleasant, and inexpensive fruit. If like the manna of the desert, it does not strike every taste, it has at least one of which one does not grow tired: equivalent to this precious quality, it is sufficient for the subsistance of entire populations who have the fill of it all year long; it is transformed into this daily food, the essence of all meals, which is found equally on the table of the rich and of the poor. And in addition to the chestnuts of the Limousin and of the Marche, I have added those of Lucienne, Lyons, and Luc. I have also applied chemical means to preserve the food; to ferment the chestnuts while preserving all their succulent molecules. The hulls are entirely stripped; the first layer offers a golden red, and the interior a dazzling white. The chestnut is chewed easily, and melts like a sweet pâté in the mouth leaving no chafe on the tongue: come forward, taste, open your pocket, and your purses.[92]

Finally, the garden crowd was regaled every evening by an abbé who sang songs and gesticulated. Accompanying himself on a guitar, his songs had titilating verses such as the following:

> *Robin a une anguille*
> *Qui fait plaisir aux filles,*
> *Quand il la met en main*
> *Maman, j'aime Robin*
> *Maman, j'aime Robin.*
>
> *Cet instrument, ma mère,*
> *Aurait de quoi vous plaire,*
> *Si vous l'aviez en main.*
> *Maman, j'aime Robin*
> *Maman, j'aime Robin.*[93]

Probably the most frequented establishments in the Palais-Royal were the cafés and restaurants. The most venerable was the Café de Foy at Number 59, established much earlier in the century, located near the rue de Richelieu and serving as a passageway to the garden.[94] Having paid Chartres 500,000 livres, Jousserand, the proprietor, alone was privileged to sell drinks in the garden under a pavilion where he had chairs but no tables. Occupying several arcades, the café was decorated with white arabesque panels and delicately sculptured *boiserie*. It catered to the highborn. Mayeur, however, believed that the café had declined. He wrote of the café's taking on the appearance of a *guinguette* and reported an aged countess, sitting with an old chevalier, taking an ice cream, to prove that she could still flirt. She was surrounded by old military men and fat, wigged financiers wearing square shoes and carrying gold-knob canes. The countess, he reported, ridiculed all the women who passed while the bantering chevalier, leaning back on his chair, legs crossed, played with his fan and talked of the *spectacles* and of last night's adventures. Next to the Café de Foy, from 4:00 p.m. until 8:00 p.m. every evening a Spanish dog displayed its abilities to read, calculate, and do tricks for 30 sous.[95]

The Café du Caveau, run by Dubuisson in a subterranean gallery at Number 89, in front of the grand alley of the old garden, used four arcades with a front of 37 feet and a depth of 29. Vaulted ceilings and columns divided the room into three parts. The absence of paneling or gilding, the large mirrors reflecting the garden, and the lamps in crystal jars supported by wreaths contributed to a rustic effect. As it was frequented by opera enthusiasts, the sides were decorated with the busts of Gluck, Sacchini, Piccini, Grétry, and Philidor. A marble table with gold-carved letters commemorated the discovery of the Montgolfiers, above which was the medallion of the two brothers. The Salon des Arts was located above the café. A cup of coffee or a glass of eau-de-vie cost six sous.

The least pretentious café in the garden was the Café de Chartres (now, of course, the Grand Véfour restaurant) at Number 80, with entrances opposite the Beaujolais and onto the garden. It was the rendezvous of businessmen, devotees of the *spectacles,* and players of chess and checkers. Always equipped with foreign newspapers, the café apparently had patrons who stared at English papers unable to read them in order to appear informed.[96] Many clerks, *avocats,* procurators, abbés, *petits-maîtres,* officers, prostitutes, courtesans, and intriguers stayed all day, pausing only to stare occasionally out of the windows or at the docile, sweet-faced seal outside who caressed passersby.

The Café Beaujolais at Number 13, with a wealth of gilding and arabesque pictures, was the smallest in the Palais. It later became a Jacobin hangout. Operated by an Italian named Carazza, it specialized in Italian and Spanish chocolate, liqueurs from Italy and the islands, maraschino, and barley sugar for colds.[97] The most curious establishment was the Café Méchanique. Two hollow cylinders with rings attached that communicated with the service area below were affixed to each table. When jerked, the ring sounded a bell below the café and opened a valve on the cylinder to receive the customer's order, which was deposited in a service lift. The Méchanique attracted the most diverse crowd in the garden: the peasant girl dressed in her Sunday finery, the recruiting sergeant and his girl, the hairdresser with a milliner, the child and his governess, the bourgeois and his wife, clerks, writers, prostitutes, and monks.[98]

In addition to these places of libation, the Palais housed the Café de Valois, a large, plain, tranquil establishment, where people played chess and dominoes; the Café Polonais, a popular spot with mirrors and plaster sculptures; and the Café des Variétés, serving sweetbreads Italian style or with milk to a large evening clientele. It had a view onto the rue de Montpensier, a passageway convenient to Variétés' patrons, and a doorway to the Camp of the Tartars. In addition to the usual coffee, punch, and liqueur, it specialized in English beer served in earthenware pots.

The cafés were, of course, a perfect place to watch the passing parade. More than any other show, people came to see the concourse of humanity, as they did on the boulevards. Outlandish dress was in vogue. Standard apparel included

> short, indecent waistcoats, lewd culottes without pockets that can hold neither a coin nor a watch; that is the strangulating dress of the day. People are too stuffed into their clothes to sit down. Adam with his fig leaf was more decently dressed than his last-born giddy children, promenading in the Palais-Royal bird-tailed. Tailors convert prelates into Adonises, magistrates into fops, dukes into potentates. In these public places dress confuses every rank and every estate.[99]

Restaurants in the palais, such as La Grotte Flamande, La Barrière, and La Taverne Angloise, tended to be large and to have tables covered with green oilcloth.[100] These expensive places were frequented habitually by chevaliers, young officers, financiers, provincials, gamblers, libertines, and prostitutes. Although one had to be well dressed to be admitted, rogues and thieves in disguise were usually present. The Grotte Flamande, with its private tables for lovers, was the favorite place of comedians from the Variétés and the Beaujolais. Upright women never went to these restaurants. Men only were seated in the rooms on the main floor and ate in silence, affecting disdain for the food and wine. Mayeur de Saint-Paul found watching the diners very amusing. He observed a hairdresser cutting his bread with a knife, then breaking it with his forefingers while sticking his other fingers in the air; an old soldier with his elbows on the table rolling a piece of meat in his jaws for three minutes because he no longer had teeth to chew it; a bloated businessman with a double chin eating slowly, seeming to choke as he swallowed his food; and the young man rubbing his hands together, trying to look important, playing on the table with the handle of his knife, and eating so vigorously that he revealed himself to be a Gascon. A few pages of a menu from a Palais-Royal restaurant indicate the kinds of cuisine available and the prices.[101]

	L. S.
Petit pâté à la béchamelle	6
Tourte de foie gras	1. 5
Tourte de Gaudiveau	1. 5
Tourte de saumon frais	2. 0
Tourte de laitances de carpe	1. 10

	L. S.
Tourte de filets de morue à la Béchamelle	1. 10
Tourte de filets de poularde à la Béchamelle	2. 5
Tourte d'anguille	2. 0
Pâté chaud de mauviettes	1. 10
Pâté chaud de grives	1. 10
Pâté chaud de bécasses	2. 0
Tourte de Turbot à la Béchamelle	2. 0

Entrées

Chapon au gros sel	9. le 1/4	2. 5
Chapon au riz	10. le 1/4	2.10
Poulet aux truffes	6. la 1/2	3. 0
Perdreau aux truffes	4.10 la 1/2	2.10
Poulet à la tartare	4. la 1/2	2. 5
Canard aux navets ou aux choux	5. le 1/4	1.15
Perdrix rouge aux choux ou au coulis de lentilles	4.10 la 1/2	2.10
Pigeon en compote		. 10
Pigeon à la crapaudine		1. 5
Ragoût mêlé de crêtes et rognons de coq		2. 0
Ris de veau à la dauphine ou glacé à l'oseille		3. 0
Ris de veau à la poulette ou en caisse		1. 10
Cervelle de veau en matelote ou frite		1. 4
— à la purée de pois et au beurre noir		1. 4
— à la poulette ou à l'Italienne		1. 4
Côtelettes de veau à la bourgeoise ou à la Schingarac		1. 0
Côtelette de veau piqué, glacé à l'oseille ou aux épinards		1. 0
Beef-stakes aux pommes de terre		1. 0
Beef-stakes à la française		1. 4
Gigot aux haricots ou aux choux		1. 0
Blanquette da veau de Pontoise		1. 5
Oreille de veau frite ou à l'Italienne		0. 18
Oreille de veau farcie frite		1. 4
Queue de veau frite ou en auchepot		1. 0
Rognons de mouton au vin de Champagne ou en brochette		0. 18
Palais de boeuf au gratin		1. 10
Palais de boeuf à la poulette ou à l'Italienne		1. 5
Fricandeau au jus ou à l'oseille		0. 18
Fricandeau aux pommes de terre		0. 18
Fricandeau à la chicorée		1. 5
Fricandeau aux épinards		1. 5
Côtelette de mouton à l'Anglaise		0. 7
Côtelette de veau en papillotte		0. 18
Béchamelle de blanc de volaille		2. 5
Béchamelle aux truffes		2. 10
Tendon de mouton en auchepot		0. 18
Tendon de veau à l'oseille		0. 18
Foies gras en caisse ou escalope de foies gras		1. 4
Choux au petit salé ou à la purée		1. 0

	L. S.
Mouton pané et grillé	0. 18
Côtellette de mouton à la jardinière	0. 18
Aileron de dindon aux navets ou à la purée	1. 5
Capiletade de poularde	2. 5
Cuisse de dinde grillée sauce Robert	2. 5
Côtelettes de porc frais sauce Robert	0. 18
Salmi de perdrau	1. 10
Salmi de faisan	1. 10
Choucroûte garnie de saucisses et de petit lard	1. 4
Mauviettes au gratin	1. 4
Fricandeau de lapereau au jus et à l'oseille	0. 18
Salmi de caille	2. 0
Filet de chevreuil à la broche, sauce piquante	1. 10

Desserts

	L. S.
Compotes de pommes ou de poires	0. 12
Cerises à l'eau-de-vie	0. 8
Chasselas de Fontainebleau	0. 12
Biscuit à la crême	0. 6
Fromage de Glocester, de Chester ou de Schabszigre	0. 8
Fromage de Gruyère ou de Neuchâtel	0. 6
Fromage de Rokfort	0. 8
Pommes de Rainette	0. 4
Gâteau de pommes	0. 12
Poire de Creusanne ou de St-Germain	0. 15
Confitures de cerises	0. 12
Gelée de pommes de Rouen	0. 12
Gelée de groseille	0. 12
Marmelade d'abricots	0. 12
Mandiens, marons de Lyon	0. 12
Olives	0. 19

Vins

	L. S.
Vin rouge	1. 0
Vin de Bourgogne	1. 5
Vin de Chablis	1. 10
Vin de Beaune	2. 0
Vin de Mercuray	2. 0
Vin de Volnay. Nuits et Pomard	3. 0
Vin de Mulseaux	2. 0
Vin de Grave	4. 0
Vin de claret	4. 10
Vin du Clos de Vougeot	4. 10
Vin de Chambertin	4. 10
Vin de l'Hermitage	4. 10
Vin de Porto	3. 0
Vin de Bordeaux	4. 0

	L. S.
Vin de Sauterne	3. 0
Vin de Bordeaux blanc	3. 0
Champagne mousseux	4. 10
Vin vieux de la Fitte	4. 10
Le petit verre de Tokai	2. 0
Muscat Frontignan	4. 0
Malaga	4. 0
Alicante	4. 0
Rota	4. 0
Le petit verre de ces quatres sortes de vin	0. 8
Malvoisie-Madère, le petit verre	0. 12
Bière forte Porter	1.
Bière blanche de Bristol	3. 0
Bière blanche	0. 10
Café	0. 6
Thé à l'Anglaise	1. 0
Chocolat	0. 12
Liqueurs fraiches	0. 6
Punch au Rhum et au Rack	3. 0
Liqueurs de toutes espèces	0. 6
Liqueurs de Madame Amphoux	0. 12
Marasquin	0. 12
Glaces	0. 12
Fruits à l'eau-de-vie	0. 12

In addition to the cafés, restaurants, theaters, and other *spectacles,* strollers in the Palais-Royal were attracted by the billiard halls that Chartres permitted.[102] The first was installed where the Grotte Flamande later moved and was called a *jeu aerostatique.* Hitting a ball into one of the springy pockets produced a small explosion hurtling several small globes from the center of the table. The entrance fee was just 2 sous. After this *jeu* failed, several others, each with distinctively shaped tables, opened on the first floors of several pavilions. A Billard Anglois was established at Number 142, and a certain M. Domale had a hall with square tables that charged 5 sous a game, 10 with a light, or 40 sous for the day or 4 livres with light. At the Grand Salon Doré one paid 45 sous a day, and at the hall at Number 26 the charge was 6 sous a game or 12 with light to play on an octagonal table. In addition, there were billiard rooms in the Hôtel de Penthièvre lighted by the three crosswalks of the garden and in the Hôtel de Montpensier, where there was a loge for ladies to watch the sport without being seen. The Montpensier also had a mechanical game in which miniature lions, rhinoceroses, elephants, wolves, deer, and a hunter appeared from a forest when the player drew the correct number. The police became alarmed about the proliferation of billiard halls when Sieur Farolet opened one on the main floor of his house in the Palais while his associate, Sieur Chaligni, also operated one on the first floor.[103]

One might expect that, with the restrictions that Chartres put on renters and entrants to his garden, the Palais-Royal would be safer and more refined than the boulevards and fairs. Although some accounts refer to the better behavior of audiences and higher caliber of plays at the Variétés than at the boulevard theaters, the garden itself was not spared crime, prostitution, and the almost inevitable invasion of *le bas peuple*.[104] The author of the *Mémoires secrets* wrote: "The garden of the Palais-Royal becomes by its new constitution, as one would have predicted, the repository of all the scoundrels of Paris, and there results from that every day, especially at night, scandalous scenes and even bloody catastrophes."[105] He described a man's assault on a girl, who was wounded with his cane when she resisted his advances. Responding to her cries, the guard arrived and tried to arrest the man in the name of the duc de Chartres. Mocking the duc, the man proclaimed his identity as the Marquis de Nesle, the first equerry of Madame, which was verified when an inspector arrived and released him.

The records of Commissaire François-Jean Sirebeau are full of reports of crimes committed in the garden and arcades: Silver plates and service were stolen from a restaurant; people were overcharged in restaurants; copper and silver canes, bottles of wine, watches, gold boxes, medallions, diamond snuffboxes, silk purses, handkerchiefs, dressing gowns, and money were stolen in the garden; scalpers sold tickets to the Variétés illegally; girls were insulted, threatened, spit on, and struck by men whom the *commissaire* usually released.[106] Indeed, fights and assaults were commonplace in the Palais.[107] Jean-Baptiste Buron, a dentist, was accosted and robbed near the Café de Foy in August 1786. Two men shouted obscenities, threw stones, and beat a man in one of the passageways in September 1786. Mademoiselle Forest, an actress at the Variétés, who in 1785 had been accosted by a coachman driving her to the theater, inflicted a contusion on the eye of Sr. Bordier, an actor. The chevalier de Blaye got into a fight with four young men over a courtesan. The chevalier wounded three of them, but the fourth slashed him four times with a sword, and he died an hour later. In the Camp of the Tartars in October 1785 a tumult occurred when a young scamp stepped on the feet of an abbé who had his arm around a ballet dancer.[108] Insults were shouted, the crowd turned on the aggressor, and a brawl ensued. It required 60 members of the Watch to break it up. The Swiss Guard, which was subsequently tripled, began dispersing three or more people walking arm in arm.

Occasionally boutiques and apartments were torn up and robbed. In October 1786 Commissaire Sirebeau investigated Sr. Deneufuille's apartment at Number 105 and found the lock of his desk smashed and the contents removed. Marie-Agnes Menin and her husband, both cooks employed by the apothecary of the duc d'Orléans, discovered that three linen housecoats, one muslin skirt, three taffeta skirts, eight handkerchiefs, seven bonnets, and eight napkins had been stolen from their apartment. In November 1786 the door of the boutique of François-Louis Caux, a jeweler, was forced open, and goods worth 4,000 to 5,000 livres were stolen. A tailor's boutique at Number 112 was robbed of the uniform of an officer of the grenadiers. Several of the merchants sent *Mémoires* to Chartres, alerting him to the dangers they faced as a result of the "prodigious concourse of *impures* under the galleries, where they attracted a multitude of unbridled libertines. . . ."[109]

Vandalism was also rampant in the Palais. In September 1786, Georges Thomassin, a music master living at Number 142, told the *commissaire* that someone had dumped urine on his merchandise from the mezzanine above his boutique. The scores of *Thémistocle* and *Nina,* six sonatas, a collection of guitar music, the overture to *Panurge,* a romance and an air for harp were so filthy they could not be sold.

Although the *commissaire's* files are crammed with reports of criminal incidents in the Palais-Royal, there was little the police could do to stop them. Indeed, the brigadier of the Guards of the Palais, who with four of his men patrolled the *spectacles,* believed that many "bad subjects" took refuge in the residences of the inhabitants because they believed the duc de Chartres would protect them. In many instances he did.[110] Spies were about the only means the police had of staying informed about activities in the Palais. There was an abundance of them, and they were useful in helping to catch thieves and villains. The only problem was that the spies were rogues themselves.[111] It cannot be assumed that these crimes were perpetrated by the lower ranks of society. Too many incidents, especially assaults, involved aristocrats. The garden was their haven. Thus the Palais was in many ways as rough as the boulevards whose atmosphere it appropriated.

Women of all types frequented the duc's garden, attended the *spectacles,* and sat in the cafés. They were often the victims of crime and assaults although their presence also provoked fights. The gardens became the favorite turf of ladies of the Opéra and celebrated courtesans, who turned the grounds into "modern Saturnalias."[112] Mercier called the garden "the empire of libertinage" at every hour of day and night at a full range of prices.[113] There is not a "*guinguette* in the world," he wrote, "more graciously depraved."[114] Mayeur identified three types of females in the Palais: wealthy, well-kept women; courtesans; and prostitutes.[115] The first had the air of persons of high rank. Courtesans were usually dressed ridiculously with huge hairdos or large plumed hats, gold necklaces, earrings, and diamonds. They had an air of disdain and were skilled in the ways of seduction. Prostitutes, who were major clients of the merchants, were usually accompanied by an old women or a servant.

Promiscuity and prostitution were as common in the Palais as on the boulevards. The girls who worked at the Variétés were no different from those who worked for Nicolet or those employed by the Opéra.[116] The time for forming liaisons was when the theaters closed. Girls in gala costumes at first affected an air of decency to mislead foreigners, but soon "they offer themselves as a merchant offers his merchandise, and as soon as their promenade ends, they lead their quarry to their houses or into the enclosure of the Palais-Royal to some spots that are called grottoes. . . ."[117] In the grottoes (subterranean restaurants), there were always other girls in case one's companion was unresponsive. At the beginning of supper, it was customary for the girl to affect the mannerisms of a great lady, but as more wine was consumed, the supper turned into an orgy. Ordinary prostitutes simply walked through the arcades and galleries at night in order "to exercise the most intolerable kind of scandalous publicity of their infamous business. . . ."[118] Chartres got Lieutenant General Lenoir to keep these girls under surveillance, prevent them from sitting down, and oblige them to keep walking until 11 p.m. Still, the Palais had the reputation of being an "immense bazaar that became the forum of idleness, of gambling, and of debauchery, the theater of shameless vice . . . opened to everyone."[119]

Because so much of the discussion of popular culture in recent years has revolved around the alleged distinction between popular and elite publics and audiences, it is germane once again, therefore, to ask who came to this pleasure garden? Certainly it did not displace the boulevards as a popular marketplace although the fairs by the late 1780s were quite dead. The prices of the restaurants, clubs, and of many *spectacles* appear too high for the lower ranks of society, yet other attractions were within their range and certainly within that of a bourgeois. The ownership of the Palais-Royal by a prince of the blood, however mercantile he had become, and its location in the heart of royalist and aristocratic Paris made it the logical playground of the highborn, and it was. Theaters such as the Opéra at the Porte Saint-Martin and the Comédie-Française in the faubourg Saint-Germain seemed far out of the way.[120] But Curtius, Séraphin, Gaillard, and Dorfeuille made the Palais equally seductive to the lowborn. Was the society, as on the boulevards truly mixed? Did the duc de Chartres' venture help to crack the social stratification of French society through the vehicle of popular entertainment? No precise data exist to answer these questions, but the testimony of keen observers of the Parisian scene, both partisans and critics of the Palais, is abundant.

The *Almanach du Palais-Royal* waxed romantic about the garden and its denizens:

> One could say that the Palais Royal is the meeting place not only of the inhabitants of the capital but of those from all over Europe. Everything combines to attract a substantial crowd of people there every day: the gaiety of the place,

its location, the protection it offers against inclement weather in every season. The cafés, the *spectacles,* the variety of things that one sees there guarantee this promenade a preference over the others, especially if women continue to enjoy coming there to augment the delights and pleasures of a moving tableau in which they appear with so much grace and elegance. Night removes none of the pleasures of this place; it only changes the beauty of the scene. The light of the torches and chandeliers, multiplied in the arcades, together with that of the theaters and apartments on the garden, produces an illumination that one cannot see for the first time without being struck with a kind of astonishment.[121]

An anonymous account of the Palais also spoke of it as a moving tableau where every style and opinion were represented in the crowd composed of flirtatious women, businessmen, and those who had no work, those who were rich, those who were hopeful, and those who were ruined. The garden was shared by all social groups.[122] Saint-Marc defined the crowd as including financiers, unemployed people, actresses, people of high society, and the demimonde.[123] Mayeur de Saint-Paul tells of the many foreigners in the garden, along with *robins,* financiers, soldiers, abbés, ladies of rank, *petits-maîtres,* courtesans, and clerks.[124] At noon the promenade included elegant people, upright women, old soldiers, officials, prostitutes, idlers, hairdressers, actors, financiers, and bachelors. Proper ladies always walked in pairs and took seats opposite each other. Soldiers and financiers sat, but young people flew about like butterflies.

> The sounds of varied voices, the rubbing of feet against the sand, the rippling of fabrics that touch, the people who blow their noses, cough, and spit—all that together produced such an incredible buzzing that, in speaking loudly, it seems that one speaks only in an ordinary tone of voice. This promenade is very amusing and makes known to the foreigner nearly every estate of life in this moving tableau. There is the rendezvous of style and the spot where the graces link love and pleasure.[125]

After dinner around 7 p.m., idlers, intriguers, and the girls dominated the side alleys; and at night, prostitutes and thieves took over when all upright people left. At any hour, it was impossible to walk in the garden "without seeing men pissing against the pilasters of the galleries, which was very disagreeable for women in general."[126]

Mayeur and Mercier summed up the Palais-Royal crowd best. Mercier referred to "the confusion of the estates, the mixture, the throng," and Mayeur declared: "All the orders of citizens are joined together, from the lady of rank to the dissolute, from the soldier of distinction to the smallest supernumerary of farms."[127] In short, the society of the Palais-Royal was a genuine mixture of rank though probably dominated by the highborn. They had embraced the culture of the people and transported it to a royalist garden whose proprietor was bent on turning it to his profit.

Epilogue

THERE IS no such thing as popular culture in the hours of life devoted to the pleasure that I have called popular entertainment if by that term one means amusements for common people as opposed to those for the elite. Although the grand theaters doubtless had their own clientele, catering primarily to classical taste and the educated, the little *spectacles* enjoyed the patronage of commoner, bourgeois, and noble alike. No separation of taste publics existed at the fairs and boulevards—and not much at the Palais-Royal—except in a relatively small distinction between seats at the little theaters. As the *Journal de Paris* put it on the occasion of street dancing in celebration of the Dauphin's birth: "At this moment equality became perfect, and the coal merchant in his working clothes was not in the least shaken to give his hand to the one whom the capital deems most elegant."[1] Moreover, the borrowing of genres and techniques between the great and little shows was too widespread for distinctions to be drawn on that basis. Even the timeliness of plays in the 1780s celebrating or spoofing the early balloon flights had been presaged in the previous century by Alard's leaping in Carolet's *Les Forces de l'amour* and in the *pièce en machines, Le Mariage en l'air* in 1737 at Saint-Germain, a parody of *Persée* at the Opéra.[2] The only real differentiation of cultures was politics, prices, and censorship. The grand theaters enjoyed monopolies that enabled them to force fair entertainers to offer productions, such as *pièces en écriteaux,* which otherwise they might not have undertaken, or to pay for the right to perform. In the first instance, the result was the creation of *opéra-comique,* one of the age's most successful and enduring cultural forms, one that breathed life into the traditional vaudeville air. *Opéra-comique* was so appealing that the faltering Comédie-Italienne could only compete with it by taking it over, removing it from the fairs, and upgrading its music and text.

Censorship was not very effective either because theaters were primarily interested in barring plays or censoring scenes resembling their repertoire, precisely those kinds of scenes that attracted audiences. In a *mémoire* calling for their privileges to be upheld and for the little *spectacles* to be confined to earlier restrictions, the Comédie-Italienne referred to the street theaters as "the amusement of *le bas peuple,* an institution that they do not serve at all if these actors are permitted to perform comedies other than those in which license and vulgarity reign . . . and if, furthermore, they are permitted to perform noble and refined works. . . ."[3] Although the government upheld the monopolies, it and the police had no desire to eradicate the diverting fare of the streets. The Opéra succeeded in bilking the popular entertainers, but although they tried for a century, the privileged theaters could not drive the *forains* out of existence. The public liked them too much, especially when they were under attack and resorted to merciless satire, and the government found them useful. The politics of privilege prevailed in ancien régime France, but its impact was to enhance the appeal of street *spectacles.*

Popular entertainment owed its attractiveness to the combination of farce and fantasy, both of which existed in many forms. All types of people were satirized in eighteenth-century Paris as long as they were types and not real persons although even specific individuals were lampooned by the song peddlers on the Pont-Neuf. Beginning with coquettes and mischievous rogues like Arlequin from commedia dell'arte, *opéra-comique* writers made fun of a bevy of stereotypical characters such as apothecaries, provincial nobles, abbés, tutors, and lackeys. They made fun of themselves as well while turning ignorant country boys and girls into models of naive virtue uncorrupted by cynicism and urban evil. Their favorite prey, however, was recognizable creatures from the world around them. At first, they satirized their rivals from the privileged theaters. Heroines from the Comédie-Française spoke in alexandrines. As the century progressed, the street theaters struck telling blows at corrupt tax collectors and other officials and at the dissipated urban aristocracy and their leering, foppish sons, the *petits-maîtres.* The humble artisan and the gruff chimney sweep became heroes in a counterculture. The defining characteristic of popular culture was that it sprang from the market-place, whose vulgar *mélée* it mirrored and directed in mockery and broad laughter at the official world of court and salon.

Fantasy often combined with farce in popular entertainment. Arlequin sailed the skies on billowy clouds to utopian lands. Miraculous transformations were commonplace, as were metamorphoses and magic. Real or contrived animals from exotic lands captivated fair crowds. By the 1780s all Parisian society seemed caught up in a wave of science, whether of the optical sort embracing everything from magic lanterns held by Savoyard girls, phantasmagoria, *ombres chinoises,* and the hypnotic effect of fireworks or of the real experiments in electricity and hydrogen gas. Childhood revery was evoked in the fantasy of street entertainment, where one could dream of imagined realities beyond time and space. E. G. Robertson, who became the master of phantasmagoria, wrote: "Since my earliest childhood, my lively and ardent imagination had delivered me to the empire of the marvelous; everything that exceeded the ordinary confines of nature, which in different ages are only the limits of our specific knowledge, excited in my spirit a curiosity, a fervor that induced me to attempt everything in order to realize the effects that I conceived."[4]

The marketplace held farce and fantasy together. The body was its image. Feats of strength and dexterity were the stock-in-trade of acrobats, equilibrists, funambulists, equestrian shows, aquatic jousts, and freaks. The actors of the Opéra-Comique were tumblers before they sang and spoke; their prowess was re-created on the stages of Nicolet and Audinot. Throughout the century, the popular theater abounded in leaping, grimacing, contorting, and mock fornication, defecation, and urination. References to the search for, and intake of, food were ubiquitous. Physical symbolism was the universal imagery of the people, the flesh of marketplace existence.

The entertainments of those who populated the Parisian marketplace were only ephemerally shaped by the transitory passage of political events and economic currents. Certainly, the politics of privilege, beginning in the reign of Louis XIV, affected them. It is also important that entertainment was commercialized on a large scale for the first time. Opéra-Comique directors became each other's competitors, as did those of the grand *spectacles.* The entrepreneurs of the Waux-Halls, the *cabinets de physique,* the cafés, the *ombres chinoises,* the menageries, and the waxworks were seeking profits, and most were successful.

But these important reservations aside, the study of popular entertainment is one of *la longue durée,* not of *histoire événementielle.* The types of entertainment in some instances went back centuries. Their themes and images would not have been difficult for one who had lived in an earlier time to recognize. The origins of many vaudevilles cannot be determined. No one is sure where or when marionettes appeared. Animal combats are at least as old as ancient Rome. Humorous derision, the farce and fantasy of the *longue durée,* encompasses the Feast of Fools, carnival, and charivari. Tumblers, conjurors, humorists, trapeze artists, jugglers, charlatans, singers, and freaks had existed in Charlemagne's time, but were chased from court for the indecency of their sport. Moreover, sacrilegious buffoonery had found its way into presentations of mystery plays, usually presented on a saint's day, and into the satirical allegories of the Enfants sans Souci, who performed in the central market while Provençal troubadors mixed comedy with their *chants*. Forming the Confrères de la Passion, pilgrims from the Crusades sang in the streets of Paris and gave Passion plays mixed with profane songs and farces to overflow crowds at the Hôpital de la Trinité. Led by the Prince of Fools, they performed farces satirizing the customs of their time. The monks of the Trinité finally turned them out in embarrassment, so the Confrères bought the Hôtel de Bourgogne, which was rented to a comedy troupe. Their rivals were the clerks of the Basoche (courts) who presented morality plays along with farces attacking birth and rank, causing an outcry from the Parlement of Paris. They had existed from the time of Philippe le Bel. Other troupes, some Italian, with similar fare were established in the sixteenth century, one of which introduced pantomimes. They enjoyed the applause of the royal court but drew the wrath of the Parlement for their indecency. Provincial troupes were performing at the Saint-Germain fair in the late sixteenth century.

The point is not that Paris had a long theatrical history, but that theatrical entertainment always echoed the derisive mockery of the streets and fairs. The *longue durée* came from the buffoonery of marketplace life wherein the elite world of orders and ranks was made the target of robust farce brimming with sacrilege and obscenity and the dreamlike wonder of the marvelous. Even the criticism of popular *spectacles* was part of the *longue durée*. The church had always lashed out at profane theater. So did the Parlement on the grounds that it was obscene and that it extracted hard-earned sous from the poor. The Comédie-Française in Louis XIV's time attacked the Italian actors for indecency. In 1696, Pontchartrain, minister of the king's household, ordered La Reynie, lieutenant general of police, to ensure that the Italians did not use equivocal language or obscene postures. But it was not just the official world that complained.

Criticism of street entertainment and popular theater, largely moralistic in character, reverberated through the centuries, but the moralistic Enlightenment probably heard more of it than any age until our own, with the birth of the American Bible Belt and its tirades against X-rated films, adult bookshops, and *Playboy*. François-Thomas-Marie de Baculard d'Arnaud wrote: "By these vulgar riddles one means this bad taste for parody, *parade, opéra-comique,* which the imbecility of a certain public and the weakness of certain authors have introduced to the stage; we have seen all Paris flock to the Opéra-Comique, to the sparks of the Italians, while the best pieces of the Molières, the Corneilles, the Racines are performed without spectators; would ignorance and gothic barbarity come back to us through a fatal revolution?"[5] The *Journal de Paris* blamed a general decadence in taste on multiple efforts to corrupt it, the opening of too many *spectacles* to all social classes, their appeal to the senses and imagination, and indecency and tumult at the theaters.[6] Invoking the authority of Cicero, Plato, Aristotle, Ovid, Quintilian, Plutarch, Luther, Calvin, Quinault, La Rochefoucauld, Boileau, La Bruyère, Racine, Bossuet, Voltaire, and Riccoboni, Desprez de Boissy argued that *spectacles* overwhelmed the senses, arousing the sexual drive at the expense of the mind and of morals.[7] He declared war on actresses who displayed their sexual attractions and appetites while dressed as divinities and also on those who looked at them. Pleasure at the *spectacle* was, for Desprez de Boissy, proof that a person was corrupt. The theater teaches female spectators how to be seductive, abandoning morality to bourgeois husbands and mothers. The anonymous author of *Pour et contre les spectacles* (maybe August Mann) also invoked a variety of authorities—Saint Augustine and the Church Fathers, cardinals, bishops, popes, and Jean-Jacques Rousseau —to justify the excommunication of actors.[8] He blamed the "pernicious lessons of impudicity" in the theater on the Encyclopedists.

Thomas Rousseau was probably the most vitriolic critic of popular theater, whose immorality, so enticing to commoners, he attributed to the censorship of the grand theaters.[9]

> If one surrenders his production to their censure, they cut, prune, trim, mutilate, and dissect it to the extent that there does not even remain for the poor child the shadow of its first form. After this blow, they return it to its father. Reduced to this state of languor, or even more annihilation, this shapeless skeleton can only revolt; he makes such a heavy fall that it appears he will never be revived; he appears, falls, dies, is buried, and everything is finished.

In this way, Rousseau contended, revolting obscenity is totally successful when good taste might otherwise have prevailed. The victims are the bourgeoisie: "I look on the faces only of the children of our bourgeois who are the most assiduous at these *spectacles forains,* and this youth forms the most numerous class and at the same time the most necessary to the state. They lose precious working time, squander their fathers' fortunes, become dull in spirit, slaves of courtesans, blind to reason." After learning the art of seduction on the boulevards, they scorn virtuous girls. Their sins spread to the provinces, where the innocence of village life, moral purity, and hard work are relinquished to the dissipation learned in the city.

The government was not blind to the criticisms of marketplace *spectacles.* It recognized the necessity to assert standards of decency and order; it understood that farces often fed the taste for libertinage and debauchery; it realized the need to upgrade entertainments from gross buffoonery in order to make them morally and socially instructive.[10] But it had no intention of eradicating them, despite the lamentations of the moralists. Du Coudray articulated the official attitude:

Madame, you agree with everyone else without doubt that *spectacles* in large cities are necessary in order to divert the man of affairs, in order to amuse upstanding people and well-to-do persons, and finally to occupy the people who, when not attached to any *spectacle,* can be induced to factionalism. You know that the populace is stirred up, thrown into confusion, flighty; it is necessary then to stabilize it: well, one cannot do it except by *spectacles,* and *spectacles* in its taste, such as marionettes, *parades,* conjurors, etc. For that reason, legislators have established different ones in every age, and I dare to suggest that it is sound politics to continue them and even to increase them. When the people go to the Danseurs de Corde or the Combat du Taureau, they will not rise up, and soldiers will not desert. If idleness is the mother of all vice, the lack of *spectacles* being an idleness, it is then a new mother of vices. . . . The days of the Virgin and the solemn fêtes that the church dedicates to the grandeur of religion, in which our theaters are closed out of respect for it, there is committed in the capital more evil on these days of every kind, whether debaucheries, drunkenness, libertinage, thefts, and even assassinations.[11]

After returning from a visit to Lieutenant General Sartine, where he reported the complaints of the grand theaters about the production of *opéras-comiques* on the boulevards, Papillon de La Ferté, intendant of the menus plaisirs, declared: "All that I understood by his reply is that he protects very strongly the *spectacles* of the boulevard."[12]

The *longue durée* of popular entertainment—popular culture in general —is with us today despite the technological revolution of the twentieth century. Aside from the cinema and television, which have removed the audience from these entertainment media, the modern life of the fairs is fully evident in 1985 in front of Beaubourg (Centre Pompidou) or on a summer night along the Boulevard Saint-Germain. I suspect farce and fantasy in some guise will always be a vital part of life and an integrating social force until the nuclear holocaust.

Notes

CHAPTER 1. The Singing Culture of the Pont-Neuf

1. Henri Lavedan, Preface to a tableau by François Boucher, quoted in Franc-Nohain, "Les Promenades à la mode," in *La Vie Parisienne au XVIIIᵉ siècle. Conférences du Musée Carnavalet* (Paris, 1928), p. 60.

2. François Colletet, *Le Tracas de Paris en vers burlesques* (Paris, 1714), p. 78.

3. Louis-Sébastien Mercier, *Tableau de Paris*, 12 vols. (Amsterdam, 1782–1788), vol. 6, pp. 192–193.

4. Jean-Georges Kastner, *Les Voix de Paris, essai d'une histoire littéraire et musicale des cris populaires de la capital, depuis le moyen âge jusqu'à nos jours* (Paris, 1857), p. v.

5. Edouard Fournier, *Histoire du Pont-Neuf*, 2 vols. (Paris, 1862), vol. 1, pp. 148–157.

6. Mercier, quoted in ibid., vol. 1, p. 293.

7. "Voyage d'un Anglais à Paris 1788," *Revue retrospective* (1889), p. 56. Translated by Frédéric Masson, this work was originally entitled "A Short Sketch of a Short Trip at Paris in 1788" and appeared in 1814 in *The Pamphleteer*.

8. Jean-Baptiste Gouriet, *Les Charlatans célèbres*, 2d ed., 2 vols. (Paris, 1819), vol. 2, pp. 1–82.

9. Paul Scarron, *La Foire Saint-Germain*, pp. 8–9, in Berthaud, *La Ville de Paris en vers burlesque* (Paris, 1692).

10. Mercier, *Tableau*, vol. 6, p. 40.

11. Alain-René Lesage and d'Orneval, *Le Théâtre de la foire ou l'opéra-comique contenant les meilleures pièces qui ont été représentées aux foires de S. Germain et de S. Laurent*, 15 vols. (Paris, 1721–1737), vol. 14, pp. 43–64.

12. Fournier, *Pont-Neuf*, Vol. 2, pp. 366–379.

13. Mercier, *Tableau*, vol. 6, pp. 42–43.

14. Emile Raunié, Preface to *Recueil Clairambault-Maurepas. Chansonnier historique du XVIIIᵉ siècle*, ed. Emile Raunié, 10 vols. (Paris, 1879–1884), vol. 1, pp. ii–iii.

15. For a discussion of this issue, see Raunié's Preface; Kastner, *Les Voix;* Victor Fournel, *Les Cris de Paris, types et physionomies d'autrefois* (Paris, 1887); Claude Brossette, *Du Vaudeville*, ed. Achille Kühnholtz (Paris, 1846). The last work cited was a discourse delivered by Brossette in 1725 at the Académie de Lyons.

16. *Journal de Paris*, 15 January 1783, p. 59.

17. [Charles Collé], *Chansons joyeuses mises au jour par un âne-onyme, onissime* (Paris, n.d.), p. 4.

18. Ibid., p. 33. The airs were, respectively "L'Eventail" and "Petite Fronde."

19. Mercier, *Tableau*, vol. 1, pp. 301–302.

20. Bibliothèque Nationale ms fr 15128, fols. 281–359. This collection includes both texts and notations.

21. BN ms fr 15130, fols. 27–32. For a slightly different notation of this vaudeville, see *La Clé du caveau à l'usage de tous les chansonniers*, ed. Pierre Capelle (Paris, 1811), pp. 130–131.

22. *Recueil Clairambault*, vol. 1, p. 32. This collection of eighteenth-century songs, one of the most important, was compiled by Pierre Clairambault, a genealogist, over a span of 70 years. After his death in 1740, his nephew, Paschal, a clerk in the ministry of Jean-Frédéric Phélypeaux, comte de Maurepas, continued the collection, which was put in the convent of the Grands-Augustins in 1772. Clairambault was a member of the Ordre du Saint-Esprit, connected to the Augustins. The collection was given to the Bibliothèque Nationale in 1792.

Evoking laughter from the multitude but anger from those whom they reviled, the Pont-Neuf songs were still controversial in the nineteenth century. In his review of the publication of the Clairambault-Maurepas collection in 1880, the noted literary scholar Ferdinand Brunetière found no redeeming literary value in the songs attacking Louis XIV and others. Charging that they fostered a bad taste for scandalous anecdotes, Brunetière contended that the anonymously composed verses distorted history by conveying incorrect impressions of historical events and figures. See Ferdinand Brunetière, "Chansonnier historique du XVIIIe siècle de M. Emile Raunié," *Revue des deux mondes* (15 August 1880): 932–943.

23. BN ms fr 15132, fols. 385–386.

24. *Recueil Clairambault*, vol. 2, p. 48. For additional verses on the scandalous life of the regent's daughter, see Jean-Frédéric Maurepas, *Mémoires*, 3d ed., 3 vols. (Paris, 1792), vol. 1, pp. 127–129, 218.

25. Charles Nisard, *Des Chansons populaires chez les anciens et chez les français: essai historique suivi d'une étude sur la chanson des rues contemporaine*, 2 vols. (Paris, 1867), vol. 1, p. 419. See also BN ms fr 15133. Most of the songs on the Saint-Médard miracles were obscene.

26. See, for example, BN ms fr 15134, fols. 739–744.

27. René Louis de Voyer de Paulmy d'Argenson, *Journal et mémoires*, ed. E. J. B. Rathery, 9 vols. (Paris, 1859–1867), vol. 5, pp. 398–399, 404, 406. See also Nisard, *Chansons*, vol. 1, pp. 393–394.

28. *Recueil Clairambault*, vol. 8, p. 313.

29. Quoted in Victor Fournel, *Tableau du vieux Paris. Les Spectacles populaires et les artistes des rues* (Paris, 1863), p. 293.

30. Fournier, *Pont-Neuf*, vol. 1, p. 243. In addition, for a discussion of charlatans, see Marie-Madeleine Rabecq-Maillard, "Jeux, Fêtes, Spectacles," in *La Vie populaire en France du Moyen Age à nos jours*, 2 vols. (Paris, n.d.), vol. 2, pp. 109–112; Victor Fournel, *Le Vieux Paris, fêtes, jeux et spectacles* (Tours, 1887), pp. 187–243; Gouriet, *Charlatans*, vol. 1, pp. 303–325.

31. Musée Carnavalet, anonymous engraving, Bb. C14. 1649.

32. Frédéric Melchior Grimm, *Correspondance littéraire, philosophique et critique*, 16 vols. (Paris, 1877–1882), vol. 10, pp. 3–5. The *Correspondance* reported on July 1, 1772, the arrest and banishment of a charlatan who had camped near the church of Saint-Roch and who claimed he could work miracles. For 10 days the streets of the quarter were full of people —"blind, deaf, lame, maimed believers whom faith and hope had brought together." Touching the people, he claimed that if they were not cured, it was because they lacked true faith. When a lame girl did not respond to the charlatan's touch, her furious mother broke her crutches on her back. Afraid to arrest the healer because of the crowd's impassioned belief in him, the police led him away on the pretext that a "great lady" needed his help; but he was taken to a *commissaire*. Unable to cure several crippled people supplied by the *commissaire*, the charlatan was taken four leagues from the city and told not to return.

33. Bibliothèque Historique de la Ville de Paris (hereafter BV), ms 619, fols. 249v–250v.

34. Gouriet, *Charlatans*, vol. 1, pp. 309–323.

35. Archives Nationales (hereafter AN), ms 0¹ 494, fol. 321.
36. Mercier, *Tableau,* vol. 3, pp. 53–55.
37. Gouriet, *Charlatans,* vol. 1, p. 323.
38. Letter from Piron to Abbé Legendre, quoted in Fournier, *Pont-Neuf,* vol. 1, p. 257. See also Edmond Jean François Barbier, *Chronique de la Régence et du règne de Louis XV* (1718–63), *ou Journal de Barbier,* 8 vols. (Paris, 1857), vol. 2, p. 81.
39. Quoted in Fournier, *Pont-Neuf,* vol. 1, pp. 261–262.

CHAPTER 2. Raillery in the Fairs

1. *Almanach forain, ou les différents spectacles des boulevards et des foires de Paris* (Paris, 1776), pp. 183–184; (1778), pp. 173–174.
2. For a description, see Fournel, *Tableau,* pp. 193–195; Florent-Carton Dancourt, *La Foire de Bezons* (Paris, 1695); the engraving by Gabriel de Saint-Aubin; Barbier, *Chronique,* vol. 1, p. 66.
3. The best information on these fairs is to be found in Emile Campardon, *Les Spectacles de la foire,* 2 vols. (Paris, 1877). Aside from the narrative history, the author provides papers of the commissaires of the Châtelet, of the Conseil d'Etat, the Parlement of Paris, and other legal bodies that pertain to the fairs. Along with Campardon, the reader should consult especially François Parfaict and Claude Parfaict, *Mémoires pour servir à l'histoire des spectacles de la foire,* 2 vols. (Paris, 1743); Henri Sauval, *Histoire et recherches des antiquités de la ville de Paris,* 3 vols. (Paris, 1724). Jean Loret's *La Muze historique, ou recueil des lettres en vers contentant les nouvelles du temps,* new ed., ed. Ch.-L. Livet, 4 vols. (1650–1665), has many evocations of the fairs; and Florent-Carton Dancourt's play *La Foire Saint-Germain* (Paris, 1696) recreates the general scene. The *Almanach forain* (1773), n.p., relates the origins and history of the fairs. For the location and a perspective of the fairs, see Louis Bretez, *Plan de Turgot* (Paris, 1966). For a plan of the fair Saint-Laurent and a discussion of the commercial activity there, see Arthur Heulhard, *La Foire Saint-Laurent, son histoire et ses spectacles* (Paris, 1878), pp. 35–43. A thorough discussion of the sources of the history of the fair theaters can be found in Georges Cucuel, "Sources et documents pour servir à l'histoire de l'opéra-comique en France," *Annales musicales* 3 (1914): 247–282. In addition to Heulhard, the best accounts of fair history in the secondary literature are Auguste Font, *Favart, l'opéra-comique et la comédie-vaudeville au XVIIe et XVIIIe siècles* (Paris, 1894), pp. 48–55; Emile Genest, *L'Opéra-comique, connu et inconnu, son histoire depuis l'origine jusqu'à nos jours* (Paris, 1925), pp. 10–30, 46–63; Maurice Albert, *Les Théâtres de la foire* (1660–1789) (Paris, 1900); Auguste Poitevin [Maurice Drack], *Le Théâtre de la foire, la comédie italienne et l'opéra-comique* (Paris, 1889), pp. 1–10; Arthur Pougin, *Dictionnaire historique et pittoresque du théâtre et des arts qui s'y rattachent* (Paris, 1885), pp. 375–386; Lionel de La Laurencie, "L'Opéra-comique" in Albert Lavignac, *Encyclopédie de la musique,* 6 vols. (Paris, 1931), vol. 3, 1457–1489; Albert Soubies and Charles Malherbe, *Précis de l'histoire de l'opéra-comique* (Paris, 1887), pp. 11–14; Eise Carel Van Bellen, *Les Origines du mélodrame* (Utrecht, 1927), pp. 16–69; Fournel, *Tableau,* pp. 90–218; Eugène d'Auriac, *Théâtre de la foire, avec un essai historique sur les spectacles forains* (Paris, 1878), pp. 1–55; V. Barberet, *Lesage et le théâtre de la foire* (Nancy, 1887), pp. 21–29; Clifford Barnes, "The 'Théâtre de la Foire' (Paris, 1697–1762): Its Music and Composers (Ph.D. dissertation, University of Southern California, 1965), pp. 22–31; G. Zetter, *Evolution des foires et marchés à travers les siècles* (Paris, 1923), pp. 97–116.
4. AN ms 0¹ 618, doss. 1, pièce 4, 1r–1v, and pièce 5.
5. See, for example, the comments of Colletet, *Tracas,* p. 20.
6. Charles Simon Favart, *Mémoires et correspondance littéraires, dramatiques et anecdotiques de C. S. Favart,* 3 vols. (Paris, 1808), vol. 1, p. 254.
7. Martin Lister, *A Journey to Paris in the Year 1698,* new ed. (London, 1823), p. 147.
8. Mercier, *Tableau,* vol. 5, p. 103.

9. Sauval, *Antiquités,* vol. 1, p. 666.

10. AN ms K 966 doss. 13, pièce 1. For documents concerning the early history of the fair along with plans of the topography, see dossiers 1–5 and 15 of this carton.

11. Joachim Christoph Nemeitz, *Séjour de Paris, c'est à dire, instructions fidèles pour les voyageurs de condition, durant leur séjour à Paris* (Leyden, 1727), p. 181.

12. Charles Sorel, *Polyandre, histoire comique* (Paris, 1648), p. 458.

13. Ibid., p. 473.

14. Barbier, *Chronique,* vol. 1, p. 191. See also Marc-René d'Argenson, *Rapports inédits du lieutenant de police René d'Argenson* (1697–1715), ed. Paul Cottin, 1891), pp. cv–cviii.

15. Germain Brice, *Nouvelle description de la ville de Paris et tout ce qu'elle contient de plus remarquable,* 8th ed. rev., 4 vols. (Paris, 1725), vol. 3, p. 401. See also Dubois de Saint-Gelais, *Histoire journalière de Paris 1716,* 2 vols. (Paris, 1716–1717), vol. 2, pp. 142–146.

16. Sorel, *Polyandre,* p. 463.

17. AN ms 0^1 849, fol. 498.

18. The archives of the commissaires are in the Y series of the Archives Nationales. My material comes principally from Y 12227, doss. 17. See also Nicholas-Toussaint Le Moyne Des Essarts, *Dictionnaire universel de police,* 7 vols. (Paris, 1786–1789), vol. 3, pp. 52–84; vol. 4, pp. 91–94; Campardon, *Spectacles,* vol. 1, pp. xl–xlvii. On the role of the lieutenant general of police in keeping order at the fairs, see D'Argenson, *Rapports,* pp. 257–259.

19. Louis Liger, *Le Voyageur fidèle, ou le guide des étrangers dans le ville de Paris* (Paris, 1715), p. 243.

20. Quoted in Heulhard, *Foire,* pp. 83–84.

21. AN ms Y 12227, doss. 17, pièce 6.

22. BV ms 631, fol. 9.

23. Des Essarts, vol. 1, p. 476.

24. Liger, *Voyageur,* pp. 78, 234.

25. Nemeitz, p. 169.

26. Des Essarts, vol. 4, p. 92.

27. Ibid., vol. 3, p. 576.

28. *Almanach historique et chronologique de tous les spectacles de Paris* (Paris, 1754), p. 182.

29. Nemeitz, p. 180.

30. Barbier, *Chronique,* vol. 1, pp. 117–118.

31. BV ms 618, 13r–13v.

32. Bibliothèque de l'Arsenal ms Bastille 12203; Antoine-Raymond-Jean-Gualbert de Sartine, *Journal des inspecteurs de M. de Sartine, 1761–1764* (Paris, 1863), p. iv.

33. Colletet, *Tracas,* pp. 37–38.

34. My discussion of this conflict is based entirely on AN ms Y 12227, doss. 17, pièces 30, 31, 34, 35, 37, and 38. A complete list of the merchants by name and establishment at Saint-Laurent from 1778 to 1780 can be found in doss. 18, pièce 12 of this carton.

35. Ibid., pièce 34, 1r.

36. Sorel, *Polyandre,* pp. 464–465.

37. Nemeitz, p. 170.

38. Mikhail Bakhtin, *Rabelais and His World,* trans. Helen Iswolsky (Cambridge, Mass., 1968), pp. 1–35.

39. *Almanach forain* (1774), p. 36. The best collection of *parades* in print is *Théâtres des boulevards* (Paris, 1756; reprint ed., with a Notice by Georges D'Heylli, Paris, 1881), 2 vols. In addition, see the "Notice" by Thomas-Simon Gueullette, the author of most of the *parades* in *Théâtre,* BA ms 52. See also BN ms fr 9328, 9340, 9341. For the career of Gueullette, a barrister of the Parlement of Paris, see Henri d'Alméras and Paul d'Estrée, *Les Théâtres libertins aux XVIIIe siècle* (Paris, 1905), pp. 7–30; Henri Nicolle, "Thomas-Simon Gueullette et les parades au XVIIIe siècle," *Revue de France* 10 (April, May, June, 1874): 768–795.

40. "Lettre à Madame sur les parades," *Théâtre des boulevards,* vol. 1, pp. 5–10.

41. *Théâtre des boulevards,* vol. 1, pp. 234, 221–239.

42. Peter Burke, *Popular Culture in Early Modern Europe* (New York, 1978), pp. 24, 29, 270–281.

43. *Journal de Paris*, 1783, pp. 1404–1405, 1411, 1474–1475, 1465–1467. On mesmerism, see Robert Darnton, *Mesmerism and the End of the Enlightenment in France* (Cambridge, Mass., 1968).

44. Liger, *Voyageur*, p. 244; Brice, *Nouvelle*, vol. 2, p. 17.

45. Quoted in John Lough, *Paris Theater Audiences in the Seventeenth and Eighteenth Centuries* (London, 1957), p. 207.

46. *Almanach forain* (1777), p. 76.

47. Nicolas-Edme Rétif de la Bretonne, *Les Nuits de Paris, ou le spectateur nocturne*, 7 vols. (London, 1788–1789), vol. 7, p. 40.

48. Anna Francesca Cradock, *Journal de Madame Cradock. Voyage en France* (1783–1786), trans. O. Delphin-Balleyguier (Paris, 1896), p. 5.

49. Ibid., p. 70.

50. Dancourt, *Foire Saint-Germain*.

51. Parfaict and Parfaict, *Mémoires*, vol. 1, p. xxiv; Scarron, *Foire Saint-Germain*, p. 9; Paul Landormy, "Le Théâtre de la foire Saint-Germain," in *Le Théâtre lyrique en France*, 2 vols. (Paris, n.d.), vol. 1, p. 104; Campardon, *Spectacles*, Vol. 1, p. xiii. For a vivid account in verse, see Colletet, *Tracas*.

52. BV ms 616, p. 56.

53. BV ms 620, p. 267.

54. Alméras and d'Estrée, *Théâtres*, has a full discussion of these theaters. See also G. Capon and R. Yve-Plessis, *Les Théâtres clandestins au XVIIIe siècle* (Paris, 1905); Mercier, *Tableau*, vol. 6, pp. 111–114.

55. Gueullette is quoted in Alméras and d'Estrée, *Théâtres*, p. 17.

56. Collé's works can be found in two collections: Charles Collé, *Parades inédites* (Paris, 1864); Charles Collé, *Théâtre de société*, 3 vols. (The Hague, 1777).

57. Grimm, *Correspondance*, cited in Alméras and d'Estrée, *Théâtres*, p. 44.

58. Alméras and d'Estrée, *Théâtres*, pp. 45–50.

59. The discussion of Delisle's plays in Capon and Yve-Plessis, *Théâtres*, is based on four volumes of his work in their possession.

60. Alméras and d'Estrée, *Théâtres*, pp. 75–152.

61. Charles Collé, *Journal et mémoires*, new ed., aug., ed. Honoré Bonhomme, 3 vols. (Paris, 1868), vol. 3, p. 105.

62. Quoted in Alméras and d'Estrée, *Théâtres*, p. 179.

63. Ibid., p. 202.

64. This piece is discussed in Capon and Yve-Plessis, *Théâtres*, pp. 42–44, who observe that the sexual activity required in such plays would have been so exhausting that the performers probably simulated the "erotic excesses" called for by authors "in order to excite satiated spectators better."

65. Quoted in ibid., p. 160.

66. Louis Petit de Bachaumont, *Mémoires secrets pour servir à l'histoire de la république des lettres en France depuis 1762 jusqu'à nos jours, ou journal d'un observateur*, 31 vols. (London, 1777–1789), vol. 6, p. 186.

67. Capon and Yve-Plessis, *Théâtres*, p. 188.

68. Bachaumont, *Mémoires*, vol. 6, p. 186.

69. See also Robert M. Isherwood, "Musical Entertainment in Eighteenth-Century Paris," *International Review of the Aesthetics and Sociology of Music* 9 (December 1978): 295–310.

70. Alméras and d'Estrée, *Théâtres*, pp. 40–41.

71. Marie-Françoise Christout in *Le Merveilleux et le théâtre du silence en France à partir du XVIIe siècle* (Paris, 1965), p. 125, calls our attention to Christine de Pisan's account of a tightrope performer who in the time of Charles V walked on a rope from the towers of Nôtre-Dame to the royal palace. Guillaume Depping in *Les Merveilles de la force et de l'adresse* (Paris, 1869), p. 188, mentions a funambulist who plunged to his death in the

Seine during an attempt to walk a rope stretched from the Tour de Nesle to the tower of the Grand-Prévôt in 1649. On the occasion of Charles IX's marriage to Emperor Maximillian II's daughter, a famous funambulist named Archange Tuccaro from Aquila accompanied the imperial entourage, danced for the French court, and became Charles's instructor in acrobatics. Tuccaro wrote a treatise in 1599 dedicated to Henri IV on tumbling, leaping, and rope walking. Funambulism and gymnastic stunts were used on occasion in the *ballets de cour* during the reigns of Louis XIII and XIV, but they found an even more receptive audience at the fairs, where as many as five troupes of *sauteurs* performed during the same fair. For a discussion of acrobatics, tightrope walking, and pantomime, see Fournel, *Tableau*, pp. 397–409; Fournel, *Vieux*, pp. 335–347; Charles Rabou, *Les Grands danseurs du roi* (Brussels, 1846), pp. 2–5; Christout, pp. 125–128; Depping, pp. 156–160.

72. The term *saltimbanque* is derived from the Italian *saltare* (to dance) *in banco* (on the bench or stand), hence *sauter sur la banque*. After the *saltimbanques* began using swords and other arms in their stunts, they were called *batalores* (*bateleurs* in French, tumblers in English). See Gaston Escudier, *Les Saltimbanques, leur vie, leurs moeurs* (Paris, 1875), p. 30; Nicolas de La Mare, *Traité de la police*, 4 vols. (Paris, 1705–1738), vol. 3, p. 436.

73. Parfaict and Parfaict, *Mémoires*, vol. 1, pp. 2–5.

74. Nemeitz, p. 176.

75. Jèze, *Journal du citoyen* (The Hague, 1754), p. 179.

76. Quoted in Christout, p. 126.

77. Wires did not replace ropes until the late eighteenth century.

78. Parfaict and Parfaict, *Mémoires*, vol. 1, p. 204.

79. *Recueil Clairambault*, vol. 3, pp. 62–64.

80. Parfaict and Parfaict, *Mémoires*, vol. 2, p. 43; Alexandre-Jacques du Coudray, *Nouveaux essais historiques sur Paris*, 3 vols. (Paris, 1781–1786), vol. 2, p. 12.

81. Jèze, *Journal*, p. 178. The figures are for 1754. Comparative prices at the Opéra-Comique were 4 livres for the first loges, amphitheather, and parquet; 2 livres for second loges; 30 sous for third; 20 for the parterre.

82. Pierre-Jean Baptiste Nougaret and Nicolas Rétif de la Bretonne, *La Mimographe, ou idées d'une honnête femme pour la réformation du théâtre national* (Amsterdam, 1770), p. 448.

83. The text of *Les Forces* is included in the collection of Poitevin, *Théâtre*, pp. 13–32; in D'Auriac, *Théâtre*, pp. 57–71; in *Almanach forain* 1773, n.p.; and in Parfaict and Parfaict, *Mémoires*, vol. 1: pp. lvi–lxxix. For an analysis of this work with special attention to the Italian influences on it, see Irène Mamczarz, *Les Intermèdes comiques italiens au XVIIIᵉ siècle en France et en Italie* (Paris, 1972), pp. 242–244; Fortunat Strowski, "Le Théâtre de la foire," in *Le Théâtre à Paris au XVIIIᵉ siècle; conférences du Musée Carnavalet (1929)* (Paris, 1930), pp. 72–75.

84. Parfaict and Parfaict, *Mémoires*, vol. 1, p. 11. The Parfaict brothers provide brief biographies of the players, most of whom were the offspring of actors and acrobats.

85. Antoine Boudet, *Les Affiches de Paris*, 5 vols. (Paris: 1746–1751), vol. 1, (n.p.).

86. Ibid., vol. 3, (n.p.).

87. Campardon, *Spectacles*, vol. 2, pp. 286–287.

88. BA ms Bastille 12203, pièce 2.

89. Boudet, *Affiches*, vol. 1, n.p. See also Campardon, *Spectacles*, vol. 2, p. 230. Jèze, *Journal*, p. 179, lists tickets at 2 to 24 sous.

90. For a discussion, see Christout, pp. 130–134; Jacques Chesnais, *Histoire générale des marionnettes* (Paris, 1947), pp. 115–124; Charles Magnin, *Histoire des marionnettes en Europe depuis l'antiquité jusqu'à nos jours* (Paris, 1862); Heulhard, *Saint–Laurent*, pp. 151–186.

91. Des Essarts, *Dictionnaire*, vol. 6, pp. 362–363.

92. AN ms Y 12227, doss. 17, pièce 6, 1v.

93. Donald F. Lach, "Asian Elephants in Europe," *Journal of Asian History* 1 (1967): pp. 133–176.

94. Lister, *Journey*, p. 149.

95. BN Cabinet des Estampes, Qbl réserve Hennin T 107, No. 9337.
96. Grimm, *Correspondance*, vol. 1, pp. 272–273; Campardon, *Spectacles*, vol. 2, pp. 312–314; Edmond-Jean-François Barbier, *Journal historique et anecdotique du règne de Louis XV*, 4 vols. (Paris, 1847), vol. 4, p. 356.
97. Campardon insisted the rhinoceros was 12 by 12 and growing larger and that it drank beer as well as water.
98. I say "apparently" because D'Argenson, *Journal*, vol. 6, p. 77, refers in his entry for 21 November 1749 to the animal seen last year at the fair.
99. Campardon, *Spectacles*, vol. 2, pp. 230–231.
100. Cradock, *Journal*, p. 68.
101. BN, Cabinet des Estampes, Catalogue de curiosité, 1772–1773, Yd 904.
102. Lister, *Journey*, p. 149.
103. Boudet, *Affiches*, vol. 3, n.p.
104. Ibid.
105. Ibid.
106. *L'Avant-coureur, feuille hébdomadaire*, 25 January 1773, n.p. Edited by Pierre-Joseph Boudier de Villemert, Jacques Lacombe, and Anne-Gabriel Meusnier de Querlon, *L'Avant-coureur* changed titles several times, especially after Panckoucke bought it in 1773. After joining it with the *Gazette de littérature, des sciences et des arts* in 1774, Panckoucke called it *Gazette et avant-coureur*. Later that year, he united it with the *Journal de politique*.
107. Mercier, *Tableau*, vol. 3, pp. 35–36.
108. Bonnet is quoted in Parfaict and Parfaict, *Mémoires*, vol. 1, pp. xlii–xliii. See also Heulhard, *Saint-Laurent*, p. 131.
109. Nemeitz, pp. 7–8.
110. Ibid., p. 10.
111. In addition to the *Almanach forain* for this period, see *Journal de Paris*, 3 February 1777, p. 4.
112. BV, ms 614, fol. 177.
113. *Journal de Paris*, 3 February 1777, p. 4.
114. Fournel, *Vieux*, pp. 371–372.
115. Bachaumont, *Mémoires*, vol. 13, p. 375.
116. Heulhard, *Saint-Laurent*, p. 133.
117. *Journal de Paris*, 12 January 1779, p. 47; 1 February 1779, p. 132.
118. BN ms n.a. fr 7812, fol. 33.
119. Nemeitz, pp. 178–179.
120. Boudet, *Affiches*, vol. 1, p. 6.
121. Ibid., n.p.
122. Ibid., vol. 2, n.p.
123. Ibid.
124. Fournel, *Vieux*, pp. 321–322.
125. *Journal de Paris*, 20 March 1783, p. 326.
126. *Affiches, annonces et avis divers*, 3 March 1785, p. 576; *Journal de Paris*, 6 March 1785, p. 270.
127. Henri Decremps, *La Magie blanche dévoilée, ou explication des tours surprenants* (Paris, 1784).
128. Boudet, *Affiches*, vol. 2, n.p.; vol. 3, n.p.
129. Elie-Catherine Fréron and Joseph de La Porte, *Lettres sur quelques écrits de ce temps*, 13 vols. (Paris, 1749–1754), vol. 3, p. 141; *Almanach forain* (1774), pp. 39–41.
130. *Journal de Paris*, 20 December 1783, p. 1458, and 3 January 1784, p. 12; Bachaumont, *Mémoires*, vol. 24, pp. 103–104; vol. 25: pp. 12–13; Fournel, *Vieux*, p. 258.
131. Loret, *La Muze historique*, vol. 2, p. 193.
132. Kircher's lantern may have been based on the various catoptrical means of distorting objects and making things disappear by using cylindrical and conic mirrors explained by the Minime scientist, Père Niceron.

133. Jean Torlais, *L'Abbé Nollet, un physicien au siècle des lumières* (Paris, 1954), pp. 29–33; Jean Torlais, "La Physique expérimentale," in *Enseignement et diffusion des sciences en France au XVIIIe siècle*, ed. René Taton (Paris, 1964), pp. 619–645; Maurice Daumas, *Les Instruments scientifiques au XVIIe et XVIIIe siècles* (Paris, 1954), pp. 186–187, 285–287; Robert Champeix, *Savants méconnus, inventions oubliées* (Paris, 1966), pp. 71–72.

134. Grimm, *Correspondance*, vol. 9, p. 110.

135. The text of Tinchet's play is in the BA, but it has not been given a number.

136. Ibid., p. 6.

137. For a discussion of some of these shows, see *Almanach forain* (1774), pp. 39–41, 69; (1776), p. 117.

138. Four books in particular have stimulated my thinking about this problem: Christout; Jean Chateau, *Le Réel et l'imaginaire dans le jeu de l'enfant. Essai sur la genèse de l'imagination* (Paris, 1946); George Jamati, *Théâtre et vie intérieure* (Paris, 1952); Marian Hannah Winter, *Le Théâtre des merveilles* (Paris, 1962).

139. Charles Alard was in fact killed after a tumble in 1709.

140. Barbier, *Chronique*, vol. 8, pp. 23–24. On the decline of Saint-Germain, see also the remarks of Du Coudray, *Nouveaux*, vol. 1, p. 253; vol. 2, p. 15.

141. See the testimony of a *limonadier* in AN ms Y 12227, doss. 17, pièce 16.

142. For accounts of the fire, see the report of Commissaire Gillespierre Chênu, AN ms K 966, pièce 10; Barbier, *Chronique*, vol. 8, pp. 22–24; Du Coudray, *Nouveaux*, vol. 3, pp. 133–135; Favart, *Mémoires*, vol. 1, pp. 254–255.

143. *Almanach forain* (1773), n.p.

144. Ibid. (1776), n.p.

145. François Métra, *Correspondance secrète, politique et littéraire*, 18 vols. (London, 1787–1790), vol. 8, p. 215.

146. On the Ruggieri family, see Henry de Chennevierres, "Les Ruggieri artificiers," *La Gazette des beaux arts* 36 (August 1887): 132–140.

147. Luc-Vincent Thiéry, *Almanach du voyageur à Paris* 5 vols. (Paris, 1783–1787), vol. 1: 601–604; vol. 2: pp. 39–40.

148. BV ms 627, 215v.

149. Bachaumont, *Mémoires*, vol. 4, p. 245.

150. Ibid., vol. 19, p. 47.

151. Ibid., vol. 6: p. 125; vol. 19, p. 180.

152. *Journal de Paris*, 3 January 1783, p. 11.

153. Bachaumont, *Mémoires*, vol. 7, p. 90.

154. Cradock, *Journal*, pp. 35–36.

155. *Journal de Paris*, 4 March 1778, pp. 251–252; 2 December 1784, p. 1427; 1 January 1785, p. 3; 23 January 1785, p. 95.

156. *Almanach forain* (1774), p. 78; (1776), pp. 113–114; (1777), p. 28.

157. BV ms 629, 52, 55.

158. *Almanach forain* (1787), p. 42.

CHAPTER 3. The Opéra-Comique

1. For the early history of French theater and theatrical entertainers in the fairs, see Parfaict and Parfaict, *Mémoires*, vol. 1, pp. xl–lxxix; *Almanach historique* (1753), pp. 3–20.

2. James R. Anthony, *French Baroque Music from Beaujoyeulx to Rameau* (New York, 1974), p. 149.

3. Some scholars believe the word *vaudeville* is derived from Vau de Vire (*vau* from *val*), a valley in lower Normandy where presumably in the fifteenth century a fuller named Olivier Basselin, who fought in the wars against England, composed patriotic songs that became popular in the region and then throughout France. See Genest, *L'Opéra comique*, pp. 65–66; Font, *Favart*, p. 9; Armand Gasté, *A Propos d'Olivier Basselin et de l'édition des vaux de vire de Louis Dubois* (Paris, 1898); Armand Gasté, *Etude sur Olivier Basselin et les compagnons*

de vau de vire, leur rôle pendant les guerres anglaises et leurs chansons (Caen, 1866); *Chansons normandes du XVe siècle*, ed. Armand Gasté (Caen, 1886); E. Prioleau, *Histoire du vaudeville* (Bordeaux. 1890), pp. 3–5. Jean le Houx, a Norman lawyer, published a collection allegedly of Basselin's songs in 1576 (or 1610). Other etymologies have been suggested including *voix de ville*, which appears in the titles of several collections of songs from the sixteenth century, including one by Jean Chardavoine published in 1588. See Julien Tiersot, *Histoire de la chanson populaire en France* (Paris, 1889), pp. 227–239; Font, *Favart*, pp. 9–12; Paul-Marie Masson, "Les Fondateurs de l'opéra-comique," in *Histoire du théâtre lyrique en France depuis les origines jusqu'à nos jours*, 2 vols. (Paris, n.d.), vol. 1, pp. 160–168, Jacques Gardien, *La Chanson populaire française* (Paris, 1948), pp. 36–39. J. -B. Wecherlin, in *La Chanson populaire* (Paris, 1886), pp. 143–146, insists that *va-de-ville* means a popular village song, the voices or songs of the country. He denies the association with *vaudevire*. In one of the most extensive and authoritative discussions of the origins of the vaudeville, Julien Tiersot repudiates the whole Basselin legend. He attributes it to Charles de Bourqueville, who, in his *Antiquités de Caen*, wanted to claim the vaudeville for the Normans. Irritated that the myth that attributed the vaudeville to the Norman countryside and to a man who may never have written songs has never been exposed, Tiersot cites song collections from the sixteenth century that bear the phrase *vaux-de-ville* and *voix-de-ville* in their titles. They contained original music by such people as Pierre de Ronsard, Adrien Le Roy, and Rémy Belleau and were published in such places as Paris, Lyons, and Chalons, indicating that vaudevilles came from French towns rather than the Norman countryside. Tiersot suggests that Jean le Houx was the actual composer of the Basselin songs. He also contends that the Norman *vaudevires* were really drinking songs whose tunes were popular in origin until the seventeenth century, when musicians such as Adam Billaud began composing them. André Campra, Louis-Nicolas Clairambault, and other well-known musicians composed the drinking songs in the two major collections of the eighteenth century: *Recueils d'airs sérieux et à boire de différents auteurs* (Paris, 1690–1732) and *Tendresses bachiques, ou duo et trio melez de petits airs tendres et à boire des meilleurs auteurs*, 2 vols (Paris, 1712 and 1718). Gardien accepts Tiersot's view (see p. 36) and states that *voix-de-ville* acquired its literal meaning from a collection of songs published in Lyons in 1579 entitled *Jardin de musique semé d'exellentes et harmonieuses chansons et voix de ville, mises en musique, à quatre parties, par Corneille de Montfort, dit de Blockland, gentilhomme Stichtois.* For an eighteenth-century account of the origins of vaudevilles, see Brossette, *Du Vaudeville*, pp. 8–28.

4. The example is from the Clairambault Collection, vol. 7, BN ms 15132, fol. 83.

5. From *Harmonicorum libri*, vol. 2, p. 164, quoted in Georges Cucuel, *Les Créateurs de l'opéra-comique français* (Paris, 1914), p. 29.

6. Brossette, p. 5.

7. *Journal des théâtres, ou le nouveau spectateur*, 15 October 1777, p. 281. Founded by Fuel de Méricourt, François-Antoine Chevrier, and Prévost d'Exmes in 1776 as *Le Nouveau spectateur ou examen des nouvelles pièces de théâtre servant de répertoire universel des spectacles,* the original publication had only four issues. Fuel de Méricourt inaugurated the fifth issue with the first title given, and it will be so designated herein. After April, 1777 the *Journal* was written by Jean-Charles Le Vacher de Charnois and Alexandre Balthazar Laurent Grimod de La Reynière.

8. Quoted in Anthony, *French Baroque*, p. 152.

9. Lesage and D'Orneval, *Théâtre*, vol. 1, Preface, n.p.

10. Jean-Jacques Rousseau, *Oeuvres complètes*, vol. 7: *Dictionnaire de musique* (Paris, 1877), pp. 335–336.

11. Mercier, *Tableau*, vol. 1, p. 301. See also Tiersot, *Histoire de la chanson*, p. 234; Cucuel, *Créateurs*, pp. 27–56; La Laurencie in Lavignac, *Encyclopédie*, vol. 3, pp. 1459–1471.

12. Michel-Jean Sedaine, *Le Vaudeville, poème didactique en 4 chants* (n.p., 1756), pp. 41–42.

13. Quoted in *Affiches*, 22 March 1781, p. 675.

14. Font, *Favart*, p. 15.

15. A *Recueil de chansons* by Coulanges was published in Paris in 1698, and other editions appeared in the eighteenth century.

16. See the Maurepas and Clairambault collections in BN ms fr 12616-12659, and BN ms fr 12686-12743.

17. Maurepas, *Mémoires,* vol. 3, pp. 1–90; Dorothy S. Packer, "'La Calotte' and the Eighteenth-Century French Vaudeville," *Journal of the American Musicological Society* 23 (Spring 1970): pp. 61–83.

18. Packer, p. 82.

19. Sedaine, *Vaudeville,* p. 47.

20. Clifford Barnes, "Vocal Music at the 'Théâtres de la Foire' (1697–1762); Part One: Vaudeville," *Recherches sur la musique française classique,* 8 (1968): 144–147.

21. Nicolas Boindin, *Lettres historiques à Monsieur* (Paris, 1717–1718), p. 18.

22. In addition to Lesage, the best early eighteenth-century collection of vaudevilles is *La Clé des chansonniers, ou recueil de vaudevilles depuis cent ans et plus,* 2 vols. (Paris, 1717). Christophe Ballard, who published this collection, printed the notation of each vaudeville along with the original text or a new one. He also indicated the *timbre* for each so that the familiar tune accompanying a new verse could be identified easily. Several examples of vaudevilles and parodies are given in Cucuel, *Créateurs.*

23. Clifford Barnes, in "The 'Théâtre de la Foire' (Paris, 1697–1762): Its Music and Composers" (Ph.D. dissertation, University of Southern California, 1965), p. 210, says that the parodied songs helped to prepare the way for the *opéras-comiques* of the second half of the century, which used newly composed ariettes, because the parodies were much longer, had more varied rhythms, were believed to be more melodically expressive, and were generally more sophisticated than the older vaudevilles derived from folk origins. Although the influence of opéra bouffe was critical in turning the *opéras-comiques* toward the ariette style, the transition was a gradual one throughout the Lesage and Favart periods toward the greater use of new vaudevilles (i.e., parodied airs), original music, and ariettes. Barnes (pp. 179–183) provides a list of all the pieces from Lully's operas used in the Lesage collection of *opéras-comiques.* Christophe Ballard published a collection of parodies in 1703 entitled *Parodies bachiques sur les beaux airs des opéras.*

24. Mamczarz, p. 249.

25. Lesage and D'Orneval, *Théâtre,* vol. 12, p. 27. See also Poitevin, *Théâtre,* p. 230; D'Auriac, *Théâtre,* pp. 73–104. For Barberet's discussion of parodies, see *Lesage,* pp. 113–116.

26. For a thorough discussion with musical examples, see Clifford R. Barnes, "Instruments and Instrumental Music at the 'Théâtres de la Foire' (1697–1762)," *Recherches sur la musique française classique* 5 (1965): 144–165. See also Cucuel, *Créateurs,* pp. 30–56.

27. Tiersot, *Histoire,* p. 235.

28. Lesage, *Théâtre,* vol. 1, n.p.

29. Barberet, *Lesage,* pp. 64–67; 116–127.

30. Letter to Comte Durazzo, 14 January 1760, in Favart, *Mémoires,* vol. 1, p. 7.

31. Although audience composition is difficult to determine, it would appear that *le bas peuple* did not frequent the grand theaters. Soldiers, prostitutes, and lackeys, who often managed to get in free, could be found at the Comédie-Française and at the Opéra, but not workers, shopkeepers, clerks, porters, and artisans. The cost of tickets must have discouraged any doubtful interest they might have had: The Opéra charged 7 livres ten sous for the first loges, 4 for the second, 2 for the parterre, and 30 sous for the gallery. Comédie-Française prices ranged from 3 livres 12 sous to 18 sous. The top seat of 1 écu at the Opéra-Comique was too high for a shopkeeper's income, but 10 sous for the amphitheater and 5 for the parterre put that show in range. See Font, *Favart,* p. 66; Pougin, *Dictionnaire,* p. 619; François Henri Jospeph Blaze [Castil-Blaze], *Mémorial du Grand-Opéra, épilogue de l'Académie Royale de Musique* (Paris, 1847), p. 61. For an excellent discussion of the social makeup of Paris theater audience, see Henri Lagrave, *Le Théâtre et le public à Paris de 1715 à 1750* (Paris, 1972), Part 2; Lough, *Paris.* In contrast to my perception, Pierre Fortassier, in "Musique et peuple au XVIIIᵉ siècle," in *Images du peuple au dix-huitième siècle. Colloque d'Aix-en-*

Provence, 25 et 26 October 1969 (Paris, 1973), pp. 327–337, argues that the Opéra was a popular theater. His case is based on several questionable contentions: (1) that opera composers used street songs (I find this practice untypical); (2) that opera became simpler and more natural (does he mean Rameau and Gluck?); (3) that there were occasions—he cites one in 1764 and one in 1770—when shouts from the parterre interrupted performances (this was true of all the theaters as A. Prat points out in 'Le Parterre au XVIIIe siècle," *La Quinzaine,* 1 February 1906, pp. 412–488, and it is not evidence that the audience was popular); (4) that there was a guard stationed at the Opéra (measures taken to preserve order at a theater constantly seething with controversy does not prove that that theater was of the people); (5) that certain performances, traditionally on opening night at a new hall, were reserved for the people; (6) that on days when few people showed up at the Opéra, the police assigned an officer to round up girls in the Palais-Royal and march them to the theater (hardly evidence of popularity!); (7) that crowd scenes were important in French lyric tragedy, making the genre itself popular; (8) that parodies of operatic airs were sung in the fair theaters; (9) that more realistic dress was adopted by operatic characters, including peasant costumes; (10) that Rousseau's concept of simple, natural melodies, as exemplified in his *Romances,* found increasing favor and that his ideas influenced Gluck (neither Rousseau's views nor his music were characteristic of eighteenth-century French opera). Fortassier concludes that there was no separation between popular music and the music of great composers and that opera audiences were socially mixed. His evidence is practically nonexistent. What he fails to discern or to admit is that vulgarity and derision also became popular among *le monde.* Nothing deterred the highborn from attending the free, accessible fairs; nothing prevented them from embracing the culture of the marketplace as their own.

32. Jacques Lacombe, *Le Spectacle des beaux arts ou considérations touchant leur nature, leurs objets, leurs effets et leurs règles principales* (Paris, 1758), p. 129.

33. Lesage, *Théâtre,* vol. 14, p. 68.

34. BN ms fr 25476, 21v.

35. BN ms fr 9251, fol. 68.

36. I translate *le fouët* in this context as fillip in its secondary meaning of something that arouses or excites. BN ms fr 25476, fol. 6.

37. The manuscript copies of these *pièces en écriteaux,* of which this is one, contain fairly explicit directions about the stage action although at one point, when Léandre, with Isabelle at his knees, succumbs and throws away his books, the author has written: "This scene can be described only imperfectly: it consists in a *grand jeu de théâtre.*"

38. For a discussion, see Chateau, *Le Réel,* p. 31.

39. BN ms fr 9251, fols. 159–165.

40. Alexis Piron, *Oeuvres complètes,* ed. Rigoley de Juvigny, 7 vols. (Paris, 1776), vol. 3, p. 456. See also Jean-Auguste Julien [Desboulmiers], *Histoire du théâtre de l'opéra-comique,* 2 vols. (Paris, 1769), vol. 1, pp. 462–463.

41. Ibid., vol. 3, pp. 580–581.

42. Ibid., vol. 4, p. 443.

43. See the discussion in Van Bellen, *Les Origines,* p. 26; Barberet, *Lesage,* pp. 127–165; Christout, pp. 121–122.

44. Lacombe, *Le Spectacle,* p. 128. See also Martin Cooper, *Opéra Comique* (London, 1949), p. 17; Nicole Wild, "Aspects de la musique sous la Régence. Les Foires: naissance de l'opéra-comique," *Recherches sur la musique française classique* 5 (1965): 129; Barberet, *Lesage,* pp. 9–10, 108–113.

45. Piron, *Oeuvres,* vol. 3, p. 105.

46. Lesage, *Théâtre,* vol. 12, pp. 108–111.

47. Julien, *Histoire,* vol. 1, pp. 95–96. The work is by Lesage, D'Orneval, and Fuzelier.

48. Lesage, *Théâtre,* vol. 1, pp. 122–125.

49. Ibid., vol. 15, pp. 73–96.

50. Piron, *Oeuvres,* vol. 3, p. 79.

51. Charles-François Panard, *Théâtre et oeuvres diverses,* 4 vols. (Paris, 1763), vol. 1, p. ii.

52. Ibid., vol. 3, pp. 261–298.

53. This three-act *pièce en écriteaux,* performed in vaudevilles at Saint-Germain, can be found in Lesage, *Théâtre,* vol. 12, pp. 3–44.

54. *Arlequin Hulla, ou la femme répudiée* (Saint-Laurent, 1716) in Lesage, *Théâtre,* vol. 12, pp. 371–412.

55. When I say, "Preoccupation," I mean that of the 34 *opéras-comiques,* selected at random from dozens that I have examined closely for the period from 1708 until 1745, 30 had themes, situations, or characters involving the marvelous.

56. *Le Tombeau de Nostradamus* in Lesage, *Théâtre,* vol. 12, pp. 97–125.

57. Piron, *Oeuvres,* vol. 3, pp. 3–61.

58. Lesage, *Théâtre,* vol. 12, pp. 129–178.

59. Ibid., vol. 13, pp. 3–53.

CHAPTER 4. **The Politics of Culture:**
The Struggle Against Privilege

1. Robert M. Isherwood, *Music in the Service of the King: France in the Seventeenth Century* (Ithaca, N.Y., 1973), pp. 182–183; 195; 200.

2. *Almanach historique* (1755), p. 109.

3. AN ms 0¹ 618, fol. 3, lr–2r.

4. Louis Travenol and J. B. Durey de Noinville, *Histoire du théâtre de l'Académie Royale de Musique en France depuis son établissement jusqu'à présent,* 2d ed., rev. (Paris, 1757), pp. 150–151; Barnes, "The 'Théâtre,'" pp. 37–39.

5. Campardon, *Spectacles,* vol. 2, pp. 286–287.

6. For a general account of the Italian theater in France, see the works of Donald J. Grout, and Napoléon-Maurice Bernardin, *La Comédie italienne en France et les théâtres de la foire et du boulevard (1570–1791)* (Paris, 1902); Van Bellen, *Origines,* pp. 22–33.

7. Jules Bonnassies, *Les Spectacles forains et la Comédie-Française, le droit des pauvres avant et après 1789* (Paris, 1875), p. 6; Adrien Peytel, "Les Théâtres musicaux subventionnés," in Lavignac, *Encyclopédie,* vol. 6, p. 3768.

8. Aside from the original manuscripts, the most important body of sources on the struggle is in Campardon, *Spectacles.* His collection consists mainly of reports of the *commissaires* of the Châtelet although documents of the Grand Conseil, the Conseil d'Etat, and the Parlement are included. The best eighteenth-century account of the struggle is in Parfaict and Parfaict, *Mémoires.* In addition see Bonnassies, *Spectacles;* Julien, *Histoire;* Heulhard, *Saint-Laurent;* Barberet, *Lesage;* Font, *Favart;* Paul-Marie Masson, "Les Fondateurs de l'opéra-comique," *Histoire du théâtre lyrique en France depuis les origines jusqu'à nos jours,* 2 vols. (Paris, n.d.) vol. 1, pp. 160–168; Cucuel, *Créateurs;* Poitevin, *Théâtre;* D'Auriac, *Théâtre;* Marcello Spaziani, *Il teatro della foire* (Rome, 1965); Sauval, *Histoire,* vol. 1; Van Bellen, *Origines,* pp. 16–69; Genest, *L'Opéra-comique,* pp. 43–139; Paul Pélissier, *Histoire administrative de l'Académie Nationale de Musique et de Danse* (Paris, 1906), pp. 22–27; Cucuel, "Sources," *Année;* Wild, "Aspects," *Recherches,* pp. 131–133; Pougin, *Dictionnaire,* pp. 375–386; Zetter, *Evolution,* pp. 77–116.

9. Although the fairs provided the setting for a uniquely French comic opera, the musical and dramatic origins of this genre lay in the Italian theater in Paris. The major collection of the Italian comedies written in French is Evariste Gherardi's *Le Théâtre italien ou le recueil général de toutes les comedies et scènes françoises jouées par les comédiens italiens du roi,* 3 vols. (Paris, 1741). The reason usually given for the expulsion of the Italians in 1697 is their plan to present a play, *La Fausse Prude,* which was taken as an insult to Madame de Maintenon.

10. For the role of the police in the actions taken against the *forains,* see BN ms fr 21625; Parfaict and Parfaict, *Mémoires,* vol. 1, pp. 14–22; Peytel, "Les Théâtres"; Lavignac, *Encyclopédie,* p. 3769. The police reports indicate strong public opposition to the attempts to exercise monopolistic privilege. Fights broke out at the Opéra and the Comédie-Française,

eliciting police orders against taking arms into these theaters, but there are no references in the reports of this period to disturbances at the fair theaters.

11. Parfaict and Parfaict, *Mémoires,* vol. 1, p. 48.

12. Heulhard, *Saint-Laurent,* p. 194.

13. The deliberations of the Grand Conseil in March and its subsequent actions in the struggle between the theaters have been printed in Campardon, *Spectacles,* vol. 2, pp. 256–259; 267–268. The *arrêts* of the Parlement between June 1706 and June 1708, along with other documents relating to the dispute until December 1711, may be found in Campardon, op. cit., pp. 257–259; 268–302.

14. Prior to the opening of the Saint-Laurent fair, Bertrand and the widow Maurice formed an association and hired Charles Dolet, his wife, and Antoine de la Place, a painter's apprentice and the son of a lemonade salesman, who had joined the Italian players in Toulouse in 1701. Selle had the other principal show at Saint-Laurent that fall, bringing into his troupe a *sauteur* named Restier, who played Gille, and Lavigne, Restier's brother-in-law who walked the rope without balancing poles and played a violin between his legs. At Saint-Germain in 1707, Dolet and La Place teemed up and tried unsuccessfully to force the widow Maurice to retire. See Parfaict and Parfaict, *Mémoires,* vol. 1, pp. 49–57.

15. The tax on actors, known as the *droit des pauvres* (later the *quart des pauvres*), was first levied on the Confrères de la Passion to support the Hôpital Saint-Julien in 1407. In the seventeenth century, Molière's company, the Théâtre du Marais, and the players of the Hôtel de Bourgogne did not pay a regular, fixed tax; but they did make charitable contributions to several religious houses and hospitals. In 1689 the Comédie-Française voluntarily contributed a portion of its proceeds each month to some of the religious orders. They gave 18 sous for candles each Sunday to the Capuchins who served the city as firefighters. The Cordeliers and the Augustins received 3 livres a month. During the last couple of decades of Louis XIV's reign, the burdens of the Hôpital-Général rose substantially, and the king sought ways to relieve the burden of the poor by increasing and regularizing the contributions of the theaters. In Pontchartrain's correspondence with Président de Harlay, the chief administrator of the Hôpital, the minister reported that establishing a fixed sum to be collected by a *receveur* or *contrôleur* would be beneficial for everyone involved. Francine, then director of the Opéra, was invited to consider what would be a reasonable sum with Harlay. The result of these initiatives was a royal ordinance issued on 25 February 1699 ordering the Opéra and the Comédie to pay one sixth of their earnings to the Hôpital-Général. See BN ms fr 21625, fol. 264. The two theaters interpreted the order, however, to be one sixth of their profits, precipitating a new ordinance issued from Versailles on 30 August 1701 ordering that one half of the one sixth be calculated on the gross receipts of the theaters rather than on the profits alone. Each time a new director of the Opéra was appointed (in 1704 and again in 1713), the Crown issued *lettres patentes* reconfirming the formula of 1701, and in 1713 the fair theaters were included in the royal order. In 1716 the Council of Regency, noting the need for new beds and rooms at the Hôtel-Dieu and the increase in the number of poor and ill persons, ordered that an additional one ninth be taken from the *spectacles,* which, in turn, were permitted to increase their ticket prices. See AN ms 0¹ 618, doss. 5, pièce 118. It soon became standard practice for the theaters to surrender one quarter of their receipts annually to the hospitals for the care of the poor. In 1732 the lieutenant general of police was instructed to supervise the collection of this *quart des pauvres* from the cashiers of the Opéra. In 1733 the Hôtel-Dieu began sending its commissioner to every performance at the Opéra in order to witness the accounting and to verify that every seat had been counted. The commissioner and the directors of the Opéra then signed the receipt sheets, copies of which were sent every month to the general receiver. The same procedure was followed at the other theaters. The Hôtel-Dieu paid the commissioner 15 deniers for every livre collected for his service. Needless to say, these mandatory contributions imposed a heavy financial burden on the theaters—the burden of poor relief was literally born by the performing arts—and provoked angry disputes between them and the hospitals. In 1762 they agreed to abandon the practice of taking a percentage of the

receipts in favor of a fixed annual subscription. By this formula the Opéra was supposed to pay 70,000 livres; the Comédie-Française, 60,000; the Comédie-Italienne, 40,000. The smaller *spectacles* on the boulevards were assessed lesser sums. See Bonnassies, *Spectacles;* Pougin, *Dictionnaire,* pp. 313–315; Peytel, "Les Théâtres," in Lavignac, *Encyclopédie,* pp. 3770–3771.

16. Lough, *Paris,* pp. 173–174; 272–273. See also Lagrave, *Théâtre.*

17. Quoted in Lough, *Paris,* p. 176.

18. The perpetually changing administration of the Opéra and its financial problems in the eighteenth century are treated in Travenol and Durey de Noinville, *Histoire,* pp. 82–104; Pélissier, *Histoire,* pp. 36–98; Peytel, "Les Théâtres," in Lavignac, *Encyclopédie,* pp. 3765–3767; Heulhard, *Saint-Laurent,* pp. 231–235.

19. Bonnassies, *Spectacles,* pp. 35–40; Albert, *Théâtres,* pp. 37–48; Parfaict and Parfaict, *Mémoires,* vol. 1, p. 108; Font, *Favart,* p. 64; Cucuel, *Créatures,* pp. 13–56; Soubies and Malherbe, *Précis,* pp. 18–19; D'Auriac, *Théâtre,* pp. 73–75; Barberet, *Lesage,* pp. 42; 77–103; Barnes, "The 'Théâtre,'" p. 52. The first three volumes of Lesage and D'Orneval, *Théâtre,* are *pièces en écriteaux.* For Lesage's discussion of these pieces, see the preface to volume 1.

20. Mamczarz, *Intermèdes,* p. 248, believes the heterogenous and spectacular character of these works is explained by the *forains'* desire to copy court divertissements and ballets and by the strong influence of the commedia dell'arte tradition. No doubt these influences were present, but the extensive use of mime, vaudevilles, dancing, and so on, seems to stem less directly from stylistic and structural influences of other types of theater than from the limitations imposed on the *forains* by the privileged theaters and the courts and by their ingenuity in getting around these restrictions.

21. BN ms fr 25476, fols. 94–109.

22. Chateau, *Le Réel,* pp. 86–90.

23. BN ms fr 25476, fols. 58–71.

24. Quoted in Bonnassies, *Spectacles,* p. 39.

25. Unsure of Lesage's motives for leaving the prestigious Comédie-Française, Barberet, *Lesage,* pp. 31–39, speculates that he wanted to air his grievances against it and could do so in the freer atmosphere of the fairs, where criticism and satire of *les Romains* were greeted with gusto. Barberet credits him with raising the genre from *parade* to farce and finally to true lyric comedy. For accounts of the new proprietors at the fairs, see Genest, *L'Opéra-comique,* pp. 59–60; Wild, "Aspects," *Recherches,* pp. 133–134; Barnes, "The 'Théâtre,'" pp. 52–58.

26. Parfaict and Parfaict, *Mémoires,* vol. 1, pp. 117–158.

27. Ibid., p. 172.

28. For the financial records of the Opéra between 1713 and 1721, see AN ms AJ[13] doss. 3, fol. 1.

29. BN ms fr 21625, fol. 266; AN ms E 1982, fols. 400–401.

30. AN ms E 1986, fols. 571–580; E 1983, fols. 643–646; K 966.

31. Peytel, "Les Théâtres," in Lavignac, *Encyclopédie,* p. 3771.

32. AN ms E 1999, fols. 219–220.

33. Two of these pieces, *La Désolation des deux comédies* and *Procès des théâtres,* are described in Wild, "Aspects," *Recherches,* pp. 137–140.

34. Lesage, *Théâtre,* vol. 12, pp. 413–432.

35. Ibid., vol. 13, pp. 149–178. In the summer of 1978 the troupe of Patrick Schmitt presented a show called "comme à la Foire Saint-Germain" outdoors on the *tréteaux* in Paris on the plateau Beaubourg (afternoons) and in the Place Saint-Germain-des-Prés (evenings). Playing to packed, standing crowds who contributed a franc or two when the hat was passed, the troupe performed fragments from eighteenth-century fair pieces, including *La Querelle.* Having thoroughly researched the fair theater, the Schmitt troupe used *écriteaux,* getting the crowd to shout the lines, and other *forain* techniques so skillfully that the nightly productions must have been very close to the originals. My understanding of the *opéras-comiques,* especially the visual buffoonery and body language, has been enhanced appreciably by the Schmitt troupe's performances.

36. *Almanach forain* (1778), pp. 44–46; *L'Année littéraire, ou suite des lettres sur quelques écrits de ce temps* 3 (1776): 327–328.

37. Campardon, *Spectacles,* vol. 2, pp. 195–196; vol. 1, pp. 9–12; BN ms fr 25471, fols. 95–112.

38. Cucuel, "Sources," *Année,* p. 254.

39. This is Barnes's explanation in "The 'Théâtre,'" pp. 67–68. For a discussion of the relations between the Italian players and the *forains,* see Emile Campardon, *Les Comédiens du roi et la troupe italienne pendant les deux derniers siècles,* 2 vols. (Paris, 1880), vol. 1, pp. xxiv–xxxvi; Albert, *Théâtres,* pp. 82–117; Bernardin, *Comédie,* pp. 180–206; Heulhard, *Saint-Laurent,* pp. 236–241.

40. Parfaict and Parfaict, *Mémoires,* vol. 1, p. 235.

41. Lesage, *Théâtre,* vol. 13, pp. 179–215.

42. Quoted in *Almanach des spectacles* (1755), p. 108.

43. For a discussion of the career of Piron, see Rigoley de Juvigny, "Vie de Piron," in Piron, *Oeuvres,* vol. 1, pp. 3–158. See also Font, *Favart,* pp. 93–105; *L'Année littéraire* 1 (1776): 203–256.

44. *Le Mariage de Momus, ou la gigantomachie,* in Piron, *Oeuvres,* vol. 5, pp. 3–62.

45. BV ms 614, pp. 132, 139.

46. René-Louis de Voyer d'Argenson, *Mémoires pour servir à l'histoire des spectacles de la foire,* 2 vols. (Paris, 1743), vol. 1, p. 13.

47. These figures are cited in a *mémoire* by Fuzelier entitled *Eclaircissement au sujet de la régie de l'Opéra-comique pour le compte de l'Académie Royale de Musique,* (n.d.), published in Cucuel, "Sources," *Année,* pp. 251–252.

48. BV ms 619, pp. 5, 7.

49. Jean Monnet, *Supplément au Roman comique, ou mémoires pour servir à la vie de Jean Monnet, ci-devant directeur de l'Opéra-Comique à Paris, de l'Opéra de Lyon, et d'une Comédie Françoise à Londres. Ecrits par lui-même.* 2 vols. (London, 1772), vol. 1, pp. 44–55. Bonnassies, *Spectacles,* questions their authenticity, but Arthur Heulhard, *Jean Monnet, vie et aventures d'un entrepreneur de spectacles au XVIIIe siècle, avec un appendice sur l'Opéra-comique de 1752 à 1758* (Paris, 1884), p. 76, refutes him.

50. Arthur Pougin, *Madame Favart: étude théâtrale, 1727–1772* (Paris, 1912), p. 7.

51. Favart, *Mémoires,* vol. 1, p. xvii.

52. These figures, which do not include the *quart des pauvres* and the Opéra's fee, come from Favart's records cited in Cucuel, "Sources," *Année,* p. 258.

53. Campardon, *Spectacles,* vol. 2, pp. 139–142.

54. *Lettre à Messieurs les comédiens françois par un de leurs zélés partisans, au sujet de l'opéra-comique* (The Hague, 1745), pp. 3–5.

Chapter 5. Time of Triumph, Time of Loss

1. Lagrave, *Théâtre,* pp. 7–11, makes a good case for viewing the period from 1715 to 1750 as a distinctive epoch in the history of the theater, especially in terms of the sweeping changes that occurred after mid-century. It is undeniable that such events as the debuts of Sedaine and Goldoni, the vogue of Italian music, and the transformation it stimulated in the Opéra-Comique, the fusion of the latter with the Comédie-Italienne, and the birth of dramatic criticism mark the period after 1750 as an innovative era, quite different from the period with which Lagrave is concerned. And he supplies the telling evidence that of 32 authors who began their careers after 1715, only 3 or 4 were still writing after 1750. The only problem is that one of these was Charles Favart, who prior to 1750 had already made significant changes in the Comique genre that looked toward the future. It seems plausible at least to consider the theatrical history of the eighteenth century in a chronology of thirds, (early opéra-comique, the 1700–1730s; the transformation period, Favart to Philidor, 1740–1760s; boulevard theater and the Revolution, 1760s–1790s) rather than demarcating it at the death of Louis XIV and in the arbitrary year of 1750.

2. *Almanach historique* (1954), pp. 1–9. See also A. Turner, *Les Transformations de l'opéra-comique* (Paris, 1865), p. 13.

3. For a list of Opéra directors, see Charles Malherbe, "Archives et Bibliothèque de l'Opéra," *La Revue musicale* 3 (15 June 1903): 277.

4. Pélissier, *Histoire,* pp. 61–62; Peytel, "Les Théâtres," in Lavignac, *Encyclopédie,* pp. 3766–3767. Despite numerous attempts at reform by the city and the directors to whom it sold the privilege, the plight of the Opéra continued to worsen. In October 1754, D'Argenson recorded that the Opéra's debts had risen to 1,400,000 livres increasing by 200,000 in the previous six months. D'Argenson blamed its difficulties in part on the fact that the directors, the Hôtel de Ville, and the secretary for Paris bowed to the demands of high-ranking persons of court that their mistresses' (female performers) salaries be increased. He believed that without the recent productions of Italian opera buffa, the Opéra would have closed its doors. See the entries for 15 November 1753 and 6 October 1754 in D'Argenson, *Journal,* vol. 8, pp. 161–162, 352. Comparative expenditures for singers and other performers show that in 1713 the Opéra paid 217,050 to its musicians. Pélissier, *Théâtre,* p. 71.

5. Monnet, *Supplément,* vol. 2, pp. 55–57; AN ms K 966, doss. 13, pièces 3 and 4.

6. *Le Retour favorable* in *Nouveau théâtre de la foire, ou recueil de pièces et opéra-comiques,* new ed., 5 vols. (Paris, 1763), vol. 1, pp. 4–14.

7. Monnet's theater was praised by everyone. The *Almanach historique* (1756), quoted in Heulhard, *Monnet,* p. 54, called it "the most beautiful hall of *spectacle* in Paris."

8. The plan of this theater can be found in the collection of the architect Dumont, *Parallèle des plans des plus belles salles de spectacle d'Italie et de France* (Paris, 1766), Plate VII. See also Heulhard, "Jean Monnet," *La Chronique* 8 (June 1875): 218. The theater survived until 1911 though not in the same location. When the Opéra-Comique merged with the Comédie-Italienne in 1762, Louis XV purchased it and incorporated it into the Hôtel des Menus Plaisirs located on the rue Bergère, where the theater was moved. It became the Conservatoire Nationale de Musique during the Revolution. See Monnet, *Supplément,* vol. 3; J. -G. Prud'homme and E. de Crauzat, *Les Menus plaisirs du roi, l'Ecole Royale et le Conservatoire de Musique* (Paris, 1929), pp. 42–49.

9. *Almanach historique* (1756), p. 100.

10. Favart turned down a lucrative offer of 1,000 livres a year plus author's fees to do two works annually exclusively for the Comédie-Italienne. See the letter from Papillon de La Ferté, intendant of the king's menus plaisirs, 27 December 1767, Favart, *Mémoires,* vol. 3, p. 62. Monnet paid him handsomely, however: 3,000 livres for each new opéra-comique and a salary of 2,000 livres for looking out for the welfare of the whole enterprise.

11. Quoted in Heulhard, "Jean Monnet," *La Chronique* pp. 222–223.

12. Monnet, *Supplément,* vol. 2, p. 62.

13. Quoted in Heulhard, *Monnet,* p. 54.

14. Cited in ibid., p. 54.

15. Monnet turned to other projects, most notably a waux-hall planned as a rustic ball for the people to be located in the Bois de Boulogne. See Monnet, *Supplément,* vol. 2, pp. 84–85. Although he was unsuccessful, his plans anticipated the rage for such entertainments in the two decades before the Revolution. His theatrical days were over, but he remained something of a legendary figure for some years. On 4 Thermidor of the year VII, a vaudeville comedy was performed in Paris called *Monnet, directeur de l'Opéra-Comique.*

16. *Almanach historique* (1761), p. 89.

17. François-Antoine Chevrier, *Observations sur le théâtre dans lesquelles on examine avec impartialité l'état actuel des théâtres de Paris* (Paris, 1755), pp. 80, 82–83.

18. For Favart's life, see Font, *Favart.* See also Cooper, *Opéra comique,* pp. 21–25; Julien Tiersot, *Lettres de musiciens du XV au XX siècle,* 2 vols. (Turin, 1924), vol. 1, p. 76.

19. Favart, *Mémoires,* vol. 1, pp. ii–iii.

20. Cited in Font, *Favart,* p. 235. See also Barberet, *Lesage,* pp. 94–95.

21. From *L'Art du dix-huitième siècle,* quoted in Cooper, *Opéra comique,* p. 24.

22. Joseph de La Porte and Jean-Marie-Bernard Clément, *Anecdotes dramatiques,* 3 vols.

(Paris, 1775), vol. 1, pp. 4–5. See also Barnes, "The 'Théâtre,'" pp. 87–88. It was customary for the price of seats to be increased substantially for final performances.

23. Favart, *Mémoires*, vol. 1, p. x.

24. Quoted in Font, *Favart*, p. 244.

25. Cooper, *Opéra comique*, p. 22.

26. Charles-Simon Favart, *Théâtre de M. Favart, ou recueil des comédies, parodies et opéras-comiques donnés jusqu'à ce jour, avec les airs, rondes et vaudevilles notés dans chaque pièce*, 8 vols. (Paris, 1763), vol. 6. Each work is paginated separately in this collection.

27. Letter to Comte de Durazzo, 14 January 1760, in Favart, *Mémoires*, vol. 1, pp. 7–8.

28. The 12 Italian works performed at the Opéra between 1 August 1752 and 12 February 1754 are listed with composers and dates in Travenol and Durey de Noinville, *Histoire*, p. 273.

29. Donald J. Grout, *A Short History of Opera*, 2d ed. (New York, 1965), p. 249.

30. Anthony, *French Baroque*, pp. 116–142, calls our attention to three operatic developments: (1) changes in the post-Lully *tragédie-lyrique* wherein the impact of the Italian concerto, cantata, and operatic style can be seen in such things as the use of obligato passages, solo instruments, more frequent changes of tempo, a wider melodic range, chromaticism, frequent modulations, and embroidered melodies; (2) the introduction of *opéra-ballet*, a new genre that tended to blur the difference between opera and *opéra-comique* because, unlike the unity of *tragédie-lyrique*, it was comprised of several self-contained acts with much emphasis on *divertissement*, comedy, satire, and a parody of serious opera; (3) the creation of ballet-héroïque, where dance and *spectacle* reigned and which used Italian concerto rhythms and ariettes. See also James R. Anthony, "The French Opera-Ballet in the Early Eighteenth Century: Problems of Definition and Classification," *Journal of the American Musicological Society*, XVII (1965): 197–206. Moreover, Irene Mamczarz, *Intermèdes*, emphasizes the fact that the Italian intermezzo and the opéra-comique developed along analogous lines in the first half of the eighteenth century. She adds (p. 279): The Italian pieces "fit quite easily into the French tradition of the divertissement."

31. Quoted in La Porte and Clément, *Anecdotes*, in Arthur Pougin, *Monsigny et son temps: L'opéra-comique et la comédie italienne, les auteurs, les compositeurs, les chanteurs* (Paris, 1908), p. 19. See also Henri de Curzon, "La 'Serva Padrona' à Paris," in *Histoire du théâtre lyrique depuis les origines jusqu'à nos jours* (Paris, n.d.), p. 154. In André Guillaume Contant d'Orville, *Histoire de l'opéra bouffon contenant les jugemens de toutes les pièces qui ont paru depuis sa naissance jusqu'à ce jour*, 2 vols. (Paris, 1768), vol. 1, p. 39, the author noted that *La Servante* had an unparalleled success: "The amateurs of music, who out of bad temper or bias had not heard the music of *La Serva Padrona* at the Opéra, thronged to admire Pergolesi at the Comédie-Italienne." He held that the piece deserved to be called a *comédie-opéra* and that it changed the whole course of musical theater in France.

32. The literature on the Querelle des Bouffons and on opera bouffe is too extensive to cite here. The best account of the controversy is still probably Louisette Eugénie Reichenburg, *Contribution à l'histoire de la "querelle des Bouffons"* (Paris, 1937). See also Alfred Richard Oliver, *The Encyclopedists as Critics of Music* (New York, 1947); Edward Lowinsky, "Taste, Style and Ideology in Eighteenth-Century Music," in *Aspects of the Eighteenth Century*, ed. Earl R. Wasserman (Baltimore, 1965), pp. 164–205; Cucuel, *Créateurs*, pp. 57–89; La Laurencie, "L'Opéra-comique," in Lavignac, *Encyclopédie*, vol. 3, pp. 1474–1477. It is worth noting that one of the pamphlets was entitled *Les Prophéties du grand prophète Monnet*.

33. Lowinsky, "Taste," *Aspects*, p. 169.

34. Rousseau contradicted his own contention somewhat with his opera *Le Devin du village*, performed first for the court at Fontainebleau in October 1752, then at the Opéra in March 1753. Although not an opera bouffe, *Le Devin* incorporated some characteristics of the Italian intermezzi. Its form was Italian in the use of continuous music, but its simple style had more the character of French vaudevilles. See Grout, *Short*, p. 256.

35. Genest, *L'Opéra-comique*, pp. 11–102. In the summer of 1978, *Les Troqueurs* was revived

for a splendid production in connection with the thirteenth annual Festival Estival in the Cour du Commerce Saint-André in Paris.

36. Monnet, *Supplément*, vol. 2, pp. 69–71.

37. With special attention to the works of Jean-Louis Laruette, the period of transition at the Opéra-Comique is clearly delineated in Paulette Letailleur, "Jean-Louis Laruette, chanteur et compositeur," *Recherches sur la musique française classique* 10 (1970): 57–86. The many adaptations and parodies of Italian intermezzi by Favart and others are discussed in detail in Mamczarz, *Intermèdes*, pp. 250–280. See also Barnes, "The 'Théâtre,'" pp. 107–114; Julien, *Histoire*, vol. 2, pp. 71–132.

38. *Almanach des muses* (Paris, 1769), p. 201. I once heard Paul Henry Lang express the view, probably not original with him, that the history of opera alternates between periods when the text dominates and periods when music is supreme.

39. Collé, *Journal*, vol. 2, p. 337.

40. Monnet, *Supplément*, p. 81. Julien, *Histoire*, vol. 2, p. 83, held the same view. Anseaume's first piece of any consequence for the Comique was a reworking of Lesage's *Le Monde renversée* in 1753. In 1754 his *Le Chinois poli en France*, a one-act parody of *Le Chinois de retour*, an Italian intermezzo, was given at the Comique. In this piece Anseaume worked with ariettes, of course, but he still used more vaudevilles than Italian music. Dealing in part with the travels of a Chinease man, Nouraddin, in France, the work appears to revert to the exoticism of the Lesage-D'Orneval period. In fact, however, it was responding to the vogue of chinoiserie. Moreover, the piece was realy a traditional love triangle, and it had no marvels, transformations, or genies. See Louis Anseaume, *Théâtre de M. Anseaume, ou recueil des comédies, parodies, opéras-comiques*, 3 vols. (Paris, 1766), vol. 1. Each piece is paginated separately.

41. Anseaume, *Théâtre*, 1.

42. Quoted in Curzon, "La 'Serva,'" *Histoire*, p. 159.

43. On Philidor see George-Edgar Bonnet, *Philidor et l'évolution de la musique francaise au XVIIIe siècle* (Paris, 1921).

44. Tiersot, *Lettres*, vol. 1, p. 84. Philidor never abandoned chess. He continued to spend about four months of every year in London demonstrating his championship skills.

45. See Louise Parkinson Arnoldson, *Sedaine et les musiciens de son temps* (Paris, 1934) for the career of Sedaine.

46. *L'Obervateur littéraire*, 18 vols. (Amsterdam, 1758–1761), vol. 2, p. 285.

47. Although *Blaise* and others of the new *opéras-comiques* were more demanding musically, the *forains* apparently continued performing the roles. The *Almanach historique* (1772), pp. 19–21, in its obituary of Trial, the Comique's conductor during these years who later became codirector of the Opéra, noted that because the actors were not musicians and had sung only vaudevilles, Trial had to exercise considerable patience in preparing works such as *Blaise*.

48. Michel-Jean Sedaine and Pierre-Alexandre Monsigny, *On ne s'avise jamais de tout, opéra-comique*, 2d ed., enl. (Paris, 1761), p. 45.

49. Quoted in Arnoldson, *Sedaine*, p. 125.

50. This is Arnoldson's opinion (in *Sedaine*), pp. 129–132.

51. Bachaumont, *Mémoires*, vol. 4, p. 235.

52. The most notable later work was *Richard Coeur de Lion* (1784) by Grétry and Sedaine. For a discussion, see Arnoldson, *Sedaine*, pp. 172–194. Reaching back into the Middle Ages for a historical work, which they bathed in pathos and melodrama, the authors filled the stage with soldiers, knights, and peasants, thus greatly increasing the importance of choruses, staging, and crowd scenes. Grétry's greatest innovation was the construction of an entire act around a medieval air sung by a servant disguised as a troubador in order to reveal his identity to the imprisoned Richard. The song was then used as a leitmotiv throughout the rest of the piece. The work earned Sedaine election to the Académie Française.

53. See, for example, Leland Fox, "Opéra-comique, a Vehicle of Classic Style," *Recherches sur la musique française classique* 4 (1964): 135, who writes: "It was not so much the comic

element in *opéra-comique* that made it so popular but rather the liberty to endorse openly the spirit of opposition. With the flood of opinion in favor of *opéra-comique*, and with the denouement of French grand opera by the Encyclopedists, *opéra-seria* failed to recognize the direction of the social evolution that was sweeping the old order out of existence."

54. Grout, *Short*, p. 258.

55. See Julien Lemer's Introduction in Jean-Joseph Vadé, *Oeuvres*, ed. Julien Lemer (Paris, 1875), pp. 1–12.

56. Quoted in Vadé, *Oeuvres*, p. 8.

57. A. P. Moore, *The Genre Poissard and the French Stage of the Eighteenth Century* (New York, 1935), pp. 3–14. This is the best study of the theatrical use of the *poissarde* and of Vadé's important role in advancing it.

58. Quoted from Charles Collé's *Manière de discours approfondi superficiellement sur l'origine inédite* in Moore, *Genre*, p. 81. For a discussion of *parades*, see ibid., pp. 78–175.

59. Moore, *Genre*, p. 178.

60. Ibid., pp. 140–141. It is important to understand that there was no fixed way of rendering the *poissard;* it varied from writer to writer. Most did not try to achieve an exact phonetic transcription of market speech, but rather mixed *poissarderie* with literary French.

61. Arnoldson, *Sedaine*, p. 69.

62. Monnet, *Supplément*, p. 78.

63. From D'Alembert, *Eloge de la chaussée*, quoted in Moore, *Genre*, p. 142.

64. From the *Mercure de France*, quoted in ibid,, p. 194.

65. Arnoldson, *Sedaine*, p. 132, remarks that the philosophes' influence on Sedaine is "too obvious to dwell on."

66. Grimm, *Correspondance*, vol. 4, p. 502.

67. Ibid., vol. 6, p. 71, quoted in Cucuel, *Créateurs*, pp. 81–82.

68. Grimm, *Correspondance*, vol. 4, p. 502, quoted in Arnoldson, *Sedaine*, pp. 101–102.

69. Ibid., vol. 5, pp. 191–192, quoted in ibid., p. 117.

70. Grimm was furious that "the public paid tribute to them by putting their opera in the ranks of these insipid and barbarous works that will be interred in the ruins of this ancient hovel the day the French come to understand what a *spectacle* in music is" (Grimm, *Correspondance*, vol. 7, pp. 31–32, 44). For more criticism, see *Almanach des muses* (1767), p. 164.

71. *L'Observateur*, vol. 1, p. 275.

72. *Almanach historique* (1762), p. 97.

73. *Almanach des muses* (1765), p. 162. See later issues for reviews of subsequent works.

74. *L'Avant-coureur* (9 February 1761): 91–92.

75. *L'Observateur*, vol. 3, pp. 316–317.

76. *L'Année* 6 (1776): 104–133. For subsequent critical reviews in *L'Année*, see issue 7 (1779): 338–356, in which Elie Catherine Fréron called Grétry's profusion of ensembles a "musical din." In issue 6 (1780): 319–336, he referred to the "moral pedantry" of the "bastard genre" at the Comédie. Jean-François Marmontel, *L'Année* declared, who "possessed a mania to indoctrinate the whole world, imagined that an *opéra-comique* could become in his hands a handsome philosophical sermon." *L'Année* proclaimed that the audience, missing the gaiety of natural airs, bored and fed up, was beginning "to desert their hall in order to rush to the boulevard *spectacles* where at least they would be sure of laughing in spite of the absurdity of the pieces played there." Still, Fréron hailed the return of Auguste de Piis, whose parodies *La Bonne femme* (parody of *Alceste*) and *L'Opéra de province* (parody of *Armide*) recalled the days of Piron, Lesage, and D'Orneval and served as an antidote to *la Dramomanie*. He greeted enthusiastically the return of vaudevilles to the Comédie: "this genre of *spectacle*, for a long time so dear to the French, the boldness and satirical strokes of the old Italian theater, emancipated from austere rules . . . the happy caprices of a lively and playful imagination. . . ." See issue 7 (1781): 146.

77. Claude-Joseph Dorat, *La Déclamation théâtrale, poème didactique en quatre chants*, 4th ed. (Paris, 1771), p. 222.

78. *Annales politiques, civiles et littéraires du dix-huitième siècle* (1777): 425. Linguet's *Annales* were a continuation of the *Journal de politique et de littérature de Bruxelles.*
79. *Le Redoteur,* 2 vols. (Amsterdam, 1775), vol. 1, p. 32. The Rondel catalog at the BA attributes this work to Nougaret, Cerfuol, and Marchand.
80. Alexandre-Jacques Du Coudray, *Lettre à Madame* (Paris, 1775), p. 13.
81. Alexandre-Jacques Du Coudray, *Il est temps de parler et il est temps de se taire* (Paris, 1779), p. 11.
82. Quoted in Pougin, *Monsigny,* p. 57.
83. Barbier, *Chronique,* vol. 8, p. 23. See also *Etat actuel de la musique,* 19 vols. (Paris, 1759–1777), vol. 1, pp. 115–122.
84. AN ms 0^1 849, fol. 48. See also Campardon, *Comédiens,* vol. 2, p. xxxviii. The intendant of the menus plaisirs fixed the figure at more than 700,000. See AN ms 0^1 849, fol. 21. A breakdown of the expenditures for the 1761–1962 season, the last before the merger and one of its better years financially, indicates the kinds of annual costs incurred by the Comédie-Italienne:

actors and actresses (26)	10,600	livres
ballet (20)	12,250	livres
orchestra (22)	13,800	livres
machinists and workers	4,962	livres
receivers and ushers	3,850	livres
supernumeraries	9,800	livres
retired actors	8,750	livres
rent of the hôtel	6,744	livres
military guard	10,000	livres
masses	560	livres
Corpus Christi	147	livres
gifts	500	livres
lights	12,000	livres
posters	2,949.15	livres
wood	2,000	livres
wine	800	livres
interest on the capital at 10%	30,000	livres
interest on money owed	4,000	livres
annuity to S. Corby	8,000	livres
annuity to M. Monet	2,000	livres
Opéra	20,000	livres
rent of the Fair Saint-Germain	2,000	livres
Total	165,712.15	livres

See AN ms 0^1 850, doss. 1, fol. 1. In addition, the Comédie, according to the records of the First Gentlemen of the Chamber, was in debt to merchants and tradesmen and in arrears in their support of the poor in the amount of 299,700.16.4 See AN ms 0^1 851, Register, pp. 11–12.

85. AN ms 0^1 851, fols. 51–52. See also Capardon, *Spectacles,* vol. 2, pp. 197–202; Pougin, *Monsigny,* pp. 58–59; Cucuel, "Sources," *Année,* pp. 261–262.
86. AN ms 0^1 851, fols. 57–58. The first gentlemen, each of whom served a quarter of the year, supervised the affairs of the Comédie-Française and the Comédie-Italienne. Some of the most eminent nobles of the realm held these positions, including the ducs d'Aumont, de Fleury, de Fronsac, de Duras, de Villequier, and the Maréchal de Richelieu. Their duties were not defined precisely, but they were responsible for inspecting the accounts of the theaters, and they had to approve all regulations and arbitrate all controversies among the actors. They frequently imposed fines and jail sentences on the personnel of the theater for indecent behavior and violation of theater rules. Their authority was final and absolute.
87. AN ms 0^1 851, fol. 48.

88. Letters to Count Durazzo dated 20 June 1761 and 8 November 1761 in Favart, *Mémoires,* vol. 1, pp. 155, 200. Giacomo Durazzo directed the Hoftheater in Vienna, where many *opéras-comiques* were performed, including several by Favart that Gluck arranged for Viennese audiences. Additional evidence that the issue of a merger was being given serious thought by many can be found in Augustin-Théodore-Vincent Le Beau de Schosne, *Lettre sur les spectacles de Paris* (Paris, 1761), pp. 2–29.

89. Favart, *Mémoires,* vol. 1, p. 203.

90. Ibid., p. 184.

91. Cucuel, "Sources," *Année,* p. 262.

92. Favart, *Mémoires,* vol. 1, p. 214.

93. Ibid., p. 220.

94. AN ms 0^1 849, fol. 30.

95. The Opéra was supervised on behalf of the king by the intendant of the menus plaisirs, who reported to the minister of the king's household. The menus plaisirs dealt with all types of royal pageantry and entertainment, hence its involvement with the Opéra, which gave frequent performances for the court at Fontainebleau. The Opéra, which was financially managed by the Bureau de Ville, had its own directors, but they reported to the intendant and negotiated regularly with him regarding personnel and decorations for balls, masquerades, ballets, and other *spectacles.* The offices and storerooms of the menus plaisirs were located after May 1763 in a large hôtel on the rue Bergère in the Faubourg Poissonnière between what is now the rue Montmartre and the rue Richer. In addition to the 0^1 series at the AN, see Denis-Pierre-Jean Papillon de La Ferté, *L'Administration des menus, journal,* ed. Ernest Boysse (Paris, 1887), pp. 2–53; Prod'homme and Crauzat, *Les Menus;* Pougin, *Dictionnaire,* pp. 401, 517–518; Barbier, *Chronique,* vol. 8, p. 23.

96. Papillon de La Ferté, *L'Administration,* p. 33.

97. AN ms 0^1 849, fol. 2.

98. Ibid., fol. 21.

99. AN ms 0^1 851, Register, pp. 32–33; Campardon, *Comédiens,* vol. 2, pp. 201–202; Cucuel, "Sources," *Année,* p. 263.

100. *Almanach historique* (1763), p. 86. For a breakdown of sums paid to different personnel, see 0^1 852, fols. 3–15.

101. Despite the fact that the Opéra kept its privileged status and the tribute that that entailed, the directors were not pleased with the settlement. By 1765, Rebel and Francoeur were demanding 45,000 livres annually in return for renewing the Comédie's lease to perform *opéras-comiques.* It required the intervention of the comte de Saint-Florentin, minister of the king's household, who worked closely with the intendant, to hold the sum to the lower figure. See Papillon de La Ferté, *L'Administration,* pp. 155–156. The new contract signed in 1766 authorized the Comédie to perform *opéras-comiques* for 18 years, beginning January 1767, but it also attempted to codify and regulate the increasingly negligible differences between the genres of the two lyric theaters. See AN ms 0^1 849, fols. 3–15. "*Spectacles* of the opéra-comique," the contract declared, consisted of "vaudevilles, dances, machines, decorations, symphonies, and pieces of song." French and Italian choruses were prohibited so that the Comédie "could not have in any way whatsoever the form of opera whether French or Italian." Borrowing pieces from the Opéra's repertoire was also prohibited. The Comédie was forbidden from importing *bouffons* from Italy and from performing intermezzi, Italian operas, or pieces constituting "continuous works of music such as *Les Troqueurs* and others of similar nature." In effect, the Opéra confined the Comédie in its lyric pieces to prose dialogue in alteration with ariettes. One clause evoked strong protest: the prohibition against adapting French words to Italian music. Insisting they had enjoyed this right since the production of *La Servante maîtresse* in 1754, the Italian players maintained that the public should not be deprived of Italian music. At issue here was the definition of parody: was it still to be broadly defined as comprising both caricature and adaptation? The matter was not resolved until 1779, when the Comédie's lease was again renegotiated. Parodies were to be confined to French operas, not French translations and

the original Italian score. The Comédie-Italienne promised not to use Italian music except for pieces such as *La Servante* and *La Colonie*, which were already in their repertoire.

Definitions and restrictions notwithstanding, the Opéra could not corral the Comédie sufficiently to win back the audiences that the Comédie had stolen away. In his *Réflexions sur la décadence de l'Opéra* (undated), Papillon de La Ferté lamented that the *pièces à ariettes* were responsible for changing taste and for the declining interest in opera. "Poets, musicians, and actors have thrown themselves onto the *tréteaux*, where people squander a fortune. . . . *Castor et Pollux* has not returned to its authors a quarter of what *Le Roy et le fermier* has produced" (quoted in Arnoldson, *Sedaine*, p. 165). The original document is in AN ms 0^1 616, fol. 86. Confronted by a mounting deficit and a stale repertoire at the Opéra, Papillon in desperation accepted two works in 1782 from Sedaine and Monsigny, *Philémon* and *Pagamin de Monèque*, the latter an *opéra-comique*. They were rehearsed, but in July 1785 the Comité of the Opéra rejected them, and they were never performed. Favart's *La Chercheuse d'esprit* and Grétry's *Colinette à la cour*, however, were successfully staged at the Opéra during the 1780s.

102. *Le Nouveau spectateur* (*Journal des théâtres*) (15 May 1776): 203.
103. *Almanach historique* (1780), p. 56.
104. In 1761, Papillon wrote that the duc de Richelieu "was very seriously occupied with joining it [the Opéra-Comique] to the Comédie-Italienne. He even had performed at court certain of the most fashionable *opéras-comiques* by the subjects of the Opéra. This genre appeared to please the royal family" (Papillon de La Ferté, *L'Administration*, p. 67). From Favart we know that performances of *Les Troqueurs* and *On ne s'avise jamais* were arranged at Versailles in 1761 by the first gentlemen. See Favart, *Mémoires*, vol. 1, pp. 184–185. The pieces were performed by personnel from the Opéra and the Comédie-Italienne.
105. There are numerous accounts in the *Journal de Paris* of the queen's attendance at the Comédie-Italienne. See, for example, 20 February 1777, p. 2.
106. Pierre-Thomas-Nicolas Hurtaut and Magny, *Le Dictionnaire historique de la ville de Paris et de ses envirous*, vol. 4, p. 670; Métra, *Correspondance*, vol. 10, p. 124.
107. Papillon de La Ferté, *L'Administration*, p. 67.
108. Quoted in Letailleur, "Laruette," *Recherches*, 10 (1970): 169. The *paradis* was the least expensive section located at the top rear of the theater.
109. Contant d'Orville, *Histoire*, vol. 1, p. 210.
110. Cited in Charles Malherbe, "Commentaire bibliographique," in Jean-Philippe Rameau, *Oeuvres complètes*, ed. C. Saint-Saëns (Paris, 1911), vol. 16, p. xliv.
111. Contant d'Orville, *Histoire*, vol. 1, p. 211,
112. Campardon, *Comédiens*, vol. 1, p. xl. The ledgers of the Comédie for May 1764 reveal that the most heavily attended productions were *opéras-comiques* such as *Le Roi et le fermier* (it earned 2,731 livres in May), *Rose et Colas*, and *Le Maréchal* whereas Italian plays, including those by Goldoni, who was brought in in 1761, did poorly. See AN ms 0^1 850, doss. 3, fol. 91. In contrast to the 1750s and early 1760s, when receipts were always lower than expenditures, the postmerger record is one of fairly steady profit. The record for the 1763–1764 season was as follows:

April, 20 performances	receipt	31,963.10
	expenses	36,729. 8. 9
	deficit	4,765.18. 9
May, 29 performances	receipt	44,099.10
	expenses	47,659.12.11
	deficit	3,560. 2.11
June, 26 performances	receipt	31,562.
	expenses	32,953.12. 5
	deficit	1,391.12. 5

July, 30 performances	receipt	35,870.
	expenses	35,113. 0. 8
	surplus	756.19. 4
August, 30 performances	receipt	33,054. 9. 4
	expenses	29,203. 1. 1
	surplus	3,851. 8. 3
September, 29 performances	receipt	50,250.18. 3
	expenses	49,957.13. 8
	surplus	293. 4. 7
October, 31 performances	receipt	55,147. 4. 7
	expenses	60,603.16. 8
	deficit	5,456.12. 1
November, 30 performances	receipt	51,680.10.
	expenses	49,528. 2. 6
	surplus	2,152. 7. 6
December, 31 performances	receipt	56,257. 7. 6
	expenses	42,909. 5.10
	surplus	13,348. 1. 8
January, 31 performances	receipt	87,906.
	expenses	73,443.11
	surplus	14,462. 9
February, 27 performances	receipt	59,702.19.
	expenses	54,550.18. 1
	surplus	5,152. 0.11
March, 30 performances	receipt	51,788. 0.11
	expenses	34,898. 8. 8
	surplus	16,889.12. 3
April 1–14, 14 performances	receipt	74,042. 6.
	expenses	75,911.17.
	deficit	1,869.10. 7

See AN 0^1 853, fols. 28–51. A breakdown for the 1764 (April 30)–1765 (March 23) season shows the following:

Expenditures

Total annual expenses for actors, orchestra, workers		248,838.14. 7
Total annual commissions and memoirs		57,109.17.11
Total annual current costs		52,541.11. 3
Total annual sum paid to tradesmen		11,636. 2. 3
Passes issued to pensioners		4,620.
	Total	374,746. 6.

Receipts

April and May	32,144.10.
June	24,274.10.
July	32,139.
August	38,417.
September	39,247.
October	47,482.
November	51,045.

December		50,253.10.
January		55,168.
February		45,433.10.
March		32,631.
	Total	448,235.
	Season Tickets	65,926.
	Total	514,161.

The profit for the year, therefore was 139,414.14 livres. See AN ms 0^1 850, doss. 3, fol. 115. For comparative figures on different pieces, see AN ms 0^1 852, the last several folios in the carton. A change occurred in the good fortune of the Comédie-Italienne in the late 1770s caused by declining performance standards, internal dissension, and the competition of the boulevard theaters (see Chapter 7). The annual receipt remained good through the 1770s, ranging from a low of 495,238 livres in 1771–1772 to a high of 709,079 in 1777–1778; but the expenditures climbed even more rapidly during the same period, amounting to 565,000 by 1780. See AN ms 0^1 850, doss. 6, fols. 230 and 234. Economies were proposed in the ballet corps and in sums spent for tradesmen. The Comédie had already begun to complain that the source of their difficulties was, of all things, the merger because it forced them to pay tribute to the Opéra and it cost them, they maintained, an extra 15,000 a month to mount *opéras-comiques*. See AN ms 0^1 849, fol. 48. The actors insisted they had gained only 5 or 6 pieces from the Comique in 1762, not counting vaudeville works, and they already had 25 lyric pieces in their repertoire prior to the merger, which they could have continued to perform without the merger. They reasoned that their success in the 1760s would have been achieved had there been no change. The actors also blamed their troubles on the declining taste for lyric theater, the suppression of French plays in 1769, the neglect of Italian pieces, and the Crown's overriding concern for *opéras-comiques* at the expense of other parts of the *spectacle*.

The intendant and the first gentlemen, however, took a very different view of the cause of the Comédie's difficulties. The intendant complained that the troupe ignored the regulations issued by the first gentlemen pertaining to administration, assemblies, debuts, new pieces, the rights of authors, and police (AN ms 0^1 849, fols. 21 and 32). See also *Almanach historique* (31 March 1781), pp. 99–100; (1783), pp. 110–113. The actors performed only when it pleased them, Papillon wrote in 1779, and the doubles insist on having their own doubles. The actors do nothing to satisfy the public, he asserted, yet they complain of rising debts. "Finally, one can say that the absence of subordination, the self-interest, the lack of zeal, the misplaced pretensions, and the indecency that actually reigns in the assemblies have changed totally the regime of this *spectacle* in comparing its present position to that of the years when all the actors took pride in uniting for the general welfare." Papillon's perception that strife was rampant at the Comédie was accurate. The lyric players and the French actors were jealous of each other and battled for supremacy (AN ms 0^1 849, fols. 22–23). The maréchal de Richelieu shared the intendant's aggravation about this discord. He reminded the players that their *spectacle* was based on variety and responded to changing taste (ibid., fol. 39). Richelieu rebuked the lyric performers for refusing to act in French plays and suggested that they might be replaced by more cooperative and talented subjects. He also expressed disgust at the lyric players' scorn for the revival of vaudevilles. "It is the case that blind prejudice against a national genre can only deliver a mortal blow to a theater whose smart politics are to multiply its resources, resources as serious, as durable as the national comedy and the national vaudeville."

113. *Journal de Paris,* 29 April 1783, pp. 496–497; 30 April 1783, p. 500. The Comédie complained about the move because it had to pay Choiseul 300,000 livres (AN ms 0^1 849, fol. 31). Most of the documents pertaining to the new theater are in the fourth and fifth dossiers of 0^1 849.

114. Jacques-Antoine Dulaure, *Nouvelle description des curiosités de Paris* (Paris, 1785), p. 548. Bachaumont, *Mémoires,* vol. 17, p. 116, held the same opinion. See also Métra, *Correspondance,* vol. 10, p. 365. Citing the repudiation of this rumor in the *Journal de la Comédie*

Italienne, BV 19277, Georges Cucuel, in "Sources," *Année:* 268, rejects the veracity of the story.

115. Grimm, *Correspondance,* vol. 5, p. 44.

116. *Journal de Paris,* 20 February 1777, pp. 2–3.

117. François-Antoine Chevrier, *L'Observateur des spectacles,* 3 vols. (The Hague, 1762–1763), vol. 1, p. 271.

118. Barbier, *Journal,* vol. 4, p. 430. The same view was expressed by Favart, *Mémoires,* 1: 276. See also Hurtaut and Magny, *Dictionnaire,* vol. 4, p. 672.

119. Pierre Jean Baptiste Nougaret, *La Mort de l'Opéra-Comique, élégie pour rire et pour pleurer* (Paris, 1762), p. 7.

CHAPTER 6. Entrepreneurial Dilemmas:
The Case of the Fair Saint-Ovide and the Champs-Elysées

1. *Almanach forain* (1773), n.p.; (1776), p. 144; (1778), p. 151; Hurtaut and Magny, *Dictionnaire,* vol. 3, p. 48; Campardon, *Spectacles,* vol. 1, p. xxx; D'Auriac, *Théâtre,* pp. 3–6; and the anonymous play *La Foire de Saint-Ovide,* BN ms fr 9250, fols. 107–120.

2. *Almanach parisien, en faveur des étrangers et des personnes curieuses* (Paris, 1765), p. 83.

3. Heulhard, *Saint-Laurent,* pp. 88–89.

4. Bachaumont, *Mémoires,* vol. 19, p. 140.

5. In addition to the *Almanach forain* (1773), n.p., see especially Campardon, *Spectacles,* vol. 1, pp. 187–188; Pierre Jean Baptiste Nougaret, *Les Historiettes du jour, ou Paris tel qu'il est,* 2 vols. (Paris, 1787), vol. 1, p. 83. Almost impossible to describe in words, the Café des Aveugles is best documented by the engraving "Grand concert extraordinaire éxécuté par un détachement des quinze-vingt au Caffé des Aveugles, foire Saint-Ovide au mois de Septembre 1771," BN Cabinet des Estampes Qb (Va fol. 234), cliché 63C 20864. For a general view of the Place and the fair shows, see the engraving entitled "La foire Saint-Ovide telle qu'elle a été décorée dans la Place Vendôme au mois de Septembre, 1763," Musée du Carnavalet, Topo p.c. 38C, and "La Foire Saint-Ovide. Vue et perspective de la Place Louis-le-Grand," BN Cabinet des Estampes, Collection Hennin Qb 1777, T 10, A 9631.

6. Early in the nineteenth century there was a Caveau des Aveugles located underground in the Palais-Royal in a former cloister. A small orchestra of blind musicians was flanked by a tall, bare-chested man covered with tattoos and wearing feathers on his back. He beat on a set of drums. Called Mahahualt, he was said to be a Delaware Indian. See Gaston Vassy, *Paris pittoresque: le Caveau des Aveugles* (Paris, 1874), pp. 7–18.

7. Bachaumont, *Mémoires,* vol. 24, p. 203.

8. All information on the operation of the fair is drawn from AN ms Y 12227, and all references to dossiers and pièces refer to documents in that carton of *commissaire* papers.

9. Paul d'Ariste and Maurice Arrivetz, *Les Champs-Elysées, étude topographique, historique et anecdotique jusqu'à nos jours* (Paris, 1913), pp. iv, 37–39; *Le Courier de l'Europe ou Mémoires pour servir à l'histoire universelle,* 9 April 1776, p. 120. Earlier in the seventeenth century, when people began strolling from the Tuileries to the Chateau de Chaillot, Marie de Médici planted the Cours-la-Reine, four lanes of trees 1500 meters long, for shade. See Du Coudray, *Nouveaux essais,* vol. 4, pp. 85–86. In addition she had a broad path laid out beyond the Tuileries gardens, leading through the area where the Place Louis XV was later built. Her plans for a gigantic garden, fountains, canals, and a labyrinth on the plain bordering the Cours never came to fruition though the Cours itself was replanted by the duc d'Antin, superintendant of the king's buildings, in 1723; and a bridge, the Pont Tournant, was installed to span the ditch where the Tuileries gardens met what is now the Place de la Concorde. In this period the Cours was a fashionable promenade, especially at night, when people walked to the Rond Point by torchlight for music and dancing.

10. The king ordered the Etoile flattened in 1768, and the original octagonal shape was changed to a circle, all with the aim of making it a fashionable area of promenade. In 1788 a school

for soldiers' orphans at the entry of the Avenue Kléber and two tollhouses linked by a barrier as a customs checkpoint for the *fermiers généraux* at the front of the Etoile were constructed. One of the latter serves now as the guardian's house in the Parc Monceau. See D'Ariste and Arrivetz, *Champs-Elysées,* pp. 291–293.

11. Franc-Nohain, *Vie Parisienne,* pp. 70–71; D'Argenson, *Journal,* vol. 9, p. 30.

12. *Affiches,* 7 November 1779, p. 2488.

13. Quoted in D'Ariste and Arrivetz, *Champs-Elysées,* p. 97.

14. *Affiches,* 12 May 1779, p. 1056; *Journal de Paris,* 8 May 1779.

15. AN ms H² 1965, doss. 14, folio 1. Many designs and locations, including the carrefour de Buci, had been proposed over the years. Reportedly, La Pompadour was furious at the actual choice of location because, despite the presence of her *hôtel* on the Champs, it put the king outside Paris. See D'Argenson, *Journal,* vol. 6, p. 146; vol. 8, pp. 252–253.

16. "Voyage," *Revue:* 47.

17. AN ms H² 1965, doss. 14, fol. 2.

18. AN ms H² 2160, doss. 1, fol. 1. Folio 3 has Gabriel's plans and the designs for the sculpted parts of the two new buildings (bas-reliefs, trophies, draperies, and so on) by Guillaume Coustou and René-Michel Slodtz, the latter to cost 170,000 livres; dossier 5, folio 2, and dossier 7 provide the designs for the scaffolding of the statue. See also D'Artiste and Arrivetz, *Champs-Elysées,* pp. 12–17.

19. *Le Courier,* 23 April 1776, p. 136; 30 August 1776, p. 284.

20. For accounts of this event, see Bachaumont, *Mémoires,* vol. 5, pp. 111–112, 134–135, 137–139; Siméon-Prosper Hardy, *Mes Loisirs, journal d'événements tels qu'ils parviennent à ma connaissance (1764–1789),* ed. Maurice Tourneux and Maurice Vitrac (Paris, 1912), pp. 194–195, 200–205.

21. Hardy, only part of whose voluminous journal was published, had a bookstore on the rue Saint-Jacques. Because of his friendship with Commissaire Convers-Desormeaux of the Place Maubert quarter, Hardy's journal is full of police information.

22. Quoted in Bachaumont, *Mémoires,* 5: 140. Hardy confirmed that the Dauphin gave three months of his *menu plaisir* fund, or 6,000 livres, to help wounded persons and children whose parents were killed.

23. Hardy, *Loisirs,* p. 203. Hardy himself contributed to the exaggerated count, making it 1,200.

24. Quoted in ibid., p. 206.

25. BV ms 628, p. 170; Mathieu-François Pidansat de Mairobert, *L'Espion anglois, ou correspondance entre Milord All'eye et Milord Alle'ar,* 6 vols. (London, 1783–1784), vol. 2, pp. 71–72; Hardy, *Loisirs,* p. 279; *Le Courier,* 20 September 1776, p. 308. George-Louis Lerouge, *Description du Colisée élevé aux Champs-Elysées sur les dessins de M. Le Camus* (Paris, 1771), p. 3, has it the other way around, claiming that the crowds on the Champs gave rise to the idea of a Colisée. In my judgment he was mistaken.

26. AN ms Y 12227, doss. 13; Campardon, *Spectacles,* vol. 1, p. 34.

27. *Mémoire* from Trudon to Sartine, AN ms Y 12227, doss. 8.

28. AN ms Y 12227, doss. 6.

29. The plan of the fair is in AN ms Y 12227, doss. 12.

30. AN ms Y 12227, doss. 11.

31. Ibid.

32. AN ms Y 12227, doss. 13; Campardon, *Spectacles,* vol. 1, pp. 33–34.

33. AN ms Y 12227, doss. 16.

34. Pidansat de Mairobert, *L'Espion,* vol. 2, pp. 69–73; Bachaumont, *Mémoires,* vol. 4, pp. 278–279, 284, 306; vol. 19, pp. 260, 266; vol. 24, p. 356.

35. Bachaumont, *Mémoires,* 4: 284.

36. Pidansat de Mairobert, *L'Espion,* vol. 2, p. 72.

37. Bachaumont, *Mémoires,* vol. 5, p. 325.

38. Ibid., p. 86.

39. Quoted in ibid., vol. 19, p. 225.

40. Ibid., p. 260.

41. Ibid., vol. 5, p. 250.
42. Ibid., vol. 24, p. 356.
43. Lerouge, *Description*, pp. 3–24; L. Gachet, *Observations sur les spectacles en général, et en particulier sur le Colisée* (Paris, 1772), pp. 46–48.
44. A catalogue of shows given at the Colisée in 1773 can be found in the *Almanach forain* (1774), p. 59. In addition to the *Almanach's* regular accounts, see Campardon, *Spectacles*, vol. 1, p. 209; Bachaumont, *Mémoires*, especially vol. 5, pp. 314, 332, 338, 377, 379, 382, and vol. 25, pp. 212, 222, 246, 237.
45. *Almanach musical* (1777), p. 33.
46. Ibid., (1778), pp. 31–32.
47. D'Artiste and Arrivetz, *Champs-Elysées*, p. 225.
48. BV ms 628.
49. Bachaumont, *Mémoires*, vol. 5, p. 323.
50. Fournel, *Vieux*, pp. 450–451.
51. Bachaumont, *Mémoires*, vol. 5, p. 349.
52. Ibid., vol. 7, pp. 225–228.
53. Ibid., vol. 9, p. 214; *Nouveau spectateur*, 1 August 1776, p. 34; 1 October 1776, pp. 321–323.
54. Bachaumont, *Mémoires*, vol. 24, p. 187.
55. Ibid., pp. 211–212.
56. Chennevierres, "Ruggieri," *Gazette*, pp. 132–139; Claude Ruggieri, *Précis historique sur les fêtes, les spectacles et les réjouissances publiques* (Paris, 1830), pp. 77–81; Frézier, *Traité des feux d'artifice pour le spectacle* (Paris, 1747), preface.
57. D'Argenson, *Journal*, vol. 3, p. 375.
58. Quoted in Rabou, *Grands*, p. 248.
59. *Almanach parisien* (1771): 50; Lerouge, *Description*, p. 23.
60. Bachaumont, *Mémoires*, vol. 5, p. 304.
61. *Nouveau spectateur*, 1 September 1776, pp. 132–134.
62. Du Coudray, *Nouveaux*, vol. 4, p. 83.
63. Gachet, *Observations*, pp. 53–54.
64. *Annales politiques* (1777): 468.
65. Mercier, *Tableau*, vol. 6, p. 244.
66. *Répons d'un artiste à un homme de lettres qui lui avoit écrit sur les Waux-halls* (Paris, 1769), p. 11.
67. Ibid., pp. 40–41.
68. Pidansat de Mairobert, *L'Espion*, vol. 2, p. 71.
69. Mercier, *Tableau*, vol. 6, p. 242.
70. Bachaumont, *Mémoires*, vol. 6, p. 182.
71. Ibid., vol. 19, p. 266.
72. Mercier, *Tableau*, vol. 6, p. 244.
73. Bachaumont, *Mémoires*, vol. 19, p. 319.
74. *Le Courier d'Avignon*, 19 September 1777, p. 304.
75. Bachaumont, *Mémoires*, vol. 19, p. 266.
76. Ibid., p. 260.
77. Pidansat de Mairobert, *L'Espion*, vol. 2, p. 72.
78. *Nouveau spectateur*, 1 October 1776, pp. 296–323.
79. AN ms 0^1 488, fol. 374.
80. The *arrêt* is printed in D'Artiste and Arrivetz, *Champs-Elysées*, p. 223.
81. See, for example, Du Coudray, *Nouveaux essais*, vol. 4, p. 92.
82. Bachaumont, *Mémoires*, vol. 10, p. 238; vol. 10, p. 255; AN ms 0^1 488, fol. 196.
83. For various accounts of the fire, see AN ms Y 12227, doss. 16; *Le Courier d'Avignon*, 3 October 1777, p. 320; 7 October 1777, p. 324; Favart, *Mémoires*, vol. 3, pp. 237–238; *Journal de Paris*, 24 September 1777, p. 3; 28 September 1777, p. 2; Métra, *Correspondance*, vol. 5, p. 187; Bachaumont, *Mémoires*, vol. 10, p. 252.
84. BV ms 630, p. 175.

85. Quoted in D'Artiste and Arrivetz, *Champs-Elysées*, p. 39. The forest meant the Bois de Boulogne.
86. Letter to an unknown official dated 26 August 1783, quoted in ibid.
87. Quoted in ibid., p. 48.

CHAPTER 7. Streets of the People

1. Thomas Rousseau, *Lettre à M. sur les spectacles des boulevards* (Paris, 1871), pp. 12–13.
2. See, for example, Hurtaut and Magny, *Dictionnaire*, vol. 1, p. 659.
3. Information on the boulevards can be found in the following works: Dulaure, *Nouvelle description*, pp. 70–72; *Le Provincial à Paris ou état actuel de Paris*, 4 vols. (Paris, 1787), vol. 3, pp. 33–34; *Almanach parisien* (1765), p. 156; Barbier, *Journal*, vol. 3, p. 475; Hurtaut and Magny, *Dictionnaire*, vol. 1, p. 660; François-Marie Mayeur de Saint-Paul, *Le Désoeuvré, ou l'espion du Boulevard du Temple* (London, 1781); Sauval, *Histoire*, vol. 1, pp. 671–672; Michel Marescot, *La Folie du jour ou la promenade des boulevards* (n.p., 1754); Thiéry, *Almanach* (1783), vol. 1, p. 145; Théodore Faucheur, *Histoire du boulevard du Temple depuis son origine jusqu'à sa démolition* (Paris, 1863); Nicolas Brazier, *Chroniques des petits théâtres de Paris*, 2 vols., 3d ed. (Paris, 1883), vol. 1, pp. 165–178; Georges Cain, *Anciens théâtres de Paris* (Paris, 1906), pp. 1–4, 37; Jacques Hillairet, *Dictionnaire historique des rues de Paris*, 2 vols. (Paris, 1963), vol. 2, pp. 541–549; Fournel, *Vieux*, pp. 111–133; Van Bellen, *Origines*, pp. 65–66; Brice, *Nouvelle*, vol. 2, pp. 69–75. When the word *boulevard* is used in the singular, the reference is to the Boulevard du Temple, which in the early modern period bent further to the north in the area of the present Place de la République than it does today. The name comes from the Templars, a religious order of knights founded in the eleventh century who, prior to their suppression in 1307, were installed in a fortress beyond the walls to the north of the city. After their suppression, Philippe le Bel gave the Temple to the knights of Saint-Jean de Jérusalem. In 1389, Charles VI built the porte du Temple on the northern side of the fortress. It was protected by a large trench and a bastion located on the present Place de la République.
4. Dulaure, *Nouvelle*, p. 72; *Le Provincial*, vol. 2, p. 43; *Almanach parisien* (1771), p. 29.
5. AN ms Y 13960, pièce dated 11 July 1767. The name Pont-aux-Choux came from a bridge over a sewer covered today by the rue de Turenne. Cabbages were once cultivated along this lane, which ran to the Porte Saint-Louis along the rampart. See Hillairet, *Dictionnaire*, vol. 2, p. 286.
6. AN ms Y 13960, pièce dated 19 October 1767, and 13926, pièce dated 14 June 1769.
7. See, for example, AN ms Y 13962, pièces dated 5 July 1769 and 16 May 1769; Y 13970, pièce dated 4 July 1771. See also Métra, *Correspondance*, vol. 7, pp. 228–229.
8. Jean-Henri Marchand and J. A. Desboulmiers, *L'Esprit et la chose* (n.p., 1767), p. 62. A provincial visitor also complained about the odor of stale tobacco smoke, the mud and filth in the streets, and the terrible smell of horse manure. (*Lettre d'un provincial à un ami sur la promenade des boulevarts* [n.p., 1760], p. 5).
9. Cited in Fournel, *Vieux*, p. 133.
10. Dulaure, *Nouvelle*, p. 72.
11. Mayeur de Saint-Paul, *Désoeuvré*, p. 11.
12. Hester Lynch Salusbury Thrale Piozzi, *The French Journals of Mrs. Thrale and Doctor Johnson*, ed. Moses Tyson and Henry Guppy (Manchester, 1932), pp. 199–200.
13. Mercier, *Tableau*, vol. 1, p. 168.
14. Nougaret, *Historiettes*, vol. 2, pp. 18–19. See also Pierre Jean Baptiste Nougaret, *Les Astuces de Paris* (Paris, 1775), p. 99; François Cognel, *La Vie Parisienne sous Louis XVI* (Paris, 1882), p. 21. The latter account by a magistrate from Nancy was written in 1787. Additional discussion of boulevard crowds can be found in Du Coudray, *Nouveaux essais*, vol. 1, p. 115; Jèze, *Journal du citoyen*, p. 192; Marescot, *La Folie*, pp. 1–7, Jean-Joseph Vadé, "Le Boulevard," in *Nouveau théâtre*, vol. 2; *La Soirée des boulevards*, in Favart, *Théâtre*, vol. 4.

15. Mayeur de Saint-Paul, *Désoeuvré*, pp. 38–41; Fournel, *Vieux*, pp. 126–128.
16. Mercier, *Tableau*, vol. 6, pp. 19–20.
17. The Turc was renamed Caffé Chinois in 1782 and redecorated at a reported cost of 80,000 livres. Bachaumont, *Mémoires*, vol. 21, pp. 100–101.
18. Métra, *Correspondance*, vol. 8, pp. 68–69.
19. Charles Théveneau de Morande, *La Gazette noire par un homme qui n'est pas blanc, ou oeuvres posthumes du gazetier cuirassé* (n.p., 1784), p. 212.
20. Nougaret, *Astuces*, pp. 19–21.
21. Mayeur de Saint-Paul, *Désoeuvré*, p. 40.
22. Ibid.
23. Fournel, *Cris*, pp. 202–207; Gouriet, *Charlatans*, vol. 1, p. 122.
24. Jacques Peuchet, *Mémoires tirés des archives de la police de Paris*, 6 vols. (Paris, 1838), vol. 2, pp. 168–186, may have had a different Fanchon in mind in his account of her career.
25. Mercier, *Tableau*, vol. 5, pp. 310–314.
26. Ibid.
27. For a discussion of the financial success of the boulevard theaters, see Michele Marie Root-Bernstein, 'Revolution on the Boulevard: Parisian Popular Theater in the Late-Eighteenth Century," (Ph.D. dissertation, Princeton University, 1981), pp. 75–79. Ms. Root-Bernstein's thesis has recently been published.
28. *Almanach parisien* (1771), p. 198. Gouriet, *Charlatans*, vol. 1, p. 117, noted that in front of Nicolet's theater there were "rows of rich carriages and horses stationed as in front of a minister's hôtel."
29. *Almanach forain* (1776), p. 41; (1778), pp. 87–88. See also Pougin, *Dictionnaire*, pp. 34, 42, 113. Accounts of the theaters can be found in Ernest Lunel, *Le Théâtre et la Révolution* (Paris, n.d.) pp. 12–22; Author Pougin, *Acteurs et actrices d'autrefois* (Paris, n.d.), pp. 33–38; Campardon, *Spectacles*, vol. 2, pp. 149–164; Henri Beaulieu, *Les Théâtres du boulevard du crime* (Paris, 1905), pp. 11–101; Nicolas Brazier, *Chroniques des petits théâtres de Paris*, 2 vols., 3d ed., (Paris, 1883), vol. 1, pp. 3–24; Rabou, *Grands danseurs*.
30. Max Aghion, *Le Théâtre à Paris au XVIIIᵉ siècle* (Paris, 1926), p. 261. Hillairet, *Dictionnaire*, vol. 2, p. 542, places his theater at the angle of the present Boulevards du Temple and Voltaire.
31. BN ms n.a. fr 3045, fol. 1; Augustin Challamel, *L'Ancien boulevard du Temple* (Paris, n.d.), pp. 9–10.
32. Campardon, *Comédiens*, vol. 2, pp. 285–289, 301–327; Du Coudray, *Nouveaux*, vol. 1, pp. 117–118.
33. Grimm, *Correspondance*, vol. 6, p. 100.
34. Campardon, *Spectacles*, vol. 1, p. xxxi.
35. Bachaumont, *Mémoires*, vol. 7, p. 88. For additional laudatory comment about *L'Enlèvement* and the art of pantomime, see "Lettre d'un grand sauteur à M. de Voltaire sur les pantomimes" and "Traité du geste" in Pierre Jean Baptiste Nougaret, *La Littérature renversé, ou l'art de faire des pièces de théâtre sans paroles avec un traité du geste* (Paris, 1775), pp. 17–54. Nougaret was convinced that if the Grands Danseurs could make mime popular enough, they could strike a blow against the arrogant censorship exercised by the privileged theaters.
36. BV ms res. 25, p. 14.
37. Grimm, *Correspondance*, vol. 11, p. 84.
38. On Taconet (1730–1774), see A. P. Moore, *The Genre Poissard and the French Stage of the Eighteenth Century* (New York, 1935), pp. 198–210; Fournel, *Tableau*, pp. 372–374. Moore spells Taconet's name with two *n*'s although most eighteenth-century sources use only one.
39. Toussaint-Gaspard Taconet, *L'Auteur ambulant, ou recueil de pièces représentées sur différents théâtres tant à Paris qu'en province*, 3 vols. (Paris, 1757–1763), vol. 2, pp. 3–62.
40. Bachaumont, *Mémoires*, vol. 3, p. 277.
41. *Journal de Paris*, 12 February 1779, p. 172; 7 February 1782, p. 152; *Affiches*, 5 March 1779, p. 512.

42. Bachaumont, *Mémoires,* vol. 13, pp. 383–384.

43. Fournel, *Vieux,* p. 346.

44. *Journal de Paris,* 1 September 1777, p. 4; 7 February 1782, p. 156.

45. Ibid., 25 June 1779, p. 720.

46. Fournel, *Vieux,* p. 348.

47. *Journal de Paris,* 28 August 1786, p. 992.

48. Métra, *Correspondance,* vol. 2, pp. 113–115.

49. Bachaumont, *Mémoires,* vol. 3, p. 160.

50. *Recueil Clairambault,* vol. 8, p. 86.

51. Mayeur de Saint-Paul, *Désoeuvré,* p. 76.

52. Nicolas-Edme Rétif de la Bretonne, *Les Contemporaines par gradation, ou avantures des jolies femmes de l'âge actuel, suivant la gradation des principaux états de la société,* 42 vols. (Paris, 1783–1785), vol. 42, p. 351.

53. Du Coudray, *Il est temps,* p. 11; Gachet, *Observations,* p. 20.

54. Bachaumont, *Mémoires,* vol. 3, p. 303.

55. For a different kind of thematic analysis with conclusions different from mine, see Root-Bernstein, "Revolution," pp. 125–165.

56. BN ms n.a. fr 2877, fols. 244–272.

57. BN ms n.a. fr 2869, fols. 361–368, 369–387.

58. BA ms 321; BN ms fr 9270 fols. 312–343.

59. BN ms n.a. fr 2864, fols. 13–25.

60. BN ms n.a. fr 2864, fols. 250–270.

61. BN ms n.a. fr 2869, fols. 341–355.

62. BN ms n.a. fr 2866, fols. 208–215.

63. Alexandre-Louis-Bertrand Robineau Beaunoir, *Jannette, ou les battus ne paient pas toujours l'amende* (Paris, 1781), pp. 5–40.

64. *Le Quiproquo de l'hôtellerie* (Paris, 1782), pp. 2–64.

65. BN ms n.a. fr 2865, fols. 88–89.

66. Ibid., fols. 190–205.

67. Louis-Archambault Dorvigny, *Le Père Duchesne, ou la mauvaise habitude* (Paris, 1789), pp. 3–51.

68. BN ms n.a. fr 2870, fols. 153–172.

69. BN ms n.a. fr 2877, fols. 244–272.

70. BN ms n.a. fr 2888, fols. 188–207.

71. BN ms n.a. fr 2871, fols. 143–167.

72. BN ms n.a. fr 2988, fol. 201.

73. BN ms n.a. fr 3017, fol. 132.

74. BN ms n.a. fr 2864, fols. 254, 257.

75. Bachaumont, *Mémoires,* vol. 29, p. 42. The best secondary accounts of Audinot and the Ambigu-Comique are Edmond Denis de Manne and C. Ménétrier, *Galérie historique des comédiens de la troupe de Nicolet* (Lyons, 1869), pp. 41–70; Heulhard, *Saint-Laurent,* pp. 28–287; see also Campardon, *Comédiens,* vol. 1, pp. 7–9; E. Deligny, *Histoire de l'Ambigu-Comique* (Paris, 1841); Mayeur de Saint-Paul, *Désoeuvré,* pp. 77–98.

76. Grimm, *Correspondance,* vol. 5, p. 44. For a contrary view, see Mayeur de Saint-Paul, *Désoeuvré,* pp. 81–82.

77. Deligny, *Ambigu,* pp. 5–9, claims that in dispair Audinot attempted suicide. Eulalie was the offspring of Audinot's mistress, Françoise Cailloux, known as la Prairie. Just eight years old when she first appeared on stage at the Ambigu, Eulalie became her father's star actress. When a second daughter was born, also the child of his mistress, Audinot posed as Françoise's husband, forged baptismal documents for both children, and gave the second child Françoise's name, which resulted in a lawsuit at the Châtelet in January 1776. He was fined and imprisoned for a time. See Mayeur de Saint-Paul, *Désoeuvré,* pp. 82–85; Métra, *Correspondance,* vol. 2, pp. 379–380; Bachaumont, *Mémoires,* vol. 9, p. 32.

78. Théodore Faucheur, *Histoire du boulevard du Temple depuis son origine jusqu'à sa démolition* (Paris, 1863), p. 18. Mayeur de Saint-Paul, *Désoeuvré,* p. 89, contended that Audinot

added a corridor that passed from the street to a grilled loge, which the Prince de Conti could use unobserved and that the director supplied his patron with pretty actresses. The theater was rebuilt in 1789, burned in 1827, built again on the Boulevard Saint-Martin in 1828, and destroyed in 1862. See Hillairet, *Dictionnaire,* vol. 2, p. 543. Drawings of both the interior and exterior of the original Ambigu, including dimensions of all parts of the theater and ink sketches of the columns, sculptures, and stuccos, can be found in AN ms N^3 1029, pièces 1–20 and N^3 1030, 1–31.

79. Challamel, *L'Ancien,* p. 24. For a description of these child actors, see *Sur l'Ambigu Comique* (n.p., n.d.), pp. 5–17. Mayeur de Saint-Paul, *Désoeuvré,* is riddled with anecdotes about boulevard actors and actresses. There is a good account of them in Root-Bernstein, "Revolution," pp. 201–225.

80. See, for example, *Almanach forain* (1778), n.p.; Gachet, *Observations,* p. 24; *Sur l'Ambigu,* pp. 32–34. The *Almanach forain* (1778), p. 81, pointed out that children had appeared in shows in 1731, 1732, and 1741 although their appearance at the Ambigu in the 1770s was unique and innovative for that period.

81. As a reward for the expense of taking the Ambigu to the fair, Audinot asked for a reduction of the *quart des pauvres.* See the documents in Campardon, *Spectacles,* vol. 1, pp. 33–34.

82. On the sexual abuse of the child actors, see Rétif de la Bretonne, *Contemporaines,* vol. 42, pp. 325–327; Pidansat de Mairobert, *L'Espion,* vol. 2, pp. 92–94. In a letter to Madame Gourdan, the proprietor of the most notorious brothel in Paris, a certain Mademoiselle Grépau charged that Audinot "controls us by kicks in the ass" (*Correspondance de Madame Gourdan* [London, 1784], p. 11). Mayeur de Saint-Paul, *Désoeuvré,* pp. 15–16, tells of Audinot's having to buy off the parents of a young actress whom he seduced. He charged that Audinot sometimes hit actors, but he also observed that the director then usually gave them a bonus. In general, Mayeur's opinion was that Audinot rewarded talent, was just and generous, and was like a father to the children.

83. *Annales politiques* (1779): 241.

84. *Almanach forain* (1773): n.p. I base this conclusion on the figures on incomes and prices supplied in Appendixes VII and VIII in George Rudé, *the Crowd in the French Revolution* (London, 1967), n.p. Two categories of laborers earned 25 and 30 sous a day; a journeyman mason earned 40 sous a day; locksmiths and carpenters earned 50 sous, and goldsmiths earned 100 sous. The figures are for the year 1789. A 4-pound loaf of bread cost about 15 sous in 1789. Adults ate about 1½ pounds a day. A laborer would have to spend about one half of a day's earnings to attend the Ambigu; a carpenter, around one fourth. For a more recent discussion, see Daniel Roche, *Le Peuple de Paris* (Paris, 1981), the chapters entitled "Fortune et infortunes populaires" (pp. 66–97) and "Savoir consommer" (pp. 131–164).

85. Bachaumont, *Mémoires,* vol. 6, pp. 6–7.

86. "Voyage, *Revue:* 63.

87. Authors' fees were guaranteed by *règlements* at the privileged theaters, but they sold their pieces outright to the boulevard directors. Audinot rarely paid over 200 livres for a piece. See Aghion, *Théâtre,* pp. 403–404.

88. Deligny, *Ambigu,* p. 28.

89. Mercier, *Tableau,* vol. 3, p. 41.

90. Ibid., vol. 8, p. 60.

91. Campardon, *Spectacles,* vol. 1, p. xxxi.

92. Bachaumont, *Mémoires,* vol. 29, p. 44.

93. *Sur l'Ambigu,* p. 22.

94. "Voyage," *Revue:* 64. The author had reference in particular to a work entitled *La Mort du capitaine Cook.*

95. *Journal de Paris,* 1 January 1781, p. 4.

96. Ibid., 16 January 1781, p. 66.

97. Ibid., 22 February 1781, p. 214.

98. Ibid., 13 August 1780, p. 920; Bachaumont, *Mémoires,* vol. 15, p. 234.

99. *Le Chat-botté, pantomime* (Paris, n.d.).

100. Nicolas-Médard Audinot, *Dorothée, pantomime à spectacle* (Paris, 1782), pp. 14–20. Again, there was no dialogue, so the published version is only a summary of the action. See also *Journal de Paris*, 14 February 1784, p. 200; 6 January 1788, p. 28.

101. Robert M. Isherwood, "The Third War of the Musical Enlightenment," *Studies in Eighteenth-Century Culture*, vol. 4, ed. Harold E. Pagliaro (Madison, 1975).

102. Nicolas-Médard Audinot, *La Musicomanie* (Paris, 1783).

103. Jean-Louis Gabiot de Salins, *Esope au boulevards* (Paris, 1784).

104. Nicolas-Médard Audinot, *Le Porte-feuille, ou la fille comme il y en a peu* (Paris, 1788).

105. Bachaumont, *Mémoires*, vol. 6, p. 7.

106. Ibid., vol. 28, p. 6.

107. Quoted in Deligny, *Ambigu*, pp. 43–44.

108. *Journal général*, 18 June 1785, pp. 291–292.

109. *Journal de Paris*, 3 June 1784, p. 673.

110. *Affiches*, 16 March 1785, p. 709.

111. Deligny, *Ambigu*, p. 31; Bachaumont, *Mémoires*, vol. 6, p. 59.

112. Ibid., p. 72. There are a number of documents in the 0^1 618 series pertaining to payments to the Opéra by Audinot and others. See especially doss. 1, pièces 32–40.

113. *Le Courier d'Avignon*, 24 December 1776, p. 122.

114. *Le Courier d'Avignon*, 11 February 1777, p. 52; Bachaumont, *Mémoires*, vol. 10, p. 25.

115. *Le Courier d'Avignon*, 26 June 1778, p. 404.

116. Bachaumont, *Mémoires*, vol. 29, pp. 110–115.

117. Bonnassies, *Spectacles*, pp. 59–60; Heulhard, *Saint-Laurent*, pp. 275–278.

118. Bachaumont, *Mémoires*, vol. 19, p. 126, quoted in Lough, *Paris*, p. 208.

119. *Sur l'Ambigu*, p. 38. For a discussion of the attitude of the police, see Root-Bernstein, "Revolution," pp. 63–73.

120. Quoted in Bonnassies, *Spectacles*, p. 57.

121. Van Bellen, *Origines*, p. 69.

122. Grimm, *Correspondance*, vol. 8, p. 232, quoted in Lough, *Paris*, pp. 207–208.

123. *Almanach forain* (1778), p. 128.

124. For a good discussion of this matter, see Root-Bernstein, "Revolution," pp. 13–19.

125. *Journal de Paris*, 19 June 1777, p. 4.

126. Grimm, *Correspondance*, vol. 24, p. 45.

127. Quoted in Louis-Henry Lecomte, *Les Variétés amusantes, 1778–1779* (Paris, 1908), p. 103, and Campardon, *Spectacles*, vol. 1, p. xxxv. See also Campardon, *Spectacles*, vol. 1, pp. 354–357; *Almanach forain* (1786), pp. 93–97. It is interesting to note that in a report on another matter to the king from the Conseil d'Etat the authors (Perdry and Goulleau) referred to the "reason of state and the secret motives" of the government in giving the Opéra control of the boulevard *spectacles* (AN ms H^2 2158, doss. 2, dated 18 August 1785).

128. Albert de Lasalle, *Les Treize salles de l'opéra* (Paris, 1875), pp. 146–147.

129. AN ms 0^1 618.

130. Manne and Ménétrier, *Galérie*, pp. 46–50. Deligny, *Ambigu*, pp. 47–48, contends that the culprit responsible for Audinot's loss of the Ambigu was a member of his troupe named Caroline, to whom Audinot owed money. Caroline allegedly seduced Lieutenant General Lenoir, who paved the way for the turnover of the theater to Caroline's lover, Dorfeuille. He also asserts that another of Audinot's actresses, Louise Masson, the comte d'Artois' mistress, used her influence with him to get Lenoir to return the privilege to Audinot in 1785. It is known that she starred in Arnauld's *La Belle au bois dormant*, which was the first production after Audinot regained his theater and which had a run of two hundred consecutive performances. For another account of Audinot's difficulties, see Bachaumont, *Mémoires*, vol. 29, pp. 26–116.

131. Vanglenne's accounts for this later December period show that the lowest amount Audinot took in for one day was 179 livres; the highest, 773 livres; and the total for 16 days, 5,734 livres, 12 sous. It is not known how much of the 2,248 livres owed the Opéra was actually

confiscated, but Vanglenne himself kept 280 livres, 8 sous, 6 deniers for his services. See Campardon, *Spectacles*, vol. 1, p. 60.

132. Métra, *Correspondance*, vol. 17, p. 243.

133. Louis Batcave, *Les Petits Comédiens du Roi au Bois de Boulogne* (Paris, 1909), pp. 4–31; Bachaumont, *Mémoires*, vol. 13, p. 285.

134. Campardon, *Spectacles*, vol. 1, p. 65; Bachaumont, *Mémoires*, vol. 29, p. 39.

135. Campardon, *Spectacles*, vol. 1, p. 69.

136. AN ms 0^1 496, p. 573.

137. Beaulieu, *Théâtres*, pp. 35–64; Faucheur, *Histoire*, pp. 16–18.

138. "Voyage," *Revue:* 65. See also Pierre Jean Baptiste Nougaret, *Tableau mouvant de Paris, ou Variétés Amusantes*, 3 vols. (Paris, 1787), vol. 1, p. 219.

139. *Almanach forain* (1786), pp. 149–150.

140. Mayeur de Saint-Paul, *Désoeuvré*, p. 45.

141. Beaulieu, *Théâtres*, p. 37.

142. Challamel, *L'Ancien*, pp. 34–37.

143. *Journal de Paris*, 8 January 1779; *Almanach forain* (1786), pp. 13–14; for titles of productions, see, for example, *Affiches*, 1 January 1780, p. 8.

144. Mayeur de Saint-Paul, *Désoeuvré*, pp. 20–36.

145. On the Variétés, see especially Lecomte, *Variétés*, pp. 1–191, which lists 294 pieces in the repertoire and has valuable summaries of several plays that were never published. See also *Almanach forain* (1786), pp. 20–28; Pougin, *Acteurs*, pp. 72–73; Campardon, *Spectacles*, vol. 1, pp. xxxiii–xxxiv; vol. 2, pp. 45–48; Moore, *Poissard*, pp. 149–156.

146. The listings of L'Ecluze's pieces in the fall of 1778 indicate that they mixed genres like those of Audinot and Nicolet, combining prose dialogue, spectacle, music, dance, and mime. See, for example, *Journal de Paris*, 6 October 1778, p. 1116.

147. Du Coudray, *Nouveaux*, vol. 1, pp. 124–126.

148. Bachaumont, *Mémoires*, vol. 14, p. 22.

149. Ibid., p. 154.

150. This case is well documented in AN ms H^2 2158 and 0^1 495, 496.

151. AN ms H^2 2158, doss. 1, pièce 3, especially pp. 11r–22r.

152. Moore, *Poissard*, p. 286. Clarence Brenner, *Le Développement du proverbe dramatique en France et sa vogue au XVIIIe siècle avec un proverbe inédit de Carmontel*, University of California Publications in Modern Philology, vol. 20 (Berkeley, 1937), pp. 1–56, states that, originating in the seventeenth-century salons, dramatic proverbs replaced Collé's gross *parades* in the private theaters at Villers-Cotterets and Bagnolet of the duc de Chartres after Madame de Montesson became his mistress in 1776. They quickly became a fad among Parisian nobles; those by Carmontel were especially popular. A collection of his proverbs can be found in BN ms fr 9326. The first one performed on the boulevards was in 1768. All the proverbs were in prose, many had vaudevilles and ariettes, and all given on the boulevards were farcical comedies like *Les Battus*.

153. Louis-Archambault Dorvigny, *Les Battus paient l'amende, proverbe-comédie-parade, ou ce que l'on voudra* (Paris, 1779).

154. Ibid., p. 43.

155. Bachaumont, *Mémoires*, vol. 14, p. 130.

156. *Le Courier d'Avignon*, 14 September 1779, p. 299. See also Du Coudray, *Nouveaux*, vol. 1, p. 126.

157. Grimm, *Correspondance*, vol. 12, p. 254.

158. Métra, *Correspondance*, vol. 10, p. 47. It is possible that his figure is accurate. The newspaper accounts certainly indicate that over five hundred performances were given, including revivals.

159. *L'Année littéraire* 2 (1782): 271.

160. *Journal de Paris*, 13 August 1780, p. 920; Charles-Jacob Guillemain, *Le Marriage de Janot avec la pantomime des ombres* (Paris, 1783).

161. See the issues of the *Affiches* for 1781.

162. Métra, *Correspondance*, vol. 9, pp. 86–87. See also Beaulieu, *Théâtres*, p. 72. Thomas Rousseau, *Lettre à M. sur les spectacles du boulevards* (Paris, 1781), p. 11, wrote of *Les Battus* that "its disgusting jargon has become the language of stylish ladies, of citizens of good breeding, and even of persons of high title."

163. Bachaumont, *Mémoires*, vol. 14, p. 368.

164. Grimm, *Correspondance*, vol. 12, p. 253.

165. Bachaumont, *Mémoires*, vol. 15, pp. 64–65.

166. Pierre Jean Baptiste Nougaret, *Les Sottises et les folies parisiennes, aventures diverses avec quelques pièces curieuses et fort rares, le tout fidèlement* (Paris, 1781), pp. 104–105.

167. *Journal de Paris*, 23 February 1780, p. 227.

168. Ibid., 28 February 1780, pp. 247–248.

169. Ibid., 14 December 1780, p. 1424.

170. Bachaumont, *Mémoires*, vol. 16, p. 76.

171. Cited in Fournel, *Vieux*, p. 304. See also Chesnais, *Histoire*, p. 124.

172. *Journal de Paris*, 10 November 1784, pp. 1324, 1332.

173. Ibid., 22 August 1784, p. 1000.

174. Ibid. See also 19 September 1784, p. 1114.

175. *Almanach forain* (1776), pp. 76–77.

176. Ibid. (1778), p. 136; Campardon, *Spectacles*, vol. 2, p. 148.

177. Nougaret, *Astuces*, p. 104.

178. Jèze, *Journal*, p. 180.

179. *Affiches*, 1 April 1785, p. 864; 1 May 1785, pp. 1159–1160.

180. *Almanach forain* (1774), pp. 39–41.

181. *L'Année* 5 (1780), p. 280.

182. *Almanach musical* (1778), p. 32.

183. Mercier, *Tableau*, vol. 12, p. 156.

184. Ibid., vol. 12, pp. 158–159.

185. *Journal de Paris*, 10 July 1780, pp. 783–784.

186. Chesnais, *Histoire*, p. 124.

187. Fournel, *Vieux*, p. 312.

188. Mercier, *Tableau*, vol. 5, pp. 315–317; Jèze, *Journal*, p. 180; Edgar Munhall, "Savoyards in French 18th Century Art," *Apollo: Magazine of the Arts* (June 1968): 86–94.

189. Mercier, *Tableau*, vol. I, pp. 19–20.

190. On Comus, see Jean Torlais, "Un Prestidigitateur célèbre chef de service d'électrothérapie au XVIIIᵉ siècle, Ledru dit Comus (1731–1807)," *Histoire de la médecine* 5 (February 1953): 13–25; Jean-Nicolas Dufort de Cheverny, *Mémoires sur les règnes de Louis XV et Louis XVI et sur la Révolution*, 2 vols. (Paris, 1886), vol. 2, p. 62.

191. Bachaumont, *Mémoires*, vol. 7, p. 16.

192. *Le Courier d'Avignon*, 1 August 1783, p. 244.

193. *Journal de Paris*, 13 May 1779, p. 535; 2 July 1778, p. 731; 1 June 1780, p. 627; 30 April 1780, p. 499; 4 May 1780, p. 515; 2 May 1782, p. 486; 9 May 1782, p. 514; 19 May 1782, p. 556; 1 September 1782, p. 997; 8 September 1782, p. 1025; 3 June 1781, p. 623.

194. Ibid., 28 July 1762, quoted in Campardon, *Spectacles*, vol. 1, p. 214.

195. Pougin, *Dictionnaire*, pp. 356–358, 465–466, 596.

196. Mayeur de Saint-Paul, *Désoeuvré*, pp. 59–60.

197. Quoted in Mercier, *Tableau*, vol. 3, p. 42.

198. See especially Fournel, *Vieux*, pp. 326–333.

199. *Affiches*, 27 March 1785, p. 824.

200. *Courier d'Avignon*, 20 March 1787, p. 96.

201. Mercier, *Tableau*, vol. 3, p. 42.

202. Mayeur de Saint-Paul, *Désoeuvré*, p. 58.

203. Ibid., p. 59.

204. Although the entry fee was only 3 sous, the loges and amphitheater each cost 3 livres. See *Affiches*, 10 May 1787, p. 1319. In 1786, however, the *Journal de Paris* reported an

admission price of 1 livre, 10 sous, and in 1789 the *Affiches* mentioned prices of 36 and 12 sous at the Waux-Hall. See the *Journal de Paris*, 14 May 1786, p. 543, and the *Affiches*, 12 April 1789, p. 1047.

205. Vaux was the name of a Frenchman who built the first hall of this type in London. See *Almanach forain* (1776), p. 114.

206. Du Coudray, *Nouveaux*, vol. 1, pp. 119–120; *L'Avant-coureur* (1769): 360; Ruggieri, *Précis*, pp. 79–80.

207. Torré used several kinds of illuminations: Chinese lanterns in clay or tin plates, tallow pots, colored glasses and lanterns, and different types of lamps.

208. Hardy, *Mes Loisirs*, p. 19.

209. Bachaumont, *Mémoires*, vol. 19, p. 26.

210. Ibid., vol. 4, p. 11.

211. Ibid., vol. 4, p. 81.

212. Papillon de La Ferté, *L'Administration*, p. 252.

213. Bachaumont, *Mémoires*, vol. 19, p. 225.

214. Ibid., vol. 9, p. 103.

215. *Le Nouveau spectateur*, 1 October 1776, p. 298.

216. Ibid., p. 301.

217. Du Coudray, *Nouveaux*, vol. 1, pp. 120–121.

218. *Journal de Paris*, 5 July 1778, p. 743.

219. *Affiches*, 10 May 1787, p. 1319.

220. Bachaumont, *Mémoires*, vol. 4, pp. 104–105; *Journal de Paris*, 14 May 1786, p. 543.

221. Cognel, *Vie Parisienne*, pp. 32–33.

222. *Affiches*, 12 April 1789, p. 1047.

223. Ibid., 9 April 1786, p. 919.

224. Ibid., 8 November 1788, p. 3095; 12 April 1789, p. 1047; *Journal de Paris*, 9 November 1788, p. 1336.

225. *Journal de Paris*, 1 January 1779, p. 4; 7 September 1777, p. 3; *Le Nouveau spectateur*, 15 July 1776, p. 511.

226. *New Larousse Encyclopedia of Mythology* (London, 1959), p. 205.

227. Bachaumont, *Mémoires*, vol. 3, pp. 60–61.

228. Cited in Du Coudray, *Nouveaux*, vol. 4, pp. 32–33.

229. *Réponse d'un artiste à un homme de lettres qui lui avoit écrit sur les Waux-halls* (Paris, 1769), pp. 3–40.

230. Nicolas-Joseph Sélis, *Lettre à un père de famille sur les petits spectacles de Paris* (Paris, 1789), p. 41.

231. Nougaret and Rétif de la Bretonne, *La Mimographe*, p. 448.

232. AN ms 0¹ 491, fol. 155.

233. For accounts, see *Le Provincial à Paris ou état actuel de Paris*, 4 vols. (Paris, 1787), vol. 3, pp. 36–38; Bachaumont, *Mémoires*, vol. 29, pp. 125; 29; 130–132; *Journal de Paris*, 7 July 1785, p. 778.

234. Ruggieri, *Précis*, pp. 77–79; Chennevierres, "Les Ruggieri," *Gazette*, pp. 132–139; Pougin *Dictionnaire*, p. 438.

235. *Affiches*, 18 October 1785, p. 2790.

236. *Journal de Paris*, 24 October 1785, p. 1225.

237. Ibid., 5 March 1789, p. 296.

238. Ibid., 8 June 1783, p. 668; 8 October 1788, p. 1248.

239. Ibid., 10 October 1783, pp. 1168–1170.

240. Ibid., 4 May 1779, p. 499.

241. Ibid., 18 June 1779, p. 666.

242. *Affiches*, 22 May 1779, p. 1136.

243. *Journal de Paris*, 5 July 1778, p. 144.

244. Bachaumont, *Mémoires*, 30: n.p.; Ruggieri, *Précis*, p. 85.

245. *Almanach parisien* (1765), pp. 154–156; Jèze, *Journal*, pp. 190–192.

246. Cited in Des Essarts, *Dictionnaire*, vol. 5, pp. 515–518.
247. BA ms 11498.
248. Ibid.
249. Mercier, *Tableau*, vol. 11, pp. 221–222.
250. Ibid., vol. 5, pp. 215–217; vol. 8, pp. 24–30.
251. Fournel, *Vieux*, pp. 421–423; Métra, *Correspondance*, vol. 15, pp. 229–230. There were other horsemen who preceded Astley but none lasted very long. They included Sieur Balp and his wife, who held riding exhibitions in 1779 on the Boulevard du Temple behind Nicolet's theater, and Sieur Hyam, who executed riding stunts. *Journal de Paris*, 11 May 1779, p. 528; Bachaumont, *Mémoires*, vol. 7, p. 205.
252. Bachaumont, *Mémoires*, vol. 21, p. 70.
253. Thiéry, *Almanach* (1784), vol. 1, p. 572; *Affiches*, 7 July 1782, n.p.
254. Bachaumont, *Mémoires*, vol. 23, p. 279; *Journal de Paris*, 14 October 1783, p. 1186; 1 January 1784, p. 4; 1 January 1785, p. 4; 23 January 1785, p. 96; 3 November 1788, p. 1314.
255. D'Artiste and Arrivetz, *Champs-Elysées*, p. 105.
256. Bachaumont, *Mémoires*, 32: 9.
257. Fournel, *Vieux*, pp. 451–452; *Affiches*, 8 May 1777, p. 591; 2 February 1778, p. 159; 26 February 1778, p. 271; 23 March 1778; 9 April 1778, p. 463; 13 August 1778, p. 1215; 3 April 1769, p. 296; 23 March 1769, p. 267; 16 March 1769, p. 240; *Journal de Paris*, 15 August 1784, p. 974; 16 November 1780, p. 1308; 15 August 1784, p. 974; 16 November 1780, p. 1308; 15 August 1782, p. 930; 27 October 1782, p. 1222; 3 November 1782, p. 1242; 8 December 1784, p. 1452; 17 March 1782, p. 304; 4 August 1782, p. 886; 2 February 1785, p. 140; Hurtaut and Magny, *Dictionnaire*, vol. 4, pp. 664, 681; Jèze, *Journal*, p. 181; Nougaret and Rétif de la Bretonne, *La Mimographe*, p. 447; *Almanach parisien* (1765), pp. 168–169; Peuchet, *Mémoires*, 1: 282; Thiéry, *Almanach* (1784), vol. 1, p. 572; Dulaure, *Nouvelle*, p. 534; Pierre Hachet-Souplet, *Le Dressage des animaux et les combats de bêtes* (Paris, 1897), pp. 143–144.
258. BN ms fr 21625, fol. 349.
259. There were 24 principal gates in Paris in 1780 leading to the main routes out of the city and through which all commodities entering the city had to pass. At least one official in a frock coat was stationed at each gate to check all persons entering the city. He inspected all vehicles for contraband or food products subject to taxes. See Nicolas-Jules-Henri Gourdon de Genouilhac, *Paris à travers des siècles*, 6 vols. (Paris, 1882–1889), vol. 4, pp. 58–59; Mercier, *Tableau*, vol. 2, pp. 55–56; vol. 5, p. 110; Jèze, *Journal*, pp. 38–41.
260. Peuchet, *Mémoires*, vol. 1, p. 282.
261. *Affiches*, 26 February 1777, p. 271; 23 March 1777, n.p.; 9 April 1777, p. 463.
262. Quoted in Fournel, *Vieux*, p. 450.
263. Du Coudray, *Nouveaux*, vol. 6, p. 240. See also Dulaure, *Nouvelle*, p. 534.
264. *Almanach parisien* (1765), p. 169.
265. Bachaumont, *Mémoires*, vol. 4, p. 110; *Journal de Paris*, 22 August 1784, p. 1000; 14 August 1784, p. 970; Ruggieri, *Précis*, p. 181; *Affiches*, 21 August 1784, p. 2200; 24 July 1769, pp. 671–672.
266. Grimm, *Correspondance*, vol. 14, pp. 259–260.
267. Ibid., 260.
268. Thiéry, *Almanach* (1784), vol. 3, p. 75. See also Des Essarts, *Dictionnaire*, vol. 1, p. 489.
269. Jèze, *Journal*, pp. 186–187.
270. Ibid., p. 187.
271. Rétif de la Bretonne, *Les Nuits*, p. 84.
272. *Journal de Paris*, 10 June 1782, p. 653; 15 July 1782, pp. 799–800.
273. Mercier, *Tableau*, vol. 11, pp. 266–267.
274. Ibid., p. 267.
275. Fournier des Ormes, "Le Procès de Ramponneau (1760)," *Feuilleton du constitutionnel* (27 September 1924): 1; *Le Provincial*, vol. 3, p. 66.

276. Fournier des Ormes, p. 2.
277. Mercier, *Tableau,* vol. 2, pp. 138–139.
278. Taconet, *L'Auteur,* vol. 2, p. 14.
279. Mercier, *Tableau,* vol. 2, pp. 139–140.
280. Fournier des Ormes, pp. 2–6; Campardon, *Spectacles,* vol. 2, p. 296. On Gaudon, see the papers of Commissaire Joron dated January 1769 in AN ms Y 13962.
281. François Marie Arouet de Voltaire, *Plaidoyer pour Genest Ramponeau cabaretier à la Courtille prononcé par lui-même contre Gaudon, entrepreneur d'un théâtre des bouleverts* (Geneva, 1760), pp. 6–10.
282. F. L. Herme de La Mothe, *Epître sur les spectacles ou mon retour à Paris* (Geneva, 1761), pp. 3–4.
283. "Le Cabaret de Ramponeau," *Magasin pittoresque,* 9 (July 1841): 233.
284. On the salons, see the excellent book by Carolyn C. Lougee, *Le Paradis des Femmes: Women, Salons, and Social Stratification in Seventeenth-Century France* (Princeton, 1976).

CHAPTER 8. The Convergence of Popular and Elite Culture: The Palais-Royal

1. Amedée Britsch, *La Jeunesse de Philippe-Egalité (1747–1785)* (Paris, 1926), pp. 311–316, 215–218; Hillairet, *Dictionnaire,* vol. 2, pp. 219–223; AN ms R⁴ 288, doss. 1; B. Saint-Marc and the marquis de Bourbonne, *Les Chroniques du Palais-Royal* (Paris, n.d.), pp. 72–165; Wilbrod Chabrol, *Histoire et description du Palais-Royal et du Théâtre Français* (Paris, 1883), pp. 110–111; Bachaumont, *Mémoires,* vol..17, pp. 287–289; François-Marie Mayeur de Saint-Paul, *Tableau du nouveau Palais-Royal,* 2 vols. (Paris, 1788), vol. 2, pp. 17–28; "Voyage," *Revue:* 35–36.
2. Chabrol, *Histoire,* p. 110, suggests that the duc also found the irregularity of the residences surrounding the garden aesthetically distasteful and became determined to seal them off from his own self-contained garden and architecturally harmonious residences.
3. J. Vatout, *Histoire du Palais-Royal* (Paris, 1830), p. 148, contended that the tree owed its name to the Parisian sympathy with the Poles when the Russians tried to conquer them. Arthur Dinaux, *Les Sociétés badines bachiques, littéraires et chantantes,* 2 vols. (Paris, 1867), vol. 1, p. 205, claimed that the word was derived from *craquer* in the sense of telling tall tales. Grimm, *Correspondance,* vol. 13, p. 12, says the tree owed its name to the partisans of the prince de Conti, who in 1697 was a competitor of the elector of Saxony for the Polish crown.
4. *Almanach parisien* (1765), p. 154.
5. Saint-Marc and Bourbonne, *Chroniques,* p. 120.
6. A plan of the arcades showing the architectural design dated 1790 can be found in AN ms R⁴ 288, pièce 26.
7. Bachaumont, *Mémoires,* vol. 17, p. 123.
8. Ibid., p. 129.
9. BN ms fr 6684, pp. 6–7.
10. Quoted in Britsch, *Jeunesse,* p. 321.
11. BN ms fr 6684, pp. 3–4. Hardy maintained that they were supported by the duc d'Orléans, who was opposed to Chartres' changes and asked the king to revoke the *lettres patentes.*
12. BN ms fr 6684, p. 8.
13. AN 0¹ 614, Book 1, fol. 148; Bachaumont, *Mémoires,* vol. 20, pp. 261–263.
14. AN ms 0¹ 624, fols. 243–259.
15. Incomplete lists of wages paid to those working on the new construction can be found in AN ms R⁴ 288, doss. 1, pièces 30–33.
16. AN ms R⁴ 288, pièces 1–20, are leases from 1781–1786, of which this is pièce 1.
17. *Courier d'Avignon,* 9 June 1786, p. 188; Saint-Marc and Bourbonne, *Chroniques,* pp. 158–159; Britsch, *Jeunesse,* p. 335; Chabrol, *Histoire,* p. 110.
18. *Lettres édifiantes du Palais Royal par un missionnaire du camp des Tartares* (Paris, 1788),

pp. 1–3; Mayeur de Saint-Paul, *Tableau,* vol. 2, pp. 38–43; Nougaret, *Tableau,* vol. 1, pp. 233–234; Saint-Marc and Bourbonne, *Chroniques,* pp. 164–165.

19. Mayeur de Saint-Paul, *Tableau,* vol. 1, pp. 109–110.

20. Hillairet, *Dictionnaire,* vol. 2, p. 219.

21. Quoted in ibid., p. 220.

22. BN ms fr 6684, p. 152.

23. *Courier d'Avignon,* 29 June 1784, p. 211.

24. Quoted in Britsch, *Jeunesse,* p. 339.

25. Rétif de la Bretonne, *Les Nuits,* vol. 1, p. 123.

26. Piozzi, *French Journals,* p. 198.

27. The cannon was put in the garden in 1784. Saint-Marc and Bourbonne, *Chroniques,* pp. 163–164, placed it between the basin and the arcades on the rue Montpensier side. Although it no longer works, the cannon is still in the basin on a pedestal covered by a plastic cube.

28. Bachaumont, *Mémoires,* vol. 27, p. 19. There had been an occasional entertainer in the garden prior to Chartres' development. See, for example, BV ms 619, p. 22v.

29. *Almanach forain* (1786), pp. 182–190; Campardon, *Spectacles,* vol. 1, pp. 107–114; Eugène Hugot, *Histoire littéraire, critique et anecdotique du Théâtre du Palais-Royal, 1784–1884,* 3d ed. (Paris, 1886); Pougin, *Acteurs,* p. 75; *Almanach du Palais Royal* (1786), pp. 97–104; Chesnais, *Histoire générale,* pp. 126–127; Mayeur de Saint-Paul, *Tableau,* vol. 1, pp. 79–85. The police gave their consent for the new theater in August. See Bachaumont, *Mémoires,* vol. 29, p. 221.

30. Chesnais, *Histoire générale,* p. 127, maintains that Delomel and Gardeur caught the public's attention when they displayed a bust of Louis XVI in their shop window amid skittle pins and chess pieces.

31. A document relevant to the construction of the theater including dimensions can be found in AN ms R^4 288, pièce 27.

32. Quoted in Louis Pericaud, *Théâtre des Petits Comédiens de S.A.S. Monseigneur le Comte de Beaujolais* (Paris, 1909), p. 15.

33. Quoted in ibid., p. 40. The most popular works in the repertoire of the Beaujolais can be found in *Almanach musical* (1788), pp. 104–110.

34. *Journal de Paris,* 22 October 1784, p. 1248.

35. BN ms fr 9244, fols. 164–175.

36. AN ms 0^1 842, pièce 257.

37. *Almanach du Palais Royal* (1786), pp. 97–99; Britsch, *Jeunesse,* pp. 343–344.

38. "Voyage," *Revue:* 68.

39. *Almanach musical* (1788), pp. 101–102.

40. Grimm, *Correspondance,* vol. 14, p. 192; Bachaumont, *Mémoires,* vol. 26, pp. 315–317.

41. BN ms fr 6685, p. 20.

42. Métra, *Correspondance,* vol. 17, p. 105; vol. 18, p. 257.

43. Grimm, *Correspondance,* vol. 14, p. 193.

44. Most of the documents relevant to the later stages of the dispute between Gaillard and Dorfeuille and their competitors can be found in AN ms V^7 492, fol. 5.

45. Saint-Marc and Bourbonne, *Chroniques,* p. 161; Vatout, *Histoire,* pp. 155–157; Mayeur de Saint-Paul, *Tableau,* vol. 1, pp. 86–88.

46. "Voyage," *Revue:* 83.

47. *Courier d'Avignon,* 7 December 1784, p. 395.

48. AN ms 0^1 842, pièce 253, dated 20 March 1786.

49. AN ms 0^1 849, pièce 29; AN ms R^4 288, pièces 31 and 32.

50. BN ms fr 6685, p. 244.

51. *Journal de Paris,* 20 April 1789, p. 500.

52. Dufort de Cheverny, *Mémoires,* vol. 2, p. 83.

53. *Almanach du Palais Royal* (1786), pp. 89–93. The *Almanach* lists all the performers and plays.

54. Métra, *Correspondance,* vol. 17, p. 2.

55. Bachaumont, *Mémoires,* vol. 28, pp. 8–9.

56. The *Affiches,* 4 June 1786, p. 1495, bracketed the Variétés with the Petits Comédiens, separate from the other *spectacles.*

57. *Almanach du Palais Royal* (1786), pp. 86–87. It is worth noting, however, that the archbishop of Paris chose this moment to make one of his harshest periodic attacks on the little *spectacles,* which he claimed were tolerated for political reasons. See the *Courier d'Avignon,* 11 March 1785, p. 53. Charging that the *spectacles* enjoyed a license unknown in earlier generations, the archbishop's main argument was that the gross farces of the time bred indigence in poor artisans who were distracted from their work, leaving their children in misery. The love of pleasure had led to a disgust for work and the dissolution of morality.

58. *Journal général,* 27 March 1787, n.p.

59. *Almanach forain* (1787), p. 1.

60. Some of the pieces from the repertoire can be found in BN ms, Collection Soleinne.

61. Charles-Jacob Guillemain, *Alexis et Rosette, mélodrame en un acte* (Paris, 1786), pp. 3–45. This piece was performed at the Beaujolais on 18 May 1786.

62. From Mayeur de Saint-Paul, *Désoeuvré,* quoted in Heulhard, *Saint-Laurent,* p. 142; *Almanach du Palais Royal* (1786), p. 116; Mayeur de Saint-Paul, *Tableau,* vol. 1, pp. 97–100; Dulaure, *Nouvelle,* p. 350; Luc-Vincent Thiery, *Guide des amateurs et des étrangers voyageurs à Paris,* 2 vols. (Paris, 1786–1787), vol. 1, p. 273.

63. *Journal de Paris,* 8 December 1784; 23 January 1785, p. 96.

64. *Almanach du Palais Royal* (1786), pp. 112–114; Chesnais, *Histoire générale,* pp. 128–130; *Feu de théâtre de Séraphin depuis son origine jusqu'à sa disparition, 1776–1870* (Paris, 1872), pp. 5–12; Thiery, *Guide,* vol. 1, p. 284; *Journal de Paris,* 5 September 1784, p. 1058; 1 January 1785, p. 4; 10 October 1784, p. 1200; Fournel, *Vieux,* pp. 315–318; Mayeur de Saint-Paul, *Tableau,* vol. 1, pp. 76–78; *Almanach forain* (1787), p. 35; Manne and Ménétrier, *Galérie,* pp. 67–69.

65. AN ms 0¹ 127, fols. 136–137.

66. Christout, *Merveilleux,* p. 134.

67. The text can be found in *Feu de théâtre,* pp. 33–43.

68. Fournel, *Vieux,* p. 317.

69. *Almanach du Palais Royal* (1786), pp. 109–110; Campardon, *Spectacles,* vol. 2, p. 287; Chesnais, *Histoire générale,* p. 125; Thiery, *Guide,* vol. 1, p. 284.

70. *Journal de Paris,* 1 January 1785, p. 4; *Almanach du Palais Royal* (1786), p. 105; Thiery, *Guide,* vol. 1, p. 278; Mayeur de Saint-Paul, *Tableau,* vol. 1, p. 92.

71. *Affiches* (Supplément), 11 September 1784, p. 2406.

72. *Affiches,* 16 April 1789, p. 1047; 27 April 1789, p. 1243.

73. *Journal de Paris,* 12 December 1784, p. 1470.

74. Ibid., 18 March 1785, p. 318.

75. *Affiches,* 8 September 1785, p. 2413.

76. *Almanach forain* (1787), p. 34.

77. *Almanach du Palais Royal* (1786), p. 115; Campardon, *Spectacles,* vol. 2, p. 146; Thiery, *Guide,* vol. 1, pp. 272–273; Mayeur de Saint-Paul, *Tableau,* vol. 1, p. 90.

78. *Almanach du Palais Royal* (1786), p. 121.

79. Métra, *Correspondance,* vol. 18, pp. 29–30.

80. *Almanach du Palais Royal* (1786), pp. 124–136; Thiery, *Guide,* vol. 1, pp. 278–279, 282–284; Métra, *Correspondance,* vol. 17, pp. 286–287.

81. Britsch, *Jeunesse,* pp. 344–345.

82. Métra, *Correspondance,* vol. 17, pp. 338–341; BN ms fr 6685, p. 60.

83. Hillairet, *Dictionnaire,* vol. 2, p. 221; Mayeur de Saint-Paul, *Tableau,* vol. 2, pp. 107–109; Chabrol, *Histoire,* p. 110; *Affiches,* 18 August 1787, p. 2302; *Journal de Paris,* 11 August 1787, pp. 126–128; Bachaumont, *Mémoires,* vol. 32, pp. 94–95; vol. 35, pp. 99–100; Saint-Marc and Bourbonne, *Chroniques,* pp. 162–163; Nougaret, *Tableau,* vol. 1, p. 232; AN ms R⁴ 288, doss. 1, pièce 22.

84. Dulaure, quoted in Grimm, *Correspondance,* vol. 15, p. 128; Bachaumont, *Mémoires,* vol. 35, p. 100.

85. *Courier d'Avignon*, 1 May 1787, p. 144.
86. AN ms 0¹ 498, dated 19 April 1787. See also *Courier d'Avignon*, 15 May 1787, pp. 159–160.
87. *Almanach du Palais Royal* (1786), pp. 152–175; Mayeur de Saint-Paul, *Tableau*, vol. 2, pp. 102–107, 122–129, 143–144, 152–190; *Affiches*, 22 October 1784, p. 2784; 20 May 1785, p. 1349; Thiéry, *Guide*, vol. 1, p. 273–275.
88. Mercier, *Tableau*, vol. 10, pp. 232–233.
89. Mayeur de Saint-Paul, *Tableau*, vol. 2, pp. 7–8.
90. Mercier, *Tableau*, vol. 2, p. 179.
91. Nougaret, *Tableau*, vol. 1, p. 232.
92. Bachaumont, *Mémoires*, vol. 34, pp. 43–45.
93. *Correspondance de Madame Gourdan*, (London, 1784–1786), p. 33.
94. *Almanach du Palais Royal* (1786), pp. 137–140; Mayeur de Saint-Paul, *Tableau*, vol. 1, pp. 29–59; Dulaure, *Nouvelle*, p. 89, 350; Nougaret, *Tableau*, vol. 1, p. 233; Hillairet, *Dictionnaire*, vol. 2, pp. 221–224.
95. *Journal de Paris*, 13 October 1784, p. 1212.
96. Mayeur de Saint-Paul, *Tableau*, vol. 1, p. 40.
97. *Affiches*, 15 March 1785, p. 700.
98. Mayeur de Saint-Paul, *Tableau*, vol. 1, p. 58.
99. Mercier, *Tableau*, vol. 10, p. 264.
100. Mayeur de Saint-Paul, *Tableau*, vol. 1, pp. 62–71; *Almanach du Palais Royal* (1786), p. 149.
101. "Voyage," *Revue:* 78–83.
102. *Almanach du Palais Royal* (1786), pp. 141–142; Mayeur de Saint-Paul, *Tableau*, vol. 2, pp. 70–73.
103. AN ms R⁴ 288, pièces 22–26.
104. Mayeur de Saint-Paul, *Tableau*, vol. 2, pp. 162–168.
105. Bachaumont, *Mémoires*, vol. 29, pp. 180–181.
106. AN ms Y 15679, doss. 1, 2 and 3, dated January–October 1785.
107. See especially AN ms Y 15680, documents from January–October 1786.
108. BN ms fr 6685, p. 216.
109. Ibid., p. 218.
110. AN ms R⁴ 288, undated *Mémoire* by Sr. Bossenet.
111. Mayeur de Saint-Paul, *Tableau*, vol. 2, pp. 136–138.
112. Pidansat de Mairobert, *L'Espion*, vol. 2, p. 74. See also *Lettres édifiantes*, pp. 25–26.
113. Mercier, *Tableau*, vol. 10, pp. 229–230.
114. Ibid., p. 222.
115. Mayeur de Saint-Paul, *Tableau*, vol. 2, p. 125.
116. Rétif de la Bretonne, *Les Contemporaines*, vol. 42, p. 307.
117. Cognel, *Vie*, p. 16.
118. BN ms fr 6685, p. 31.
119. Saint-Marc and Bourbonne, *Chroniques*, p. 160.
120. Métra, *Correspondance*, vol. 17, p. 215.
121. *Almanach du Palais Royal* (1786), pp. 41–42; *Almanach parisien* (1786), p. 154.
122. *Lettre écrite du Palais-Royal aux quatre parties du monde* (Paris, 1785), pp. 5–7.
123. Saint-Marc and Bourbonne, *Chroniques*, p. 141. See also "Voyage," *Revue:* 35.
124. Mayeur de Saint-Paul, *Tableau*, vol. 1, pp. 3–6.
125. Ibid., pp. 133–134.
126. Ibid., vol. 2, p. 98.
127. Mercier, *Tableau*, vol. 10, p. 242; Mayeur de Saint-Paul, *Tableau*, vol. 2, p. 113.

EPILOGUE

1. *Journal de Paris*, 28 October 1781, p. 1213.
2. Jules Duhem, "Les Parodies aéronautiques dans la comédie ancienne," in *Bulletin du Bibliophile*, pp. 110–112.

3. AN ms 0¹ 849, doss. 2, pièce 52, p. 4.

4. E. G. Robertson, *Mémoires récréatifs, scientifiques et anecdotiques,* 2 vols. (Paris, 1831), vol. 1, p. 143.

5. François-Thomas-Marie de Baculard d'Arnaud, *Les Dégoûts du théâtre* (Paris, 1746), p. 18.

6. *Journal de Paris,* 31 March 1788, p. 402.

7. Ch. Desprez de Boissy, *Lettres sur les spectacles,* 2 vols., 4th ed., enl. (Paris, 1771), vol. 1, pp. 2–160.

8. *Le Pour et contre des spectacles* (Mons, 1782), pp. 4–29. See also Sélis, *Lettre;* BN ms fr 21625.

9. Rousseau, *Lettre sur les spectacles,* pp. 7–10, 17.

10. Des Essarts, *Dictionnaire,* vol. 1, pp. 51–150.

11. Du Coudray, *Lettre à Madame,* pp. 1–2.

12. Papillon de La Ferté, *L'Administration,* p. 69. See also BN ms fr 9557, p. 3.

Bibliography

Manuscripts

Archives Nationales

E. Conseil du roi
    1982–1999. Arrêts.
H². Bureau de Ville de Paris
    1778–1880. Registres et délibérations du Bureau.
    1881–1960. Documents.
    1961–2212. Administration.
    1965. Place Louis XV.
    2213. Place Louis-le-Grand
    2158. Théâtre des Variétés Amusantes et de l'Ambigu, 1785–1786.
    2160. Place Louis XV.
    2169. Magasin de décors de l'Opéra.
    2204. Arrêts.
K. Monuments historiques de Paris
    966. Foire Saint-Germain.
    967–972. Abbaye de Saint-Germain-des-Prés.
N³. Plans
    259. Salle de la Foire Saint-Germain.
    260. Salle de la Foire Saint-Germain (section judiciaire).
    262. Salle projeté dans le préau de la foire.
    1029. Salle d'Audinot.
    1030. Ambigu-comique.
O¹. Ministre de la maison du roi
    487–501. Minutes et correspondance (1775–1790).
    613. Opéra administration. Arrêts et règlements, 1672–1757.
    614. Académie Royale de Musique.
    615. Correspondance.

616. Intendant des Menus Plaisirs.

617. Intendant des Menus Plaisirs.

618. Privilèges de l'Opéra, relativement aux autres spectacles, ordonnances, lettres patentes, extraits du Conseil, mémoires, théâtres, écoles.

619. Directeurs de l'Académie Royale de Musique.

620. Délibérations du Comité de l'Opéra.

621. Répertoire.

622. Personnel.

623. Personnel.

624. Comptes, pensions, abonnements, bals.

625. Recettes et dépenses.

626. Recettes et dépenses.

627. Représentations.

628. Matériel, bâtiments, travaux de salles, comptes.

629. Salles projetées.

842. Grand Chambellan.Théâtres divers.

846–847. Comédie-Française.

848. Comédie-Italienne.

849. Correspondance, notes, mémoires (1761–1789); mémoires divers (1760–1779); auteurs, répertoire (1785–1789); loges louées, construction, projets (1788); salle construction (1782); recettes et dépenses (1740–1781).

850. Comtes (1762–1781).

851. Etats de recettes, appointements, représentations, mémoires, ordres divers (1761–1762). Gentilshommes de la Chambre.

852. Comptes (1762–1763).

853. Comptes (1763–1767).

854. Comptes (1767–1770).

857. Grands Ecuyers de France; pièces personnelles divers (1708–1782).

3263–3264. Fêtes publiques.

R^4. 288. Duc d'Orléans.

V^5. 680, 683. Grand Conseil.

V^7. 391. Opéra privilèges.

V^7. 492. Grande Chancellerie et Conseil.

Y. Châtelet de Paris.

11035. Procès verbaux.

12166–12193. Delaporte, Temple et Saint-Denis (1766–1791).

12227. Mutel, Saint-Laurent et Saint-Ovide (1763–1783).

13209–13237. Parent, Luxembourg (1723–1726). Saint-Germain-des-Prés (1727–1747) Saint-André-des-Arts (1748–1750).

13515–13582. Guyot, Les Halles (1756–1757), Saint-Germain (1758–1789).

13763–13781. Thiot, Saint-André-des-Arts (1755–1758), Saint-Germain (1759–1770).

13959–13982. Joron, Temple (1765–1770), Saint-Antoine (1771–1790).

13999–14027. Hubert, Saint-Germain (1730–1771).

14545. Tilloy, Saint-Germain (1755–1758).

14558–14559. Monnaye, Saint-Germain (1773–1775).

14560–14573. Leseigneur, Saint-Germain (1775–1783).

15260–15280. Duchesne, Saint-Paul, Saint-Denis, Saint-Martin.

15557–15626. Glou, Temple, Marais (1724–1753).

15626–15694. Sirebeau, Palais-Royal (1755–1784).

15969–16008. Vanglenne, Temple (1770–1790).

Z¹ᴴ. Bureau de Ville. Prévôt des Marchands.

Bibliothèque de l'Arsenal

Bastille 3866. Le Postillon de Paris, 1742–1743.

Bastille 4840–4843. Recueil de chansons historiques.

Bastille 6541–6544. Recueil de Tralage.

Bastille 10235. Meusnier.

Bastille 11480. Arnaud.

Bastille 11498. Mouhy, Charles de Fieux de. Le Postillon de Paris, 1741–1745.

Bastille 12203. Sartine.

Rondel, no number. Tinchet Abbel. L'Heureuse pêche.

Rondel 321. Le Bal masqué.

Rondel 3348–3355. D'Argenson, Notices sur les ouvrages.

Bibliothèque Historique de la Ville de Paris

538–542. Recueil de chansons historiques et chronologiques sur les différens événemens arrivés depuis l'année 1600 jusqu'en 1752.

614–631. Gazette à la main, 1731–1744.

C.P. 3684. Règlements de la foire, procès et règlements des droits des locataires, plans (1482–1744).

C.P. 4437. Journal de la Comédie-Italienne, représentations des pièces, débuts d'acteurs. 1781.

Bibliothèque Nationale

6680–6687. Hardy, Siméon-Prosper. Mes Loisirs, ou journal d'événemens tels qu'ils parviennent à ma connoissance (1764–1789).

6815–6817. Extraits et dépouillements de toutes les gazettes de France, contenant ce qui s'est passé de plus remarquable depuis 1631 jusqu'en 1723.

9242–9341. Collection de pièces de théâtre formée par M. de Soleinne.

9557. Mélanges: Spectacles inférieurs de Paris. 1764.

12355. Parfaict, Claude, and François Parfaict. Histoire de l'Académie Royale de Musique depuis son établissement jusqu'à présent.

12616–12659. Chansonnier dit de Maurepas.

12686–12743. Chansonnier dit de Clairambault.

13679–13690. Journaux historiques des années 1711–1722.

13694–13712. Nouvelles à la main.

15048-15061. Duval, Henri. Dictionnaire des ouvrages dramatiques depuis Jodelle jusqu'à nos jours.

15127–15134. Recueil de chansons choisies en vaudevilles pour servir à l'histoire anecdote, depuis 1600 jusque et compris le mois d'Aoust 1744.

16207. Mélanges juridiques, historiques et scientifiques.

21545–21808. Collection formée par Nicolas Delamare sur l'administration et la police de Paris et de la France.

22156–22165. Journal de l'Inspecteur d'Hémery, 1750–1769.

22566–22569. Recueil de chansons, épigrammes, satires, épitaphes, sur les personnages et sur les événements des règnes de Louis XIV et Louis XV.
25471. Pièces du théâtre de la foire qui n'ont point été imprimé par Le Sage et
 d'Orneval.
25476. Recueil de pièces du théâtre de la foire.
25480. Recueil de pièces du théâtre de la foire et de parodies.

BN Nouvelles Acquisitions

2842–3060. Collection de pièces de théâtre.
7561–7978. Collection de copies de pièces sur l'histoire de France sous le nom
 Portefeuilles de Fontanieu.

Printed Sources

Affiches, annonces et avis divers (Paris), 1751–1811.
Alletz, Pons-Augustin. *Les Leçons de Thalie, ou les tableaux des divers ridicules que la
 comédie présente.* 2 vols. Paris: Nyon, 1751.
Almanach dauphin, ou tablettes royales du vrai mérite des artistes célèbres, et d'indication générale des principaux marçhands, artistes et fabricans (Paris,
 1772–1774, 1777).
Almanach des Beaux-Arts (Paris, 1753).
*Almanach des ballons, ou globes aérostatiques; étrennes du jour physico-historiques et
 chantantes* (Paris, 1784).
Almanach des muses, ou choix des poésies fugitives de Paris (Paris, 1765–1833).
Almanach du Palais Royal (Paris, 1786).
*Almanach forain, ou les différens spectacles des boulevards et des foires de Paris; avec
 un catalogue des pièces, farces et parades tant anciennes que nouvelles qui y
 ont été jouées, et quelques anecdotes plaisantes qui ont rapport à cet objet*
 (Paris, 1773–1787).
Almanach historique et chronologique de tous les spectacles de Paris (Paris, 1752–1815).
Almanach musical (Paris, 1775–1783).
Almanach parisien en faveur des étrangers et des personnes curieuses (Paris,
 1762–1789).
Annales politiques, civiles et littéraires du dix-huitième siècle. 19 vols. London: n.p.,
 1777–1792.
L'Année littéraire, ou suite des lettres sur quelques écrits de ce temps. 56 vols. Paris:
 C. J. Panckoucke, 1754–1791.
Anseaume, Louis. *Théâtre de M. Anseaume, ou recueil des comédies, parodies, opéras-
 comiques.* 3 vols. Paris: Musier, 1749.
Antonini, Annibale. *Mémorial de Paris et de ses environs à l'usage des voyageurs,* 2
 vols., new rev. ed. Paris: Musier, 1749.
Apologie de messieurs les comédiens françois en forme de réplique à deux écrits. Paris:
 n.p., 1746.
D'Argenson, Marc-René. *Rapports inédits du lieutenant de police René d'Argenson
 (1697–1715).* Ed. Paul Cottin, Paris: Plon, 1891.
D'Argenson, René-Louis de Voyer de Paulmy. *Journal et mémoires.* Ed. E. J. B.
 Ratberg, 9 vols. Paris: V. Renouard, 1859–1867.
———. *Mémoires pour servir à l'histoire des spectacles de la foire.* 2 vols. Paris:
 Priasson, 1743.

————. *Notices sur les oeuvres de théâtre, depuis le théâtre grec jusqu'au XVIIIe siècle.* Paris: Gueullette, n.d.

D'Argenville, Antoine Nicolas Dézallier. *Voyage pittoresque de Paris.* 6th ed. Paris: De Bure, 1778.

Arnaud de Saint-Maurice. *L'Observatoire volant et le triomphe héroïque de la navigation aérienne et des vésicatoires amusants et célestes, poëme en quatre chants.* Paris: Cussac, 1784.

Arnould, Jean-François. *Arlequin soldat magicien, ou le canonier, pantomime.* Paris: Herissant, 1764.

Audinot, Nicolas-Médard, *Dorothée, pantomime à spectacle, précédée des preux chevaliers, prologue-pantomime.* Paris: Cailleau, 1782.

————. *La Musicomanie.* Paris: Cailleau, 1783.

————. *Le Porte-feuille, ou la fille comme il y en a peu.* Paris: Cailleau, 1788.

L'Avant-coureur, feuille hebdomadaire, où sont annoncés les objets particuliers des sciences de la littérature, des arts, des métiers de l'industrie, des spectacles, et les nouveautés en tous genres. 13 vols. Paris: Lambert, 1760–1774.

Bachaumont, Louis Petit de. *Mémoires secrets pour servir à l'histoire de la république des lettres en France depuis 1762 jusqu'à nos jours, ou journal d'un observateur.* 31 vols. London: J. Adamson, 1777–1789.

Baculard d'Arnaud, François-Thomas-Marie de. *Les Dégoûts du théâtre.* Paris: n.p., 1746.

Barbier, Edmond-Jean-François. *Chronique de la Régence et du règne de Louis XV (1718–1763), ou journal de Barbier.* 8 vols, Paris: Charpentier, 1857.

————. *Journal historique et anecdotique du règne de Louis XV.* 4 vols. Paris: Renouard, 1847.

Beaunoire, Alexandre-Louis-Bertrand Robineau. *L'Hymen et le dieu jaune.* Paris: Cailleau, 1782.

————. *Jannette, ou les battus ne paient pas toujours l'amende, parade.* Paris: n.p., 1781.

Beguillet, Edme. *Description historique de Paris et de ses plus beaux monuments gravés en taille-douce par F.-N. Martinet.* 3 vols. Paris: Duchesne, 1779–1881.

Bibliothèque dramatique de Monsieur Soleinne. 5 vols. Paris: Alliance des Arts, 1844–1845.

Bodard de Tezay, Nicolas-Marie-Félix. *Le Ballon ou la physicomanie.* Paris: Cailleau, 1783.

Boindin, Nicolas. *Lettres historiques à Monsieur D. sur la nouvelle comédie italienne dans lesquelles il est parlé de son établissement du caractère, des acteurs qui la composent, des pièces qu'ils ont représentées jusqu'à présent.* Paris: Prault, 1717–1718.

————. *Lettres historiques sur tous les spectacles de Paris.* Paris: Prault, 1719.

Boissy, Louis de. *La Frivolité, comédie en un acte et en vers.* Paris: n.p., 1753.

Boudet, Antoine. *Les Affiches de Paris, des provinces et des pays étrangers.* 5 vols. Paris: Thiboust, 1746–1751.

Bricaire de la Dixmérie, Nicolas. *Les Deux âges du goût et du génie français sous Louis XIV et sous Louis XV; parallèle des efforts du génie et du goût dans les sciences, dans les arts et dans les lettres, sous les deux règnes.* Amsterdam: Vlam, 1770.

————. *Lettres sur l'état présent de nos spectacles, avec des vues nouvelles sur chacun d'eux; particulièrement sur la Comédie Française et l'Opéra.* Amsterdam: n.p., 1765.

Brice, Germain. *Nouvelle description de la ville de Paris et tout ce qu'elle contient de plus remarquable.* 4 vols. 8th ed., rev. and enl. Paris: J. M. Gandouin, 1725.

Bridard de La Garde, Philippe. *Les Annales amusantes ou mémoires pour servir à l'histoire des amusements de la nation en tout genre.* Paris, n.p., 1741.

Brossette, Claude. *Du Vaudeville.* Ed. Achille Kühnholtz. Paris: Comon et Cie, 1846.

Burney, Charles. *An Eighteenth-Century Musical Tour in France and Italy.* Ed. Percy A. Scholes. London: Oxford University Press, 1959.

Buvat, Jean. *Journal de la Régence (1715–1723).* 2 vols. Paris: H. Plon, 1865.

Campardon, Emile. *Les Comédiens du roi et la troupe italienne pendant les deux derniers siècles.* 2 vols. Paris: Berger-Levrault, 1880.

———. *Les Spectacles de la foire. Théâtre, acteurs, sauteurs et danseurs de corde, monstres, géants, nains, animaux curieux ou savants, marionnettes, automates, figures de cire et jeux mécaniques des foires Saint-Germain et Saint-Laurent, des boulevards et du Palais-Royal, depuis 1595 jusqu'à 1791. Documents inédits recueillis aux Archives Nationales.* 2 vols. Paris: Berger-Levrault, 1877.

Carrogis, Louis [Carmontel]. *Amusemens de société, ou proverbes dramatiques.* 2 vols. Paris: Merlin, 1768 .

———. *Jardin de Monceau.* Paris: Jorry, n.d.

Carrière-Doisin, A. *Les Etrennes de mon cousin, ou l'Almanach pour rire.* Paris: Desenne, 1789.

Catalogue de curiosité, 1772–1773. Paris: n.p., n.d.

Catalogue de musique française et autres qui se vendent chez Christoph Ballard. Paris: Ballard, 1704.

Challamel, Augustin. *L'Ancien boulevard du Temple.* Paris: Société des gens de lettres, n.d.

Chansonnier François, ou recueil de chansons, ariettes, vaudevilles et autres couplets choisis. 4 vols. Paris: n.p., 1760–1762.

Charpentier, Louis. *Les Causes de la décadence du goût sur le théâtre.* Paris: Dufour, 1768.

Le Chat-Botté, pantomime. Paris: n.p., n.d.

Chaussard, Pierre-Jean-Baptiste. *Le Nouveau diable boiteux, tableau philosophique et moral de Paris.* 3 vols. Paris: Barba, 1803.

Chevrier, François-Antoine. *Almanach des gens d'esprit par un homme qui n'est pas sot, ou calendrier pour l'année 1762 et le reste de la vie.* Paris: Jean Nourse, 1762–1763.

———. *L'Observateur des spectacles, ou anecdotes théâtrales.* 3 vols. The Hague: Constapel, 1762–1763.

———. *Observations sur le théâtre dans lesquelles on examine avec impartialité l'état actuel des théâtres de Paris.* Paris: Bure, 1755.

———. *Le Retour du goût, comédie en 1 acte en vers libre avec un divertissement.* Paris: n.p., 1754.

———. *Les Ridicules du siècle.* London: Jean Nourse, 1774.

La Clé du Caveau à l'usage de tous les chansonniers français, des amateurs, auteurs, acteurs du vaudeville et de tous les amis de la chanson. Collected by Pierre-Adolph Capelle. Paris: Capelle et Renaud, 1811.

La Cléf des chansonniers, ou recueil de vaudevilles depuis cent ans et plus. Collected by Jean-Baptiste Christophe Ballard. 2 vols. Paris: Mont-Parnasse, 1717.

Clément, Pierre. *Les Cinq années littéraires, ou lettres de M. Clément sur les ouvrages de littérature qui ont paru dans les années 1748–1752.* 2 vols. Berlin: n.p., 1755.

Cognel, François. *La Vie Parisienne sous Louis XVI.* Paris: Levy, 1882.

Collé, Charles. *Chansons joyeuses mises au jour par un ane-onyme onissime.* new ed. Paris: Ispahan, n.d.

———. *Journal et mémoires sur les hommes de lettres, les ouvrages dramatiques et les événéments les plus mémorables du règne de Louis XV (1748–1772).* new rev. ed. Ed. Honoré Bonhomme. Paris: n.p., 1868.

———. *Parades inédites.* Paris: n.p., 1864.

———. *Théâtre de société.* 3 vols. The Hague: P.-F. Gueffier, 1777.

Colletet, François. *Le Tracas de Paris en vers burlesques, contenant la foire S. Laurent, les marionnettes, les subtilités du Pont-Neuf, le départ des coches, l'intrigue des servantes, le pain de gonnesse, l'affeterie des bourgeoises de Paris, le vin d'Espagne, les mauvais lieux qu'on fait sauter, les crieurs d'eau-de-vie, les aveugles, les gobelins, les étrennes, et divers autres descriptions plaisantes et récréatives.* Paris: Nicolas Oudot, 1714.

Confession générale d'Audinot. Geneva: Crammer, 1774.

Contant d'Orville, André Guillaume. *Histoire de l'opéra bouffon, contenant les jugemens de toutes les pièces qui ont paru depuis sa naissance jusqu'à ce jour. Pour servir à l'histoire des théâtres de Paris.* Amsterdam: Grangé, 1768.

Correspondance de Madame Gourdan, dite la Comtesse augmentée de dix lettres inédites dont deux facsimilées suivie de la description de sa maison et de diverses curiosités qui s'y trouvent avec un recueil de chansons à l'usage de ses soupers. London: Jean Nourse, 1784.

Le Courier d'Avignon (Avignon), 1733–1768, 1775.

Le Courier de l'Europe ou Mémoires pour servir à l'histoire universelle (London), 1776–1792.

Cradock, Anna Francesca. *Journal de Madame Cradock. Voyage en France (1783–1786).* Translated by O. Delphin-Balleyquier. Paris: Perrin, 1896.

Critique sur la folie du jour, ou la promenade des boulevards. Paris: n.p., 1754.

Dancourt, Florent-Carton. *La Foire de Besons.* Paris: T. Guillain, 1695.

———. *La Foire Saint-Germain.* Paris: T. Guillain, 1696.

Decremps, Henri. *La Magie blanche dévoilée ou explication des tours surprenants qui font depuis peu l'admiration de la capitale et de la province.* Paris: Langlois, 1784–1785.

Des Essarts [Nicolas-Toussaint Le Moyne]. *Dictionnaire universel de police.* 7 vols. Paris: Moutard, 1786–1789.

Desprez de Boissy, C. *Lettres sur les spectacles.* 2 vols. 4th ed. Paris: Butard, 1771.

Dorat, Claude-Joseph. *La Déclamation théâtrale, poème didactique en quatre chants.* 4th ed. Paris: Delalain, 1771.

Dorvigny, Louis-Archambault. *Les Battus paient l'amende, proverbe-comédie-parade, ou ce que l'on voudra.* Paris: L. Jorry, 1779.

———. *Les Folies à la mode.* Paris: Cailleau, 1782.

———. *Le Père Duchesne, ou la mauvaise habitude.* Paris: Cailleau, 1789.

Dubois de Saint-Gelais. *Histoire journalière de Paris, 1716.* 2 vols. Paris: E. Ganeau, 1716–1717.

Du Coudray, Alexandre-Jacques. *Anecdotes intéressantes et historiques de l'illustre voyageur pendant son séjour à Paris.* Paris: Ruault, 1777.

———. *Il est temps de parler et il est temps de se taire.* Paris: Ruault, 1779.

————. *Lettre à Madame la comtesse de T. sur un second théâtre françois à Paris et sur le retour de l'ancien Opéra Comique.* Paris: Durand, 1775.

————. *Lettre à M. Palissot sur le refus de ses 'Courtisannes,' comédie en 3 actes et en vers.* Paris: Duchesne, n.d.

————. *Lettre au public sur le mort de M. M. de Crébillon, censeur royal, Gresset, de l'Académie française, Parfaict, auteur de l'histoire du théâtre français.* Paris: Durand, 1777.

————. *Lettre d'un Parisien à son ami en province sur le nouveau spectacle des Elèves de l'Opéra.* Paris: n.p., 1779.

————. *Lettre historique et critique sur l'installation des Comédiens françois à la nouvelle salle, suivie du projet d'une école dramatique sous les ordres de M. M. les premiers gentilshommes de la chambre, et de la suppression des théâtres forains, conforme aux vues du gouvernement.* Paris: Belin, n.d.

————. *Mélange drammatique, contenant Vénus Pélerine, Lettre au public, Il est tems de parler, et Il est tems de se taire,* Paris: Ruault, 1779.

————. *Nouveaux essais historiques sur Paris pour servir de suite et de supplément à ceux de M. de Saintfoix.* 3 vols. Paris: Belin, 1781–1786.

————. *Repertoire général de toutes les pièces de théâtre qui se représentent ordinairement, tant à Paris que dans la plupart des autres grandes villes du royaume de France.* Paris: n.p., n.d.

Duduit de Maizières. *Les Muses françoises.* Paris: Duchêne, 1764.

Dufort de Cheverny, Jean-Nicolas. *Mémoires sur les règnes de Louis XV et Louis XVI et sur la Révolution.* 2 vols. Paris: E. Plon, 1886.

Dulaure, Jacques-Antoine. *Nouvelle description des curiosités de Paris.* Paris: Lejay, 1785.

Dumont, Gabriel-Martin. *Parallèle de plans des plus belles salles de spectacles d'Italie et de France, avec des détails de machines théâtrales.* Paris, n.p., n.d.

Engel, M. *Idées sur le geste et l'action théâtrale.* 2 vols. Paris: Barrois, 1788.

Etrennes aux sociétés qui font leur amusement de jouer la comédie, ou catalogue raisonné et instructif de toutes les tragédies, comédies des théâtres François et Italien, actes, d'Opéra, Opéra-Comiques, Pièces à Ariettes et Proverbes qui peuvent facilement se représenter sur les théâtres particuliers. Paris: Bradel, 1782.

L'Esprit des journaux françois et étrangers; oeuvre périodique et littéraire. 480 vols. Liège: J. J. Tutot, 1772–1818.

Etat actuel de la musique de la chambre du roi et des trois spectacles de Paris. Paris: Vente, 1759–1777.

Fagan, Barthélemy-Christophe. *Nouvelles observations au sujet des condamnations prononcées contre les comédiens.* Paris: Chaubert, 1751.

Favart, Charles-Simon. *Mémoires et correspondance littéraires, dramatiques et anecdotiques de C. S. Favart.* 3 vols. Paris: Léopold Collin, 1808.

————. *Théâtre de M. Favart, ou recueil des comédies, parodies et opéras-comiques donnés jusqu'à ce jour, avec les airs, rondes et vaudevilles notés dans chaque pièce.* 8 vols. Paris: Duchesne, 1763.

Les Fêtes du Colisée. Poème en un chant dédié au beau sexe. Paris: n.p., 1771.

Fouques, François-Georges [Desfontaines]. *Histoire universelle des théâtres de toutes les nations depuis Thespis jusqu'à nos jours, par une société de gens de lettres.* 13 vols. Paris: Duchesne, 1779–1781.

Framery, Nicolas-Etienne. *De l'Organization des spectacles de Paris ou essai sur leur forme actuelle; sur les moyens de l'améliorer, par rapport au public et aux acteurs; dans lequel on discute les droits respectifs de tous ceux qui concourent à leur existence, et où l'on traite les principales questions relatives à ce sujet.* Paris: Beusson, 1790.

Fréron, Elie-Catherine, and La Porte, Joseph de. *Lettres sur quelques écrits de ce temps.* 13 vols. Paris: Duchesne, 1749–1754.

Frézier. *Traité des feux d'artifice pour le spectacle.* Paris: Jollet, 1747.

Gabiot de Salins, Jean-Louis. *Esope aux boulevards.* Paris: Bélin, 1784.

Gachet, L. *Observations sur les spectacles en général, et en particulier sur le Colisée.* Paris: Le Prieur, 1772.

Garcin, Laurent. *Traité du mélodrame, ou réflexions sur la musique dramatique.* Paris: Vallat-La-Chapelle, 1772.

Gabriel. *Examen des causes destructives du théâtre de l'Opéra, des moyens qu'on pourait employer pour le rétablir; ouvrage spéculatif, par un amateur de l'harmonie.* Paris: Duchesne, 1776.

Gazette de France (Paris), 1750–1792.

Gazette de littérature, des sciences et des arts (Paris), July 1786–July 1789.

Gherardi, Evariste. *Le Théâtre italien ou le recueil général de toutes les comédies et scènes françoises jouées par les comédiens italiens du roi.* 6 vols. Amsterdam: Michel Charles, 1721.

Gouriet, Jean-Baptiste. *Les Charlatans célèbres, ou tableau historique des bateleurs, des baladins, des jongleurs, des bouffons, des opérateurs, des voltigeurs, des escamoteurs, des filous, des escrocs, des devins, des tireurs de cartes, des diseurs de bonne aventure, et généralement de tous les personnages qui se sont rendus célèbres dans les rues et sur les places publiques de Paris depuis une haute antiquité jusqu'à nos jours.* 2 vols. 2d ed. Paris: Lerouge, 1819.

Grimm, Frédéric Melchior. *Correspondance littéraire, philosophique et critique.* 16 vols. Paris: Garnier, 1877–1882.

Guillemain, Charles-Jacob. *Alexis et Rosette, mélodrame en un acte.* Paris: Cailleau, 1786.

———. *Le Mariage de Janot, avec la pantomime des ombres.* Paris: Cailleau, 1783.

Guyot, Edme-Gilles. *Récréations physiques et mathématiques.* 3 vols. Paris: Gueffier, 1769.

Hardy, Siméon-Prosper. *Mes Loisirs, journal d'événements tels qu'ils parviennent à ma connaissance (1764–1789).* Ed. Maurice Tourneux and Maurice Vitrac. Paris: Picard, 1912.

Herme de La Mothe, F. L. *Epître sur les spectacles ou mon retour à Paris.* Geneva: n.p., 1761.

L'Homme a cornes, tragi-comédie. Paris: n.p., 1787.

Hurtaut, Pierre-Thomas-Nicolas, and Magny. *Le Dictionnaire historique de la ville de Paris et de ses environs.* 4 vols. Paris: Moutard, 1779.

Imbert de Boudeaux, Guillaume. *La Chronique scandaleuse ou mémoires pour servir à l'histoire de la génération présente.* Ed. Jean Hervez. Paris: Bibliothèque des Curieux, 1912.

Jèze. *Journal du citoyen.* The Hague: n.p., 1754.

Joly, Joseph Romain. *Lettres historiques et critiques sur les spectacles adressées à Mlle. Clairon, dans lesquelles on prouve que les spectacles sont contraires à la religion Catholique, selon les canons et les sentimens des PP. de l'Eglise.* Avignon: Libraires Associés, 1762.

Journal de musique par une société d'amateurs. Paris; Ruault, 1773–1774, 1777.

Journal de Paris (Paris), 1777–1811.

Journal de politique et de littérature, contenant les principaux événemens de toutes les cours; les nouvelles de la république des lettres (Paris), 1774–1781.

Journal des beaux-arts et des sciences (Paris), 1768–1774.

Journal des dames (Paris), 1759–1769, 1774–1775.

Journal des théâtres, ou le nouveau spectateur, servant de répertoire universel des spectacles (Paris), 1777–1778.

Journal encyclopédique (Liège), 1756–1793.

Journal étranger; ouvrage périodique (Paris), 1754–1762.

Journal général de France (Paris), 1785–1792.

Journal économique ou mémoires, notes et avis divers sur les arts, l'agriculture et le commerce (Paris), 1751–1757, 1758–1772.

Julien, Jean-Auguste [Desboulmiers]. *Histoire anecdotique et raisonnée du théâtre italien depuis son rétablissement en France jusqu'à l'année 1769. Contenant les analyses des principes pièces et un catalogue de toutes celles, tant italiennes que françaises données sur ce théâtre avec les anecdotes les plus curieuses et les notices les plus intéressantes de la vie et des talens des auteurs et acteurs.* 7 vols. Paris: Lacombe, 1769.

———. *Histoire du théâtre de l'opéra-comique.* 2 vols. Paris: Lacombe, 1769.

Karamzin, N. M. *Letters of a Russian Traveler 1789–1790.* Trans. Florence Jonas. New York: Columbia University Press, 1957.

Lacepede, Bernard Germain Etienne Laville de. *La Poëtique de la musique.* 2 vols. Paris: Imprimerie de Monsieur, 1785.

Lacombe, Jacques. *Le Spectacle des beaux arts ou considérations touchant leur nature, leurs effets et leurs règles principales.* Paris: Hardy, 1758.

La Garde, Philippe Bridard de. *Annales amusantes ou mémoires pour servir à l'histoire des amusemens de la nation en tout genre.* Paris: n.p., 1742.

———. *L'Echo du public sur les ouvrages nouveaux, sur les spectacles et sur les talents.* Paris: Didot, 1740.

———. *Lettres de Thérèse ou mémoires d'une jeune demoiselle de province pendant son séjour à Paris.* The Hague: J. Neaulme, 1739.

La Harpe, Jean-François de. *Correspondance littéraire (1774–1791) adressée à son altesse impériale Mgr. le Grand-Duc, aujourd'hui empereur de Russie, et à M. le Comte André Schowalow.* 5 vols. Paris: Migneret, 1801–1807.

La Mare, Nicolas de. *Traité de la police, où l'on trouvera l'histoire de son établissement, les fonctions et prérogatives de ses magistrats, toutes les loix et tous les règlemens qui la concernent.* 4 vols. Paris: J.-F. Hérissant, 1705–1738.

La Porte, Joseph de. *Dictionnaire dramatique, contenant l'histoire des théâtres, les règles du genre dramatique, les observations des maîtres célèbres, et des réflexions nouvelles sur le génie et la conduite de tous les genres, avec les notices des meilleures pièces, le catalogue de tous les drames, at celui des auteurs dramatiques.* 3 vols. Paris: Lacombe, 1776.

———, and Clémont, Jean-Marie-Bernard. *Anecdotes dramatiques contenant toutes les pièces de théâtre, tragédies, pastorales jouées à Paris et en province depuis l'origine des spectacles en France jusqu'en 1775.* 3 vols. Paris: Duchesne, 1775.

Le Brun, Pierre. *Discours sur la comédie, ou traité historique et dogmatique des jeux de théâtre et des autres divertissemens comiques soufferts ou condamnés depuis le premier siècle de l'église jusqu'à présent.* Paris: Delaulne, 1694.

Leris, Antoine de. *Dictionnaire portatif historique et littéraire des théâtres contenant l'origine des différens théâtres de Paris.* 2d ed. Paris: Jombert, 1763.

Lerouge, Georges-Louis. *Nouveau voyage de France, géographique, historique, et curieux.* 3 vols. Paris: Libraires Associés, 1771.

———. *Description du Colisée élevé aux Champs-Elysées sur les dessins de M. Le Camus.* Paris: Le Rouge, 1771.

Lesage, Alain-René, and d'Orneval. *Le Théâtre de la foire ou l'Opéra comique contenant les meilleures pièces qui ont été représentées aux foires de S. Germain et de S. Laurent.* 15 vols. Paris: Etienne Ganeau, 1721–1737.

Lettre à Messieurs les comédiens françois par un de leurs zélés partisans au sujet de l'opéra comique. The Hague: n.p., 1745.

Lettre à M. Linguet, auteur du Journal de politique et de littérature sur son article 'Spectacles' inséré dans le no. 3 du dit Journal. Paris: n.p., 1774.

Lettre à M. sur le cirque qui se construit au milieu du jardin du Palais Royal. Paris: Le Jay, 1787.

Lettre de Madame à une de ses amies sur les spectacles et principalement sur l'opéra comique. Paris: n.p., 1745.

Lettre d'un Parisien à son ami en province sur le nouveau spectacle des Elèves de l'Opéra. Paris: n.p., 1779.

Lettre d'un provincial à un ami sur la promenade des boulevards. Paris: n.p., 1760.

Lettre écrite du Palais-Royal aux quatre parties du monde. Paris: Cailleau, 1785.

Lettres édifiantes du Palais Royal par un missionnaire du camp des Tartares. Paris: Gattieres, 1788.

Liger, Louis. *Le Voyageur fidèle, ou le guide des étrangers dans la ville de Paris.* Paris: Ribou, 1715.

Lister, Martin. *A Journey to Paris in the Year 1698.* 2d ed. London: J. Tonson, 1699.

Luynes, Charles-Philippe d'Albert de. *Mémoires sur la cour de Louis XV (1735–1758).* 17 vols. Paris: Firmin Didot, 1860–1865.

Marais, Mathieu. *Journal et mémoires sur la Régence et le règne de Louis XV (1715–1737).* Ed. M. de Lescure. 4 vols. Paris: Didot, 1863–1868.

Marchand, Jean-Henri, and Desboulmiers, J. A. *L'Esprit et la chose.* Paris: n.p., 1767.

Marescot, Michel. *La Folie du jour ou la promenade des boulevards.* Paris: n.p., 1754.

Maupoint. *Bibliotèque des théâtres, contenant le catalogue alphabétique des pièces dramatiques, opéras, parodies, et opéra-comiques.* Paris: Prault, 1733.

Maurepas, Jean-Frédéric Phelypeaux. *Mémoires.* 3 vols. 3d ed. Paris: Buisson, 1792.

Mayeur de Saint-Paul, François-Marie. *Le Désoeuvré, ou l'espion du Boulevard du Temple.* London: n.p. 1781.

———. *Le Fou par amour, ou la fatale épreuve.* Paris: Cailleau, 1768.

———. *Tableau du nouveau Palais-Royal.* 2 vols. Paris: Maradan, 1788.

Mercier, Louis-Sébastien. *Tableau de Paris.* 12 vols. new ed. Paris: n.p., 1782–1788.

Le Mercure de France (Paris), 1678–1820.

Métra, François. *Correspondance secrète, politique et littéraire, ou mémoires pour servir à l'histoire des cours, des sociétés et de la littérature en France depuis la mort de Louis XV.* 18 vols. London: Adamson, 1787–1790.

Monnet, Jean. *Supplément au Roman comique, ou mémoires pour servir à la vie de Jean Monnet, ci-devant directeur de l'Opéra-Comique à Paris, de l'Opéra de Lyon, et d'une Comédie Françoise à Londres. Ecrits par lui-même.* 2 vols. London: n.p., 1772.

Moufle d'Angerville, Barthélémy-François. *Le Cannevas de la Paris, ou mémoires pour servir à l'histoire de l'Hôtel du Roule*. 2 vols. Brussels: Gay, 1886.

Mouhy, Charles de Fieux de. *Abrégé de l'histoire du théâtre français depuis son origine jusqu'au premier juin de l'année 1780, précédé du dictionnaire de toutes les pièces de théâtre jouées et imprimées, du dictionnaire des auteurs dramatiques et du dictionnaire des acteurs et actrices*. 4 vols., new ed. Paris: L. Jorry, 1780.

———. *L'Ami de vertu ou mémoires et aventures de Monsieur d'Argicourt*. Liège: D. de Boubers, 1764.

———. *Les Dangers des spectacles, ou les mémoires de M. le duc de Champigny*. 4 vols. Paris: L. Jorry, 1780.

———. *Paris, ou le mentor à la mode*. Paris: P. Ribou, 1735.

———. *Le Papillon, ou lettres parisiennes, ouvrage qui contiendra tout ce qui se passe d'intéressant, de plus agréable et de plus nouveau dans tous les genres*. 4 vols. Paris: n.p., 1746–1751.

Le Mouton, le canard, et le coq. Fable dialoguée. Paris: Hardouin, 1783.

Musard, Jacques-Antoine [Dumont]. *Le Désoeuvré mis en oeuvre ou le revers de médaille, pour servir d'opposition à l'Espion du boulevard du Temple, et de préservatif à la prévention*. Paris: Les Marchands de Nouveautés, 1782.

Nemeitz, Joachim Christoph. *Séjour de Paris, c'est à dire instructions fidèles pour les voiageurs de condition, comment ils se doivent conduire, s'ils veulent faire un bon usage de leur tems et argent durant leur séjour à Paris*. Leiden: Jean Van Abcoude, 1727.

Nisard, Charles. *Des Chansons populaires chez les anciens et chez les français. Essai historique suivi d'une étude sur la chanson des rues contemporaine*. 2 vols. Paris: E. Dentu, 1867.

Nougaret, Pierre-Jean-Baptiste. *Ainsi va le monde*. Amsterdam: n.p., 1769.

———. *Anecdotes des beaux-arts, contenant tout ce que la peinture, la sculpture, la gravure, l'architecture, la littérature, la musique, et la vie des artistes offrent de plus curieux et de plus piquant chez tous les peuples du monde depuis l'origine de ces différens arts, jusqu'à nos jours*. 3 vols. Paris: J.-F. Bastien, 1776–1780.

———. *Anecdotes secrètes du dix-huitième siècle, rédigées avec soin d'après la "Correspondance secrète, politique et littéraire," pour faire suite aux "Mémoires de Bachaumont."* 2 vols. Paris: L. Collin, 1808.

———. *De l'Art du théâtre ou il est parlé des différents genres de spectacles, et de la musique adaptée au théâtre*. 2 vols. Paris: Cailleau, 1769.

———. *Les Astuces de Paris, anecdotes parisiennes dans lesquelles on voit les ruses que les intriguans et certaines jolies femmes mettent communément en usage pour tromper les gens simples et les étrangers*. Paris: Cailleau, 1775.

———. *Aventures galantes de Jerôme, frère Capucin*. Paris: G. Davois, 1814.

———. *Doutes patriotiques sur le nouveau règne*. Paris: J. B. Brunet, 1774.

———. *La Folle de Paris, ou les extravagances de l'amour et de la crédulité*. 2 vols. Paris: Bastien, 1787.

———. *Les Historiettes du jour, ou Paris tel qu'il est*. 2 vols. Paris: Duchesne, 1787.

———. *Il n'y a plus d'enfans, comédie; la Guinguette, ambigu-comique; le Chat botté, pantomime*. Paris: P. -R. -C. Ballard, 1772.

———. *La Littérature renversé, ou l'art de faire des pièces de théâtre sans paroles avec un traité du geste*. Paris: n.p., 1775.

———. *Lucette, ou les progrès du libertinage*. London: J. Nourse, 1765.

———. *Les Mille et une folies, contes français.* 4 vols. Paris: Duchesne, 1771.

———. *La Mort de l'Opéra-Comique, élégie pour rire et pour pleurer, par un jeune homme de 17 ans.* Paris: Partout, 1762.

———. *Les Sottises et les folies parisiennes, aventures diverses avec quelque pièces curieuses et fort rares, le tout fidèlement.* Paris: Duchesne, 1781.

———. *Tableau mouvant de Paris, ou variétés amusantes.* 3 vols. Paris: Duchesne, 1787.

Nougaret, Pierre-Jean-Baptiste, and Rétif de la Bretonne, Nicolas-Edme. *La Mimographe, ou idées d'une honnête femme pour la réformation du théâtre national.* Amsterdam: Changuion, 1770.

Nouveau théâtre de la foire, ou recueil de pièces et opéra-comiques. 5 vols. Paris: Duchesne, 1763.

Nouvelles de la cour et de la ville, contenant le monde, les arts, les théâtres et les lettres (1734–1738). Paris: Rouveyre, 1879.

Nouvelles parodies bachiques, mêlées de vaudevilles. 3 vols. Paris: C. Ballard, 1700–1702.

L'Observateur littéraire (Amsterdam), 1758–1761.

Ordre chronologique des principales troupes qui ont paru successivement sur les différens théâtres de la foire. Paris: n.p., 1751.

Origny, Antoine-Jean-Baptiste-Abraham d'. *Annales du Théâtre-italien depuis son origine jusqu'à ce jour.* 3 vols. Paris: Duchesne, 1788.

Panard, Charles-François. *Théâtre et oeuvres diverses.* 4 vols. Paris: Duchesne, 1763.

Papillon de La Ferté, Denis-Pierre-Jean. *L'Administration des menus, journal.* Ed. Ernest Boysse. Paris: P. Ollendorff, 1887.

Parfaict, Claude, and Parfaict, François. *Dictionnaire des théâtres de Paris.* 7 vols. Paris: Rozet, 1767.

———. *Histoire du théâtre françois depuis son origine jusqu'à présent.* 15 vols. Paris: P. G. Le Mercier, 1735–1749.

———. *Histoire de l'ancien Théâtre italien depuis son origine en France jusqu'à sa suppression en l'année 1697.* Paris: Rozet, 1767.

———. *Mémoires pour servir à l'histoire des spectacles de la foire.* 2 vols. Paris: Briasson, 1743.

Paris sous Louis XV. Rapports des inspecteurs de police au roi. 2 vols. Ed. Camille Piton. Paris: Mercure de France, 1906–1908.

Perrinet d'Orval. *Essai sur les feux d'artifice pour le spectacle et pour la guerre.* Paris: Coustelier, 1745.

Peuchet, Jacques. *Mémoires tirés des archives de la police de Paris.* 6 vols. Paris: Levasseur, 1838.

Pidansat de Mairobert, Mathieu-François. *L'Espion anglois, ou correspondance entre Milord all'eye et Milord alle'ar.* 6 vols. London: Adamson, 1783–1784.

Piganiol de La Force, Jean-Aymar. *Description historique de la ville de Paris et de ses environs.* 10 vols. new ed. Paris: G. Desprez, 1765.

Piozzi, Hester Lynch Salusbury Thrale. *The French Journals of Mrs. Thrale and Doctor Johnson.* Ed. Moses Tyson and Henry Guppy. Manchester: The Manchester University Press, 1932.

Poitevin, Auguste [Drack, Maurice]. *Le Théâtre de la foire, la comédie italienne et l'opéra-comique. Recueil de pièces choisies, jouées de la fin du XVIIe siècle aux premières années du XIXe siècle, avec étude historique, notes et table chronologique (1658–1720).* Paris: Firmin-Didot, 1889.

Piron, Alexis. *Oeuvres complètes.* 7 vols. Ed. Rigoley de Juvigny. Paris: Lambert, 1776.

Pleinchesne, Roger-Timothé-Regnarde de. *Don Quichotte, pantomime en trois actes, précédée d'un prologue pantomime; le tout sur des airs connus.* Paris: Grands Danseurs, 1778.

Le Porte-Feuille de Madame Gourdan dite la Comtesse pour servir des moeurs du siècle et principalement de celles de Paris. n.p.: n.p., 1783.

Le Pour et contre les spectacles. Mons: C. J. Beugnies, 1782.

Le Pour et contre, ouvrage périodique d'un goût nouveau. 20 vols. Paris: Didot, 1733–1740.

Précis pour les locataires du Palais Royal. Paris: Prault, 1788.

Le Prévost d'Exmes, François. *Le Nouveau spectateur, ou examen des nouvelles pièces de théâtre dans lequel on a ajouté les ariettes notées.* Paris: Valade, 1770.

Le Provincial à Paris, ou état actuel de Paris; ouvrage indispensable à ceux qui veulent connoître parcourir Paris sans faire aucune question. 4 vols. Paris: Watin, 1787.

Prud'homme, Louis-Marie. *Miroir historique, politique, et critique de l'ancien et du nouveau Paris, et du départment de la Seine.* 6 vols., 3d ed. Paris: Prudhomme fils, 1807.

Pujoulx, Jean-Baptiste. *Paris à la fin du XVIIIᵉ siècle.* Paris: B. Mathé, 1801.

Le Quiproquo de l'hôtellerie, comédie en deux actes en prose. Paris: Cailleau, 1782.

Rainguet, Pierre-Damien. *Biographie Saintongeaise, ou dictionnaire historique de tous les personnages qui se sont illustrés par leurs écrits ou leurs actions dans les anciennes provinces de Saintonge et d'Aunis.* Saintes: Niox, 1851.

Recueil Clairambault-Maurepas. Chansonnier historique du XVIIIᵉ siècle. 10 vols. Ed. Emile Raunié. Paris: A. Quantin, 1879–1884.

Recueil des plus belles et excellentes chansons en formes de voix de villes, tirée de divers auteurs et poètes français. Paris: Clos Bruneaux, 1576.

Recueil d'opéras-comiques de différens auteurs. 5 vols. Paris: Vente, 1781.

Recueil général des ariettes, airs, récitatifs, romances et vaudevilles. 2 vols. Geneva: Gallay, 1778.

Le Redoteur. 2 vols. Amsterdam: Rey, 1775.

Regnard, Jean-François. *La Foire Saint-Germain.* Paris: n.p., 1878.

Réponse d'un artiste à un homme de lettres qui lui avoit écrit sur les Waux-halls. Paris: Dufour, 1769.

Rétif de la Bretonne, Nicolas-Edme. *Les Contemporaines par gradation, ou aventures des jolies femmes de l'âge actuel suivant la gradation des principaux états de la société.* 42 vols. Paris: Duchesne, 1783–1785.

———. *Les Nuits de Paris, ou le spectateur nocturne.* 7 vols. London: n.p., 1788–1789.

———. *Le Palais-Royal.* Paris: Guillot, 1790.

Richer, Adrien. *Théâtre du monde, où par des exemples tirés des auteurs anciens et modernes, les vertus et les vices sont mis en opposition.* 4 vols. Paris: n.p., 1775–1788.

Rivarol, Antoine de. *Lettre écrite à Monsieur le Président de . . . sur le globe aérostatique sur les têtes parlantes et sur l'état présent de l'opinion à Paris.* Paris: Cailleau, 1783.

Rivery, Claude-François-Félix Boulenger de. *Recherches historiques et critiques sur quelques anciens spectacles, et particulièrement sur les mimes et sur les pantomimes.* Paris: Mérigot, 1751.

Robertson, E. G. *Mémoires récréatifs, scientifiques et anecdotiques.* 2 vols. Paris: by the author, 1831.

Rousseau, Thomas. *Lettre à M. sur les spectacles des boulevards.* Paris: n.p., 1781.

Saint-Foix, Germain-François Poulain de. *Essais historiques sur Paris.* 3 vols. Paris: Duchesne, 1759.

Saint-Marc, B., and Bourbonne. *Les Chroniques du Palais-Royal.* Paris: Belin, n.d.

Sartine, Antoine-Raymond-Jean-Gualbert de. *Journal des inspecteurs de M. de Sartine, 1761–1764.* Paris: Dentu, 1863.

Saugrin, Claude-Marin. *Curiosités de Paris, de Versailles, Marly, Vincennes, Saint-Cloud, et des environs.* 2 vols., new ed. Paris: Libraires Associés, 1779.

Sauval, Henri. *La Chronique scandaleuse de Paris.* Paris: H. Daragon, 1910.

————. *Histoire et recherches des antiquités de la ville de Paris.* 3 vols. Paris: C. Moette, 1724.

Scarron, Paul. *La Foire Saint-Germain.* Berthaud. *La Ville de Paris en vers burlesque, augmentée de la Foire S. Germain, par le sieur Scarron.* Paris: A. Rafflé, 1692.

Schosne, Augustin-Théodore-Vincent Le Beau de. *Lettre sur les spectacles de Paris.* Paris: Cailleau, 1761.

Sébastien-Roch, Nicolas Chamfort. *Dictionnaire dramatique contenant l'histoire des théâtres, les règles du genre dramatique, les observations des maîtres les plus célèbres, et des réflexions nouvelles sur les spectacles, sur le génie et la conduite de tout les genres, avec les notices des meilleures pièces, le catalogue de tous les drames, et celui des auteurs dramatiques.* 3 vols. Paris: Lacombe, 1776.

Sedaine, Michel-Jean. *Théâtre.* Edited by Georges d'Heylli. Paris: Librairie Générale, 1877.

————. *Le Vaudeville, poème didactique en 4 chants.* Paris: n.p., 1756.

Sedaine, Michel-Jean, and Monsigny, Pierre-Alexandre. *On ne s'avise jamais de tout, opéra-comique.* 2d ed. rev. Paris: Claude Herissant, 1761.

Sélis, Nicolas-Joseph. *Lettre à un père de famille sur les petits spectacles de Paris.* Paris: Garnéry, 1789.

Sigaud de La Fond, Joseph-Aignan. *Description et usage d'un cabinet de physique expérimentale,* 2 vols. Paris: P. -F. Gueffier, 1775.

Sorel, Charles. *Polyandre, histoire comique.* Paris: N. Cercy, 1648.

Le Spectateur françois, ou recueil de tout ce qui a paru imprimé sous ce titre (Paris), June 1721–September 1724.

Sur l'Ambigu-Comique. Paris: n.p., n.d.

Le Tableau des théâtres, almanach nouveau (Paris, 1748–1749, 1752).

Taconet, Toussaint-Gaspard. *L'Auteur ambulant, ou recueil de pièces représentées sur différens théâtres tant à Paris qu'en province.* 3 vols. Paris: different publishers, 1757–1763.

Tendresses bacchiques, ou duo et trio mêlez de petits airs, tendres et à boire, des meilleurs auteurs. 2 vols. Paris: Ballard, 1712–1718.

Théâtre des boulevards. 2 vols., ed. Georges d'Heylli. Paris: Rouveyre, 1881.

Théveneau de Morande, Charles. *La Gazette noire par un homme qui n'est pas blanc, ou oeuvres posthumes du gazetier cuirassé.* Paris: n.p., 1784.

————. *Le Philosophe cynique.* Paris: n.p., 1771.

Thiébault, Adrien-Paul-François-Charles-Henry. *Mémoires.* 5 vols. Paris: Plon, 1893–1895.

Thiéry, Luc-Vincent. *Almanach du voyageur à Paris* (Paris, 1783–1787).

————. *Guide des amateurs et des étrangers voyageurs à Paris, ou description raisonnée de cette ville et de tout ce qu'elle contient de remarquable.* 2 vols. Paris: Hardouin et Galley, 1786–1787.

Tiersot, Julien. *Lettres de musiciens écrites en français du XV au XX siècle.* 2 vols. Turin: Bocca, 1924.

Tournon, Antoine. *La Vie et les mémoires de Pilâtre de Rosier.* Paris: Tournon, 1786.

Travenol, Louis and Durey de Noinville, J. B. *Histoire du théâtre de l'Académie Royale de Musique en France depuis son établissement jusqu'à présent.* 2d ed. rev. Paris: Duchesne, 1757.

Le Triomphe des comédiens françois sur l'opéra comique. Algeria: n.p., n.d.

Vadé, Jean-Joseph. *Oeuvres.* Ed. Julien Lemer. Paris: Garnier Frères, 1875.

Le Vol plus haut, ou l'espion des principaux théâtres de la capitale. Memphis: Sincere, 1784.

Voltaire, François-Marie Arouet de. *Plaidoyer pour Genest Ramponeau cabaretier à la Courtille prononcé par lui-même contre Gaudon, entrepreneur d'un théâtre des bouleverts.* Geneva: Cramer, 1760.

"Voyage d'un Anglais à Paris 1788," *Revue retrospective* (1889).

Wille, Johann Georg. *Mémoires et journal.* 2 vols. Ed. Georges Duplessis. Paris: Renouard, 1857.

Secondary Works

Aghion, Max. *Le Théâtre à Paris au XVIIIe siècle.* Paris: n.p., 1926.

Albert, Maurice. *Les Théâtres de la foire (1660–1789).* Paris: Hachette, 1900.

Alméras, Henri d', and Estrée, Paul d'. *Les Théâtres Libertins au XVIII siècle.* Paris: Daragon, 1905.

Anthony, James R. *French Baroque Music from Beaujoyeulx to Rameau.* New York: W. W. Norton, 1974.

Ariste, Paul d', and Arrivetz, Maurice. *Les Champs-Elysées. Etude topographique, historique et anecdotique jusqu'à nos jours.* Paris: Emile-Paul, 1913.

Arnoldson, Louise Parkinson. *Sedaine et les musiciens de son temps.* Paris: L'Entente linotypiste, 1934.

Auriac, Eugène d'. *Théâtre de la foire avec un essai historique sur les spectacles forains. Recueil de pièces représentées aux foires Saint-Germain et Saint-Laurent.* Paris: Garnier, 1878.

Banville, Théodore de. *La Lanterne magique, camées parisiens.* Paris: Pincebourde, 1883.

Barbeau, M. "Le Théâtre des Tuileries sous Louis XIV, Louis XV et Louis XVI." *Bulletin de la Société Historique de Paris* 22 (1895): 130–188.

Barberet, V. *Lesage et le théâtre de la foire.* Nancy: Paul Sordoillet, 1887.

Barbier, Pierre, and Vernillat, France. *Histoire de France par les chansons.* 8 vols. Paris: Gallimard, 1956–1959.

Barnes, Clifford R. "Instruments and Instrumental Music at the 'Théâtres de la Foire' (1697–1762)." *Recherches sur la musique française classique* 5 (1965): 142–168.

————. "The 'Théâtre de la foire' (Paris, 1697–1762). Its Music and Composers." Ph.D. dissertation, University of California at Los Angeles, 1965.

————. "Vocal Music at the 'Théâtres de la foire' (1697–1762); Part One: Vaudeville." *Recherches sur la musique française classique* 8 (1968): 141–160.

Batcave, Louis. *Les Petits Comédiens du Roi au Bois de Boulogne (1778–1789)*. Paris: J. Schemit, 1909.

Beaulieu, Henri. *Les Théâtres du boulevard du crime*. Paris: Daragon, 1905.

Bernardin, Napoléon-Maurice. *La Comédie italienne en France et les théâtres de la foire et du boulevard (1570–1791)*. Paris: Revue Bleue, 1902.

Bizard, L., and Chapon, J. "La Foire Saint-Laurent et son théâtre." *Mercure de France* 235 (April 1932): 60–85.

Blaze [Castil-Blaze], François Henri Joseph. *Mémorial du Grand-Opéra, épilogue de l'Académie Royale de Musique, histoire littéraire, musicale, chorégraphique, pittoresque, morale, critique, facétieuse, politique et galante de ce théâtre de 1645 à 1847*. Paris: by the author, 1847.

Blum, André. *L'Estampe satirique et la caricature en France au XVIIIe siècle*. Paris: Gazette des Beaux-Arts, 1910.

Blum, Ernest. "Souvenirs d'un vaudevilliste; le Boulevard du Crime." *Figaro, supplément littéraire*. 17 August 1907, pp. 1–32.

Bonnardot, H. "Le Colisée." *Bulletin de la Société Historique de Paris* (1879): 117–118.

Bonnassies, Jules. *Les Spectacles forains et la Comédie-Française d'après des documents inédits*. Paris: E. Dentu, 1875.

Bonnet, George-Edgar. *Philidor et l'évolution de la musique française au XVIIIe siècle*. Paris: Delagrave, 1921.

Bossuet, Pierre. *Histoire administrative des rapports des théâtres et de l'état*. Paris: Henri Jouve, 1909.

Brazier, Nicolas. *Le Boulevard du Temple*. Paris: n.p., 1832.

———. *Chroniques des petits théâtres de Paris*. 2 vols. Paris: Rouveyre et Blond, 1883.

Brennan, Thomas, "Cabarets and Laboring Class Communities in Eighteenth-Century Paris." Ph.D. dissertation, The Johns Hopkins University, 1981.

Brenner, Clarence. *Le Développement du proverbe dramatique en France et sa vogue au XVIIIe siècle avec un proverbe inédit de Carmontelle*. University of California Publications in Modern Philology, vol. 20, no. 1, Berkeley: University of California Press, 1937.

———. *The Théâtre Italien: Its Repertory, 1716–1793, With a Historical Introduction*. Berkeley: University of California Press, 1961.

Briqueville, Eugène de. *L'Abbe Arnaud et la réforme de l'opéra au XVIIIe siècle*. Avignon: Leguin, 1881.

Britsch, Amédée. *La Jeunesse de Philippe-Egalité (1747–1785)*. Paris: Payot, 1926.

Brock, A. de St. H. *A History of Fireworks*. London: G. Harraps, 1949.

Brown, Frederick. *Theater and Revolution: The Culture of the French Stage*. New York: Viking Press, 1980.

Brunetiére, Ferdinand. Review of *Chansonnier historique du XVIII siècle*. Ed. Emile Raunié. *Revue des deux mondes*, 15 August 1880, pp. 932–943.

Buguet, Henry, and d'Heylii, Georges. *Foyers et coulisses*. 13 vols. Paris: Tresse, 1873–1882.

"Le Cabaret de Ramponneau." *Magasin pittoresque*, July 1841, pp. 233–244.

Cain, Georges. *Anciens théâtres de Paris*. Paris: Charpentier et Fasquelle, 1906.

———. *Tableaux Parisiens d'autrefois*. Paris: n.p., n.d.

Capon, Gaston. *Les Petites maisons galantes de Paris au XVIIIe siècle*. Paris: Daragon, 1902.

Capon, G., and Yve-Plessis, R. *Les Théâtres clandestins au XVIIIe siècle*. Paris: Plessis, 1905.

Carlson, Marvin. *The Theatre of the French Revolution*. Ithaca: Cornell University Press, 1966.

Carmody, Francis J. *Le Répertoire de l'opéra-comique en vaudevilles de 1708 à 1764*. University of California Publications in Modern Philology, vol. 16, no. 4. Berkeley: University of California Press, 1932–1933.

Catalogue de curiosité, 1772–1773. Paris: n.p., n.d.

"La Catastrophe de la rue Royale, 30 Mai 1770." *Revue des questiones historiques* (1900): 414–418.

Chabrol, Wilbrod. *Histoire et description du Palais-Royal et du Théâtre Français*. Paris: Plon, 1883.

Challamel, Augustin. *L'Ancien boulevard du Temple*. Paris: Gauthier-Villars, n.d.

Chaponnièrre, Paul. "Les Comédies de moeurs du théâtre de la foire." *Revue d'histoire littéraire de la France* 20 (1913): 828–844.

———. *Piron, sa vie et ses oeuvres*. Geneva: Journal de Genève, 1910.

Chapuis, Alfred. *Les Automates, histoire et technique*. Neuchâtel: Griffon, 1949.

Chateau, Jean. *Le Réel et l'imaginaire dans le jeu de l'enfant. Essai sur la genèse de l'imagination*. Paris: J. Vrin, 1946.

Chennevierres, Henry de. "Les Ruggieri, artificiers." *La Gazette des Beaux Arts* 36 (1 August 1887): 132–140.

Chesnais, Jacques. *Histoire générale des marionnettes*. Paris: Bordas, 1947.

Chevalier, A. "Un Charlatan du XVIIIe siècle, Le Grand Thomas." *Mémoires de la Société Historique de Paris* (1880): 61–78.

Christout, Marie-Françoise. *Le Merveilleux et le 'théâtre du silence' en France à partir du XVIIe siècle*. Paris: Mouton, 1965.

Colombey, Emile. *Ruelles, salons et cabarets*. 2 vols. Paris: E. Dentu, 1895.

Cooper, Martin. *Opéra comique*. London: Max Parrish, 1949.

Cucuel, Georges. *Les Créateurs de l'opéra-comique français*. Paris: Félix Alcan, 1914.

———. "La Critique musicale dans les revues du XVIIIe siècle." *L'Année musicale* 8 (1912): 127–203.

———. "Sources et documents pour servir à l'histoire de l'opéra-comique en France." *L'Année musicale* 3 (1914): 247–282.

Curzon, Henri de. "La 'Serva Padrona' à Paris." In vol. 1 of *Histoire du théâtre lyrique depuis les origines jusqu'à nos jours*. pp. 151–159. Paris: Radio-Paris, n.d.

Dagen, Georges. "Les Femmes du monde à Paris à la fin du XVIIIe siècle: cabarets, cafés, tabagies." *Courier d'Epidaure* (November, 1937): n.p.

Daumas, Maurice. *Les Instruments scientifiques au XVIIe et XVIIIe siècle*. Paris: n.p., 1953.

Deligny, E. *Histoire de l'Ambigu-Comique*. Paris: Lacombe, 1841.

David, Hans. "The Cultural Functions of Music." *Journal of the History of Ideas* 3 (June 1951): 423–429.

Demuth, Norman. *French Opera. Its Development to the Revolution*. Sussex: Artemis Press, 1963.

Depping, Guillaume. *Les Merveilles de la force et de l'adresse*. Paris: Hachette, 1869.

Desnoireterres, Gustave Le Brisoys. *La Comédie satyrique au XVIIIe siècle. Histoire de la société française par allusion, la personnalité et la satire au théâtre: Louis XV, Louis XVI, la Révolution*. Paris: E. Perrin, 1885.

Dictionnaire des journalistes (1600–1789). Ed. Jean Sgard. Grenoble: Presses Universitaire de Grenoble, 1976.

Dinaux, Arthur. *Les Sociétés badines, bachiques, littéraires et chantantes.* 2 vols. Paris: Bachelin-Deflorenne, 1867.

Du Bled, Victor. *La Comédie de société au XVIIIᵉ siècle.* Paris: Calmann Levy, 1893.

Duhem, Jules. "Les Parodies aéronautiques dans la comédie ancienne," *Bulletin du bibliophile* (n.d.): 110–121.

Escudier, Gaston. *Les Saltimbanques, leur vie, leurs moeurs.* Paris: Michel Levy, 1875.

Farge, Arlette. *Vivre dans la rue à Paris au XVIIIᵉ siècle.* Paris: Gallimard, 1979.

Faucheur, Théodore. *Histoire du boulevard du Temple depuis son origine jusqu'à sa démolition.* Paris: E. Dentu, 1863.

Feu de théâtre de Séraphin depuis son origine jusqu'à sa disparition, 1776–1870. Paris: Rouquette, 1872.

Font, Auguste. *Favart, l'opéra-comique et la comédie-vaudeville aux XVIIᵉ et XVIIIᵉ siècles.* Paris: Fischbacher, 1894.

Fontaine, Léon. *La Censure dramatique au 18ᵉ siècle.* Lyon: Pitrat, 1892.

———. *Le Théâtre et la philosophie au dix-huitième siècle,* Paris: Cerf, 1878.

Fortassier, Pierre. "Musique et peuple au XVIIIᵉ siècle." In *Images du peuple au dix-huitième siècle. Colloque d'Aix-en-Provence 25 et 26 Octobre 1969,* pp. 327–331. Paris: Armand Colin, 1973.

Fouquier, Marcel. *Paris au XVIIIᵉ siècle. Ses folies.* Paris: Emile-Paul, 1912.

Fournel, Victor. *Les Cris de Paris, types et physionomies d'autrefois.* Paris: Firmin-Didot, 1887.

———. *Du Rôle des coups de bâton dans les relations sociales et en particulier dans l'histoire littéraire.* Paris: A. Delahays, 1858.

———. *Tableau du vieux Paris. Les Spectacles populaires et les artistes des rues.* Paris: E. Dentu, 1863.

———. *Le Vieux Paris, fêtes, jeux et spectacles.* Tours: A. Mame, 1887.

Fournier, Edouard. *Histoire du Pont-Neuf.* 2 vols. Paris: E. Dentu, 1862.

———, and Michel, Francisque. *Le Livre d'or des métiers. Histoire des hôtelleries, cabarets, hôtels garnis, restaurants et cafés, et des anciennes communautés et confréries d'hôteliers, de marchands de vins, de restaurateurs, de limonadiers.* 2 vols. Paris: Librairie Historique, 1851.

Fournier des Ormes. "Le Procès de Ramponneau (1760)," *Feuilleton du Constitutionnel* (27 September 1924): 1–2.

Fox, Leland. "Opéra-comique, a Vehicle of Classic Style." *Recherches sur la musique française classique* 4 (1964): 133–145.

Gardien, Jacques. *La Chanson populaire française.* Paris: Larousse, 1948.

Garnier, Jacques. *Forains d'hier et d'aujourdhui.* Orléans: by the author, 1968.

Gaxotte, Pierre. *Paris au XVIIIᵉ siècle.* Paris: Arthaud, 1967.

Genest, Emile. *L'Opéra-comique, connu et inconnu, son histoire depuis l'origine jusqu'à nos jours.* Paris: Fischbacher, 1925.

Ginisty, Paul. "Les Théâtres disparus." *Je sais tout* 1 (14 August 1912): 105–113.

Gourdon de Genouilhac, Nicolas-Jules-Henri. *Paris à travers des siècles. Histoire nationale de Paris et des Parisiens depuis la fondation de Lutèce jusqu'à nos jours.* 6 vols. Paris: F. Roy, 1882–1889.

Gouriet, J. -B. *Personnages célèbres dans les rues de Paris.* 2 vols. Paris: Lerouge, 1811.

Grand-Carteret, John. *Les Almanachs français. Bibliographie-iconographie, 1600–1895.* Paris: J. Alisié, 1896.

————. *L'Histoire, la vie, les moeurs et la curiosité par l'image, le pamphlet et le document (1450–1900).* 5 vols. Paris: Librairie de la Curiosité et des Beaux-Arts, 1928.

Grégoire, Edouard G. J. *Les Gloires de l'opéra et de la musique à Paris.* 3 vols. Brussels: n.p., 1878–1881.

Grout, Donald J. *A Short History of Opera.* 2d ed. New York: Columbia University Press, 1965.

Gruber, Alain-Charles. *Les Grandes fêtes et leurs décors à l'époque de Louis XVI.* Geneva: Droz, 1972.

"Un Guide de Paris à l'usage des dessinateurs pour étoffes." *Bulletin de la Société Historique de Paris* (1905): 202–206.

Hachet-Souplet, Pierre. *Le Dressage des animaux et les combats de bêtes.* Paris: Firmin-Didot, 1897.

Hénard, Robert. *Les Jardins et les squares.* Paris: Renouard, 1911.

Heulhard, Arthur. *La Foire Saint-Laurent, son histoire et ses spectacles.* Paris: Alphonse Lemerre, 1878.

————. "Jean Monnet." *La Chronique musicale; revue bi-mensuelle de l'art ancien et moderne* 7 (15 March 1875): 241–251; 8 (1 June 1875): 217–223.

————. *Jean Monnet, vie et aventures d'un entrepreneur de spectacles au XVIII siècle, avec un appendice sur l'Opéra-Comique de 1752 à 1758.* Paris: Lemerre, 1884.

Hillairet, Jacques. *Dictionnaire historique des rues de Paris.* 2 vols. Paris: Editions de Minuit, 1963.

Hugot, Eugène. *Histoire littéraire, critique et anecdotique du Théâtre du Palais-Royal, 1784–1884.* 3d ed. Paris: Paul Ollendorff, 1886.

Hunn, James Martin. "The Balloon Craze in France, 1783–1799: A Study in Popular Science." Ph.D. dissertation, Vanderbilt University, 1982.

Iacuzzi, Alfred. *The European Vogue of Favart; the Diffusion of the opéra-comique.* New York: Institute of French Studies, 1932.

Isherwood, Robert M. "Entertainment in the Parisian Fairs in the Eighteenth Century." *Journal of Modern History* 53 (March 1981): 24–48.

————. *Music in the Service of the King: France in the Seventeenth Century.* Ithaca: Cornell University Press, 1973.

————. "Popular Musical Entertainment in Eighteenth-Century Paris." *International Review of the Aesthetics and Sociology of Music* 9 (December 1978): 295–310.

————. "The Third War of the Musical Enlightenment." In vol. 4, *Studies in Eighteenth-Century Culture,* Ed. Harold E. Pagliaro, pp. 223–245. Madison: University of Wisconsin Press, 1975.

Jousse, Marcel. *Anthropologie de geste.* Paris: n.p., 1969.

Kastner, Jean-Georges. *Les Voix de Paris, essai d'une histoire littéraire et musicale des cris populaires de la capitale depuis le moyen âge jusqu'à nos jours, précédé de considérations sur l'origine et le caractère du cri en général et suivi de les cris de Paris, grande symphonie humoristique vocale et instrumentale.* Paris: G. Brandus, Dufour et Cie, 1857.

Lagrave, Henri. *Le Théâtre et le public à Paris de 1715 à 1750.* Paris: C. Klincksieck, 1972.

La Laurencie, Lionel. "L'Opéra-comique." In Albert Lavignac. *Encyclopédie de la musique.* 6 vols. Paris: Delagrave, 1931. vol. 3: 1457–1489.

Landormy, Paul. "Le Théâtre de la Foire Saint-Germain." In *Histoire du théâtre lyrique depuis les origines jusqu'à nos jours.* vol. 1, pp. 103–110. Paris: Radio-Paris, n.d.

Lasalle, Albert de. *Les Treize salles de l'opéra.* Paris: Sartorius, 1875.

Lecomte, Louis Henry. *Les Variétés Amusantes, 1778–1779.* Paris: n.p., 1908.

Lenôtre, G. *Paris et ses fantômes.* Paris: n.p., 1933.

Letailleur, Paulette. "Jean-Louis Laruette chanteur et compositeur." *Recherches sur la musique française classique* 8 (1968): 161–189; 10 (1970): 57–86.

Lindsay, Frank W. *Dramatic Parody by Marionettes in Eighteenth-Century Paris.* New York: King's Crown Press, 1946.

Lough, John. *Paris Theater Audiences in the Seventeenth and Eighteenth Centuries.* London: Oxford University Press, 1957.

Lowinsky, Edward. "Taste, Style and Ideology in Eighteenth-Century Music." In *Aspects of the Eighteenth Century.* Ed. Earl R. Wasserman. Baltimore: Johns Hopkins University Press, 1965. pp. 163–205.

Lunel, Ernest. *Le Théâtre et la Révolution.* Paris: H. Daragon, n.d.

Magnin, Charles. *Histoire des marionnettes en Europe depuis l'antiquité jusqu'à nos jours.* Paris: Michel-Lévy, 1862.

Malcolmson, Robert W. *Popular Recreations in English Society, 1700–1850.* Cambridge: Cambridge Univeristy Press, 1973.

Malherbe, Charles. "Archives et Bibliothèque de l'Opéra." *La Revue musicale* 3 (15 June 1903): 269–276.

―――. "Commentaire bibliographique." In *Oeuvres complètes* by Jean-Philippe Rameau. Ed. C. Saint-Saëns. Paris: A. Durand, 1911. vol. 16, pp. 13–135.

Mamczarz, Irène. *Les Intermèdes comiques italiens au XVIIIᵉ siècle en France et en Italie.* Paris: Editions du Centre National de la Recherche Scientifique, 1972.

Manne, Edmond Denis de, and Ménétrier, C. *Galérie historique des comédiens de la troupe de Nicolet.* Lyons: N. Scheuring, 1869.

Masson, Chantal. "Journal du Marquis de Dangeau, 1684–1720; extraits concernant la vie musicale à la cour." *Recherches sur la musique française classique* 2 (1961–1962): 193–223.

Masson, Paul-Marie, "Les Fondateurs de l'opéra-comique." In *Histoire du théâtre lyrique en France depuis les origines jusqu'à nos jours.* Paris: Radio-Paris, n.d. pp. 160–168.

Moore, A. P. *The Genre Poissard and the French Stage of the Eighteenth Century.* New York: Institute of French Studies, 1935.

Mourey, Gabriel. *Fêtes foraines de Paris.* Paris: Renouard, 1906.

Munhall, Edgar. "Savoyards in French Eighteenth-Century Art." *Apollo: Magazine of the Arts* (June 1968): 86–94.

Nansouty, Max de. *Les Trucs du théâtre, du cirque et de la foire.* Paris: Armand Colin, 1909.

Nicolle, Henri. "Thomas-Simon Gueullette et les parades au XVIIIᵉ siècle." *Revue de France* 10 (May 1874): 768–795.

Nuitter, Charles. "Curiosités des archives de l'Opéra. Les Origines de l'opéra-comique." *La Chronique musicale* 1 (1873): 60–67.

Oliver, Alfred Richard. *The Encyclopedists as Critics of Music.* New York: n.p., 1947.

Packer, Dorothy S. "'La Calotte' and the Eighteenth-Century French Vaudeville." *Journal of the American Musicological Society.* 23 (Spring 1970): 61–83.

Pélissier, Paul. *Histoire administrative de l'Académie Nationale de Musique et de Danse.* Paris: Bonvalot-Jouve, 1906.

Pellison, Maurice. "Les Gens de lettres et les comédiens au XVIIIe siècle." *La Grande Revue* 20 (25 October 1911): 734–756.

Pericaud, Louis. *Théâtre des Petits Comédiens de S. A. S. Monseigneur le Comte de Beaujolais.* Paris: E. Jorel, 1909.

Peytel, Adrien. "Les Théâtres musicaux subventionnés." In Albert Lavignac. *Encyclopédie de la musique.* 6 vols. Paris: Delagrave, 1931. vol. 6, pp. 3748–3833.

Pitsch, Marguerite. *La Vie populaire à Paris au XVIIIe siècle.* Paris: Picard, 1949.

Poete, Marcel. *La Promenade à Paris au XVIIe siècle.* Paris: Armand Colin, 1913.

––––––. *Une Vie de cité. Paris de sa naissance à nos jours.* 2 vols. Paris: Picard, 1924.

Ponet, L. *Fanchon, ou la vielleuse du boulevard du Temple.* Paris: Renard, 1803.

Pougin, Arthur. *Acteurs et actrices d'autrefois.* Paris: F. Juven et Cie, n.d.

––––––. "André Philidor." *La Chronique musicale* 7 (February 1875): 111–119; 8 (1875): 20–26.

––––––. *Dictionnaire historique et pittoresque du théâtre et des arts qui s'y rattachent.* Paris: Firmin-Didot, 1885.

––––––. *Madame Favart: étude théâtrale, 1727–1772.* Paris: Fischbacher, 1912.

––––––. *Monsigny et son temps. L'Opéra-Comique et la comédie italienne, les auteurs, les compositeurs, les chanteurs.* Paris: Fischbacher, 1908.

Prat, A. "Le Parterre au XVIIIe siècle." *La Quinzaine* (1 February 1906): 388–412.

Prioleau, E. *Histoire du vaudeville.* Bordeaux: Feret, 1890.

Prod'homme, J.-G., and Crauzat, E. de. *Les Menus plaisirs du roi, l'Ecole Royale et le Conservatoire de Musique.* Paris: Delagrave, 1929.

Rabou, Charles. *Les Grands Danseurs du Roi.* Brussels: Meline, 1846.

Raymond, Louis. *Les Mimes du Palais-Royal, ou réflexions sur divers points concernant le spectacle des Beaujolais.* Paris: n.p., n.d.

Réal, Antony. *Histoire philosophique et anecdotique du baton depuis les temps les plus reculés jusqu'à nos jours.* Paris: Société des Gens de Lettres, n.d.

Reichard, Henri-Auguste-Ottokar. *Guide des voyageurs en Europe.* 2 vols. Paris: n.p., 1792.

Reichenburg, Louisette Eugénie. *Contribution à l'histoire de la "querelle des bouffons."* Paris: n.p., 1937.

Roche, Daniel. *Le Peuple de Paris: essai sur la culture populaire au XVIIIe siècle.* Paris: Aubier Montaigne, 1981.

Root-Bernstein, Michelle Marie. "Revolution on the Boulevard: Parisian Popular Theater in the late Eighteenth Century." Ph.D. dissertation, Princeton University, 1981.

Ruggieri, Claude. *Précis historique sur les fêtes, les spectacles et les réjouissances publiques.* Paris: Bachelier, 1830.

Saisselin, Rémy. *Taste in Eighteenth-Century France.* Syracuse, New York: Syracuse University Press, 1965.

Salvatore, Paul J. *Favart's Unpublished Plays. The Rise of the Popular Comic Opera.* New York: Institute of French Studies, 1935.

Soubies, Albert, and Malherbe, Charles. *Histoire de l'opéra-comique.* 2 vols. Paris: Marpon et Flammarion, 1892–1893.

––––––. *Précis de l'histoire de l'opéra-comique.* Paris: A. Dupret, 1887.

Strehly, Georges. *L'Acrobatie et les acrobates.* Paris: Delagrave, 1903.

Strowski, Fortunat. "Le Théâtre de la foire." In *Le Théâtre à Paris au XVIIIe siècle; conférences du Musée Carnavalet (1929).* Paris: Payot, 1930. pp. 68–87.

Thurner, A. *Les Transformations de l'opéra-comique.* Paris: Castel, 1865.

Tiersot, Julien. "Gossec et les noëls." *Le Ménestral* 69 (1903): 411–412.

———. *Histoire de la chanson populaire en France.* Paris: Plon, 1889.

Tissandier, Gaston. *Bibliographie aéronautique. Catalogue de livres d'histoire, de science, de voyages et de fantaisie traitant de la navigation aérienne ou des aérostats.* Paris: H. Launette et Cie, 1887.

———. *Histoire des ballons et des aéronautes célèbres, 1783–1800.* Paris: H. Launette, 1887.

Torlais, Jean. "Un Prestidigitateur célèbre chef de service d'électrothérapie au XVIIIe siècle, Ledru dit Comus (1731–1807)." *Histoire de la médicine* 5 (February 1953): 13–25.

Van Bellen, Eise Carel. *Les Origines du mélodrame.* Utrecht: Kemink, 1927.

Vassy, Gaston. *Paris pittoresque: le Caveau des Aveugles.* Paris: Alcan-Lévy, 1874.

Vatout, J. *Histoire du Palais-Royal.* Paris: Gaultier et Lacuionie, 1830.

Veinstein, André. *Bibliothèque et musées des arts du spectacle dans le monde.* Paris: Editions du Centre National de la Recherche Scientifique, 1960.

La Vie populaire en France du Moyen Age à nos jours. 2 vols. Paris: Editions Diderot, n.d.

Weckerlin, J.-B. *La Chanson populaire.* Paris: Firmin-Didot, 1886.

Wild, Nicole. "Aspects de la musique sous la Régence. Les Foires: Naissance de l'opéra-comique." *Recherches sur la musique française classique* 5 (1965): 129–141.

Winter, Marian Hannah. *The Theatre of Marvels.* New York: Benjamin Blom, Inc., 1964.

Zetter, G. *Evolution des foires et marchés à travers les siècles.* Paris: Comité de la foire de Paris, 1923.

Index